Sustainability and Global Environmental Policy: New Perspectives

Sustainability and Global Environmental Policy

New Perspectives

Andrew K. Dragun and Kristin M. Jakobsson
Swedish University of Agricultural Sciences

Edward Elgar
Cheltenham, UK. Lyme, US.

Published by
Edward Elgar Publishing Limited
8 Lansdown Place
Cheltenham
Glos GL50 2HU
UK

Edward Elgar Publishing, Inc.
1 Pinnacle Hill Road
Lyme
NH 03768
US

A catalogue record for this book
is available from the British Library

Library of Congress Cataloguing-in-Publication Data
Sustainability and global environmental policy : new perspectives /
    Andrew K. Dragun and Kristin M. Jakobsson [editors].
        Includes indexes
            1. Sustainable development. 2. Environmental policy.
        3. Environmental protection. 4. Environmental economics.
        5. Industries—Environmental aspects. I. Dragun, Andrew K.
        II. Jakobsson, Kristin M., 1957–
        HC79.E5S8663 : 1997
        363.7—dc21   97-14363
                                                                        CIP

ISBN 1 85898 630 3
Printed and bound in Great Britain by Hartnolls Limited, Bodmin, Cornwall

Dedication

To Haakan and Asher

Contents

List of Figures

List of Tables

List of Contributors

Graciela Chichilnisky holds the UNESCO Chair in Mathematics and Economics and Director, Program on Information and Resources, Columbia University. She is also a member of the Board of Trustees of the National Resources Defence Council (NRDC), US.

Robert Costanza is a Professor at the University of Maryland, Institute for Ecological Economics, Center for Environmental and Estuarine Studies, US.

Herman Daly is a Senior Research Scholar, School of Public Affairs, University of Maryland, US.

Andrew Dragun is a Professor in Economics at the Swedish University of Agricultural Sciences, Uppsala, Sweden.

Paul Ekins is a Senior Lecturer, Environmental Policy Unit, Department of Economics, Keele University, UK. He is also a Director of Forum for the Future where he is director of its sustainable economy unit. Additionally, he is an advisor to the UK government's Advisory Committee on Business and the Environment.

Sylvie Faucheux is Professor and Vice Director of the Centre d'Économie and d'Éthique pour l'Environnement et le Développement (C3ED), Université de Versailles à Saint-Quentin-en-Yvelines, France.

Robert Goodland is currently a Special Environmental Adviser with the Environment Department of The World Bank, Washington DC.

Ian Hodge is currently Gilbey lecturer in Land Economy at the University of Cambridge in the UK.

Terrance Hurley is Visiting Scientist at the Center for Agricultural and Rural Development, Department of Economics, Iowa State University, US.

Kristin Jakobsson is an Associate Professor in Economics at the Swedish University of Agricultural Sciences, Uppsala, Sweden.

Jack L. Knetsch is a Professor in Economics at the Simon Fraser University, Canada.

Martin O'Connor is Professeur-Associé en Sciences Economiques,Centre d'Économie and d'Éthique pour l'Environnement et le Développement (C3ED), Université de Versailles à Saint-Quentin-en-Yvelines, France.

Matthias Ruth is a Professor at the Center for Energy and Environmental Studies, Boston University, US.

Jason Shogren is Thomas Stroock Distinguished Professor of Natural Resource Conservation and Management, Department of Economics and Finance, University of Wyoming, US.

Clem Tisdell is a Professor of Economics, The University of Queensland, Brisbane, Australia, where he is also Head of Department. He is also Deputy Director of the School of Marine Sciences at the University of Queensland and an honorary professor of the People's University of China.

Hans-Erik Uhlin is a Docent with the Department of Economics, the Swedish University of Agricultural Sciences, Uppsala, Sweden.

Preface

The forum for the initial presentation of the papers included in this volume was a special colloquium entitled *New Dimensions in Environmental Policy* held in the Department of Economics at the Swedish University of Agricultural Science, at Uppsala in June of 1996. Almost all the papers presented to the original colloquium are included here, with the addition of several papers prepared by other participants at the colloquium. Substantively, all the papers included here are original and have not been published elsewhere.

It was our objective as editors of this volume to facilitate and enable the presentations which have been included here, maintaining editorialising to a minimum. In this way we have not sought to obtain unanimity of argument or thinking amongst the contributors and it should be expected that there might be many disagreements on theory and issues amongst the contributors.

Of the participants of the original colloquium, we especially wish to thank Associate Professor Lars Drake for his support and advice on a wide range of matters and Elisabeth Wakeman for her enduring and efficient administrative assistance. In addition a number of colloquium participants contributed to the discussions and deserve special thanks, including Johan Andersson, Magnus Arnek, Mats Björsell, Mark Brady, Stefan Bäckman, Kaisu Haataja, Thomas Hahn, Lars Hallgren, Rasmus Heltberg, Ruben Hoffman, Fredrik Holstein, Seif Khamis, Tatiana Kluvankova, Lenka Kovarova, Asko Miettinen, Richard Porter, Basim Saifi, Sirajo Seidi, Elie Storesletten, Elisabeth Wakeman, Stephan Vermeulen and Tadesse Zerihun.

This book has been assembled in a very short timescale since the original colloquium as a result of a high level of cooperation from all contributors, for which the editors are extremely grateful, and with the foresight of Dymphna Evans at Elgars who was categorical in her support for the project.

Andrew Dragun
Kristin Jakobsson
Uppsala

1. Introduction: New Environmental Policy Dimensions

Andrew Dragun and Kristin Jakobsson

This book explores the cutting edge of contemporary environmental economic policy. A group of internationally well known environmental economic researchers were asked to elucidate on areas and issues which they considered to be important in the setting of new and different ways to deal with environmental problems into the new millennium. The theme of *New Dimensions* was to develop the idea that governments and societies have a range of new social and environmental problems as well as approaches or environmental policy instruments available to achieve environmental goals. What are the problems on one hand and how do they emerge - and subsequently, what are the new approaches or instruments, how do they work and what are their impacts?

The background to this introspection on current environmental policy is rooted in the widespread dramatic transformation of the international political scene in recent years, with a fundamental reappraisal of social governance in general and environmental policy in particular. The face of environmental policy has evolved significantly since the beginning of the decade of the 1990s, as a range of environmental problems have assumed international concern and as globalisation spreads.

Interestingly, seven of the participants focussed directly on issues of sustainability while the remaining six contributions raised a range of specific policy concerns which could best be described as involving issues of equity and decision making on environmental issues. The chapters are grouped accordingly, with the general sustainability contributions first.

In Chapter 2, 'Reconciling internal and external policies for sustainable development' Professor Herman Daly presents four interrelated policies for sustainable development, focussing on the US, but with general application. Professor Daly begins the paper by describing the basic point of view, or pre-analytic vision, from which the policies logically arise. In this point of view, the economy is seen as a subsystem of the total ecosystem which supports it, raising the fundamental question of how big the economic subsystem can become before the resources available in the total ecosystem become limiting

1

or unsustainable. Global levels of environmental degradation and poverty indicate that resources have already have become limiting.

The four policy suggestions described were first, to stop counting consumption of natural capital as income and introduce a system of 'green accounting'. Second, to tax labour and income less and tax resource throughput more. The third policy is to maximise the productivity of natural capital in the short run and invest in increasing its supply in the long run. Professor Daly argues that in general, natural and man made capital are complements, not substitutes. Declining natural capital cannot be replaced by man made capital to any significant degree.

The fourth policy suggestion is to move away from the ideology of global economic integration by free trade. In his view nations should develop domestic production for their own markets first and focus on international trade second. Professor Daly counters the argument that any problems of globalisation will be more than compensated for by the resulting economic growth and increase in welfare by showing that the link between growth and welfare (usually assumed to be positive and closely correlated) is highly questionable. More growth may even reduce welfare. Ricardo's theory of comparative advantage is often used as a supporting argument for the ideology of globalisation and free trade, but his theory applied to the free trade of goods under the assumption of capital immobility. The same results cannot be expected when capital (and to some extent labour) is also freely mobile.

Professor Daly concludes that nations must consume less and become more self sufficient. Nations are the 'major unit of community capable of carrying out any policies for the common good'. Increasing globalisation reduces the ability of nations to develop and carry out both national and international environmental policies.

Paul Ekins considers the issue of 'Sustainability as the basis of environmental policy' in Chapter 3, defining the basic meaning of sustainability as 'the capacity for continuance more or less indefinitely into the future'. Mr Ekins concludes that, in aggregate, current human ways of life are not sustainable because of the destruction of their environmental support systems and their adverse environmental effects. Mr Ekins draws the distinction between environmental, economic and social sustainability and considers their interactions. Failure to take these interactions into account is likely to result in ineffective or even counterproductive policies.

There is a moral basis for environmental concern, which Mr Ekins terms the 'ethic of sustainability' which will strongly influence the environmental policies chosen. 'How a society uses its environment depends first and foremost on its world view, its perception of the nature of the world and the status of human beings and other life forms within it.' This world view will also determine how a society perceives environmental justice (relative rights of current and future humans and non-human forms of life), how a society values and makes decisions about the environment and who is considered to be responsible for promoting environmental sustainability.

Mr Ekins provides a set of sustainability conditions which can be used to derive sustainability standards and to set targets and overall objectives for environmental policy. The chapter sets out a methodology for making the concept of environmental sustainability operational by tracing out its causes and identifying instruments to bring economic activity within defined standards of sustainability. The standards of sustainability derived from the conditions defined in this chapter can be used to set clear directions and targets for changes in the economy's biophysical throughputs and in the production of biomass.

Chapter 4, 'Biophysical and objective environmental sustainability' by Dr Robert Goodland, deals with the issue of what sustainability is, with a view that if sustainability is not well defined and cannot be made an operational concept, it is difficult to develop policies to promote sustainability. Environmental sustainability, social sustainability and economic sustainability are each separately defined. Defining each 'component' of sustainability distinctly may then become an organizing principle for action for the activities required to approach sustainability in real life, even though these distinct activities will necessarily be interconnected. The focus of the chapter is on environmental sustainability, which is tightly defined by the rigorous biophysical principles on which it is based.

Dr Goodland subsequently discusses the relationship of sustainability, development and growth. Environmentally sustainable development implies sustainable levels of both production and consumption rather than sustained economic growth. 'The need for sustainability arose from the recognition that the profligate, extravagant and inequitable nature of current patterns of development, when projected into the not too distant future, leads to biophysical impossibilities ... The tacit goal of economic development is to narrow the equity gap between the rich an poor. Almost always this is taken to mean raising the bottom, rather than lowering the top of redistribution'. However, it will not be possible to bring the low income countries up to the affluence levels in the high income countries through growth alone. Sharing and population stability will be necessary to achieve greater equality.

Environmental sustainability seeks to maintain global life support systems indefinitely. It can be defined by the two fundamental environmental services, the source and sink functions, that must be maintained unimpaired during the period over which sustainability is required. Environmental sustainability is subject to biophysical laws, rather than human laws and so can be considered 'universal and rigorous'. However, the paths needed by each nation to approach sustainability will not be the same. Some countries may need to reduce pollution, others to stabilise population and the affluent nations may need to reduce per capita consumption.

Professor Tisdell's contribution in Chapter 5, 'Agricultural sustainability and conservation of biodiversity: Competing policies and paradigms', provides an overview of sustainability issues related to agriculture and biodiversity, policies for the conservation of biodiversity and their implications for agriculture.

Professor Tisdell argues that mainstream economic approaches to environmental policy have tended to be technocratic, top down and mechanistic, in part as a natural consequence of econometric model building and the use of mathematical models of a relatively deterministic nature. The failure of these policy approaches to include such considerations as irreversibility, hysteresis, uncertainty and learning, institutional arrangements and several other factors has had unfortunate consequences for biodiversity conservation and agricultural sustainability.

Some responses to improve environmental policy making and implementation which Professor Tisdell mentions include greater participation in policy making by those directly affected by the policies, greater consideration of the complexities of the systems involved and use of the concept of total economic valuation in decision making. However, Professor Tisdell cautions that these are also not straightforward and will not guarantee favourable outcomes.

The uncertainty and complexity associated with biodiversity conservation, agricultural sustainability and their interrelationships do not allow for simple solutions. 'New approaches to environmental policy making are needed which are less mechanical and more organic than neoclassical approaches appear to be'.

The issue of energy use and sustainability in modern agriculture is considered by Dr Hans-Erik Uhlin in Chapter 6, 'Energy productivity and sustainability in Swedish agriculture - some evidence and issues'. Modern agriculture, with the high use of fossil fuels, is normally considered as an entropy destructive strategy and a non-sustainable system. The standard conclusion of energy and agriculture studies in the 1970s was that energy productivity in agriculture was decreasing, prompting a call for policies to reduce the reliance of agriculture on external energy inputs such as fossil fuels and man made energy.

More recent studies indicate that there may have been a shift to an increasing energy productivity in agriculture. Dr Uhlin concludes from Swedish data over the period 1956 to 1993 that energy productivity in agriculture has increased over time as a result of technical and structural changes, even when all indirect energy costs are included.

The increasing energy productivity of agriculture suggests a change in policy proposals away from focussing on agricultural systems with low man-made and fossil fuel energy inputs, which may be slow contributors to entropy increases but may also have a limited capacity to feed a large population. Dr Uhlin recommends a deeper look into the importance of solar energy, land, land use and the opportunity cost aspects of alternatives and the development of agricultural systems to capture solar energy. Agriculture has a potential to use natural and biological resources in ways that increase the binding of solar radiation into biomass. Careful 'use' of solar radiation for biomass can be seen as lowering entropy. Dr Uhlin suggests a strategy of using 'surplus' land, made available through a fertiliser based agriculture, plus technical and structural change, for harvesting the sun through the use of special energy crops.

The impetus for Professor Sylvie Faucheux's analysis in Chapter 7, is the long term environmentally-motivated technological transformation which focuses on proactive prevention of environmental despoliation, instead of the traditional end-of-pipe approach of capturing pollutants after they have been generated. Particularly, Professor Faucheux is concerned with the institutional arrangements and economic instruments required to incorporate environmental concerns into an industrial strategy affecting firms directly. Thus the title, 'Technological change, ecological sustainability and industrial competitiveness'.

To explore the complicated relationships between the three components noted in the title, Faucheux introduces the discussion by reviewing the role of technological change in the implementation of sustainable development. The analysis is then focussed by appraising the endogenous disposition of technological change in the possible dynamics of transition to sustainable development. Subsequently, Faucheux presents an evolutionary approach to technological change focussing on notions of strategy which might reconcile competitiveness with norms of sustainability. The roles of firms' strategies for giving effect to the norms of sustainability are then explained relative to the endogenisation of technological change. The case is then made that an apparently beneficial role of firms towards sustainability only emerges contingently from the new tests of commercial viability. Finally Professor Faucheux considers a range of institutional factors considered relevant to technological change trajectories at the different national and international levels.

Professor Martin O'Connor's study 'Environmental valuation: From the point of view of sustainability' in Chapter 8, is motivated by a concern that various forms of sustainability - economic, ecological and social - bring the long term future into conflict with the considerations of the present. Professor O'Connor explores the process of reconciling preoccupations with the present as against a consideration for the future, by initially surveying the traditional methodologies of economic valuation, focussing on the issues of discounting and obtaining a net present value. The connection of a maximised NPV to distributional conflicts between the present and the future is then introduced demonstrating the difficulties of applying cost-benefit approaches based on time discounting, to large-scale and long-term environmental problems. The selection of discount rates is recognised to implicitly or explicitly involve intertemporal distributional choices.

In relation to this conundrum, an alternative approach to environmental valuation is developed in the second part of the chapter where the impetus is to enlarge the scope of consideration from commodity production systems to focus on the ecosystems of the planet as well as the long run. Here, sustainable development may be represented as a symbiosis between economic production and ecological *re*production with a need to manage habitats which are identified as life support systems in addition to commodity production systems. Consequently, valuation for sustainability is identified as inseparable from the notion of a habitat as a place to live with social and community significance and meaning. Thus, questions of ecological, economic and social sustainability are identified to involve explicit choices of the redistribution of economic opportunity and access through time. The issue is then the distribution of sustainability with respect to ecosystems, habitats, economic opportunity as well as environmental bads and individuals.

Part three of Professor O'Connor's analysis presents an example of how the understanding of valuation as action for and against sustainability may be applied. The demonstration involving small forest pockets in an agricultural region of France near Paris, illustrates how the value of the forest may be seen to be inseparable from the collective or shared interest and investment. The overall conclusion emphasises how this approach to the valuation for sustainability implies a distinctive epistemological view of living in nature and living in time, involving an unavoidable collective sharing of the distribution of sustainability.

In Chapter 9, 'Environment, equity and welfare economics', Professors Dragun and Jakobsson, consider the applicability of modern welfare economic theory to environmental problems in general. The focus here is not so much on the particular methodological flaws raised in the wide range of alternative valuation approaches suggested by the Pigovian approach, but rather on the ability to delineate consistent policy results.

The analysis reviews a range of valuation methodologies developed in the Pigovian perspective as well as the alternative Public Choice interpretation of welfare economics. While the different Pigovian approaches may be recognised to yield insight in some non-market situations more fundamental theoretical problems are not circumvented. The meaning of individual preferences and the problem of inconsistent ordinal rankings are not dealt with very well in the mainstream theory as attested by the alternative Public Choice approach to welfare economics. But the Public Choice approach does not escape the same conundrums of welfare economics.

What is left in welfare economics are a range of weak allocative efficiency propositions, which are made weak by an inability to deal with distributional issues. In the setting of environmental policy, where problems of property rights specification - especially in the developing country context - seem to imply that distributional issues are certainly not less prevalent than elsewhere in the economy, conventional welfare economic theory can do little more than provide background to a more explicit social consideration of the distributional issues which seem to be unavoidable.

Chapters 10 and 11, by Professor Jack Knetsch and Professor Jason Shogren, both deal with aspects of people's behaviour and how they express their preferences and make choices and the implications for environmental policy. Professor Knetsch discusses the issue of economic valuation in 'Evaluation and environmental policies: Recent behavioural findings and further implications'. The growing recognition of the economic value of the amenities and productivity of natural environments has greatly increased demands to take such values into account in the design of environmental policies. Many long-held valuation principles, however, involve various assertions of people's behaviour that may not be sustainable. The results from many surveys, experiments and other behavioural studies suggest that many common assertions provide neither a very good prescription of people's preferences nor very useful predictions of their reactions to real choices. The areas of risk perception and time preferences are good examples.

Another well-documented behavioural finding that is seriously inconsistent with nearly all current environmental policy analyses, is that people commonly value losses much more than they do commensurate gains. As most environmental valuation studies uses willingness to pay measures to assess both losses and gains, the valuation disparity has significant practical importance. The long-standing conventional assumption is that in most cases willingness to pay and willingness to accept compensation measures will give essentially the same answer, but empirical evidence shows large and systematic valuation disparities between the two measures. It seems people value possible gains very differently to possible losses, for an identical entitlement.

The implications of the valuation disparity for particular environmental policies are then discussed. The general implication is that the use of willingness to pay measures to value losses will result in systematic understatements of values and too great an allocation of resources to activities with negative environmental impacts.

Professor Jason Shogren uses experimental economics to explore the motivations for individual's behaviour and discusses how the results could be applied to functional environmental policies in Chapter 11, 'Tournament incentives in environmental policy'. Economic prescriptions for environmental problems usually presume that absolute payoffs motivate individual behaviour. But evidence from experimental economics suggests that people are not exact in their ability to discern and react to trivial differences in payoffs. Trivial payoff differences do not really punish deviations from optimal behaviour. One response is to impose an institutional incentive that provides sufficiently high rewards for trivial differences in measurable performance such that relative payoffs matter, that is, a tournament.

The behavioural findings from such tournament experiments can be used to design practical environmental policies, for example, in the control of nonpoint pollution, that are less costly in terms of the information required than alternative policies.

The theme of Chapter 12, 'The production of biodiversity: Institutions and the control of land' by Dr Ian Hodge, is that new innovative institutions, especially in relation to land use, may be needed to deal with the problem of species decline or biodiversity loss. The motivation for this study is that human development is generating increasing pressures on land use which in turn is causing an apparent decline in biodiversity, which is manifest at a global scale both in terms of causes and impacts. In many resource situations such circumstances can be explained as a function of poorly defined property rights which can lead to less sustainable uses and a failure to account all local values.

While biodiversity problems have similar characteristics to some other environmental problems, Dr Hodge identifies that land users do not seem to have the same duty to protect the environment with respect to biodiversity as they appear to have in connection to pollution. Instead positive initiatives may be established towards the provision of biodiversity which might be characterised as either beneficiary pays or provider gets in contrast to the alternative polluter pays concept. According to Dr Hodge, this implies the need to innovate payment mechanisms to transfer funds from beneficiaries or the tax system to the providers, consistent with the underlying distribution of property rights.

Dr Hodge is concerned to establish newer wider institutional arrangements that can provide all interested parties with an appropriate opportunity to have an influence on resource allocation decisions. These institutions could stand in for the functions of a market. In practice it is considered that there could be a vast array of institutional alternatives which can carry out the recognised functions of expressing values, legitimating interests, establishing linkage mechanisms and controlling land. Several market models of articulation, the attenuated market model and the extended market model are mentioned and then the analysis turns to alternative models including the management agreement model, the CART model and the hypothecated fund model.

According to Dr Hodge, these alternative models will be found to be appropriate in different settings where a diversity of institutions may yield a diversity of species. Crucial here is the need to provide positive incentives to landholders and to distribute costs in a low cost manner where benefits might be shared very widely, where the role of the state in terms of institutional building and support is a key.

In Chapter 13, Professor Graciela Chichilnisky's analytical motivation is clearly expressed in the title 'Development and global finance: The case for an International Bank for Environmental Settlements'. Professor Chichilnisky is concerned to redress the current environmental imbalance, where it is perceived that humanity has the ability to rapidly destroy the massive global habitat which supports the survival of the human species, with a new innovative global financial institution. The objective through the International Bank for Environmental Settlements (IBES) is to obtain market value from environmental resources without destroying them.

Professor Chichilnisky seeks to merge the interests of private financial markets with international development policy, using such instruments as emissions trading, the global reinsurance of environmental risks and the securitisation of biodiversity resources in a manner harmonious to the use of the world's resources.

Particularly, Professor Chichilnisky is concerned with the impact on developing countries where an efficiency rationale is conceived for allocating more of the property rights to the global commons to developing countries which own relatively few private goods. In the first case, it is established that environmental abatement should increase with the level of income in a country. Secondly, a fundamental insight developed here, is that conventional trading markets for certain environmental considerations may not be efficient and that new institutions like the IBES are needed to complement a market where the trade is in privately produced public goods. The insight here, which cuts across the traditional Coasian interpretation, is that personalised markets (which is Lindahl's solution), can be replaced by an appropriate choice of property rights, thus facilitating international cooperation.

Throughout the chapter Professor Chichilnisky examines which policy instruments are preferable for controlling emissions and when do market prices reflect the value of resources. Subsequently, the institutional structures are identified that will lead to efficient allocations of environmental resources, consistent with the efficiency and integrity of the market. The impact on developing countries is considered, particularly in relation to the question of whether such countries should have more of the property rights to the global commons and also how an acceptable degree of equity can be ensured for the use of the global commons.

The final contribution in this volume is entitled 'Dynamic systems modelling for scoping and consensus building' authored by Professors Robert Costanza and Matthias Ruth. While broadly outlining the various types and uses of models for complex environmental systems, the authors are primarily concerned with the use of systems models in a social setting, to build consensus on problems and policies. Fundamentally, the authors are concerned to enable and foster a high degree of consensus on the appropriateness of the assumptions of system models, as well as the results achieved by the models. The approach is thus directed to promoting a high degree of compliance with the policy options derived from the models.

Professors Costanza and Ruth thus envisage a new role for system modelling, as a tool for actually building and securing a broad consensus not only between the science and policy practitioners, but also including the stakeholders in the public sphere. In this connection the link is made to the Rawlsian notion of fairness in overlapping consensus, which is then related to robust and effective sustainable solutions which are fair and equitable.

In application the authors identify a three step process for developing system models moving from very simplified and high generality models used for scoping and consensus building, to a more realistic research modelling phase and then on to a high precision management model stage. The tradeoff between these models is identified in terms of the criteria of realism, precision and generality.

Subsequently, Professors Costanza and Ruth proceed to apply their vision to a series of case studies including studies of: US iron and steel production; US pulp and paper production; South African fynbos ecosystems; Louisiana coastal wetlands; the Florida everglades; the Patuxent river watershed in Maryland; and the Banff National Park.

The authors conclude by noting how the modelling exercise achieved a detailed set of conclusions by embodying the input and expert judgement of a broad range of stakeholders. The consensus achieved in such processes is seen as a prerequisite for the successful management of complex ecological economic systems.

2. Reconciling Internal and External Policies for Sustainable Development

Herman Daly

INTRODUCTION

The main thrust of this chapter is to present four interrelated policies for sustainable development. The policies are presented from the perspective of the US, but should apply to any country in principle. Before getting to the specific policies, I discuss a basic point of view within which the policies appear most sensible and urgent, even though I think they are also defensible to a degree within the standard neoclassical framework. The four policies are then presented in order of increasing radicalism. The first two are fairly conservative, fundamentally neoclassical and should be relatively noncontroversial, although often they are not. The third will be hotly debated by many and the fourth will be considered outrageous by most economists. It would be politic to omit the fourth, but I really cannot, since it is the complementary external policy that is logically required if the first three internal policies are not to be undercut by free trade and capital mobility. In conclusion I will spend a few pages defending the fourth and most controversial suggestion against the two most frequently raised objections.

POINT OF VIEW

Much depends on which paradigm one accepts, the economy as subsystem versus the economy as total system. For those who, understandably, have become allergic to the word 'paradigm', I suggest Joseph Schumpeter's earlier and more descriptive term, 'pre-analytic vision'. Since I think pre-analytic visions are fundamental, I will take the time to illustrate their importance for the issue at hand with a story about the evolution of the World Bank's 1992 World Development Report, *Development and the Environment*.

An early draft of the 1992 World Development Report had a diagram entitled 'The relationship between the economy and the environment'. It consisted of a square labelled 'economy', with an arrow coming in labelled 'inputs' and an arrow going out labelled 'outputs', nothing more. I worked in the Environment Department of the World Bank at that time and was asked to review and comment on the draft. I suggested that the picture was a good idea, but failed to show the environment and that it would help to have a larger box containing the one depicted and that the large box would represent the environment. Then the relation between the environment and the economy would be clear; specifically that the economy is a subsystem of the environment and depends on the environment both as a source of raw material inputs and as a sink for waste outputs. The text accompanying the diagram should explain that the environment physically sustains the economy by regenerating the low-entropy inputs that it requires and by absorbing the high-entropy wastes that it cannot avoid generating, as well as by supplying other ecological services. Environmentally sustainable development could then be defined as development which does not destroy natural support functions.

The second draft had the same diagram, but with an unlabelled box drawn around the economy, like a picture frame, with no change in the text. I commented that the larger box had to be labelled 'environment' or else it was merely decorative and that the text had to explain that the economy was related to the environment in the ways just described. The third draft omitted the diagram altogether. There was no further effort to draw a picture of the relation of the economy and the environment. I thought that was very odd.

By coincidence a few months later the Chief Economist of the World Bank, Lawrence Summers, under whom the 1992 World Development Report was being written, happened to be on a review panel at the Smithsonian Institution discussing the book *Beyond the Limits*. In that book there was a diagram showing the relation of the economy to the ecosystem as subsystem to total system, identical to what I had suggested (Figure 2.1). In the question and answer time I asked the Chief Economist if, looking at that diagram, he felt that the issue of the physical size of the economic subsystem relative to the total ecosystem was important and if he thought economists should be asking the question, 'What is the optimal scale of the macro economy relative to the environment that supports it?' His reply was immediate and definite: 'That's not the right way to look at it', he said.

Reflecting on these two experiences has strengthened my belief that the difference truly lies in our pre-analytic visions. My pre-analytic vision of the economy as subsystem leads immediately to the questions: How big is the subsystem relative to the total system? How big *can it be* without disrupting the functioning of the total system? How big *should it be*, what is its optimal scale, beyond which further growth in scale would be anti-economic - would increase environmental costs more than it increased production benefits? The Chief Economist had no intention of being sucked into these subversive questions, that is not the right way to look at it and any questions arising from that way of looking at it are simply not the right questions.

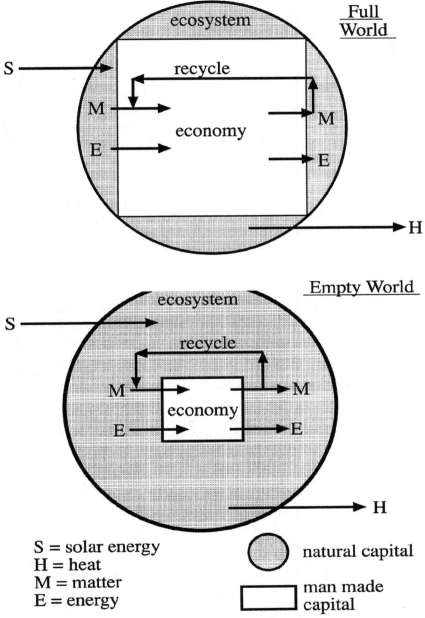

Figure 2.1   *Economy as an open subsystem of ecosystem*

That attitude sounds rather unreasonable and peremptory, but in a way that had also been my response to the diagram in the first draft of *Development and the Environment* showing the economy receiving raw material inputs from nowhere and exporting waste outputs to nowhere. That is not the right way to look at it, I basically said, and any questions arising from that picture, say, how to make the economy grow as fast as possible by speeding up throughput from an infinite source to an infinite sink, were not the right questions. Unless one has in mind the pre-analytic vision of the economy as subsystem, the whole idea of sustainable development, of an economic subsystem being sustained by a larger ecosystem whose carrying capacity it must respect, makes no sense whatsoever.

It was not surprising, therefore, that the 1992 World Development Report was incoherent on the subject of sustainable development, placing it in solitary confinement in a half page box where it was implicitly defined as nothing other than good development policy. It is the pre-analytic vision of the economy as a box floating in infinite space that allows people to speak of sustainable *growth* (as opposed to *development*) - a clear oxymoron to those who see the economy as a subsystem of a finite and non-growing ecosystem. The difference could not be more fundamental, more elementary, or more irreconcilable.

It is interesting that so much should be at stake in such a simple picture. The required tool of thought here is not a thousand equation general equilibrium model on a Cray computer. All we really need is a wide lined Big Chief Tablet with one crayola! Once you draw the boundary of the environment around the economy, you have implicitly admitted that the economy cannot expand forever. You have said that John Stuart Mill was right, that populations of human bodies and populations of capital goods cannot grow forever. At some point quantitative growth must give way to qualitative development as the path of progress and we must come to terms with Mill's vision of the classical stationary state.

But the World Bank cannot say that, at least not yet and not publicly, because growth is the official solution to poverty. If growth is physically limited, or if it begins to cost more than it is worth at the margin and thereby becomes uneconomic, then how will we lift poor people out of poverty? We pretend there is no answer, but the answer is painfully obvious: By population control; by redistribution; and by improvements in resource productivity, both technical and managerial. But population control and redistribution are considered politically impossible. Increasing resource productivity is considered a good idea until it conflicts with capital and labor productivity, until we realize that historically we have bought high productivity and high incomes for capital and labor by using resources lavishly, thereby sacrificing resource productivity in exchange for a reduction in class conflict between capital and labor. Yet resources are the limiting factor in the long run, the very factor whose productivity economic logic says should be maximized.

When we draw that containing boundary of the environment around the economy we move from 'empty world' economics to 'full world' economics. Economic logic stays the same, but the perceived pattern of scarcity changes radically and policies must change radically if they are to remain economic. That is why there is such resistance to a simple picture. The fact that the picture is so simple and so obviously realistic is why it cannot be contemplated by the growth economists. That is why they react to it much the way vampires react to crucifixes: 'No, no, take it away, please! That's not the right way to look at it!' But let us persevere in looking at it that way and turn now to consider some economic policies consistent with this full world vision.

FOUR POLICY SUGGESTIONS

Stop Counting the Consumption of Natural Capital as Income

Income is by definition the maximum amount that a society can consume this year and still be able to consume the same amount next year. That is, consumption this year, if it is to be called income, must leave intact the capacity to produce and consume the same amount next year. Thus sustainability is built into the very definition of income. But the productive capacity that must be maintained intact has traditionally been thought of as man-made capital only, excluding natural capital. We have habitually counted natural capital as a free good. This might have been justified in yesterday's empty world, but in today's full world it is anti-economic. The error of implicitly counting natural capital consumption as income is customary in three areas: (1) The System of National Accounts (SNA); (2) evaluation of projects that deplete natural capital; and (3) international balance of payments accounting.

The first (SNA) is well recognized and efforts are under way to correct it. Indeed, the World Bank played a pioneering role in this important initiative and I hope will regain its earlier interest in 'greening the GNP'.

The second (project evaluation) is well recognized by standard economics which has long taught the need to count user cost (depletion charges) as part of the opportunity cost of projects that deplete natural capital. World Bank *best* practice counts user costs, but World Bank *average* practice ignores it. Uncounted user costs show up in inflated net benefits and an overstated rate of return for depleting projects. This biases investment allocation toward projects that deplete natural capital and away from more sustainable projects. Correcting this bias is the logical first step toward a policy of sustainable development. User cost must be counted not only for depletion of nonrenewables, but also for projects that divest renewable natural capital by exploiting it beyond sustainable yield. The sink or absorptive services of natural capital, as well as its source or regenerative services, can also be depleted if used beyond sustainable capacity.

Therefore a user cost must be charged to projects that deplete sink capacity, such as the capacity of a river to carry off wastes, or, most notably, the atmosphere's ability to absorb CO_2. Measuring user cost is admittedly highly uncertain, but attempting to avoid the issue simply means that we assign to depleted natural capital the precise default value of zero, which is frequently not the best estimate.[1] Even when zero is the best estimate it should be arrived at not by default, but by reasoned calculation based on explicit assumptions about backstop technologies, discount rates and reserve lifetimes (Kellenberg and Daly 1994).

Third, in balance of payments accounting the export of depleted natural capital, whether petroleum or timber cut beyond sustainable yield, is entered in the current account and thus treated entirely as income. This is an accounting error. Some portion of those nonsustainable exports should be treated as the sale of a capital asset and entered on capital account. If this were properly done, some countries would see their apparent balance of trade surplus converted into a true deficit, one that is being financed by drawdown and transfer abroad of their stock of natural capital.

Reclassifying transactions in a way that might convert a country's balance of trade from a surplus to a deficit would trigger a whole different set of IMF recommendations and actions. This reform of balance of payments accounting should be the initial focus of the IMF's new interest in environmentally sustainable development. The World Bank should warmly encourage its sister institution to get busy on this; it does not come naturally to them.

Tax Labor and Income Less and Tax Resource Throughput More

In the past it has been customary for governments to subsidize resource

---

[1] Depletion of a nonrenewable resource has two costs: the opportunity cost of labor, capital, and other resources used to extract the resource in question, and the opportunity cost of not having the resource tomorrow because we used it up today. The latter is referred to as 'user cost' and is calculated by estimating the extra cost per unit of the best substitute that will have to be used when the resource in question is depleted, and then discounting that cost difference from the estimated date of depletion back to the present. That discounted amount is then added to the current cost of extraction to get the proper price that measures full opportunity cost.

throughput to stimulate growth.[2] Thus energy, water, fertilizer and even deforestation, are even now frequently subsidized. To its credit the World Bank has generally opposed these subsidies. But it is necessary to go beyond removal of explicit financial subsidies to the removal of implicit environmental subsidies as well. By implicit environmental subsidies I mean external costs to the community that are not charged to the commodities whose production generates them.

Economists have long advocated internalizing external costs either by calculating and charging Pigovian taxes (taxes which when added to marginal private costs make them equal to marginal social costs), or by Coasian redefinition of property rights (such that values that used to be public property and not valued in markets, become private property whose values are protected by their new owners). These solutions are elegant in theory, but often quite difficult in practice.

A blunter, but much more operational instrument would be simply to shift our tax base away from labor and income on to throughput. We have to raise public revenue somehow and the present system is highly distortionary in that by taxing labor and income in the face of high unemployment in nearly all countries, we are discouraging exactly what we want more of. The present signal to firms is to shed labor and substitute more capital and resource throughput, to the extent feasible. It would be better to economize on throughput because of the high external costs of its associated depletion and pollution and at the same time to use more labor because of the high social benefits associated with reducing unemployment - a 'double dividend' in terms of efficiency.

As a bumper sticker slogan the idea is, 'tax bads, not goods'. In more theoretical terms the idea is to stop taxing value added and start taxing that to which value is added, namely the natural resource flow yielded by natural capital (Daly 1995). Since the latter is the limiting factor in the long run (a point to be argued in the next section) and since its true opportunity cost is only poorly reflected in markets, it is reasonable to raise its effective price through taxation. Shifting the tax base to throughput induces greater resource efficiency and internalizes, in a gross, blunt manner the externalities from depletion and pollution. It also avoids the distortions of taxing income. True, the exact external costs will not have been precisely calculated and attributed

---

[2] The term 'throughput' is an inelegant but highly useful derivative of the terms input and output. The matter-energy that goes in to a system and eventually comes out is what goes through - the 'throughput' as engineers have dubbed it. A biologist's synonym might be 'the metabolic flow' by which an organism maintains itself. This physical flow connects the economy to the environment at both ends, and is of course subject to the physical laws of conservation and entropy.

to exactly those activities that caused them, as with a Pigovian tax that aims to equate marginal social costs and benefits for each activity. But those calculations and attributions are so difficult and uncertain that insisting on them in the interests of 'crackpot rigor' would be equivalent to a full employment act for econometricians.

Politically the shift toward ecological taxes could be sold under the banner of revenue neutrality. However, the income tax structure should be maintained so as to keep progressivity in the overall tax structure by taxing very high incomes and subsidizing very low incomes. But the bulk of public revenue would be raised from taxes on throughput either at the depletion or pollution end, but especially the former. The goal of the vestigial income tax would be redistribution, not net public revenue.

The shift could be carried out gradually by a preannounced schedule to minimize disruption (von Weizsacker 1992). Ecological tax reform should be a key part of structural adjustment, but should be pioneered in the North. Indeed, sustainable development itself must be achieved in the North first. It is absurd to expect much sacrifice for sustainability in the South if similar measures have not first been taken in the North.[3] The major weakness in the World Bank's ability to foster environmentally sustainable development is that it only has leverage over the South, not the North. Some way must be found for the World Bank to serve as an honest broker, an agent for reflecting the legitimate demands of the South back to the North.

Maximize the Productivity of Natural Capital in the Short Run and Invest in Increasing its Supply in the Long Run

Economic logic requires that we behave in these two ways toward the *limiting* factor of production, maximize its productivity today and invest in its increase tomorrow. Those principles are not in dispute. Disagreements do exist about whether natural capital is really the limiting factor. Some argue that man-made and natural capital are such good substitutes that the very idea of a limiting

---

[3] Even in its 1992 World Development Report (*Development and the Environment*) the World Bank has proved unable to face the most basic question: Is it better or worse for the South if the North continues to grow in its resource use? The standard view is that it is better, because growth in the North increases markets for Southern resource exports, as well as funds for aid and investment by the North in the South. The alternative view is that it makes things worse by preempting the remaining resources and ecological space needed to support Southern growth. Northern growth also increases income inequality and world political tensions. The alternative view urges continued *development* in the North, but not *growth*. The two answers to the basic question cannot both be right. The absence of that fundamental question from World Bank policy research represents a failure of both nerve and intellect, as well as a continuing psychology of denial regarding limits to growth.

factor, which requires that the factors be complementary, is irrelevant.[4] It is true that without complementarity there is no limiting factor. So the question is, are man-made capital and natural capital basically complements or substitutes? Here again we can provide perpetual full employment for econometricians and I would welcome more empirical work on this, even though I think it is sufficiently clear to common sense that natural and man-made capital are fundamentally complements and only marginally substitutable[5] (see Appendix for arguments).

In the past natural capital has been treated as superabundant and priced at zero, so it did not really matter whether it was a complement or a substitute for man-made capital. Now remaining natural capital appears to be both scarce and complementary and therefore limiting. For example, the fish catch is limited not by the number of fishing boats, but by the remaining populations of fish in the sea. Cut timber is limited not by the number of sawmills, but by the remaining standing forests. Pumped crude oil is limited not by man-made pumping capacity, but by remaining stocks of petroleum in the ground. The natural capital of the atmosphere's capacity to serve as a sink for CO_2 is likely to be even more limiting to the rate at which petroleum can be burned than is the source limit of remaining oil in the ground.

In the short run raising the price of natural capital by taxing throughput, as advocated above, will give the incentive to maximize natural capital productivity. Investing in natural capital over the long run is also needed. But how do we invest in something which by definition we cannot make? If we could make it, it would be man-made capital! For renewable resources we have the possibility of fallowing investments, or more generally 'waiting' in the Marshallian sense, allowing this year's growth increment to be added to

---

[4] Both goods and factors of production can be either complements or substitutes. For consumer goods shoes and socks are complements (used together); shoes and boots are substitutes (one used instead of the other). In building a house, bricks and wood are substitutes; bricks and masons are complements. If factors are good substitutes the absence of one does not limit the usefulness of the other. For complements, the absence of one greatly reduces the usefulness of the other. The complementary factor in short supply is then the *limiting factor*.

[5] No one questions that some resources can be substituted for others, for example, bricks for wood. But to substitute capital stock (saws and hammers) for wood is only marginally possible if at all. Capital is the agent of transformation of the natural resource flow from raw material to finished product. Resources are the *material cause* of the finished product; capital is the *efficient cause*. One material cause may substitute for another and one efficient cause for another. But, efficient cause and material cause are related as complements rather than substitutes. If man-made capital is complementary with the natural resource flow, then it is also complementary with the natural capital stock that yields that flow.

next year's stock rather than consuming it.[6] For nonrenewables we do not have this option. We can only liquidate them. So the question is how fast do we liquidate and how much of the proceeds can we count as income if we invest the rest in the best renewable substitute? And of course how much of the correctly counted income do we then consume and how much do we invest?

One renewable substitute for natural capital is the mixture of natural and man-made capital represented by tree plantations, fish farms and so on, which we may call *cultivated natural capital*. But even within this important hybrid category we have a complementary combination of natural and man-made capital components. For example, a plantation forest may use man-made capital to plant trees, control pests and choose the proper rotation, but the complementary natural capital services of rainfall, sunlight, soil and so on are still there and eventually still become limiting. Also, cultivated natural capital usually requires a reduction in biodiversity relative to natural capital proper.

From the familiar biological yield curve (Figure 2.2), it is clear that a sustainable harvest of H will be yielded either at a stock of P1 or P2. In general, P1 is the *natural capital* mode of exploitation of a wild population. P2 is the *cultivated natural capital* mode of exploitation of a bred population. At P1 we have a large population taking up a lot of ecological space, but providing, in addition to a yield of H, other natural services, as well as maintaining a larger amount of biodiversity and general resiliency. Costs are basically harvest cost of the wild population. At P2 we have a much smaller stock giving the same yield of H, requiring much less ecological space, but requiring greater maintenance, breeding, feeding and confinement costs as cultivated natural capital. The appeal of cultivated natural capital is to get H from a low P, making ecological room for other exploited (or wild) populations. But management costs are high. The appeal of P1 and the mode of natural capital proper is that management service is free and the biodiversity of larger stocks is greater. A large human scale forces more and more reliance on cultivated natural capita. In the limit, all other species become cultivated natural capital, bred and managed at the smaller population size to make more room for humans. Instrumental values such as redundancy, resiliency, stability, sustainability, would be sacrificed, along with the intrinsic value of life enjoyment by sentient subhuman species, in the interests of efficiency, defined as anything that increases the human scale.

For both renewable and nonrenewable resources, investments in enhancing

---

[6] Forgone consumption today in exchange for greater consumption tomorrow is the essence of investment. Consumption is reduced either by reducing per capita consumption or population. Therefore investment in natural capital regeneration includes investment in population control, and in technical and social structures that demand less resource use per capita.

throughput productivity are needed. Increasing resource productivity is indeed a good substitute for finding more of the resource. But the main point is that investment should be in the limiting factor and to the extent that natural capital has replaced man-made capital as the limiting factor, the World Bank's investment focus should shift correspondingly. I do not believe that it has. In fact, the failure to charge user cost on natural capital depletion, noted earlier, surely biases investment away from replenishing projects.

The three policies suggested all require the recognition and counting of costs heretofore not counted. It is difficult to imagine a global authority imposing a more complete and uniform cost accounting regime on all nations. It is also difficult to imagine nations agreeing on an international treaty to that effect. What is easy to imagine is just what we observe; different national cost accounting standards leading to an international standards lowering competition to reduce wages, environmental controls, social security standards and so on. The best way to avoid the latter is to give up the ideology of global economic integration by free trade and free capital mobility and accept the need for national tariffs to protect, not inefficient industries, but efficient national standards of cost accounting, as will be argued below.

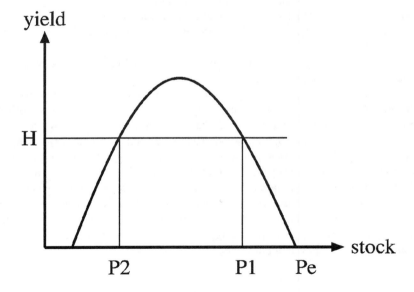

Figure 2.2   *Biological yield curve*

Move from the Ideology of Global Economic Integration by Free Trade

Free capital mobility, and export led growth - and move toward a more nationalist orientation that seeks to develop domestic production for internal markets as the first option, having recourse to international trade only when clearly much more efficient.[7]

At the present time global interdependence is celebrated as a self-evident good. The royal road to development, peace and harmony is thought to be the unrelenting conquest of each nation's market by all other nations. The word globalist has politically correct connotations, while the word nationalist has come to be pejorative. This is so much the case that it is necessary to remind ourselves that the World Bank exists to serve the interests of its members, *which are nation states, national communities* not individuals, not corporations, not even NGOs. It has no charter to serve the one world without borders cosmopolitan vision of global integration - that of converting many relatively independent national economies, loosely dependent on international trade, into one tightly integrated world economic network upon which the weakened nations depend for even basic survival.

The model of international community upon which the Bretton Woods institutions rests is that of a 'community of communities', an international federation of *national* communities cooperating to solve global problems under the principle of *subsidiarity*. The model is not the cosmopolitan one of direct global citizenship in a single integrated world community without intermediation by nation states.

To globalize the economy by erasure of national economic boundaries through free trade, free capital mobility and free, or at least uncontrolled migration, is to wound fatally the major unit of community capable of carrying out any policies for the common good. That includes not only national policies for purely domestic ends, but also international agreements required to deal with those environmental problems that are irreducibly global (CO_2 build up, ozone depletion). International agreements presuppose the ability of national governments to carry out policies in their support. If nations have no control over their borders they are in a poor position to enforce national laws designed to serve the common good, including those laws necessary to secure national compliance with international treaties.[8]

---

[7] For an earlier analysis tending strongly in this direction see Lewis (1978).

[8] As a thought experiment imagine first a world of free migration. What reason would there be in such a world for any country to try to reduce its birth rate? Now imagine that people do not migrate, but capital and goods, under free trade, migrate freely. In both cases, wages tend to equality worldwide and cheap labor is a competitive advantage. There would be no incentive for any country to reduce its birth rate, especially that of its working class majority. Does anyone think the United Nations will limit the global birth rate?

Cosmopolitan globalism weakens national boundaries and the power of national and sub-national communities, while strengthening the relative power of transnational corporations. Since there is no world government capable of regulating global capital in the global interest, and since the desirability and possibility of a world government are both highly doubtful, it will be necessary to make capital less global and more national. I know that is an unthinkable thought right now, but take it as a prediction - ten years from now the buzz words will be 'renationalization of capital' and the 'community rooting of capital for the development of national and local economies', not the current shibboleths of export led growth stimulated by whatever adjustments are necessary to increase global competitiveness. 'Global competitiveness' (frequently a thought substituting slogan) usually reflects not so much a real increase in resource productivity as a standards lowering competition to reduce wages, externalize environmental and social costs and export natural capital at low prices while calling it income (Daly 1993).

The World Bank should use the occasion of its fiftieth birthday to reflect deeply on the forgotten words of one of its founders, John Maynard Keynes:

> I sympathize therefore, with those who would minimize, rather than those who would maximize, economic entanglement between nations. Ideas, knowledge, art, hospitality, travel - these are the things which should of their nature be international. But let goods be homespun whenever it is reasonably and conveniently possible; and, above all, let finance be primarily national. (Keynes 1933)

REPLIES TO THE TWO MOST FREQUENT OBJECTIONS TO ABANDONING FREE TRADE

Growth Will Compensate

Some globalists will admit that the problems just outlined are real, but whatever costs they entail are, in their view, more than compensated by the welfare increase from economic growth brought about by free trade and global integration. While it may be true that free trade increases economic growth, the other link in the chain of argument, that growth increases welfare, is shown below to be devoid of empirical support in the US since 1947.

It is very likely that we have entered an era in which growth is increasing environmental and social costs faster than it is increasing production benefits. Growth that increases costs by more than it increases benefits is anti-economic growth and should be called that. But Gross National Product can never register anti-economic growth because nothing is ever subtracted. It is much too gross.

Although economists did not devise GNP to be a direct measure of welfare, nevertheless welfare is assumed to be highly correlated with GNP. Therefore if free trade promotes growth in GNP, it is assumed that it also promotes growth in welfare. But the link between GNP and welfare has become very questionable and with it the argument for deregulated international trade and indeed for all other growth promoting policies.

Evidence for doubting the correlation between GNP and welfare in the United States is taken from two sources.

First Nordhaus and Tobin (1972) asked, 'is growth obsolete?' as a measure of welfare and hence as a proper guiding objective of policy. To answer their question they developed a direct index of welfare, called Measured Economic Welfare (MEW) and tested its correlation with GNP over the period 1929-1965. They found that for the period as a whole GNP and MEW were indeed positively correlated. For every six units of increase in GNP there was, on average, a four unit increase in MEW. Economists breathed a sigh of relief, forgot about MEW and concentrated on GNP.

Some twenty years later John Cobb, Clifford Cobb and I (1989) revisited the issue and began development of our Index of Sustainable Economic Welfare (ISEW) with a review of the Nordhaus and Tobin MEW. We discovered that if one takes only the latter half of the period (that is, the eighteen years from 1947-1965) the correlation between GNP and MEW falls dramatically. In this most recent period, which is surely the more relevant for projections into the future, a six unit increase in GNP yielded on average only a one unit increase in MEW. This suggests that GNP growth at this stage of United States' history may be a quite inefficient way of improving economic welfare and certainly less efficient than in the past.

The ISEW was then developed to replace MEW, since the latter omitted any correction for environmental costs, did not correct for distributional changes and included leisure, which dominated the MEW and introduced many arbitrary valuation decisions.[9] The ISEW, like the MEW, though less so, was correlated with GNP up to a point beyond which the correlation turned slightly negative.

Neither the MEW nor ISEW considered the effect of individual country GNP growth on the global environment and consequently on welfare at geographic levels other than the nation. Nor was there any deduction for harmful products, such as tobacco or alcohol. Nor did we try to correct for diminishing marginal utility of income. Such considerations, we suspect, would further weaken the correlation between GNP and welfare. Also, GNP,

---

[9] For critical discussion and the latest revision of the ISEW, see Cobb and Cobb *et al.* (1994). For a presentation of the ISEW see Appendix of *For the Common Good*, Daly and Cobb (1994). See also Cobb *et al.* (1995).

MEW and ISEW all begin with Personal Consumption. Since all three measures have in common the largest single category there is a significant autocorrelation which makes the poor correlations to GNP all the more dramatic.

Measures of welfare are difficult and subject to many arbitrary judgments, so sweeping conclusions should be resisted. However, it seems fair to say that for the United States since 1947, the empirical evidence that GNP growth has increased welfare is *very* weak. Consequently any impact on welfare via free trade's contribution to GNP growth would also be very weak. In other words, the 'great benefit', for which we are urged to sacrifice community standards and industrial peace, turns out on closer inspection not to exist.

Comparative Advantage Proves that Global Integration is Beneficial

Since I am an economist and really do revere David Ricardo, the great champion of classical free trade, I think it is important to point out that if he were alive now, he would *not* support a policy of free trade and global integration as it is understood today.

The reason is simple: Ricardo was very careful to base his comparative advantage argument for free trade on the explicit assumption that capital was immobile between nations. Capital, as well as labor, stayed at home; only goods were traded internationally. It was the fact that capital could not, in this model, cross national boundaries, that led directly to replacement of absolute advantage by comparative advantage. Capital follows absolute advantage as far as it can within national boundaries. But since by assumption it cannot pursue absolute advantage across national boundaries, it has recourse to the next best strategy which is to reallocate itself within the nation according to the principle of comparative advantage.

For example, if Portugal produces both wine and cloth cheaper than does England, then capital would love to leave England and follow absolute advantage to Portugal where it would produce both wine and cloth. But by assumption it cannot. The next best thing is to specialize domestically in the production of cloth and trade it for Portuguese wine. This is because England's disadvantage relative to Portugal in cloth production is less than its disadvantage relative to Portugal in wine production. England has a comparative advantage in cloth, Portugal a comparative advantage in wine. Ricardo showed that each country would be better off specializing in the product in which it had a comparative advantage and trading for the other, regardless of absolute advantage. Free trade between the countries and competition within each country, would lead to this mutually beneficial result.

Absolute advantage is the rule for maximizing returns to capital when capital is mobile. Comparative advantage is the rule for maximizing returns to capital subject to the constraint that capital stays at home. The relevant comparison for comparative advantage is the difference between the internal cost ratios of the two countries - the unit cost ratio of cloth to wine in England compared to the unit cost ratio of cloth to wine in Portugal. Note that the units in which costs are measured may be different in each country without affecting the comparison of ratios - the units cancel out in each ratio. This means of course that absolute cost differences between countries do not matter for comparative advantage. It also means that in Ricardo's world, where capital stays at home, nations would unilaterally be able to adopt different standards of internalization of environmental and social costs, without upsetting the principle of comparative advantage - that is, harmonization would not be necessary. It is only when capital is mobile and absolute advantage reigns, that differing national cost-internalization practices would initiate an international standards-lowering competition to keep and attract capital.

Economists have been giving Ricardo a standing ovation for this demonstration ever since 1817. So wild has been the enthusiasm for the conclusion that some economists forgot the assumption upon which the argument leading to that conclusion was based; namely, internationally immobile capital. Whatever the case in Ricardo's time, in our day it would be hard to imagine anything more contrary to fact than the assumption that capital is immobile internationally. It is vastly more mobile than goods.

The argument for globalization based on comparative advantage is therefore embarrassed by a false premise. When starting from a false premise, one would have a better chance of hitting a correct conclusion if one's logic were also faulty! But Ricardo's logic is not faulty. Therefore I conclude that he would not be arguing for free trade - at least not on the basis of comparative advantage which requires such a wildly counterfactual assumption. Unlike some of today's economists and politicians, Ricardo would *never* argue that because free trade in goods is beneficial, adding free trade in capital must be even more beneficial! To use the conclusion of an argument that was premised on capital *immobility*, to support an argument in favour of capital *mobility*, is too illogical for words. To get away with something that illogical you have to hide it under a lot of intimidating, but half-baked, mathematics.

In their July 1993 draft, 'Trade and Environment: Does Environmental Diversity Detract from the Case for Free Trade?' Bhagwati and Srinivasan reaffirm the view that free trade remains the optimal policy in spite of environmental issues. But their conclusion is based on what they call 'a fairly general model ... but one where resources, such as capital, do not move across countries' (p. 11). Of course if capital is immobile between nations comparative advantage arguments still hold. The point is that in today's world capital is highly mobile. Nor do they advocate restricting capital mobility to make the world conform to the assumptions of their argument - much the contrary! Their willingness to draw concrete policy conclusions from such an injudiciously abstracted model is a classic example of what Whitehead called the 'fallacy of misplaced concreteness'. At least they honestly pointed out their assumption and did not leave it under a pile of mathematics - but without noting the triviality of their conclusion, given that assumption.

In the classical vision of Smith and Ricardo the national community embraced both national labor and national capital and these classes cooperated, albeit with conflict, to produce national goods which then competed in international markets against the goods of other nations, produced by their own national capital-labor teams.

Nowadays, in the globally integrated free trade world, it no longer makes sense to think of national teams of labor and capital. Global capitalists now communicate by mobile telephone with their former national workers in the following manner:

Sorry to inform you of your dismissal, old Union Joe, but as everybody knows, we live in a global economy now - I can buy labor abroad at one tenth the wage your union wants and with lower environmental and social taxes and still sell my product in this market or any other. Your severance check is in the mail. Good luck, Joe. - What's that? What do you mean "bonds of national community"? I just told you that we live in a global economy and have abandoned all that nationalistic stuff that caused two World Wars. Haven't you heard of Smoot and Hawley? Factor mobility is necessary for maximum efficiency and without maximum efficiency we will lose out in global competition. Yes, of course there will be a tendency to equalize wages worldwide, but profits will also equalize. Well, yes, of course wages will be equalized downward and profits equalized upward. What else would you expect in a global economy that reflects world supply and demand? I can't change the law of supply and demand, Joe. Besides, don't you want the Chinese and Mexican workers to be as rich as you are? You're not a racist, are you, Joe? Furthermore, economists have proved that free trade benefits everyone. So be grateful and now that you have some time, why not enrol in Econ 101 at your local community college - try to learn some economics, Joe. It will help you feel better.

At this stage in the dialogue there is not much community left. We have here the abrogation of a basic social agreement between labor and capital over how to divide up the value that they jointly add to raw materials. That agreement has been reached nationally, not internationally. It was not reached by economic theory, but through generations of national debate, elections, strikes, lockouts, court decisions and violent conflicts. That agreement on which national community and industrial peace depend, is being repudiated in the interests of global integration. That is a very poor trade, even if you call it 'free trade'.

Free trade, specialization and global integration, mean that nations are no longer free *not* to trade. Yet freedom not to trade is surely necessary if trade is to remain mutually beneficial. National production for the national market should be the dog and international trade its tail. But the globalist free traders want to tie the dogs' tails together so tightly that the international knot will wag the national dogs in what they envision as a harmoniously choreographed canine ballet. But I foresee a multilateral dogfight. High consuming countries, whether their high consumption results from many people, or from high consumption per capita, will, in a finite and globally integrated full world, more and more be at each others throats.

To avoid war, nations must both consume less and become more self sufficient. But free traders say we should become less self sufficient and more globally integrated as part of the overriding quest to consume ever more. That is the worst advice I can think of.

Appendix

A point sure to be contested is the assertion that man-made and natural capital are complements. Many economists insist that they are substitutes. It is therefore necessary to argue the case for complementarity.

(a) One way to make an argument is to assume the opposite of what you want to demonstrate and then show that it is absurd. If man-made capital were a near perfect substitute for natural capital, then natural capital would also be a near perfect substitute for man-made capital. But in the empty world we already had an abundance of natural capital, which, as a near perfect substitute for man-made capital, would have made the effort to accumulate man-made capital absurd, since we already possessed an abundant supply of a near perfect substitute. But historically we did accumulate man-made capital, precisely because it is complementary to natural capital.

(b) Man-made capital is itself a physical transformation of natural resources which are the flow yield from the stock of natural capital. Therefore, producing more of the alleged substitute (man-made capital), physically requires more of the very thing being substituted for (natural capital) - the defining condition of complementarity!

(c) Man-made capital (along with labor) is an agent of transformation of the resource flow from raw material inputs into product outputs. The natural resource flow (and the natural capital stock that generates it) are the *material cause* of production; the capital stock that transforms raw material inputs into product outputs is the *efficient cause* of production. One cannot substitute efficient cause for material cause, as one cannot build the same wooden house with half the timber no matter how many saws and carpenters one tries to substitute. Also, to process more timber into more wooden houses, in the same time period, requires more saws, carpenters and so on. Clearly the basic relation of man-made and natural capital is one of complementarity, not substitutability. Of course one could substitute bricks for timber, but that is the substitution of one resource input for another, not the substitution of capital for resources. In making a brick house one would face the analogous inability of trowels and masons to substitute for bricks.

Regarding the house example I am frequently told that insulation (capital) is a substitute for resources (energy for space heating). If the house is considered the final product, then capital (agent of production, efficient cause) cannot end up as a part (material cause) of the house, whether as wood, brick, or insulating material. The insulating material is a resource like wood or brick, not capital. If the final product is not taken as the house but the service of the house in providing warmth, then the entire house, not only insulating material, is capital. In this case more or better capital (a well-insulated house) does reduce the waste of energy. Increasing the efficiency with which a resource is used is certainly a good substitute for more of the resource. But these kinds of waste-reducing efficiency measures (recycling prompt scrap, sweeping up sawdust and using it for fuel or particle board, reducing heat loss from a house and the like) are all rather marginal substitutions that soon reach their limit.

The complementarity of man-made and natural capital is made obvious at a concrete and commonsense level by asking: What good is a sawmill without a forest; a fishing boat without populations of fish; a refinery without petroleum deposits; an irrigated farm without an aquifer or river? We have long recognized the complementarity between public infrastructure and private capital - what good is a car or truck without roads to drive on? Following Lotka and Georgescu-Roegen we can take the concept of natural capital even further and distinguish between endosomatic (within skin) and exosomatic (outside skin) natural capital. We can then ask, what good is the private endosomatic capital of our lungs and respiratory system without the public exosomatic capital of green plants that take up our carbon dioxide in the short run, while in the long run replenishing the enormous atmospheric stock of oxygen and keeping the atmosphere at the proper mix of gases (the mix to which our respiratory system is adapted) and therefore complementary.

If natural and man-made capital are obviously complements, how is it that economists have overwhelmingly treated them as substitutes? First, not all economists have done so. Leontief's input-output economics with its assumption of fixed factor proportions treats all factors as complements. Second, the formal, mathematical definitions of complementarity and substitutability are such that in the two factor case the factors must be substitutes. Since most textbooks are written on two-dimensional paper this case receives most attention.

The usual definition of complementarity requires that for a given constant output a rise in the price of one factor would reduce the quantity of both factors. In the two factor case both factors means all factors and it is impossible to keep output constant while reducing the input of all factors. But complementarity might be defined back into existence in the two factor case by avoiding the constant output condition. For example, two factors could be considered complements if an increase in one alone will not increase output, but an increase in the other will - and perfect complements if an increase in neither factor alone will increase output, but an increase in both will. It is not sufficient to treat complementarity as if it were nothing more than limited substitutability. That means that we could get along with only one factor well enough, with only the other less well, but that we do not need both. Complementarity means we need both and that the one in shortest supply is limiting. Imagine the L-shaped isoquants that depict the case of perfect complementarity. Now erase the right angle and replace it with a tiny 90-degree arc. This seems to me the most realistic case - a very marginal range of substitution quickly giving way to a dominant relation of complementarity.

Third, mathematical convenience continues to dominate reality in the general reliance on Cobb-Douglas and other constant elasticity of substitution production functions in which there is near infinite substitutability of factors, in particular of capital for resources.

Georgescu-Roegen deserves to be quoted at length on this point. He writes the Solow-Stiglitz variant of the Cobb-Douglas function as:

$$Q = K^{a_1} . R^{a_2} . L^{a_3} \qquad (2.1)$$

Where Q is output, K is the stock of capital, R is the flow of natural resources used in production, L is the labor supply and $a_1 + a_2 + a_3 = 1$ and of course, $a_i > 0$.

From this formula it follows that with a constant labor power, L_0, one could obtain any Q_0, if the flow of natural resources satisfies the condition

$$R^{a_2} = \frac{Q_0}{K^{a_1} . L^{a_3}_0} \qquad (2.2)$$

This shows that R may be as small as we wish, provided K is sufficiently large. Ergo, we can obtain a constant annual product indefinitely even from a very small stock of resources $R > 0$, if we decompose R into an infinite series $R = \text{Sum } R_i$, with $R_i \rightarrow 0$, use R_i in year i and increase the stock of capital each year as required by (2). But this ergo is not valid in actuality. In actuality , the increase of capital implies an additional depletion of resources. And if $K \rightarrow$ infinity, then R will rapidly be exhausted by the production of capital. Solow and Stiglitz could not have come out with their conjuring trick had they borne in mind, first, that any material process consists in the transformation of some materials into others (the flow elements) by some agents (the fund elements) and second, that natural resources are the very sap of the economic process. They are not just like any other production factor. A change in capital or labor can only diminish the amount of waste in the production of a commodity: No agent can create the material on which it works. Nor can capital create the stuff out of which it is made. In some cases it may also be that the same service can be provided by a design that requires less matter or energy. But even in this direction there exists a limit, unless we believe that the ultimate fate of the economic process is an earthly Garden of Eden.

> The question that confronts us today is whether we are going to discover new sources of energy that can be safely used. No elasticities of some Cobb-Douglas function can help us to answer it (Georgescu-Roegen, in Smith 1979, p. 98).

To my knowledge neither Solow nor Stiglitz has ever replied to Georgescu-Roegen's critique.

REFERENCES

Cobb, C.W. and Cobb, J.B. Jr. *et al.* 1994. *The Green National Product.* New York: University Press of America.

Cobb, C.W. *et al.* 1995. 'If the GDP is up, why is America down?' *Atlantic Monthly,* October.

Daly, H.E. 1993. 'The perils of free trade', *Scientific American,* November.

Daly, H.E. 1995. 'Consumption and welfare: Two views of value added', *Review of Social Economy,* LIII(4), 451-73.

Daly, H.E. and Cobb, J. 1994. *For the Common Good* (Appendix). Boston: Beacon Press (second edition).

Kellenberg, J. and Daly, H.E. 1994. 'Counting user costs in evaluation of projects that deplete natural capital'. Working Paper, ENVPE, World Bank.

Keynes, J.M. 1933. 'National self-sufficiency', in Moggeridge, D. (ed.), *The Collected Writings of John Maynard Keynes,* Vol. 21. London: Macmillan and Cambridge University Press.

Nordhaus, W.D. and Tobin, J. 1972. 'Is growth obsolete?', in *Economic Growth, Fiftieth Anniversary Colloquium,* Vol. 5. New York: National Bureau of Economic Research.

Lewis, W.A. 1978. *The Evolution of the International Economic Order.* Princeton University Press.

Smith, V.K. (ed.) 1979. *Scarcity and Growth Reconsidered.* Baltimore: RFF and Johns Hopkins Press, 98 pp.

von Weizsacker, E. 1992. *Ecological Tax Reform.* London: Zed Books.

3. Sustainability as the Basis of Environmental Policy

Paul Ekins

GENERAL DEFINITIONS AND DETERMINANTS

The basic meaning of sustainability is the capacity for continuance more or less indefinitely into the future. It is now clear that, in aggregate, current human ways of life do not possess that capacity, either because they are destroying the environmental conditions necessary for their continuance, or because their environmental effects will cause unacceptable social disruption and damage to human health. The environmental effects in question include climate change, ozone depletion, acidification, toxic pollution, the depletion of renewable resources (for example, forests, soils, fisheries and water) and of non-renewable resources (for example, fossil fuels) and the extinction of species.

A way of life is a complex bundle of values, objectives, institutions and activities, with ethical, environmental, economic and social dimensions. While current concern about unsustainability largely has an ecological basis, it is clear that human situations or ways of life can be unsustainable for social and economic reasons as well. The pertinent questions are: For the environment, can its contribution to human welfare and to the human economy be sustained? For the economy, can today's level of wealth creation be sustained? And for society, can social cohesion and important social institutions be sustained?

Provided that the inter-relatedness of the different dimensions is borne in mind, it can be useful to distinguish between the implications for sustainability of human mores, relationships and institutions (the social dimension); of the allocation and distribution of scarce resources (the economic dimension); and of the contribution to both of these from, and their effects on, the environment and its resources (the ecological dimension). Clearly human relationships may be socially unsustainable (for example, those leading to civil war) independently of economic or ecological factors; and a particular allocation of resources may be economically unsustainable (leading, for example, to growing budget deficits) independently of social or ecological factors.

33

Similarly, a given level of economic growth may be unsustainable for purely economic reasons, insofar as it is leading to increased inflation or balance of payments deficits; on the other hand, it may be socially unsustainable insofar as it is increasing income inequalities or undermining structures of social cohesion such as the family or community; or it may be environmentally unsustainable insofar as it is depleting resources on which the economic growth itself depends.

One way of illustrating the complexities involved is through the matrix shown in Table 3.1, where the rows show the types of sustainability and the columns the influences on those types, across the same dimensions. In the example above, the sustainability of economic growth would be considered across the second row, with environmental influences (for example, resource depletion) in box A, economic influences (for example, inflation, balance of payments) in box B and social influences (for example, social cohesion) in box C. A fourth column has been added to the matrix to indicate the importance for sustainability of ethical influences. Relevant influences in box E, for example, would be concern for future generations or non-human forms of life; in box F they could be attitudes to poverty and income distribution.

Table 3.1. Types of sustainability and their interactions

Types of Sustainability	Influences on Sustainability			
	Ethical	Environmental	Economic	Social
Environmental	E		D	
Economic		A	B	C
Social	F			

Environmental sustainability may always be considered a desirable characteristic of a human situation, though some states of such sustainability may be better than others. In contrast, economic and social sustainability have no such happy connotation. As Hardoy *et al.* stress: 'When judged by the length of time for which they (were) sustained, some of the most successful societies were also among the most exploitative, where the abuse of human rights was greatest' (Hardoy *et al.* 1993, pp. 180-1). Also, poverty and the evils which go with it may be all too sustainable. Similarly, in many countries structural unemployment is showing worrying signs of long term sustainability.

This chapter's principal focus is the environment economy relationship (boxes A and D in Table 3.1). But such a focus necessarily includes all the above dimensions, the implications of which for environmental sustainability will now be briefly explored. In a situation of any complexity, the dimensions of sustainability will generally interact in a multiplicity of ways. Any attempt to proceed from the symptoms of unsustainability to their practical remediation which fails to take these interactions into account will be in grave danger of ineffective and perhaps counterproductive, intervention.

THE ETHICS OF SUSTAINABILITY

According to the Brundtland Report: 'Even the narrow notion of physical sustainability implies a concern for social equity between generations, a concern that must logically be extended to equity within each generation. ... Our inability to promote the common interest in sustainable development is often a product of the relative neglect of economic and social justice within and amongst nations'. (WCED 1987, pp. 43,49). The UK Government, in its environment White Paper, also emphasised the moral basis of environmental concern: 'The ethical imperative of stewardship ... must underlie all environmental policies. ... We have a moral duty to look after our planet and hand it on in good order to future generations' (HMG 1990, p. 10).

How a society uses its environment depends first and foremost on its world view, its perception of the nature of the world and the status of human beings and other life forms within it. It is likely, for example, that a secular, anthropocentric world view will sanction different uses of the environment and permit more environmental destruction, than a world view in which the earth and all life within it is perceived as sacred.

From its world view a society will derive its concept of environmental justice: The relative rights of non-human forms of life, of future human generations and of current human generations to benefit from, share or just exist in 'the environment'. Environmental sustainability gains in strength as an imperative the more it is perceived that the well being and opportunities of future humans and non-human beings should not be sacrificed for present human advantage.

From its world view, too, a society will derive its means for valuing and taking decisions about the environment. If the environment is viewed primarily as an economic resource, then techniques of environmental economic valuation will be perceived as the most important environmental inputs into decision making processes.

It is likely that a society's norms of environmental justice will be related to its norms of economic and social justice. If basic personal and civil rights are denied, then environmental rights are unlikely to be respected, or even recognised. Thus sustainability and democracy are related. Further, if non-environmental economic wealth is unequally distributed, access to environmental goods is also likely to be inegalitarian. This has an obvious and direct importance for sustainability, if indeed it is true that poverty is a great destroyer of the environment, as is often asserted.

The ethics of sustainability will also determine to a considerable extent where the responsibility for promoting environmental sustainability is perceived to lie and the degree of coercion in its enforcement that is considered justified. The Polluter Pays Principle, acceded to by OECD countries as early as 1972, but by no means fully implemented, is not only a maxim of economic efficiency; it is also a statement of moral responsibility. If polluters under prevailing economic and social arrangements do not pay and governments are invoked to make them do so, how governments proceed with this task will depend on the political and social contract between governors and governed, on balances of rights and responsibilities and the institutions that express and enforce them. This leads naturally to consideration of sustainability's social dimension.

THE SOCIAL DIMENSION OF SUSTAINABILITY

Social sustainability refers to a society's ability to maintain, on the one hand, the necessary means of wealth creation to reproduce itself and, on the other, a shared sense of social purpose to foster social integration and cohesion. Partly this is a question of having a sustainable economy, as discussed below. Partly it is a question of culture and values. Social sustainability is likely to be a necessary condition for the widespread commitment and involvement which *Agenda 21*, the document to emerge from the United Nations Conference on Environment and Development, sees as critical to the achievement of sustainable development: 'Critical to the effective implementation of the objectives, policies and mechanisms ... of *Agenda 21* will be the commitment and genuine involvement of all social groups'. (*Agenda 21*, Chapter 23, Preamble, *Earth Summit '92*, p. 191).

Western industrial societies are often called 'consumer societies', presumably because it is perceived that in these societies consumption is the most important contributor to human welfare. Certainly the principal objective of public policy in these societies is the growth of the GNP. The importance that these societies attach to consumption is not only problematic environmentally, because of the level of consumption and consequent environmental impacts, to which such an emphasis can and often does lead. It is also problematic socially. A dominant social goal of increasing competitive, individualistic consumption does not seem likely to foster social cohesion, especially in an economic system that is subject to cyclical recession and increasing inequality.

Poverty is always an economic problem in the sense that it denotes chronic scarcity at an individual level. It is an ethical problem because this scarcity often induces acute suffering. In some industrialised countries, relative (and sometimes absolute) poverty is also a growing social problem, in terms of its impacts on the social fabric and on the social sense of security, which act to reduce the well being of the non-poor.

The sense of identity and social purpose of very many people, as well as their income, derives in large part from their employment. Extended unemployment, therefore, not only leads to poverty, but also to the loss of these other characteristics, which is probably more to blame than poverty for unemployment's high correlation with ill health, mental stress and family breakdown. Unemployment is not just a waste of economic resources, in terms of the unemployed's lost production. It is socially destructive as well, and, at levels not much higher than those presently pertaining in Europe, may be expected to be socially unsustainable. Welfare states were established, both to give practical expression to a sense of social justice and to maintain social cohesion, at far lower levels of unemployment. At current levels they find it difficult to sustain the necessary transfer payments to accomplish these objectives, especially in a climate of growing international competition and taxpayer resistance.

Another contributor to people's sense of identity is their membership of and involvement in their local community. In an era of globalisation, the economic life of local communities tends to become increasingly extended. The concept of a local economy that contributes to local livelihoods and responds to local priorities is increasingly unrealistic. To a lesser extent, even national economic options are becoming externally determined. Yet the principal political institutions, that are expected to promote wealth creation and foster wider well being, operate at the national and sub-national level. Globalisation damages a sense of social connectedness, of community, while the mismatch between economic and political realities undermines confidence in political processes. Neither phenomenon is helpful for social sustainability. It is possible that local environmental action - both political and practical - will help to maintain or regenerate local social purpose and identity.

THE ECONOMIC DIMENSION OF SUSTAINABILITY

Economic sustainability is most commonly interpreted as a condition of non-declining economic welfare projected into the future (Pezzey 1992). It is well established that economic optimality (the maximisation of the present value of consumption) is quite distinct from sustainability and that in fact optimality is compatible with unsustainability.

Economic welfare derives from, *inter alia*, income and from the environment, which performs various functions, some of which contribute to production and therefore income, others of which contribute to welfare directly. Income is generated by stocks of capital, including manufactured, human and natural capital. Natural capital also performs the welfare creating environmental functions. Non-declining economic welfare requires, *ceteris paribus*, that the stock of capital be maintained (Pezzey 1992).

There is then the issue as to whether it is the total stock of capital that must be maintained, with substitution allowed between various parts of it, or whether certain components of capital, particularly natural capital, are non-substitutable, that is, they contribute to welfare in a unique way that cannot be replicated by another capital component. 'Weak' environmental sustainability conditions derive from a perception that welfare is not normally dependent on a specific form of capital and can be maintained by substituting manufactured for natural capital. 'Strong' sustainability conditions derive from a different perception that substitutability of manufactured for natural capital is seriously limited by such environmental characteristics as irreversibility, uncertainty and the existence of 'critical' components of natural capital, which make a unique contribution to welfare (Pearce and Atkinson 1992, Turner 1992). An even greater importance is placed on natural capital by those who regard it in many instances as a complement to man-made capital (Daly 1992).

To some extent it is possible to view the process of industrialisation as the application of human and social capital to natural capital to transform it into human-made capital. But it is now clear that such substitutability is not complete. If our current development is unsustainable, it is because it is depleting some critical, non-substitutable components of the capital base on which it depends.

The difference between weak and strong sustainability is important to the argument about the compatibility of sustainability and GDP growth. In general, it may be said that value added (GDP) is generated by transforming energy and materials from the natural environment into human-made goods and services. Fewer environmental goods can be permanently transformed into human-made capital under strong sustainability than under the weak version. *Ceteris paribus*, strong sustainability conditions could therefore be expected to make the generation of GDP more difficult. The general conditions for compatibility of GDP growth and environmental sustainability will be explored in more detail later, but it should be noted here that the fewer the substitution possibilities allowed, the more stringent the conditions in practice become.

CONSIDERATIONS OF ENVIRONMENTAL SUSTAINABILITY

The contribution of the environment to the human economy and to human life in general can be regarded as taking place through the operation of a wide range of 'environmental functions'. This concept was first employed in economic analysis by Hueting (1980) and has been extensively developed by de Groot (1992). De Groot defines environmental functions as 'the capacity of natural processes and components to provide goods and services that satisfy human needs' (de Groot 1992, p. 7). These 'natural processes and components' can in turn be identified as the stocks of and flows from 'natural capital' (though de Groot does not use the term), which features in various definitions of sustainability and sustainable development (see, for example, Pearce *et al.* 1989). De Groot identifies thirty seven environmental functions, which he classifies under four headings: Regulation, carrier, production and information (*ibid.* p. 15).

More simply, environmental functions can be grouped under three headings: Provision of resources for human activity; absorption of wastes from human activity; and provision of environmental services independently of or interdependently with human activity.

These two classifications are not contradictory. The resource functions in the second typology correspond broadly to the production functions of the first, but also include some carrier functions. The waste absorption functions are included among the regulation functions; and the provision of services includes the information functions and some regulation and carrier functions.

With the increase of the human population and the scale of its activities, the environmental functions are increasingly in competition with each other. Choices have to be made between them and some functions are lost. Lost functions represent costs to be ascribed to the chosen functions. It is in this sense that the environment has become an economic factor: It is increasingly scarce; the uses to which it is put are increasingly competing; and it is an important ingredient of human welfare. The choices between environmental functions are therefore precisely analogous to other economic choices.

The environmental sustainability of human ways of life refers to the ability of the environment to sustain those ways of life. The environmental sustainability of economic activity refers to the continuing ability of the environment to provide the necessary inputs to the economy to enable it to maintain economic welfare. Both these sustainabilities in turn depend on the maintenance of the requisite environmental functions, according to some classification as above. Which functions are important for which ways of life and which economies and the level at which they should be sustained, will vary to some extent by culture and society, although there are obviously basic biophysical criteria for human production, consumption and existence. Such considerations provide the context for the setting of standards of sustainability, to be discussed below.

As has been seen, partly the concern over the environmental unsustainability of current ways of life has an ethical basis: Some consider it wrong to diminish the environmental options of future generations below those available today; others consider wrong the impacts on other life forms that unsustainability implies. Partly the concern derives from perceived self interest. Unsustainability threatens costs and disruption to ways of life in the future that are or may be greater than those incurred by moving voluntarily towards sustainability now. The self-interested concern about unsustainability will obviously become stronger as the time scale within which the costs and disruption will be experienced is perceived to shorten. This is probably the reason for the current strengthening of public anxiety about the environment.

While some would view environmental sustainability as an ethical imperative and it is becoming an increasingly important, though not yet dominant, objective of public policy, it is not usually viewed as an end in itself. It is, rather, a present desirability with regard to future human development; and yet the conditions for sustainability can act as a constraint on present development. Sustainability guarantees certain life opportunities in the future at the cost of the modification or sacrifice of life opportunities in the present. The political argument and the tension in the concept of sustainable development, is over the acceptability of and uncertainties involved in the tradeoffs. The task for science is to clarify the uncertainties as far as possible. The task for economic analysis is to elaborate the economic implications of moving towards sustainability and show how the costs can be minimised, once the definition of and need for sustainability have been accepted.

COSTS OF UNSUSTAINABILITY

To apply the standard economic approach to problems of unsustainability, one should seek to equate the marginal benefit produced by the activity causing the unsustainability with the marginal cost of that unsustainability. Where both costs and benefits are expressed in well functioning markets with socially just property rights, this job can be left to those markets. Unfortunately, environmental problems are often not mediated by such markets. Most of the effects escape the market mechanism (they are externalities) and there can be insuperable problems, with regard to basic feasibility and the level of transaction costs, to applying the Coasian remedy of defining property rights in order to create those markets (Pearce and Turner 1990).

Where costs or benefits escape markets and markets cannot be created to capture them, the economic approach is to apply some valuation technique in order nevertheless to express the cost or benefit in monetary terms and so bring it into the calculus. Environmental systems have many different kinds of values, relating to their different functions. Pearce (1993, p. 22) considers that the total economic value (TEV) of these systems can be expressed as:

TEV = Direct use value + Indirect use value + Option value + Existence value

Where the direct use value relates broadly to the production of at least potentially measurable, marketable outputs; the indirect use value relates to other uses of production functions and of the regulation, carrier and information functions; the option value relates to people's desire to sustain these functions for possible future use even if they are not being used currently; and existence value relates to people's desire to sustain these functions irrespective of their use. Pearce considers existence value to capture at least part (the humanly defined part) of 'intrinsic' value (*ibid.* p. 15).

Within this basic formulation of value, there are several possible ways of trying to calculate the value of environmental functions and thence the economic implications of their loss.

Costs in surrogate markets
People's valuation of environmental functions may be deducible from the costs they are prepared to incur to make use of them (for example, by paying more for well situated houses or paying to travel to parks).

Damage costs
The impairment or loss of a function may damage economic productivity or human welfare. Such damage may or may not be remedied and may or may not give rise to compensation, which might include actual payments, the provision of substitutes or hypothetical willingness to accept valuations. Any of the costs of the damage, its remedy or compensation for it may be used as a valuation of the environmental function.

Maintenance and protection costs
The costs of maintaining and protecting environmental functions can be regarded as expressions of their worth to human society. These costs may be actual payments made or hypothetical costs, as in willingness to pay evaluations; or they may be opportunity costs, that is, the costs of foregoing otherwise beneficial activities which would unacceptably impair or destroy an environmental function.

Restoration costs
The costs associated with the impairment or loss of a function may under some circumstances be equated to the cost of restoring that function to some agreed level.

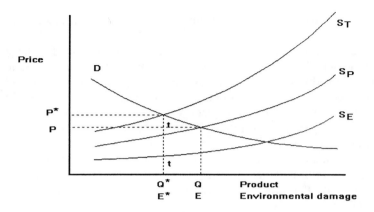

a   **Supply and demand of a good with an environmental externality**

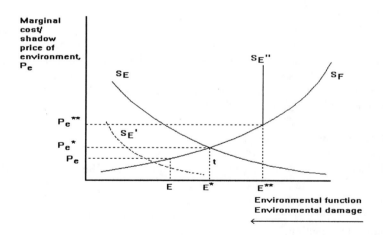

b   **Costs related to environmental damage**

Figure 3.1.   Environmental costs and their internalization

Figure 3.1 illustrates the economic problem and the necessity for cost evaluation in order to arrive at a solution. In Figure 3.1a the horizontal axis has two variables on different scales: The output of a good and the environmental damage associated with its production, which rises in proportion to output. S_P is the (private) supply curve of the good. S_E is the marginal external environmental cost curve and can be thought of as the 'supply curve' of the environmental damage, which is an unintended output of production. The combined social supply curve of the good is therefore represented by S_T, where $S_T = S_P + S_E$. The good's demand curve is D. The optimal economic solution to the problem is to levy a tax, t, equal to the difference between the private and combined cost curves at the optimal output level Q^*. The tax, t, is also equal to the marginal external social cost at that output.

Figure 3.1b reverses the horizontal axis for the environmental damage, so that S_E can now be viewed as the demand curve for the environmental function(s) affected by the good's production. S_F is the marginal cost curve for preventing or remedying the environmental damage and can be regarded as the supply curve of the relevant environmental function(s) for this use. Expenditures on preventing environmental damage will change the relationship between output and environmental damage and thus may enable damage to be reduced without reducing output. In this formulation, the economic problem becomes the location of E^*, the optimal level of the environmental function, where the current level of the function is given by E (the E and E^* are the same levels of environmental damage/function as in Figure 3.1a).

The various techniques for measuring the kinds of costs described under A, B and C above represent attempts to determine the S_E curves in Figure 3.1, the 'total economic value' (as earlier defined) of the environmental sacrifice. Both de Groot and Pearce acknowledge the controversial nature of some of these techniques, especially contingent valuation (willingness to pay/accept, WTP/WTA), for arriving at a credible valuation of environmental functions. Option and existence value are particularly difficult to measure. As Pearce says, only contingent valuation can be used in these cases (Pearce 1993, p. 74).

De Groot considers that 'accurate economic quantification of existence values attached to ecosystems is quite impossible' (de Groot 1992, p. 134) and that 'it is quite difficult if not impossible to assign a monetary value to the option value of natural ecosystems' (de Groot 1992, p. 136). It must also be borne in mind that the environmental costs (or benefits) may be incurred in the future, in which case the calculation of their present value involves the use of a discount rate, the appropriate value of which for distant, large environmental effects is a further matter of great controversy (de Groot 1992 and Pearce 1993, as well as Cline 1993 and Birdsall and Steer 1993 for further discussion).

The values of environmental functions produced by these techniques can vary enormously. Pearce 1993 (p. 166) reports implicit willingness to pay valuations for tropical forests that vary by a factor of 400 without any evidence that this difference relates to difference in forest quality. Again, different methods of valuing the potential benefits in OECD countries of medicinal forest plants under threat of extinction produced results that varied between $17.2 billion and $720 billion (*ibid.* p. 86). Another example that enters into some environmental valuations is the value of a human 'statistical life', $1 million in one study and $4 million in another (*ibid.* pp. 45, 87). Such variations, undermine the credibility and usefulness of the techniques.

These differences in valuation are not surprising given the common characteristics of many of the symptoms of unsustainability, which make them most intractable for economic analysis and which include chronic uncertainty often verging on the indeterminate; irreversibility; profound social and cultural implications; actual or potential grave damage to human health, including threats to life; global scope; and a long-term intergenerational time-scale.

There is rarely any generally acceptable way of putting a money value on costs with these characteristics, especially when the characteristics are combined. Microeconomic techniques of hedonic pricing, contingent valuation and cost-benefit analysis are not able realistically to assess the economic costs of displacing millions of people from low-lying coastal areas (global warming); of hundreds of thousands of extra eye-cataracts and skin cancers (ozone depletion); of other processes of large-scale environmental degradation, such as current rates of deforestation, desertification and water depletion, which entail considerable national or international threats to life and livelihood; of the possible unravelling of ecosystems (species extinction); of the persistent release of serious toxins (for example, radiation) or the effects of major disasters (for example, Chernobyl, Bhopal).

A danger of seeking to arrive at a money valuation of effects such as these is that they will be underestimated and decisions will be taken in favour of the far more certain, near term benefits that accrue from environmental destruction. This amounts to the derivation of only a partial demand curve such as S'_E in Figure 3.1b), which leads to an excessive level of environmental damage. It is here that the concept of sustainability can be useful.

The rhetoric in favour of environmental sustainability at gatherings such as the Rio Summit suggest that it is an increasingly important human priority. Insofar as it is taken to be an over-riding priority, the implicit costs of unsustainability can be thought of as approaching infinity. In Figure 3.1b, if E** is taken to be the minimum sustainable level of the environmental function(s), then accepting the priority of environmental sustainability amounts to deriving a demand curve for the function(s) of S''_E. E** will not necessarily be the same as the efficient level of the environmental function (E*), for, as

Pearce (1993, p. 47) says: 'An efficient use of resources need not be a sustainable one'. S_F has already been identified as the marginal restoration or abatement cost associated with supplying the environmental function(s) and corresponding to costs type D in the earlier discussion. These costs normally *are* determinable to acceptable levels of accuracy.

The point of intersection of the S_F curve with the S''_E curve gives the shadow price of environmental sustainability (P_c^{**}), which in turn puts a value on the extent to which the environment is underpriced (= $P_c^{**} - P_c$), leading to unsustainable levels of economic activity. The E** levels of environmental quality are derived from sustainability standards, as discussed below. The first step in deriving the S_F curve is to trace the causes of unsustainability.

MAPPING UNSUSTAINABLE PROCESSES

Unsustainability arises from activities of production and consumption. At a certain level these cause competition between environmental functions. Following Hueting (1980) again this competition can be quantitative, qualitative or spatial. Quantitative competition results from the extraction and depletion of resources. Qualitative competition results from the emission of substances (or noise) at or resulting in disruptive levels or concentrations. Spatial competition arises from occupation of space resulting in congestion. Unsustainability arises from some of the effects of the depletion, concentration and congestion on living things, including people (biotic effects), or on the human way of life.

All competition between environmental functions entails costs and is appropriate for economic analysis. However, not all such competition results in problems of unsustainability. Noise is an example of qualitative competition which can be disruptive but which is not therefore necessarily a problem of unsustainability as such. It is an economic problem but need not be a sustainability problem. The boundary between the two is defined by the sustainability conditions and standards.

It is, however, important to attempt the economic evaluation of even non-sustainability problems, because, in the event of them being resolved as a by-product of measures which are directed at sustainability problems, the net cost of these measures is reduced by the now foregone cost of the resolved (non-sustainability) problem. Examples are where a transport policy aimed at reducing emissions also reduces noise because of a diminution of road traffic (cost foregone); or where an agricultural policy aimed at reducing pesticide concentrations results in a landscape of greater aesthetic or amenity value (benefit gained). While the cost and benefit may be incidental to the achievement of sustainability they should still be accounted for when computing the cost of the sustainability measure itself.

In mapping processes of unsustainability, the following steps are required, with reference to Figure 3.2:

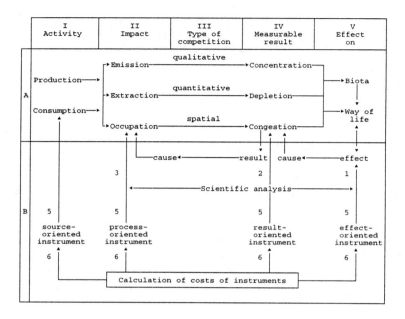

A - causal sequences; B - analytic sequences
Numbers 1-6 refer to the numbered paragraphs

Figure 3.2.   Mapping processes of unsustainability

1. The effects on the biota or human way of life (V) must be identified and, if possible, quantified.

2. The causes of these effects must be determined scientifically: Whether they are due to concentration, depletion or congestion (IV) and of what.

3. These causes will themselves be the result of qualitative, quantitative or spatial competition between environmental functions (III) and must in turn be related to the emissions, extraction or occupation patterns of particular

human activities (II). The boundaries and levels of these activity patterns and their effects must be established (see next section). Thus far the task is one of scientific analysis and the production of appropriate environmental statistics.

4. Standards must be set for the effects on biota and the human way of life which are compatible with sustainability. These standards must then be traced back through the lines of cause and effect established in 2 and 3, to arrive at sustainability standards for emission, depletion and occupation.

5. Instruments, which might be market based, regulatory or technical, must be devised to meet these standards (see Opschoor and Vos 1989 for a discussion of economic instruments in general). These instruments can either be effect-oriented (applied to the effects), result-oriented (applied to the concentrations, depletion or congestion), process-oriented (applied to the emissions, extraction or occupation) or source-oriented (applied to the activity, either reducing its volume or changing its nature). The instruments themselves might have environmental implications (for example, the quarrying and transport of lime for use in counteracting the acidification of lakes), which should themselves be subject to the mapping process of Figure 3.2. Say, for example, that the unsustainability effect was health problems caused by water pollution (an example of qualitative competition). An effect-oriented instrument would be the administration of a drug to affected persons; a result-oriented instrument would be water purification; a process-oriented instrument would be emission controls; and a source-oriented instrument would be the restriction of production or the replacement or reduction of the pollutant's use. Not all the types of instrument will be appropriate or feasible for all problems. Alternatively, effective tackling of a problem may require the use of instruments in several or all categories.

6. The costs of the instruments need to be calculated, 1. for comparison between them so as to be able to choose the most cost-effective option; 2. to estimate, through the use of an appropriate economic model, their sectoral and macroeconomic implications; and 3. to permit the computation of an adjustment to GNP in order for it to approximate sustainable income.

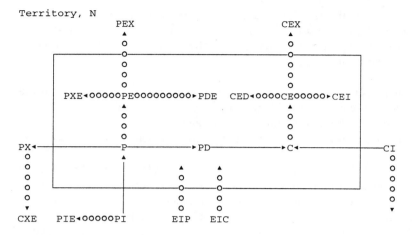

Key to Figure 3.3

Solid lines are processes of production or consumption. Lines of O are associated environmental impacts.
E terms: E appearing in any sequence of letters signifies an environmental impact, such as emission,
extraction or occupation.

Activity: Production,P Consumption,C

N	=	Territorial boundary of nation-state
P	=	Production within N
PE	=	Environmental impacts due to production in N
PI	=	Imports for production (capital goods)
PIE	=	Environmental impacts outside N due to PI
PD	=	Domestic product for home consumption
PX	=	Domestic product for export
CXE	=	Environmental effects outside N due to consumption of exports
PDE	=	Environmental impacts due to production of home-consumed domestic product
PXE	=	Environmental impacts due to production of exports

Production equation: P = PD + PX

C	=	Consumption within N
CE	=	Environmental impacts due to consumption in N
CED	=	Environmental impacts in N due to consumption of domestic product
CEI	=	Environmental impacts in N due to consumption of imports
CI	=	Imports consumed in N
CIE	=	Environmental effects outside N due to production of imports of consumer good

Consumption equation: C = PD + CI

PEI,CEI	=	Import of environmental effects due to production and consumption abroad
PEX,CEX	=	Export of environmental effects due to domestic production and consumption

Environmental effects equations:

PE	=	PDE + PXE + PEX
TPE	=	Total environmental impacts (in and outside N) due to production in N
	=	PE + PIE + CXE
CE	=	CED + CEI + CEX
TCE	=	Total environmental effects (in and outside N) due to consumption in N
	=	CE + CIE

Figure 3.3.   *Production, consumption and environmental impacts of and
in country N*

BOUNDARIES OF SUSTAINABILITY

Environmental impacts can be felt at global, continental, (bio)regional, national and local levels. To be effective, public policy will have to be formulated at a level appropriate to the impact concerned. Because of the primacy of national governments in political decision-making, it makes sense to think of boundaries of sustainability, initially at least, in terms of the nation-state.

Figure 3.3 is a schematic representation of the domestic production and consumption of a country, N and the environmental impacts caused by these, together with imported pollution.

Of course, the environmental effects will not generally be measurable in the same units, so that the additions are descriptive rather than computable. Most of the environmental effects identified are obvious and need no exemplification here. EIP, EIC, PEX, CEX, the imports and exports of environmental effects, are likely to be in the form of air- or water-borne pollutants. CIE might be exemplified by the destruction of tropical forests due to hardwood imports, CXE by damage to human health or the environment by the export of pesticides or other dangerous chemicals.

It is possible to identify three meaningful sets of boundaries:

1. The total environmental impacts in N due to domestic production and consumption are:
$$PE + CE - PEX - CEX = PDE + PXE + CED + CEI$$

2. The total environmental impacts in N are:
$$PDE + PXE + CED + CEI + EIP + EIC$$

3. The total environmental effects of domestic production and consumption are:
$$TPE + TCE = PE + CE + PIE + CIE + CXE$$

Which of these boundaries are relevant and can be made operational will depend on the issue in question and on possibilities of measurement. The measurement of impacts in N is likely to include the contribution of imported impacts (EIP and EIC, as in 2). The measurement of domestic emissions will probably include those that are subsequently exported (PEX and CEX). PIE, CIE and CXE are likely to be impossible to measure without the co-operation of the exporting/importing country, but may be among the principal contributors to unsustainability. The boundaries must also be borne in mind in the choice of instruments. Tackling domestic emissions may not improve the domestic concentration of pollutants if the pollutants are mainly imported (EIP, EIC), in which case the cheapest way to improve environmental quality may be to subsidise emission-reduction in the neighbouring polluting countries (though this has obvious implications for the observation or otherwise of the Polluter Pays Principle). Similarly, purifying domestic soil or water will not decrease the emissions that are exported to neighbours.

In accounting situations involving more than one country only case 2 allocates all effects to one country and one only. In case 1, no country is considering the impacts of pollution imports and exports (PEX, CEX, EIP, EIC). In case 3, more than one country (N and the countries importing from or exporting to N) will be considering, and perhaps taking responsibility for, CXE, CEI, PXE, PIE, CIE. (CXE for one country is the equivalent to CEI for the other; PXE is similarly equivalent to the sum of PIE and CIE). While untidy in accounting terms, acceptance of shared responsibility for these effects is likely to produce the best environmental outcome.

SUSTAINABILITY CONDITIONS AND STANDARDS

Unsustainability in general has been earlier defined as an effect on biota or the human way of life which prevents the way of life, or incurs an unacceptable risk of preventing it in the future, from continuing. Environmental unsustainability comes about when environmental functions which are important for human ways of life and welfare are not sustained or put at risk. Given the uncertainties involved in matters of sustainability the question of risk is crucial, not least because risk, through insurance premia, for example, incurs present real, rather than hypothetical future, costs.

The problems of unsustainability arise, as has been seen, from chronic competition between environmental functions:

1. Qualitative = excessive emissions lead to excessive concentrations which lead to unsustainable effects.
2. Quantitative = excessive extraction leads to excessive depletion which leads to unsustainable effects.
3. Spatial = excessive occupation (of space) leads to excessive congestion which leads to unsustainable effects.

What counts as an 'unsustainable effect' rather than a sustainable economic cost is a matter of judgement which can only partially be resolved by science. Ethics and the attitude to risk also play a significant role here. It is important that the basis of judgement is articulated clearly, especially as to who is responsible for the effects and who is bearing their costs and differentiating the contributions played by science, ethics and risk acceptance or aversion.

Environmental sustainability derives its legitimacy as a fundamental objective of public policy from a number of sources, discussed in Perrings *et al.* (1995). Most important, perhaps, is the issue of intergenerational equity, whereby it is perceived that present generations have an obligation to leave future generations no worse off in terms of environmental functions, in acknowledgement of the fact that these functions provide the basis for wealth creation and economic activity, for human welfare and ways of life, and, indeed, for life itself.

The environmental functions produced by complex ecosystems are in many cases not substitutable by human-made alternatives. Moreover, such ecosystems are often characterised by threshold effects and irreversibilities that make unwelcome changes impossible both to predict and undo. As Perrings *et al.* (1995, p. 22) observe: 'Ecosystems typically continue to function in the short term even as resilience declines. Indeed, they often signal loss of resilience only at the point at which external shocks at previously sustainable levels flip these systems into some other basis of attraction and so some other regime of behaviour'.

Other 'regimes of behaviour' may be substantially less hospitable to humans than the present one. Munasinghe and Shearer (1995, pp. xviii, xix) consider that 'sustaining the global life support system is a prerequisite for sustaining human societies', yet 'the increasing concentration of greenhouse gases in the atmosphere, the weakening ozone shield, increased local and regional pollution and the decreasing capability of the atmosphere to oxidize biogenic and anthropogenic emissions are symptoms of progressive and unsustainable deterioration of the life support system provided by the global atmosphere'. In the Foreword to Munasinghe and Shearer (1995, p. ix), de Souza and Serageldin warn bluntly that in the face of current over exploitation of natural resources, 'the quality of the environment and of human life is likely to decline rapidly, accompanied by widespread suffering'.

It is therefore the importance of environmental functions for human welfare that justifies the adoption of environmental sustainability as an important, and perhaps preeminent, policy objective. Even so, not all environmental functions everywhere can be sustained. Some assessment must be made of those functions that play a particularly important role in life support and policy for sustainability must be geared towards these. The following are put forward as a preliminary set of sustainability conditions:

1. Destabilisation of global environmental features such as climate patterns or the ozone layer must be prevented. Most important in this category are the maintenance of biodiversity (see below), the prevention of climate change, by the stabilisation of the atmospheric concentration of greenhouse gases, and safeguarding the ozone layer by ceasing the emission of ozone depleting substances.

2.   Important ecosystems and ecological features must be absolutely protected to maintain biological diversity. Importance in this context comes from a recognition not only of the perhaps as yet unappreciated use value of individual species, but also of the fact that biodiversity underpins the productivity and resilience of ecosystems. Resilience, defined as 'the magnitude of the disturbance that can be absorbed before the system changes its structure by changing the variables and processes that control its behaviour' (Folke *et al.* 1994, p. 6) depends on the functional diversity of the system. This depends in turn, in complex ways, not just on the diversity of species but on their mix and population and the relations between the ecosystems that contain them. 'Biodiversity conservation, ecological sustainability and economic sustainability are inexorably linked; uncontrolled and irreversible biodiversity loss ruptures this link and puts the sustainability of our basic economic environmental systems at risk' (Barbier *et al.* 1994, p. 41).

3.   The renewal of renewable resources must be fostered through the maintenance of soil fertility, hydrobiological cycles and necessary vegetative cover and the rigorous enforcement of sustainable harvesting. The latter implies basing harvesting rates on the most conservative estimates of stock levels, for such resources as fish; ensuring that replanting becomes an essential part of such activities as forestry; and using technologies for cultivation and harvest that do not degrade the relevant ecosystem and deplete neither the soil nor genetic diversity.

4.   Depletion of non-renewable resources should seek to balance the maintenance of a minimum life-expectancy of the resource with the development of substitutes for it. On reaching the minimum life expectancy, its maintenance would mean that consumption of the resource would have to be matched by new discoveries of it. To help finance research for alternatives and the eventual transition to renewable substitutes, all depletion of non-renewable resources should entail a contribution to a capital fund. Designing for resource efficiency and durability can ensure that the practice of repair, reconditioning, re-use and recycling (the 'four Rs') approach the limits of their environmental efficiency.

5.   Emissions into air, soil and water must not exceed their critical load, that is the capability of the receiving media to disperse, absorb, neutralise and recycle them, nor may they lead to life-damaging concentrations of toxins. Synergies between pollutants can make critical loads very much more difficult to determine. Such uncertainties should result in a precautionary approach in the adoption of safe minimum standards.

6. Risks of life-damaging events from human activity must be kept at very low levels. Technologies, such as nuclear power, which threaten long-lasting ecosystem damage at whatever level of risk, should be foregone.

Of these six sustainability principles, 3, 4 and, to some extent, 2 seek to sustain resource functions. 5 seeks to sustain waste absorption functions; 1 and 2 seek to sustain life supporting environmental services; and 6 acknowledges the great uncertainties associated with environmental change and the threshold effects and irreversibilities mentioned above. The principles give clear guidance how to approach today's principal perceived environmental problems. They may need to be supplemented as new environmental problems become apparent.

The principles are also reflected in a number of international treaties, conventions and principles, including the Montreal Protocol to phase out ozone depleting substances (2 above), the Convention on International Trade in Endangered Species and the establishment of World Biosphere Reserves to maintain biodiversity (3 above) and the Precautionary Principle, endorsed by the United Nations Conference on Environment and Development in *Agenda 21*, to limit environmental risk taking (5 and 6 above). None of these international agreements was the outcome of detailed application of environmental evaluation techniques in a framework of cost benefit analysis. They rest on a simple recognition that they represent the humane, moral and intelligent way for humans to proceed in order to maintain their conditions for life and are argued for on that basis.

The different forms of competition (qualitative, quantitative, spatial) will need to be addressed by different kinds of standards, which can be clarified through the expression of a few simple sustainability constraints relating to the various environmental inputs and outputs. Ecological capital has here been split into the parts corresponding to the two different kinds of functions it performs: Resource functions (EC1) and waste absorption functions (EC2).

Qualitative Constraints

Sustainability condition 5 implies:

$$Wes \leq Aes$$

and

$$Wec2 \leq Aec + Iec$$

Where Wes and Wec2 are the waste emissions into the environment which potentially affect the environmental services directly (Wes), or which affect the ecological capital which produces those services and ecological resources (Wec2), Aes and Aec are environmental absorptive/neutralising capacities and

Iec is investment in the regeneration of ecological service producing capital.

It is important to emphasise that not all wastes or emissions cause pollution. They only do so when they exceed the extent to which the environment can absorb, neutralise or recycle them. In the non-human bioeconomy there is no such thing as pollution. All emissions or waste products from one process are transformed into resources for another in a multitude of interlinked cyclical processes powered by the sun, which provides the necessary external energy input to decrease entropy in the biosystem overall, as life forms become increasingly varied and complex.

The distinction between Wec2 and Aec on the one hand and Wes and Aes on the other is important. Wastes Wec2 impact on the environmental capital stock which produces environmental services; wastes Wes may affect the services themselves. The distinction may be exemplified as that between emissions which cause fundamental atmospheric and climate change (Wec2) and those which cause smog (Wes). Both ultimately interfere with the climatic experiences of those affected, but effects on the capital stock itself tend to be less easily remedied. Against that it may be argued that the capital stock itself is less easily affected than the services it provides (Aec > Aes). The emissions that produce a local smog are lower than those needed to cause a global change in climate. One of the more serious characteristics of the present environmental situation is that it derives from fundamental degradation of the basic stock (atmosphere, ozone layer, soil, forest systems) rather than a simple interference with the services they provide. Regenerating this capital stock is likely to be a more formidable task than removing interference with its services.

In general for qualitative constraints, a standard can be set at each of the stages of the unsustainable process:

1. Effect, for example, a tolerated level of sickness from pollution or disruption from noise.
2. Concentration, for example, maximum levels of pollutants in soil, water, air, organisms.
3. Emissions, for example, maximum emissions levels.

Quantitative Constraints

A basic sustainability equation for resources is
$$E \leq Iec1 + Wec1$$

Where E is the total outflow of renewable and non-renewable resources into the economic process, Iec1 is the generation of new ecological resources by investment and Wec1 is the addition to the resource stock achieved by recycling. The renewable component of Iec1 includes the replenishment of natural resources by human intervention or non-human processes (for example, the sun). The non-renewable component of Iec1 implies new discoveries or the development of new technologies, materials or processes to substitute for depleting resources.

For renewable resources the basic sustainability standard is clear: The definition of a minimum acceptable stock and then the definition and enforcement of a strictly sustainable harvest. For non-renewable resources, the situation is more complex and various methods have been developed in order to address explicitly the issue of how a non-renewable resource can be used 'sustainably', when all depletion of such a resource must bring closer its exhaustion. The approach of Hueting *et al.* (1992, p. 15) is to determine the maximum sustainable rate of depletion in any period, according to the improvements in use efficiency, recycling or development of substitutes for the resource during the period in question. Where $r(t)$ is the rate of such improvements, $d(t)$ is the rate of depletion and $s(t)$ is the stock of the resource, they posit the equation

$$d(t) \leq r(t) * s(t) \qquad\qquad 3.1$$

Another way of seeking to ensure sustainable use is to set a minimum life expectancy of the resource, L_{min}. Where d_1 is the depletion rate in period 1 from a stock level of S_1, then

$$d_1 \leq S_1/L_{min}$$

As is shown in Appendix 1, where d_2 is the rate of depletion in period 2 and D_1 is the amount of the resource discovered in period 1, then, operating at maximum depletion rates

$$d_2 = d_1 [1 + (D_1 - d_1)/S_1] \qquad\qquad 3.2$$

The interpretations of sustainability given by equations (3.1) and (3.2) are quite different. The effect of (3.1), strictly in accordance with the principle of strong sustainability, is to ensure that the stock of the given resource maintains its capacity to perform its environmental function at its current level. More stock may be drawn down into use (consumed) only insofar as technical advances enable the stock remaining to perform the same level of function as the initial stock. Discoveries, which add to the quantity of known stock, mean that the stock is able to maintain a higher level of environmental function than was originally thought and it is this higher level that then becomes the standard for sustainability. Obviously, under equation (3.1), if no technical advance takes place in a given period, even if there are substantial discoveries, then the sustainable level of resource consumption in that period is zero.

Equation (3.2) interprets sustainability as the maintenance of the current level of environmental function for a certain minimum length of (finite) time. Discoveries increase the possible depletion rate by increasing the stock, that is, the sustainable level of environmental function is not adjusted upward as in the Hueting method. With no discoveries and operating at the maximum depletion rate consistent with the minimum life expectancy, this depletion rate will decline over time, according to the ratio of depletion in the previous period to the undepleted stock (as seen by setting $D_1 = 0$ in equation (3.2)). Technical advance does not enter into equation (3.2). If it occurs, but depletion stays the same, then the consumed resources will have increased their productivity of useful services delivered. But this will not change the minimum life expectancy of the resource.

In terms of the strict maintenance of environmental functions over an indefinite time period, the Hueting method would appear to be correct. For non-renewable resources, the level of environmental function depends only on the stock, whether discovered or not. As discoveries are made, so that the quantity of the known stock is revised upward, so is the level of function that needs to be sustained. Only recycling, more efficient use, or the development of (renewable and renewed) substitutes can add to the environmental function of a given stock, so that it is only by the amount of these advances that the stock can be sustainably depleted.

The minimum life expectancy method, on the other hand, treats discoveries as windfalls which will either enable the stock to last longer or, at constant life expectancy, allow greater annual consumption. Here it is only the current level of environmental function that is to be sustained and only for a definite period. With no discoveries, the sustainable level of depletion according to this decision rule would gradually decline.

The problem with the Hueting method is in its practical implications. Technical advance is inherently unpredictable, so that at any time it would not be clear whether a resource was being sustainably used or not. A burst of technical advance in one year might permit substantial depletion in that year, a lack of it would imply that almost all resource use in that year was unsustainable. Such fluctuations do not facilitate effective planning of resource use, sustainable or otherwise. It is also no easy matter to estimate advances in recycling, efficiency or substitutes on a year by year basis. In contrast, the minimum life expectancy method requires no information beyond discoveries, initial stock and depletion rates, which are already widely available. Year on year changes in sustainable depletion, at least insofar as they reduced it, are likely to be small.

These differences between the methods perhaps suggest that they are suited for different tasks. The Hueting method would provide a rigorous method for calculating the gap between current and sustainable depletion; the minimum life expectancy method could be used as a target for actual depletion policy.

Setting the minimum life expectancy for different resources would be somewhat arbitrary, but should perhaps be between 30 and 50 years, based on the timescale required for the development and diffusion of new technologies, if these were needing to be deployed once a resource was exhausted.

How much of a non-renewable resource can be used sustainably is one issue; how receipts from that use should be accounted is another. Given that use of a non-renewable resource amounts to the liquidation of natural capital, it is clearly incorrect that all the receipts from such depletion should be accounted as income, as they are as present. Correct national accounting for sustainable income is beyond the scope of this chapter; for the present it can be noted that El Serafy (1989) has proposed that the receipts (net of extraction costs) be divided into two streams, one representing current income, the other either to fund research into substitutes for the resource or to generate a permanent income stream in the future equal to that consumed as income in the present. El Serafy calculated a formula by which this proportion can be computed (derived in Appendix 2), relating it to the discount rate and the life expectancy of the resource.

The formula is:

$$I/R = 1/(1 + r)^{n+1}$$

Where

$I =$ that part of receipts to be considered as capital

$R =$ receipts

$r =$ discount rate

$n =$ life expectancy of the resource

It may be noted that, if the Hueting method is an application of the strong sustainability principle, the El Serafy method is an example of the weak sustainability principle. The monetary receipts are divided into two parts, broadly a capital and income component, but there is no requirement for the capital component to be invested such that specific substitutes for the depleted resource are provided. To the extent that the capital component is so invested, of course, the strong sustainability principle will be being followed.

The Hueting, minimum life expectancy and El Serafy methods could be applied as alternatives or together, with their different implications summarised thus. The Hueting method would guarantee strong sustainability but at the price of abrupt changes in permitted depletion if it were to form the basis of depletion policy. The second method would guarantee to future generations a continuing flow of the resource in question but, depending on new discoveries, it could be a diminishing one. Reductions in sustainable depletion would be gradual. El Serafy's method could result in total exhaustion of the resource but should have ensured the development of a substitute or an equivalent income stream from another source. This would only be compatible with strong sustainability where the asset producing the income stream was a perfect substitute for the depleted resource.

Given that the whole notion of sustainable use of a non-renewable resource is somewhat contradictory, a case can be made for applying the methods together and therefore reaping all of their different sustainability insights.

Spatial Constraints

The principal unsustainability effect from spatial competition is species extinction. Because of its irreversibility and the uncertainties involved, an appropriate standard would appear to be that no species be knowingly extinguished. This is rendered the more imperative by the fact that many extinctions are currently occurring and many more undoubtedly will occur, as a result of processes already underway which cannot be immediately halted (though for sustainability they must be over time). Other potentially unsustainable examples of spatial competition are waste-dumping and traffic congestion. Both these are likely to be much ameliorated by sustainability measures to reduce emissions and depletion, so it may not be necessary to formulate sustainability standards in these areas (although as noted earlier, the cost savings associated with dealing with these problems must be computed and subtracted from the costs of the measures of the sustainability measures in the other areas.)

CONCLUSION

This chapter has set out a methodology for making the concept of environmental sustainability operational by tracing out its causes and identifying instruments to bring economic activity within defined standards of sustainability. The determined application of these instruments across the whole range of activities implicated in unsustainability could have profound implications for the macroeconomy, as well as for economic growth, though despite a heated debate on this issue since the 1970s, no consensus on the growth sustainability relationship has yet emerged.

Standards of sustainability derived from the conditions set out earlier will set clear directions and targets for changes in the economy's biophysical throughputs and in the production of biomass. The instruments necessary to achieve these targets can be modelled by an appropriate macroeconomic model to estimate the instruments' impacts on GNP growth and other macroeconomic variables. Another use of the cost figures associated with certain of the instruments of environmental policy is to compute adjustments to GNP figures to take account of environmental damage.

APPENDICES

1. Deriving the formula for the depletion rate at minimum life expectancy

Let:

S	=	Resource reserves (stock)
d	=	Depletion in a given time period, then
L	=	Life expectancy $=$ S/d
L_{min}	=	Agreed minimum life expectancy
D	=	Discoveries

Subscripts $_{1,2}$ refer to time-periods, then

$$S_2 = (S_1 - d_1) + D_1$$

At L_{min}:

$$
\begin{aligned}
L_{min} &= S_1/d_1 = S_2/d_2 \\
&= [(S_1 - d_1) + D_1]/d_2 \\
\Rightarrow d_2 &= d_1[S_1 - d_1) + D_1]/S_1 \\
&= d_1[1 + (D_1 - d_1)/S_1]
\end{aligned}
$$

2. Derivation of capital/income shares of receipts from depletion of a non-renewable resource (after El Serafy 1989, p. 17)

Let:

R	=	Constant stream of receipts from total depletion of a resource over n years
X	=	Constant income derived from R in each year of depletion and indefinitely thereafter from capital fund, S
I	=	Constant capital component of R, which contributes to S in each year of depletion
$\Rightarrow R$	=	$X + I$ in each period
r	=	Interest rate

The task is to convert a finite stream of income, R in each year for n years, into an indefinite stream of income, X in each year. This can be done by converting each stream to a present value, and equating the present values.

For X

$$\sum_0^\infty \frac{X}{(1+r)^i} = \frac{X}{1 - 1(1+r)}$$

For R

$$\sum_0^\infty \frac{R}{(1+r)^i} = \sum_0^n \frac{R_i}{(1+r)^i} = \sum_{n+1}^\infty \frac{R_i}{(1+r)^i}$$

Now present value of $R_{n+1} = R/(i+r)^{n+1}$

This implies

$$\sum_{n+1}^{\infty} \frac{R}{(1+r)^i} = \frac{\dfrac{R}{(1+r)^{n+1}}}{1 - \dfrac{1}{(1+r)}}$$

This implies

$$\sum_0^n \frac{R}{(1+r)^i} = \frac{R}{1 - \dfrac{1}{(1+r)}} - \frac{\dfrac{R}{(1+r)^{n+1}}}{1 - \dfrac{1}{(1+r)}} = \frac{R[1 - \dfrac{1}{(1+r)^{n+1}}]}{1 - \dfrac{1}{(1+r)}}$$

Now let

$$\sum_0^{\infty} \frac{X}{(1+r)^i} = \sum_0^n \frac{R}{(1+r)^i}$$

This implies

$$\frac{X}{1 - \dfrac{1}{(1+r)}} = \frac{R[1 - \dfrac{1}{(1+r)^{n+1}}]}{1 - \dfrac{1}{(1+r)}}$$

This implies

$$\frac{X}{R} = 1 - \frac{1}{(1+r)^{n+1}}$$

and

$$\frac{I}{R} = \frac{1}{(1+r)^{n+1}}$$

REFERENCES

Barbier, E., Burgess, J. and Folke, C. 1994. *Paradise Lost? The Ecological Economics of Biodiversity*. London: Earthscan.

Birdsall, N. and Steer, A. 1993. 'Act now on global warming - but don't cook the books', *Finance and Development*, International Monetary Fund, Washington DC, March 6-8.

Cline, W. 1993. 'Give greenhouse abatement a fair chance', *Finance and Development*, International Monetary Fund, Washington DC, March 3-5.

Daly, H. 1992. 'From empty world to full world economics', in Goodland, R., Daly, H. and El Serafy, S. 1992. *Population, Technology and Lifestyle: The Transition to Sustainability*. Washington DC: Island Press.

de Groot, R. 1992. *Functions of Nature*. Groningen: Wolters-Noordhoff.

El Serafy, S. 1989. 'The proper calculation of income from depletable natural resources', in Ahmad, Y., El Serafy, S. and Lutz, E. (eds), *Environmental Accounting for Sustainable Development*. Washington DC: World Bank, pp. 10-18.

Folke, C., Holling, C.S. and Perrings, C. 1994. 'Biodiversity, ecosystems and human welfare', Beijer Discussion Paper Series No.49. Stockholm: Beijer International Institute of Ecological Economics.

Hardoy, J., Mitlin, D. and Satterthwaite, D. 1993. *Environmental Problems in Third World Cities*. London: Earthscan.

HMG (HM Government) 1990. *This Common Inheritance*. London: HMSO.

Hueting, R. 1980. *New Society and Economic Growth*. Amsterdam: North Holland.

Hueting, R., Bosch, P. and de Boer, B. 1992. *Methodology for the Calculation of Sustainable National Income*. Statistical Essay M44, Netherlands Central Bureau of Statistics, Vonberg/Heeslan.

Munasinghe, M. and Shearer, W. (eds) 1995. *Defining and Measuring Sustainability: The Biogeophysical Foundations*. For the United Nations University and World Bank. Washington DC: World Bank.

Opschoor, J.B. and Vos, H.B. 1989. *Economic Instruments for Environmental Protection*. Paris: Organisation for Economic Cooperation and Development.

Pearce, D. 1993. *Economic Values and the Natural World*. London: Earthscan.

Pearce, D. and Atkinson, G. 1992. 'Are national economies sustainable? Measuring sustainable development', CSERGE Discussion Paper GEC 92-11, University College London.

Pearce, D., Markandya, A. and Barbier, E. 1989. *Blueprint for a Green Economy*. London: Earthscan.

Pearce, D. and Turner, R.K. 1990. *Economics of Natural Resources and the Environment*. Hemel Hempstead: Harvester Wheatsheaf.

Perrings, C., Turner, K. and Folke, C. 1995. 'Ecological economics: The study of interdependent economic and ecological systems', Beijer Discussion Paper Series No.55. Stockholm: Beijer International Institute of Ecological Economics.

Pezzey, J. 1992. *Sustainable Development Concepts: An Economic Analysis*. World Bank Environment Paper No.2. Washington DC: World Bank.

Turner, K. 1992. 'Speculations on weak and strong sustainability', CSERGE Working Paper GEC 92-26, CSERGE, University of East Anglia, Norwich.

United Nations 1992. *Agenda 21*, Chapter 23, Preamble, *Earth Summit '92*. United Nations Conference on Environment and Development. London: Regency Press.

WCED (World Commission on Environment and Development) 1987. *Our Common Future* (The Brundtland Report). Oxford/New York: Oxford University Press.

4. Biophysical and Objective Environmental Sustainability

Robert Goodland[1]

INTRODUCTION

Prime Minister Brundtland's United Nations Commission (WCED 1987) garnered wide political consensus on the urgent need for sustainability. Many countries and institutions then started grappling with the same problem: Precisely what is sustainability and specifically what does it mean for this sector or that region? This chapter first outlines the concept of sustainability in general, but then focuses on one subset, namely environmental sustainability.[2]

Detractors are terrified of defining environmental sustainability precisely because they know it would change their behaviour. To postpone such a horrific result, two evasions are common. The first evasion is to dilute the concept by loading all desiderata, such as poverty alleviation, freedom, democracy, gender balance, equality, equity, employment, feminism, peace, social security and justice, onto the sustainability bandwagon. The second evasion is to refuse to define the concept; keep it ambiguous and interpretive, they say. Some detractors claim sustainability cannot be defined or made operational. Detractors keep the concept trite and insipid precisely so that it will not cause specific action. This chapter does the opposite. Environmental

[1] In addition to World Bank colleagues, comments on earlier drafts were warmly welcomed from Bill Adams, Jeroen van den Bergh, Frank Golley, Don Ludwig, Raymond Mikesell, Johannes Opschoor, Michael Redclift, Jan van der Straaten, Salah El Serafy, Fulai Sheng and Tom Tietenberg. This paper is an updated synthesis of Goodland (1995), Goodland and Daly (in press) and Serageldin, Daly and Goodland (1995). This paper honors Herman Daly, the world's leading sustainability theoretician, on whose work this paper is based. His enormous and generous contributions are warmly acknowledged.

These personal opinions should in no way be construed as representing the official position of the World Bank Group.

[2] Some readers may prefer the term 'ecological sustainability', but to the extent ecology is the study of the environment, it seems less precise. Biophysical sustainability seems a close synonym. Similarly, does sustainability seem passive or intransitive? In this case, 'sustentation' should be preferred for the act of sustaining, the state of being sustained, or maintainable.

sustainability is tightly defined by the rigorous biophysical principles on which it is based.

This chapter seeks to focus the definition of environmental sustainability partly by sharply distinguishing environmental sustainability from social sustainability and to a lesser extent from economic sustainability. The challenge to social scientists is to produce their own definition of social sustainability, rather than to conflate social sustainability with environmental sustainability. There is overlap among the three and important linkages which must be strengthened. Economic sustainability and environmental sustainability have especially strong linkages. Social sustainability needs to be disaggregated and defined separately in sociological terms by different disciplines. Social scientists are best able to define social sustainability and environmentalists do not have a major role in that area. Environmental sustainability should be defined more by environmentalists, ecologists and biophysical scientists. The disciplines best able to analyse each type of sustainability are different; each follows different laws and methods. It is not clarifying to heap all priorities on to a single type of sustainability. Defining each 'component' of sustainability distinctly may then become an organizing principle for action for the activities required to approach sustainability in real life, even though these distinct activities will necessarily be interconnected.

Similarly with economic sustainability; let economists define it or use previous and robust definitions of economic sustainability, such as by extending that of Hicks (1946) for 'Hicksian' income. The three types of sustainability - social, environmental and economic - are clearest and most effective when kept separate. Environmental sustainability is derived closely from and overlaps economic sustainability. They should be treated more closely than is the case here. Once agreement on the definitions is converging, it may prove possible to synthesize the three. The main reason they are separated here is that the economic approach to sustainability has been well analysed already. This chapter seeks to focus more on the biophysical and environmental aspects of sustainability. There may be a case for separating social sustainability and welfare objectives, while lumping economic and environmental sustainability together. Possibly too in the future a 'general' sustainability will come to be based on all three of them.

Historically, economics has focussed on efficiency and, to a much lesser degree, on equity. Recent recognition of the pervasive economic significance of environmental 'externalities' forces two changes. First, the relatively new criterion of scale must now be added to the traditional criteria of allocation and efficiency (Daly 1992, Opschoor 1992). Second, markets are almost invariably deficient when natural resources are concerned. To a large degree, scale relates to environmental sustainability; the growth debate devolves on the scale of the growing human economic subsystem relative to the finite ecosystem. Ecologists and other biophysical scientists need to take more responsibility for leading the thinking on sustainable development and seeing that it is implemented promptly.

Economic sustainability focuses more on that portion of the natural resource base that provides physical inputs, both renewable and exhaustible, into the production process. Environmental sustainability adds to the physical inputs into production, more emphasis of environmental life support systems without which neither production not humanity could exist. These life support systems include atmosphere, water, oceans and soil that are healthy. Healthy here means that their environmental service capacity is maintained; soil organisms assimilate carcasses for example; the ozone shield prevents ultraviolet 'b' damage to biota such as humans and crops. Continuous depletion or damage by human activities to these irreplaceable and unsubstitutable services would be incompatible with sustainability.

SOCIAL SUSTAINABILITY

After survival, that is, achievement of environmental sustainability, some measure of social sustainability is essential. Clearly, achieving environmental sustainability is necessary but insufficient for any definition of an adequate life. Full environmental sustainability without some social sustainability cannot be a worthy objective. Poverty reduction is the main goal of social sustainability. Redclift (1987, 1989, 1994) claims that poverty reduction is the primary goal of sustainable development, even before environmental quality can be fully addressed. Poverty is increasing in the world in spite of global and national economic growth. Growth has so far failed to alleviate poverty. Poverty reduction has to come more from qualitative development, from redistribution and sharing, from population stability and community sodality, rather than from trickle down quantitative throughput growth. Politicians will doubtless want the impossible goal of increasing throughput growth, increasing consumption by all.

Countries truly sustaining themselves environmentally, rather than liquidating their resources, will be more peaceful than countries with unsustainable economies (Goodland 1994). Unsustainable economies face certain future decline. Unsustainable economies, those liquidating their own natural capital, or those importing liquidated capital from other countries, or belonging to mankind in general, are more likely to wage war than are sustainable economies. Peace needs work; it is not automatic. The poor and vulnerable minorities need best efforts by the relatively rich and powerful to alleviate their poverty and empower them to democratically enact rules for the common good. Social sciences are needed precisely because the environment has now become a major constraint on human progress. Fundamentally important though social sustainability is, environmental sustainability or maintenance of life support systems, is a prerequisite for social sustainability. The conditions to support life itself comes first, even before freedom, equality and so on. Social sustainability is not here amplified further. The rest of this chapter refers instead to environmental sustainability.

Dumping social desiderata onto environmental sustainability, as is happening at present, should be resisted because social and environmental sustainability follow different laws. Aggregation of social sustainability with environmental sustainability guts sustainability into a dim blur. People versed in the biophysical laws of environmental sustainability cannot contribute as much to social sustainability as social scientists can. When social sustainability has been clarified, possibly it will be re-linked with environmental sustainability, the whole contributing to sustainable development. Just as much of the world is not yet environmentally sustainable, neither is it socially sustainable. Disaggregation of social unsustainability will show what needs to be changed.

SUSTAINABILITY AND DEVELOPMENT

Clarification of environmental sustainability is the purpose of this chapter. Sustainable development should integrate social, environmental and economic sustainability and use these three to start to make development sustainable. The moment the term 'development' is introduced, the discussion becomes quite different and more ambiguous. This chapter is not focussed on sustainable development, here assumed to be development which is socially, economically and environmentally sustainable, or development without throughput growth beyond environmental carrying capacity and which is socially sustainable. WWF's (1993) definition of sustainable development is similar: 'Improvement in the quality of human life within the carrying capacity of supporting ecosystems'. These definitions need the social parts clarified, but they are less ambiguous than the Brundtland (WCED 1987) definition of 'development that meets the needs of the present without compromising the ability of future generations to meet their own needs'. According to United Nations Secretary General Boutros-Ghali (1994) development is a 'fundamental human right which requires, *inter alia*, democracy and good governance ... Economic growth is the engine of development ... sustained economic growth'.[3] This chapter offers the case that environmental sustainability cannot admit generalized economic growth, much less the sustained economic growth in the UN definition. On the contrary, environmentally sustainable development implies sustainable levels of both production (sources) and consumption (sinks) rather than sustained economic growth.

Recent emphases on social development, economic development, development with equity and development and basic needs suggests that development has become so vague as to require a sanctifying adjective. These phrases, as well as social and environmental qualifiers, should be carefully distinguished and defined anew by interdisciplinary teams: That is a challenge for development specialists and is not the focus of this review of environmental sustainability. The priorities of development should be the reduction of poverty, illiteracy, hunger, disease and inequity. While these goals are fundamentally important, they are quite different from the goals of environmental sustainability, namely maintaining human life support systems, environmental sink and source capacities, unimpaired.

The need for sustainability arose from the recognition that the profligate, extravagant and inequitable nature of current patterns of development, when projected into the not too distant future, leads to biophysical impossibilities. The transition to environmental sustainability is urgent because the deterioration of global life support systems imposes a time limit. We do not have time to dream of creating more living space or more environment, such as colonizing the moon or building cities beneath the ocean; we must save the remnants of the only environment we have and allow time for and invest in the regeneration of what we have already damaged.

The tacit goal of economic development is to narrow the equity gap between the rich and the poor. Almost always this is taken to mean raising the bottom, rather than lowering the top or redistribution (Haavelmo and Hansen 1992). Only very recently is it admitted that bringing the low income countries up to the affluence levels in OECD countries, in 40 or even 100 years, is a totally unrealistic goal. To prevent accusations of attacking a straw man (whoever would be foolish as to claim that global equality at current OECD levels was remotely possible?), note that most politicians and most citizens have not yet accepted the unrealistic nature of this goal. Most people would

---

[3]   This UN definition does not distinguish among the different concepts of growth and development. While development can and should go on indefinitely for all nations, throughput growth cannot. Sustainability will be achieved only when development supplants growth; when the scale of the human economy is kept within the capacity of the overall ecosystem on which it depends. Acknowledging the finite nature of our planet, 'sustainable growth' is a bad oxymoron (Daly 1988, 1990a,b, 1996a,b). Throughput growth has to be kept within carrying capacity or within the capacity of the environmental services of assimilation and regeneration.

accept that it is *desirable* for low income countries to be as rich as the North and then leap to the false conclusion that it must therefore be *possible*. They are encouraged in this *non sequitur* by the realization that if greater equality cannot be attained by growth alone, then sharing and population stability will be necessary. Politicians find it easier to revert to wishful thinking than to face those two issues. Once we wake up to reality, there is no further reason for dwelling on the impossible and every reason to focus on what *is* possible.

Serageldin (1993a,b) makes the persuasive case that achieving per capita income levels in low income countries of $1,500 to $2,000, rather than OECD's $21,000 average, is quite possible. Moreover, that level of income may provide 80 per cent of the basic welfare provided by a $20,000 income, as measured by life expectancy, nutrition, education and other measures of social welfare. This tremendously encouraging case remains largely unknown, even in development circles. It needs to be widely debated and accepted as the main goal of development. Its acceptance would greatly facilitate the transition to environmental sustainability. Colleagues working on Northern overconsumption should address the corollary not dealt with by Serageldin (1993a,b). Can $21,000 per capita countries cut their consumption by a factor of 10 and suffer 'only' a 20 per cent loss of basic welfare? If indeed both raising the bottom (poor income rises to $2000) and lowering the top (OECD income declines to $16,000) prove feasible, that would be tremendously encouraging and would speed environmental sustainability.

INTERGENERATIONAL AND INTRAGENERATIONAL SUSTAINABILITY

Sustainability in economic terms can be described as the maintenance of capital, sometimes phrased as non-declining capital. Historically, at least as early as the Middle Ages, the merchant traders used the word capital to refer to human-made capital. The merchants wanted to know how much of their trading ships cargo sales receipts could be consumed by their families without depleting their capital. Economics Nobelist Sir John Hicks encapsulated the sustainability concept in 1946 when he defined income as 'the amount one could consume during a week and still be as well off at the end of the week'. Thus Hicksian income is a concept designed to inform prudential (sustainable) consumption if one wants to avoid inadvertent impoverishment. El Serafy (1989, 1991, 1993) extended Hick's definition from financial capital to natural capital. Now that natural capital, rather than human-made capital, is often the limiting factor, the concept of Hicksian income is now extended as the basis of sustainability. Sustainability to Solow (1974, 1993a,b) is a less clear obligation or injunction 'to conduct ourselves so that we leave to the future the option or the capacity to be as well off as we are ... not to satisfy ourselves by impoverishing our successors' (Solow 1993a,b).

Today's OECD societies have already reduced environmental source and sink capacities. Most extinctions and atmospheric damage have been and are caused by industrial nations. Most people in the world today are already impoverished or barely above subsistence; poverty is numerically increasing. By no stretch of the imagination can developing countries ever be as well off as indicated by today's OECD average income. Our successors or future generations seem more likely to be more numerous and poorer than today's generation. Sustainability indeed has an element of not harming the future (intergenerational equity) and some find the intergenerational equity component of sustainability to be its most important element (WCED 1987). Intergenerational equity is important for sustainability, but addressing only the future diverts attention from today's lack of sustainability. If the world cannot move towards intragenerational sustainability during this generation it will be greatly more difficult to achieve intergenerational sustainability sometime in the future. The capacity of environmental services will be lower in the future than it is today.

The second reason for tackling intragenerational sustainability first is that world population soars by 100 million new souls each year, some of them OECD over-consumers, most of them poverty stricken; world population doubles in a single human generation, say every 40 years. This means that achieving intergenerational equity is more difficult. Achieving intergenerational equity will likely reduce total population growth. Every year we continue to add 100 million people, we increase in intra- as well as inter-generational inequity, since the new additions arrive overwhelmingly to the poor. Rather than focussing on the intergenerational equity concerns of environmental sustainability, the stewardship approach of safeguarding life support systems today is preferable.

WHAT SHOULD BE SUSTAINED?

Having cleared the decks of the important issues of development and social sustainability and having deliberately focussed on only the environmental form of sustainability, we can now make sense of the question: 'What must be sustained?' The answer is clear: Environmental sustainability seeks to sustain global life support systems indefinitely; principally those systems maintaining human life. Global life support systems are the enabling conditions for human life to continue. These systems can be divided into two capacities: The source capacity of the global ecosystem to provide raw material inputs (food, water, air, energy) and the sink capacity to assimilate outputs or wastes. These source and sink capacities are large but finite; sustainability requires that they be maintained. Overuse of a capacity impairs that capacity to provide life support services. For example, it is clear that the capacity to assimilate CFCs has been exceeded. Accumulation of CFCs is damaging the capacity of the atmosphere to protect humans and other biota from harmful UVb radiation. Life support systems are the capacity of the ecosystem to provide sources and sinks for humanity; they are the services provided by the environment to support life. Seen in this light, the question 'what should be sustained?' (Gale and Cordray 1994) becomes moot. Environmental sustainability is essential for humanity to survive. Survival is an essential prerequisite for concern with social sustainability, poverty alleviation or economic development. Now we have to make planetary survival politically popular.

The qualifier 'principally' used above acknowledges first, that human life is the main reason anthropocentric humans seek sustainability. Second, it acknowledges the utilitarian argument that human life depends on some other species, such as for food, shelter, pollination, waste assimilation and other environmental life support services. The huge instrumental value of non-human species to humans is grossly undervalued by economics. Third, non-human life, those other species with which we share the earth, has intrinsic worth whether useful to humans or not. Non-human species of no present value to humans have intrinsic worth, but this consideration is almost entirely excluded in economics, exceptions being existence and option values. The question is rarely posed and not yet answered: With how many 'non-useful' other species is humanity willing to share the earth, or should they all be sacrificed to make room for more and more of the single human species? It is arrogant folly to extinguish a species just because we think it is useless today. The anthropocentric and ecocentric views are contrasted in Goodland and Daly (1993a,b, 1996).

Although biodiversity conservation seems recently on the way to becoming a general ideal for nations and development agencies, there is no agreement on how much should be conserved, nor at what cost. Leaving aside the important fact that we have not yet learned to distinguish useful from non-useful species, agreeing on how many other species to conserve is not central to the definition of environmental sustainability. Reserving non-human habitat for other species to divide among themselves is important; let evolution select the mix of species, not us. But reserving a non-human habitat requires limiting the scale of the human habitat. 'How much habitat should be conserved?', while important to ascertain, is moot because the answer is probably 'no less than today's remnants'. This brings us to the precautionary principle: In cases of uncertainty, sustainability mandates that we err on the side of prudence. Because practically all the workings of global life support systems are uncertain, we should be very conservative in our estimation of the various input and output capacities and the role of apparently 'useless' species.

Many writers (Brown *et al.* 1995, Brown and Kane 1994, Costanza 1991, Costanza and Daly 1992, Daly and Cobb 1989, Jansson *et al.* 1994, Goodland 1992, Hardin 1993, Korten 1991, Meadows *et al.* 1992, Simonis 1990) are convinced that the world is hurtling away from environmental sustainability at present, although consensus amongst economists that the world is becoming less sustainable has not yet been reached. But what is not contestable is that the current modes of production prevailing in most parts of the global economy are causing the exhaustion and dispersion of a one time inheritance of natural capital, such as topsoil, groundwater, tropical forests, fisheries and biodiversity. The rapid depletion of these essential resources, coupled with the degradation of land and atmospheric quality show that the human economy, as currently configured, is already inflicting serious damage on global supporting ecosystems and is probably reducing future potential biophysical carrying capacities by depleting essential natural capital stocks (Daily and Ehrlich 1992, Daily, Ehrlich and Ehrlich 1994).

A POTTED HISTORY OF SUSTAINABILITY

If one addresses only the last century or so, some notion of economic sustainability was firmly embodied in the writings of Mill (1848) and Malthus (1798, 1836). Mill (1848) emphasized that environment ('Nature') needs to be protected from unfettered growth if we are to preserve human welfare before diminishing returns set in. Malthus emphasized the pressures of exponential population growth on the finite resource base. The modern version (Neo-Malthusianism) is exemplified by Ehrlich and Ehrlich (1989a,b; 1991) and by Hardin (1968, 1993). Daly's *Toward a Steady State Economy* (1972, 1973, 1974) and *Steady State Economics* (1977, 2nd ed. 1991) synthesized and extended these population and resources viewpoints. Daly's steady state economics is the seminal work in which population and consumption pressures on environmental sources and sinks are clearly demonstrated and magisterially extended into the single critical factor of scale - the throughput of matter and energy from the environment, used by the human economy and released back into the environment as wastes.

Neither Mill nor Malthus is held in great esteem by today's economists who follow the technological optimism of Ricardo (1817) who rightly believed that human ingenuity and scientific progress would postpone the time when population would overtake resources or 'the niggardliness of nature'. As poverty is increasing worldwide, that postponement seems to have ended.

The definition of environmental sustainability hinges on distinguishing between throughput growth and development. The 'growth debate' started becoming mainstream two decades after World War II. Boulding (1966, 1968, 1992), Mishan (1967, 1977) and Daly (1972, 1973, 1974, 1977), for example, seriously questioned the wisdom of infinite throughput growth in a finite earth. Throughput growth is defended by most economists including Beckerman (1974, 1992a,b), who still rejects the concept of sustainability (1994, 1995; but see Daly 1995). *The Limits to Growth* (Meadows *et al.* 1972) and *Beyond the Limits* (Meadows *et al.* 1992) shook the convictions of the technological optimists. Meadows *et al.* (1972) concluded that 'it is possible to alter these growth trends and establish a condition of ecological and economic stability that is sustainable into the future'. Barney's 1980 US Global Report to the President amplified and clarified the limits argument. Large populations, their rapid growth and affluence are unsustainable. The Ricardian tradition still dominates conventional economics and is exemplified by the Cornucopians Simon and Kahn in their 1984 response to the Global 2000 report (Barney 1980). Panayotou (1993), Summers (1992) and Fritsch *et al.* (1994) find growth compatible with sustainability and even necessary for it. The 1980 World Conservation Strategy by IUCN and WWF (IUCN 1980) and Clark and Munn's 1987 IIASA report *Sustainable Development of the Biosphere* reinforced the limits conclusions. Daly and Cobb's (1989) prizewinning *For the Common Good* estimated that growth, at least in the US, actually decreased well being. The growth debate and sustainability are usefully synthesized by Korten (1991).

The most consensualist definition of sustainable development is that of the 1987 UN Brundtland Commission: 'Development that seeks to meet the needs and aspirations of the present without compromising the ability to meet those of the future'. Part of the success of the Brundtland Commission's definition stems from its opacity (Hueting 1990) and they defined sustainability in a growth context. But when WCED (1992) reconvened five years later, calls for growth were striking for their absence. HRH Prince Charles commended WCED in the same publication (WCED 1992) on dropping their 1987 call for huge 5 to 10 fold increases in economic growth. They also elevated the population issue higher on the agenda to achieve sustainability (WCED 1992). Toman (1994) claims that World Development Report (1992) basically treats sustainability as another way of espousing economic efficiency in the management of services derived from the natural endowment.

Few economics Nobelists write on sustainability. Haavelmo and Hansen (1992) and Tinbergen and Hueting (1992) repudiate throughput growth and urge the transition to sustainability. Solow's earlier writings (1974) questioned the need for sustainability, but recently he is modifying that position (1993a,b). The World Bank adopted environmental sustainability in principle rather early on in 1984 and is promoting it actively (Ahmad *et al.* 1989, Lutz 1993, Serageldin 1993a,b, Serageldin, Daly and Goodland 1995. Daly and

Cobb (1989) is the most influential and durable of these publications because it shows more growth has started to do more harm than good. It outlines pragmatic operational methods to reverse environmental damage and reduce poverty. Goodland, Daly and El Serafy (1992), supported by two economics Nobelists, Tinbergen and Haavelmo, made the case that there are indeed limits, that the human economy has reached them in many places, that it is impossible to grow into sustainability, that source and sink capacities of the environment complement human-made capital which cannot substitute for their environmental services and that there is no way the South can ever catch up with the North's current consumerist lifestyle.

Since the late 1980s, there has been a substantial corpus of literature on 'ecological economics' (Costanza 1991), largely espousing stronger types of sustainability, as outlined below (Hueting 1980, Collard *et al.* 1987, Archibugi and Nijkamp 1989, Tisdell 1992, IIASA 1992, Barbier 1993, Turner 1993, Netherlands 1994, Jansson *et al.* 1994).

GROWTH COMPARED WITH DEVELOPMENT

When something grows it gets quantitatively bigger; when it develops it get qualitatively better or at least different. Growth is a physical or material and quantitative expansion; development is qualitative improvement. Quantitative growth and qualitative improvement follow different laws. Our planet develops over time without growing (Daly 1992, 1994a,b). Our economy, a subsystem of the finite and non-growing earth must eventually adapt to a similar pattern of development without throughput growth. The time for such adaptation is now. Historically, standard evolution of economies starts with quantitative throughput growth as infrastructure and industry is built and eventually matures into a pattern with less throughput growth but more qualitative development. While this pattern of evolution is encouraging, qualitative development needs to be distinguished from quantitative throughput if environmental sustainability is approached.

It is helpful to distinguish various forms of quantitative growth from qualitative improvement. There is wide agreement that the economy's throughput growth (physical matter and energy) is not a sufficient condition for development; now the debate devolves on the extent to which throughput growth is a necessary condition for development or welfare improvement. Throughput growth cannot be indefinitely sustained. As GNP today embodies so much throughput growth, neither can GNP growth be sustained. If efficiency, substitution, changes in composition of input and output of production and other changes were to be included in GNP, then such a new GNP could keep growing. Biomass and topsoil growth can be sustainable, although left alone they would eventually reach a steady state. Development and welfare can increase indefinitely, but that should not be confused with growth.

It is neither ethical nor helpful to the environment to expect poor countries to cut or arrest their conventional development, which tends to be highly associated with throughput growth. Poor, small, developing economies need both throughput growth and development. Therefore, the high consuming countries, which are responsible for most environmental damage so far and whose material well being can sustain halting or even reversing throughput growth, must take the lead in this respect. That is clearly in the North's self interest, rather than altruism and certainly not sacrifice; GNP increases mean decreases in welfare in OECD countries. Poverty reduction will require considerable growth, as well as development, in developing countries. But global environmental constraints, such as atmospheric CO_2 accumulation, ozone shield damage and acid rain are real and more growth for the South must be balanced by negative throughput growth in the North, if environmental sustainability is to be achieved. Negative Northern growth need not decrease welfare very much, to the extent that $2,000 per capita gains 80 per cent of basic welfare, as mentioned earlier.

Development by the North must be used to free resources for growth and development so urgently needed by the poorer nations. Large scale transfers to the poorer countries also will be required, especially as the impact of economic stability in Northern countries may depress terms of trade and lower economic activity in developing countries. Higher prices for the exports of poorer countries, as well as debt relief, therefore will be required. Most importantly, population stability is essential to reduce the need for growth everywhere. This includes where population growth impacts the most, in the Northern high consuming nations, as well as where population growth is highest, in the poor, low consuming countries.

THE DEFINITION OF ENVIRONMENTAL SUSTAINABILITY

The 'maintenance of natural capital' definition of environmental sustainability is the input/output rule below, building on the economic definition of sustainability as non-declining wealth per capita. As wealth is so difficult to measure, environmental sustainability is now defined by the two fundamental environmental services, the source and sink functions, that must be maintained unimpaired during the period over which sustainability is required (Daly 1977, 1980, 1988, 1994a,b). Daly's is the most useful short definition of environmental sustainability so far and is gaining adherents. For example

Opschoor (1992, 1994), Opschoor and van der Straaten (1993) and Dietz and van der Straaten (1992) encapsulate it in one sentence: 'The (aggregate) environmental impacts shall not impair the functioning of resource regenerative systems and waste assimilative systems and the use of nonrenewable resources of which is compensated for by equivalent increases in supplies of renewable or reproducible substitutes'. Thus environmental sustainability is a set of constraints on four major activities regulating the scale of the human economic subsystem: Pollution and waste assimilation on the sink side and the use of renewables and nonrenewables on the source side. The fundamental point to note about this definition is that environmental sustainability is a natural science concept and obeys biophysical laws, rather than human laws.[4] This general definition seems to be robust and irrespective of country, sector or future epoch; that is why environmental sustainability seems to be universal and rigorous. Even so, environmental sustainability can in turn be disaggregated.

The emphasis on maintenance of natural capital is to be expected, first for intergenerational equity: Our descendants should have as much choice as we have. Second, as the scale of the human economic subsystem relative to the overall ecosystem increases or matures, production is no longer for growth but increasingly for maintenance. Production is the maintenance cost of the stock and should be minimized (Daly 1994b). Sustainability demands that production and consumption be equal so that we maintain capital stocks. Efficiency demands that the maintenance cost (production equal to consumption) be minimized, given the capital stock.

Although environmental sustainability seems to be universal, the paths needed by each nation to approach sustainability will not be the same. Although all countries need to follow the input/output rules, all countries differ in the balance of attention between output and input that will be needed for that country to achieve environmental sustainability. For example, some countries or regions, such as the former centrally planned economies, need to concentrate more on controlling pollution; some countries, such as the tropical timber exporting countries, need to pay more attention to bringing harvest rates of their renewable resources down to regeneration rates; other countries may need to bring their population to below carrying capacity; while others, such as the OECD countries, need to reduce their per capita consumption.

There are compelling reasons why industrial countries should lead in devising paths towards sustainability. First, industrial countries must take the lead in approaching sustainability. They have to adapt far more than do developing countries. If OECD countries cannot act first and lead the way, it is less likely that developing countries will choose to do so (von Weizsacker

---

[4] See Bartlett's laws and hypotheses relating to sustainability (Bartlett 1994).

1992). Not only would it be enlightened self interest for the North to act first, but it could also be viewed as a moral obligation. Second, developing countries are rightly pointing out (Beijing Declaration 1991, Agarwal and Narain 1991) that OECD countries have already consumed substantial amounts of environmental sink capacity as well as of source capacity. Third, OECD countries can afford the transition to sustainability because they are richer. The rich would do themselves good by using the leeway they have for cutting overconsumption and waste.

THE CAUSES OF UNSUSTAINABILITY

Human societies and cultures, not nature, are largely responsible for the absence of sustainability (Redclift 1994). The overall cause of environmental unsustainability is that the scale of the human economic subsystem has grown large relative to the scale of the overall ecosystem which supports it as the sole source of all raw materials and the sole sink for all waste. When the human economic subsystem was small, the regenerative and assimilative capacities of the environment appeared infinite. However, we are now painfully learning that the overall ecosystem, the environmental sources and sinks, are finite. These capacities were indeed very large, but in non-trivial pervasive cases the scale of the human economy has exceeded source and sink capacities.

Source and sink capacities have now become scarce. As economics deals only with scarcities, formerly source and sink capacities of the environment did not have to be taken into account. But the growth of the human economic subsystem is infinite; indeed conventional economists call for more of it. Conventional economists hope or claim economic growth is infinite or at least that we are not yet reaching limits to growth. But, the scale of the human economy is a function of throughput - the flow of materials and energy from the sources of the environment, used by the human economy and returned to environmental sinks as waste. The scale of throughput has exceeded environmental capacities: That is the definition of unsustainability.

Throughput growth is, in its turn, a function of population growth and consumption at given levels of technology. Throughput growth translates into increased rates of resource extraction and pollution. Ideology, culture, institutions and the science of economics itself are hampering the recognition of unsustainability. Population is beginning to be agreed to be a problem, although consensus is far off. At the 1994 UN Population Conference in Cairo, maternal and child health and gender equality almost totally eclipsed the issue of the massive environmental damage from mainly OECD overconsumption and mainly southern overpopulation. Family size still is incorrectly believed to be a case of individual preference. The right to life itself, that is, functioning life support systems or environmental sustainability, is not yet widely recognized as more important than individual preferences for family size, freedom, equality and so on.

There is very little admission yet that more consumption above sufficiency is not an unmitigated good. There is even less admission that more economic growth is doing more harm than good (WCED 1987). The scale of the human economy has become unsustainable because it is living off inherited and finite capital, because we do not account for losses of natural capital, nor do we admit the costs of environmental harm. For example, substantial fractions of the populations of polluted cities die or are sickened by respiratory disease; more than a quarter of deaths in Mexico City, Hong Kong and elsewhere. But because this morbidity is not accounted for, we continue to tolerate internal combustion engines downtown. The fact of unsustainability is well documented by Meadows *et al.* (1972, 1992) and Hardin (1993). Daly and Cobb (1989) and Cobb and Cobb (1994) unimpeachably estimate that economic growth is decreasing welfare, at least in the USA.

The reasons for unsustainability are best codified by Opschoor (1992) and Opschoor and van der Straaten (1993). First, market failures mean environmental externalities are not internalized. Marketization is sweeping the globe, but market economies prefer to externalize costs so that they are borne by all society, rather than internalizing such costs to the correct site, namely the firm responsible. Today's resistance to the 'polluter pays principle' is a case in point. Polluter pays is a precursor of environmental sustainability, extended to mean users of all environmental services should pay full costs. Full cost accounting is a useful step towards environmental sustainability. But because it is difficult if not impossible to ascertain indirect and complex costs over the long term and because paying does not always mean maintaining, even paying full cost will not achieve environmental sustainability. Some economists believe it 'economically impeccable' to export toxic waste to 'under polluted' Third World countries. Individual preferences as expressed through the market, the basis for economic decision making, is effective in reaching optimal allocation, but dangerously misleading in determining optimal scale.

The second reason for unsustainability is related to the first: Government failure to admit that pollution and fast population growth are doing more harm than good. Part of government failure is lack of valuation techniques, institutions or instruments. Nearly a quarter of Europe's forests are badly damaged by air pollution and acid rain and in three countries (Czech Republic, Moldova, Poland) this has risen to 50 per cent or more. Lack of clear ownership and defensibility inherent in open access resources means that market principles cannot be applied to air, for example,[5] and international bargaining over air pollution damage has achieved little.

THE URGENCY OF ENVIRONMENTAL SUSTAINABILITY

Approaching sustainability is urgent. It is not some desire for future generations. If we, the present generation, cannot become sustainable, future generations are less likely to be able to become sustainable. Every day that unsustainability prevails makes sustainability more difficult. Furthermore, much unsustainability is irreversible, for example, loss of biodiversity, or loss of topsoil, would take far too long to repair to be of much survival interest to humans. Every passing year means sustainability has to be achieved for an additional 100 million extra people. Though environmental sources and sinks until recently seemed to have been vast and resilient and have been providing humanity with their free services for the last million years, we have at last succeeded in exceeding them and damaging them worldwide. Where environmental services are substitutable, there is less urgency, but as discussed, achieved substitution has been marginal. Most natural capital or environmental services cannot be substituted for and their self regenerating properties are slow and cannot be significantly hastened. That is why environmental sustainability has a time element.

Much of the resistance to accepting sustainability today is that it is felt to be politically unacceptable - controlling consumerism and waste, halting population growth and probably reducing population size, phasing out of much coal and relying instead on renewable energy. These are all felt to be politically risky, if not suicidal, so they are not promoted as much needed societal goals. Instead society calls for incremental progress such as the polluter pays principle, women's reproductive health, educating girls and clean technology, but no redistribution from rich to poor. It is impossible for us to grow out of poverty and environmental degradation. It is precisely the nonsustainability of throughput growth beyond a certain scale that gives urgency to the concept of sustainability (Daly 1980, 1988, 1990a,b). All forms of growth are unsustainable, whether in the number of trees, people, great whales, atmospheric CO_2 or GNP.

Erecting misleading goals means the world will take longer to become sustainable. Unsustainability will have to worsen before sustainability ceases to be a euphemism. The world will become sustainable. The only choice we

---

[5] This highlights the need for environmental policies which are a collective responsibility.

have is to select the timing and nature of the transition, or to let depletion and pollution dictate the abruptness of the inevitable transition. The former will be painful; the latter deadly. The longer we delay agreement on goals for sustainability, the more the source and sink capacities will be damaged, the more people will have to be accommodated and the more difficult will be the transition. For example, species extinctions are fast now and accelerating. If that continues for several decades before we reach sustainability, the sustainability we do eventually reach will be at a poorer and less resilient level. Even relatively reversible damage, such as that to the ozone shield, will not return to its pre-CFC state for a century after we stop releasing CFCs.

Irreversibility means there is an important time element in reaching sustainability. It is urgent to reach it as soon as possible and every year that passes makes it more difficult. First we need to agree what sustainability really is. The second change is to act much faster when a dangerously unsustainable process has been identified. We can no longer afford manufacturers' denial that a product is harmful, followed by reluctant agreement to phase out the harmful substance as soon as substitutes can be economically manufactured, as if corporate solvency is more important than global survival. Third, we need to accelerate the internalization of externalities. For example, when automobiles have to pay their way fully, public transportation will become more popular. Why does rail have to earn commercial returns on capital from fares paid by users? Roads are not held to the same economic criteria. On the contrary, they are subsidized. Why do coal-fired thermal projects refuse to internalize CO_2 emissions? We need to apply the best economics we can across the board, not just selectively. Fourth, politically unpalatable biophysical imperatives have to be faced as soon as possible, rather than covered up. The sooner population is stabilized, the better off individuals and aggregate society can become. That is not an absolute precondition for poverty reduction, but it would help enormously.

NATURAL CAPITAL AND SUSTAINABILITY

Of the four kinds of capital, environmental sustainability refers to natural capital. So defining environmental sustainability includes at least two further terms, namely 'natural capital' and 'maintenance' or at least 'non-declining'. Natural capital is basically the natural environment and is defined as the stock of environmentally provided assets, such as soil, atmosphere, forests, water and wetlands, which provide a flow of useful goods or services. The flow of useful goods and services from natural capital can be renewable or non-renewable and marketed or non-marketed. Sustainability means maintaining environmental assets, or at least not depleting them. Income is sustainable by the generally accepted Hicksian definition of income (Hicks 1946). Any consumption that is based on the depletion of natural capital is not income and should not be counted as such. Prevailing models of economic analysis tend to treat consumption of natural capital as income and therefore tend to promote patterns of economic activity that are unsustainable. Consumption of natural capital is liquidation, or disinvestment, the opposite of capital accumulation. Correction of the System of National Accounts to reflect depletion of natural capital (Ahmad *et al.* 1989, Lutz 1993), such as green accounts or green GNP are most effective means to promote sustainability.

Natural capital is distinguished from other forms of capital, namely human capital (people, their capacity levels, education, information, knowledge),[6] human-made capital (houses, roads, factories, ships) and social capital (the institutional and cultural basis for a society to function). From the mercantilists until very recently capital referred to the form of capital in the shortest supply, namely human-made capital. Investments were made in the limiting factor, such as sawmills and fishing boats, because their natural capital complements, forests and fish, were abundant. That idyllic era has ended.

Now that the environment is so heavily used, the limiting factor for much economic development has become natural capital. Fish have become limiting, rather than fishing boats. Timber is limited by remaining forests, not by saw mills; petroleum is limited by geological deposits and atmospheric capacity to absorb CO_2, not by refining capacity. As natural forests and fish populations become limiting we begin to invest in plantation forests and fish ponds. This introduces an important hybrid category that combines natural and human-made capital, a category we may call cultivated natural capital.[7] This category is vital to human well being, accounting for most of the food we eat and a good deal of the wood and fibres we use. The fact that humanity has the capacity to cultivate natural capital dramatically expands the capacity of natural capital to deliver services. But cultivated natural capital (agriculture) is separable into human-made capital, such as tractors, diesel irrigation pumps, chemical fertilizers and biocides and natural capital, such as topsoil, sunlight and rain. Eventually the natural capital proves limiting.

---

[6] Human capital formation, by convention is left out of the national accounts for various reasons, one of which is that, if it is truly productive, it will eventually be reflected, through enhanced productivity, in a higher GDP. Realization of the values of education and administration, for example, are lagged, and are conventionally assumed to be equal to their costs. The loss of natural capital, if not recorded, as largely is the case today, may take some time before it will reflect itself in income and productivity measurements.

[7] The subcategory of marketed natural capital, intermediate between human capital and natural capital, is 'cultivated natural capital' such as agriculture products, pond-bred fish, cattle herds, and plantation forests.

Natural Capital is Now Scarce

In an era in which natural capital was considered infinite relative to the scale of human use, it was reasonable not to deduct natural capital consumption from gross receipts in calculating income. That era is now past. Environmental sustainability needs the conservative effort to maintain the traditional (Hicksian) meaning and measure of income now that natural capital is no longer a free good, but is more and more the limiting factor in development. The difficulties in applying the concept arise mainly from operational problems of measurement and valuation of natural capital, as emphasized by Ahmad *et al.* (1989), Lutz (1993) and El Serafy (1989, 1991, 1993).

Three Degrees of Environmental Sustainability

Sustainability can be divided into three degrees; weak, strong and absurdly strong, depending on how much substitution one thinks there is among the four types of capital (Daly and Cobb 1989):

Human-made capital; manufactured capital
Infrastructure, factories, ships. This is the one usually considered in financial and economic accounts.

Natural capital
The stock of environmental assets which provide useful goods and services, often referred to as source and sink capacities (Daly 1994a). (Leaving for the moment the hybrid sub-category of cultivated natural capital, such as agriculture, aquaculture, tree plantations and cattle ranches).

Human capital
Investments in education, health and nutrition of individuals.

Social capital
The institutional and cultural basis for a society to function.

Weak Environmental Sustainability

This is maintaining total capital intact without regard to the composition of that capital between the different kinds of capital (natural, human-made, social or human). This would imply that the different kinds of capital are more or less substitutes, at least within the boundaries of current levels of economic activity and resource endowment. Given current liquidation and gross inefficiencies in resource use, weak sustainability would be a vast improvement as a welcome first step, but would by no means constitute environmental sustainability. Weak sustainability is a necessary but not sufficient condition for environmental sustainability.

Weak sustainability is rejected by Beckerman (1994), but is finding some acceptance in economic circles. It means we could convert all or most of the world's natural capital into human-made capital or artifacts and still be as well off! For example, society would be better off, it is claimed by those espousing weak sustainability, by converting forests to houses and oceanic fish stocks into nourished humans. Human capital, educated, skilled, experienced and healthy people, is largely lost at death, so has to be renewed each generation, whereas social capital persists in the form of books, knowledge, art, family and community relations. Society would be worse off because natural and human-made capital are not perfect substitutes. On the contrary, they are complements to a great extent.

Strong Environmental Sustainability

This requires maintaining different kinds of capital intact separately. Thus, for natural capital, receipts from depleting oil should be invested in ensuring that energy will be available to future generations at least as plentifully as enjoyed by the beneficiaries of today's oil consumption. This assumes that natural and human-made capital are not perfect substitutes. On the contrary, they are complements to some extent in most production functions. A sawmill (human-made capital) is worthless without the complementary natural capital of a forest. The same logic would argue that if there are to be reductions in one kind of educational investment they should be offset by other kinds of education, not by investments in roads.

Of the three degrees of sustainability, strong sustainability seems greatly preferable mainly because of lack of substitutability for much natural capital, the fact that it and not human-made capital is now limiting and for prudence in the face of many irreversibilities and uncertainties. Pearce *et al.* (1988, 1989, 1990), Costanza (1991), Costanza and Daly (1992), Opschoor (1994), van den Bergh (1993), van den Bergh and Nijkamp (1991), most ecologists and most ecological economists prefer, or are coming round to, some version of strong sustainability.

Absurdly Strong Environmental Sustainability

Here, we would never deplete anything. Non-renewable resources, absurdly, could not be used at all. All minerals would remain in the ground. For renewables, only net annual growth increments could be harvested in the form of the over mature portion of the stock. Some ecologists fear we may be reduced to part of this type of sustainability - harvesting only over-mature growth increments of renewables, in which case this sustainability is better called 'superstrong' sustainability (Opschoor 1994).

The choice between weak and strong sustainability highlights the tradeoffs between human-made capital and natural capital. Economic logic requires us to invest in the limiting factor which now is often natural capital rather than human-made capital. Investing in non-marketed natural capital is essentially an infrastructure investment on a grand scale, that is the biophysical infrastructure of the entire human niche. Investment in such infrastructure maintains the productivity of all previous economic investments in human-made capital, public or private, by rebuilding the natural capital stocks that have come to be limiting.

Environmental or resource accounting will be required to ensure that the per capita national or world product is indeed maintained. Such accounts should deduct from gross output not only depletion of mineral resources, topsoil and other environmental inputs to production, but also damage to life support systems or the environmental services provided by natural capital, such as damage to the atmosphere, greenhouse gas accumulation and ozone shield damage. Properly calculated net national product provides a measure of sustainability performance, although not of damage to life support systems.

SUSTAINABILITY AND SUBSTITUTABILITY

Ecology has paid inadequate attention to the extent of substitutability between natural and human-made capital so far, yet it is central to the issue of sustainability. Substitutability is the ability to offset a diminished capacity of environmental source and sink services to absorb wastes and provide healthy air, atmosphere and so on. The importance of substitutability is that if it prevails, then there can be no limits. If an environmental good is destroyed, a substitute can replace it. Conventional economics and technological optimists depend heavily on substitutability being the rule rather than the exception. Alfred Marshall's traditional economics and especially his emphasis on investment in waiting or fallow for regeneration of natural capital is a welcome exception.

In all fairness, substitutability has been reliable historically. When white pine or sperm whales became scarce, there were other acceptable substitutes. When surficial oil flows were exhausted, drilling technology enabled very deep deposits to be tapped. In Europe, when the native forest was consumed, timber for houses was replaced with brick. If bricks did not substitute for local timber, then it was imported. Uncertainty or scarcity of copper imports led to aluminum substitutes and now all new telecommunication networks use fibre optics made from superabundant silica sand.

The realization that substitutability is the exception, rather than the rule, is not yet at all widespread, in spite of Ehrlich's (1989) warning. However, once limits of imports cease masking substitutability, then it becomes plain that most (not all) forms of capital are more complementary or neutral and are less substitutable. Natural capital cannot substitute for human capital; an abundance of timber or bricks will not get a house built without the human capital of carpenters and masons. Economists who hope, questionably, that natural capital and human-made capital are substitutes, then claim total capital (the sum of natural and human-made capital) can be maintained constant in some aggregate value sense (Daly 1994a). This reasoning, built on the questionable premise that human-made capital is substitutable for natural capital, means it is acceptable to divest natural capital as long as an equivalent value has been invested in human-made capital. Even this weak sustainability is not required by national accounting rules. Indeed, our national accounts simply count natural capital liquidation as income (El Serafy 1991, 1993).

Unfortunately, that is also the way the world is being run at the micro or firm level; user costs are rarely calculated (Kellenberg and Daly 1994). We consume environmental source capacity by releasing many wastes into the air because we claim the investment in energy production and refrigeration substitute for healthy air or atmosphere. We extinguish species by converting jungle to cattle ranches because the human-made capital is a substitute for the natural capital of biodiversity. This belief, weak sustainability, has not yet been achieved and it would be a great improvement were it attained. But, because human-made and natural capital are far from perfect substitutes, weak sustainability is a dangerous goal. It would be risky even as an interim stage on the way to any reliable concept of sustainability.

Ecologists attach great importance to Baron Justus von Liebig's Law of the Minimum; the whole chain is only as strong as its weakest link. The factor in shortest supply is the limiting factor because factors are complements, not substitutes. If scarcity of phosphate is limiting the rate of photosynthesis, then it would be useless to increase another factor, such as nitrogen or light or water or CO_2. If one wants faster photosynthesis one must ascertain which factor is limiting and then invest in that one first, until it is no longer limiting. More nitrogen fertilizer cannot substitute for lack of phosphate, precisely because they are complements. Environmental sustainability is based on the conclusion that most natural capital is a complement for human-made capital and not a substitute. Complementarity is profoundly unsettling for conventional economics because it means there are limits to growth, or limits to environmental source and sink capacities. Human-made capital is a very poor substitute for most environmental services and substitution for some life support systems is impossible. Some cities try to increase one sink capacity by collecting sewage, treating it and discharging treated effluent into the nearest creek. This expensive and wasteful course is not working. Treated sewage is killing many rivers and estuaries worldwide, damaging their source and sink capacities. Even many coastal waters are affected. People increasingly accept the fact that local limits are being exceeded, but become more spatially myopic when the limit being reached is a global one, such as atmospheric carbon dioxide accumulation.

A compelling argument that human-made capital is only a marginal substitute for natural capital is the *reductio ad absurdum* case in which all natural capital is liquidated into human-made capital. We might survive the loss of fossil fuels, but what would substitute for the loss of topsoil and breathable air? Only in science fiction could humanity survive by breathing bottled air from backpacks and eating only hydroponic greenhouse food. If there is insufficient substitutability between natural capital and human-made capital, then throughput growth must be severely constrained and eventually cease. While new technology may postpone the transition from quantitative growth to qualitative development and environmental sustainability, current degradation shows that technology is inadequate.

> For natural life support systems no practical substitutes are possible and degradation may be irreversible. In such cases (and perhaps in others as well), compensation cannot be meaningfully specified. (Toman 1994).

CRITERIA FOR ENVIRONMENTAL SUSTAINABILITY

From the above maintenance of natural capital approach to environmental sustainability, we can draw practical rules of thumb to guide the design of economic development. As a first approximation, the design of investment strategies should be compared with the input/output rules of environmental sustainability in order to assess the extent to which an action is sustainable.

The implications of implementing environmental sustainability are immense. We must learn how to manage the renewable resources for the long term; we have to reduce waste and pollution. In fact, because the capacity of natural systems to absorb our wastes is limited and cannot be expanded, sustainable societies will eliminate waste by optimizing the full life cycle of products and processes. No throw aways will be permissible; recyclability and reparability will be integrated during manufacture; ephemeral fads and fashions will become errors of the past. We must learn how to use energy and materials with scrupulous efficiency; we must learn how to use solar energy in all its forms and we must invest in repairing the damage, as much as possible, done to the earth in the past few decades by unthinking industrialization and violence in many parts of the globe. Environmental sustainability needs enabling conditions which are not integral parts of environmental sustainability: Not only economic and social sustainability but ability to negotiate conflicts and resolve disputes, democracy, human resource development, empowerment of women and much more investment in human capital than is common today (Orr 1992).

The sooner we start to approach environmental sustainability the easier it will become. For example, the demographic transition took a century in Europe, but only a decade in Taiwan; technology and education make big differences. But the longer we delay, the worse the eventual quality of life, especially for the poor who do not have the means to insulate themselves from the negative effects of environmental degradation.

Yet, what is galling, is that in spite of spending capital inheritance rather than just income, most of the world consumes at barely subsistence levels. Can humanity attain a more equitable standard of living which does not exceed the carrying capacity of the planet? The transition to environmental sustainability will inevitably occur. However, whether nations will have the wisdom and foresight to plan for an orderly and equitable transition to environmental sustainability, rather than allowing biophysical limits to dictate the timing and course of this transition, remains in doubt.

It is obvious that if pollution and environmental degradation were to grow at the same rate as economic activity, or even population growth, the damage to ecological and human health would be appalling and the growth itself would be undermined and even self defeating. Fortunately, this is not necessary. A transition to sustainability is possible, although it will require big changes in policies and the way we humans value things. The key to the improvement of the wellbeing of millions of people lies in the increase of the added value of output after properly netting out all the environmental costs and benefits, and after differentiating between the stock and flow aspects of the use of natural resources. This is the key to sustainable development. Without this adjustment in thinking and measurement, the pursuit of economic growth that does not account for natural capital and counts depletion of natural capital as income generation will not lead to sustainable development.

The global ecosystem, which is the source of all the resources needed for the economic subsystem, is finite and has now reached a stage where its regenerative and assimilative capacities have become very strained. It looks inevitable that the next century will witness double the number of people in the human economy, depleting sources and filling sinks with their increasing wastes. If we emphasize the latter, it is because human experience seems to indicate that we have tended to overestimate the environment's capacity to cope with our wastes, even more than we overestimated the 'limitless' bounty of its resources, such as the fish in the sea.

THE BASIC CONDITIONS FOR ENVIRONMENTAL SUSTAINABILITY[8]

Maintenance of natural capital, the basic definition of environmental sustainability can now be extended and disaggregated. But even if natural capital is maintained, population growth will undermine sustainability and welfare. That is why the per capita dimension becomes necessary. The main needs for approaching sustainability are first, decrease Northern overconsumption and overuse of environmental sources and sinks; second stabilize or even reduce Northern population; third, increase in throughput growth for developing countries, but transforming growth to development before growth starts to decrease wellbeing, or before carrying capacities are exceeded. Fourth, stabilize population size in developing countries. Stating the conditions for sustainability in per capita terms calls attention to the importance of stopping population growth.

Stopping throughput of matter and energy from growing, or holding throughput constant is the condition for environmental sustainability. Sustainability does not imply optimality. Sustainability is a necessary but not sufficient condition of optimality (Daly 1994a,b). Optimality means stabilizing population on the demand side and improving resource productivity or 'dematerializing' the economy on the supply side. Resource productivity has increased already, for example, improvements in energy efficiency, more production with less energy and fewer materials, tight recycling, repair, reuse and the transition to renewables such as wind, photovoltaics and hydrogen.

ENVIRONMENTAL SUSTAINABILITY INVOLVES PUBLIC CHOICE

Environmental sustainability as biophysical security is connected to welfare and both are somewhat connected to economics, especially efficiency. Biophysical sciences follow biophysical laws irrespective of public choice. Public choice governs the rate at which society elects to approach environmental sustainability voluntarily and purposefully, or as at present, to

---

[8] 1. Maintenance of human-made capital; 2. Maintenance of renewable natural capital; 3. Maintenance of non-renewable substitutable natural capital; 4. Maintenance of non-substitutable, non-renewable natural resources; 5. All economic consumption should be priced to reflect full cost of all capital depletion; 6. The per capita stock of all kinds of capital could remain constant as long as the stocks grew at the same rate as population; 7. Constant per capita net national product (or net world product) will need to be financed from savings (Dr Raymond Mikesell, *pers. comm.* 1994).

recede away from environmental sustainability. Society has the choice of an orderly transition to environmental sustainability on our terms, or letting biophysical damage dictate the timing and speed of the transition.

If society lets biophysical deterioration make the transition to environmental sustainability for us it is likely to be unacceptably harsh for humans. That is why clarity and education are so important in the race to approach environmental sustainability. Partly because recognition of the need for environmental sustainability is so recent, political will and institutional capacity now have to catch up. There will be powerful losers when society decides to move towards environmental sustainability and making polluters pay. Institutional strengthening therefore is a necessary condition for environmental sustainability.

WHY DOESN'T ECONOMICS TAKE CARE OF EXPLOITATION?

Current economic thinking exaggerates the efficiency of markets making it economically rational to destroy a resource if its natural growth rate is lower than the economic opportunity cost of capital, even for sole owners. Clark (1973) worked this out for the great whales, which breed slowly, but the argument applies to all natural resources which grow slower than the interest rate, which is usually less than the opportunity cost. Projects based on natural resources that grow at say 2 per cent a year will be rejected if the investor has to borrow at, say, 8 per cent.[9]

Financial rates of return on natural resource projects tend to be lower than the cost of borrowing capital. This explains the reluctance to invest in tree plantations, regeneration, fallows, rotations or Marshallian investments in 'waiting'. Conventional economics compares such natural resources with a human artifact (the interest rate) which is volatile, hence a grossly misleading guide to maintenance of natural capital. Ludwig (*pers. comm.* 1995) concludes that nothing will be spared in the long run under the present economic regime. Unless we are aware of the deficiencies of the free market in guiding investment needed to maintain and expand natural capital, *laissez faire* cannot be expected to take care of this problem.

---

[9] The weakness of the putative economic argument comes from reliance on market signals rather than on economic or social signals. In the area of project appraisal, financial, economic and social rates of return have been distinguished, the latter two involving the calculation of shadow prices that would correct the financial analysis. Markets are notoriously inadequate in reflecting optimal pricing for natural resources that would capture externalities and bring in considerations of sustainability. I am grateful to Salah El Serafy for this clarification.

A single measure - population times per capita consumption of natural capital - encapsulates an essential dimension of the relationship between economic activity and environmental sustainability. This scale of the growing human economic subsystem is judged, whether large or small, relative to the finite global ecosystem on which it so totally depends and of which it is a part. The global ecosystem is the source of all material inputs feeding the economic subsystem and is the sink for all its wastes. Population times per capita consumption of natural capital is the total flow, or throughput, of resources from the global ecosystem to the economic subsystem, then back to the global ecosystem as waste.

In the long gone empty world case, the scale of the human economic subsystem is small relative to the large, but non-growing global ecosystem. In the full world case, the scale of the human economic subsystem is large and still growing, relative to the finite global ecosystem. The economic subsystem has already started to interfere with global biospheric processes, such as altering the composition of the atmosphere or the now nearly global damage to the ozone shield.

PRIORITIES TO APPROACH GLOBAL ENVIRONMENTAL SUSTAINABILITY

The main means to accelerate the two crucial transitions to sustainability, to population stability and to renewable energy are:

Human capital formation

1. Education, training and employment creation, particularly for girls equivalent to that for boys, the poor and vulnerable minorities.
2. Empowerment of women; women's reproductive and health rights.
3. Meeting unmet family planning demand, delaying marriage slightly, postponing first birth marginally, spacing births optimally.

Technological transfer

1. For the South and East to leapfrog the North's environmentally damaging 'smoke stack' stage of economic evolution.
2. For the developing countries, this requires creating an incentive framework conducive to efficient investment (Daly and Duffy 1996).
3. For industrial countries, this requires adequate investment in renewable energy and clean technologies.

Direct poverty alleviation

1. Direct poverty alleviation, including social safety nets and targeted aid (Goodland and Daly 1993a,b).

CONCLUSION

This chapter reviews the current status of the debate about the concept of environmental sustainability and mentions its related aspects of growth, limits, scale and substitutability. The chapter suggests that environmental sustainability is a clear concept and that it is universal and rigorous. While the many paths leading to environmental sustainability in each country or sector will differ, the goal remains constant. The monumental challenge of ensuring that possibly ten billion people are decently fed and housed within less than two human generations, without damaging the environment on which we all depend, means that the goal of environmental sustainability must be reached as soon as humanly possible.

REFERENCES

Agarwal, A. and Narain, S. 1991. 'Global warming in an unequal world', *International Journal of Sustainable Development*, 1(1), 98-104.

Ahmad, Y., El Serafy, S. and Lutz, E. (eds) 1989. *Environmental Accounting*. The World Bank: Washington DC, 100 pp.

Archibugi, F. and Nijkamp, P. (eds) 1989. *Economy and Ecology: Towards Sustainable Development*. Dordrecht: Kluwer, 348 pp.

Barbier, E. (ed.) 1993. *Economics and Ecology: New Frontiers and Sustainable Development*. London: Chapman and Hall, 205 pp.

Barney, G.O. (ed.) 1980. *The Global 2000 Report to the President of the USA: Entering the 21st century*. Harmondsworth: Penguin, 2 vols.

Bartlett, A.A. 1994. 'Reflections on sustainability', *Population and Environment*, 16(1), 5-35.

Beckerman, W. 1974. *In Defence of Economic Growth*. London: Jonathan Cape.

Beckerman, W. 1992a. 'Economic growth: Whose growth? Whose environment?', *World Development*, 20, 481-492.

Beckerman, W. 1992b. *Economic Development: Conflict or Complementarity?* Washington DC: The World Bank, WPS 961, 42 pp.

Beckerman, W. 1994. '"Sustainable development": Is it a useful concept?', *Environmental Values*, 3, 191-209.

Beckerman, W. 1995. *Small is Stupid: Blowing the Whistle on the Greens*. London: Duckworth, 202 pp.

Beijing Declaration 1991. Beijing ministerial declaration on environment and development. Beijing, People's Republic of China, Ministerial Conference of (41 Ministers of) Developing Countries on Environment and Development, 18-19 June 1991, 9 pp.

Boulding, K.E. 1966. 'The economics of the coming spaceship earth', in Jarret, H. (ed.) *Environmental Quality in a Growing Economy*. Baltimore: Johns Hopkins.

Boulding, K.E. 1968. *Beyond Economics*. Ann Arbor: University of Michigan, 302 pp.

Boulding, K.E. 1992. *Towards a New Economics: Ecology and Distribution*. Aldershot: Edward Elgar, 344 pp.

Boutros-Ghali, B. 1994. *An Agenda for Development*. New York: United Nations, NGO Liaison Service 46, 20 pp.

Brown, L.B. *et al.* 1995. *State of the World: 1995*. Washington DC: Worldwatch Institute, 255 pp.

Brown, L.B. and Kane, H. 1994. *Full House: Reassessing the Earth's Population Carrying Capacity*. New York: Norton, 261 pp.

Clark, C. 1973. 'The economics of over exploitation', *Science*, 181, 630-34.

Clark, W.C. and Munn, R.E. (eds) 1987. *Sustainable Development of the Biosphere*. Cambridge: Cambridge University Press, 491 pp.

Cobb, C.W. and Cobb, J.B. 1994. *The Green National Product: A Proposed Index of Sustainable Economic Welfare*. Lanham MD: The University Press of America.

Collard, D., Pearce, D.W. and Ulph, D. (eds) 1987. *Economics, Growth and Sustainable Environments*. New York: St. Martin's Press, 205 pp.

Costanza, R. (ed.) 1991. *Ecological Economics: The Science and Management of Sustainability*. New York: Columbia University Press.

Costanza, R. and Daly, H.E. 1992. 'Natural capital and sustainable development', *Conservation Biology*, 6, 37-46.

Daily, G.C. and Ehrlich, P.R. 1992. 'Population, sustainability and the earth's carrying capacity', *BioScience*, 42(10), 761-71.

Daily, G., Ehrlich, P.R. and Ehrlich, A. 1994. 'Optimum population size', *Population and Environment*, 15(6), 469-75.

Daly, H.E. 1972. 'In defense of a steady-state economy', *American Journal of Agricultural Economics*, 54(4), 945-54.

Daly, H.E. (ed.) 1973. *Toward a Steady State Economy*. San Francisco: Freeman.

Daly, H.E. 1974. 'The economics of the steady state', *American Economic Review*, May, 15-21.

Daly, H.E. 1977 (1991 2nd ed.). *Steady state economics*. Washington DC: Island Press, 302 pp.

Daly, H.E. (ed.) 1980. *Economics, Ecology and Ethics: Essays Toward a Steady-State Economy*. San Francisco: Freeman.

Daly, H.E. 1988. 'On sustainable development and national accounts', in Collard, D., Pearce, D.W. and Ulph, D. (eds), *Economics, Growth and Sustainable Environments*. New York: St. Martin's Press, 205 pp.

Daly, H.E. 1990a. 'Toward some operational principles of sustainable development', *Ecological Economics*, 2, 1-6.

Daly, H.E. 1990b. 'Sustainable growth: An impossibility theorem', *Development*, (SID) 3/4.

Daly, H.E. 1992. 'Allocation, distribution and scale: Towards an economics that is efficient, just and sustainable', *Ecological Economics*, 6(3), 185-193.

Daly, H.E. 1994a. 'Operationalizing sustainable development by investing in natural capital', in Jansson, Å, Hammer, M., Folke, C. and Costanza, R. (eds) *Investing in Natural Capital: The Ecological Economics Approach to Sustainability*. Washington DC: Island Press, pp. 22-37.

Daly, H.E. 1994b. Consumption: Value added, physical transformation and welfare (30 pp. Draft). Public Affairs, University of Maryland, College Park.

Daly, H.E. 1995. 'On Wilfrid Beckerman's critique of sustainable development', *Environmental Values*, 4, 49-55.

Daly, H.E. 1996a. 'Avoiding uneconomic growth'. Stockholm, Right Livelihood Award, 12 pp.

Daly, H.E. 1996b. *Beyond Growth: The Economics of Sustainable Development*. Boston: Beacon Press, 253 pp.

Daly, H.E. and Cobb, J.B. 1989. *For the Common Good*. Boston: Beacon Press.

Daly, H.E. and Duffy, J. 1996. 'Ecological tax reform', *Perspectives on Business*, 10 (2), 17-24.

Dietz, F.J. and van der Straaten, J. 1992. 'Rethinking environmental economics: Missing links between economic theory and environmental policy', *Journal of Economic Issues*, 26(1), 27-51.

Ehrlich, P.R. 1989. 'The limits to substitutability: Meta-resource depletion and a new economic-ecological paradigm', *Ecological Economics*, 1, 9-16.

Ehrlich, P.R. and Ehrlich, A. 1989a. 'Too many rich folks', *Populi*, 16(3), 3-29.

Ehrlich, P.R. and Ehrlich, A. 1989b. 'How the rich can save the poor and themselves', *Pacific and Asian Journal of Energy*, 3, 53-63.

Ehrlich, P.R. and Ehrlich, A. 1991. *Healing the Planet*. Boston: Addison-Wesley.

El Serafy, S. 1989. 'The proper calculation of income from depletable natural resources', in Ahmad, Y.J. *et al.*, *Environmental Accounting for Sustainable Development*. Washington DC: World Bank/UNEP Symposium, pp. 25-39.

El Serafy, S. 1991. 'The environment as capital', in Costanza, R. (ed.), *Ecological Economics*. New York: Columbia University Press, pp. 168-75.

El Serafy, S. 1993. 'Country macroeconomic work and natural resources', The World Bank: Washington DC, Environment Working Paper No. 58, 50 pp.

Fritsch, B., Schmidheiny, S. and Seifritz, W. 1994. *Towards an Ecologically Sustainable Growth Society: Physical Foundations, Economic Transitions and Political Constraints*. Berlin: Springer, 198 pp.

Gale, R.P. and Cordray, S.M. 1994. 'Making sense of sustainability: Nine answers to "what should be sustained?"', *Rural Sociology*, 59(2), 311-32.

Goodland, R. 1992. 'The case that the world has reached limits', *Population and Environment*, 13(2), 167-82.

Goodland, R. 1994. 'Environmental sustainability: Imperative for peace', in Graeger, N. and Smith, D. (eds), *Environment, Poverty, Conflict*. Oslo: International Peace Research Institute (PRIO), pp. 19-46.

Goodland, R. 1995. 'The concept of environmental sustainability', *Annual Review of Ecology*, 26, 1-24.

Goodland, R. and Daly, H.E. 1993a. 'Why Northern income growth is not the solution to Southern poverty', *Ecological Economics*, 8, 85-101.

Goodland, R. and Daly, H.E. 1993b. 'Poverty alleviation is essential for environmental sustainability', Environment Working Paper No. 42. Washington DC: The World Bank, 34 pp.

Goodland, R. and Daly, H.E. in press. 'Environmental sustainability: Universal and non-negotiable', *Ecological Applications*.

Goodland, R., Daly, H.E. and El Serafy, S. 1992. *Population, Technology, Lifestyle: The Transition to Sustainability*. Washington DC: Island Press, 154 pp.

Haavelmo, T. and Hansen, S. 1992. 'On the strategy of trying to reduce economic inequality by expanding the scale of human activity', in Goodland, R., Daly, H.E. and El Serafy, S. 1992. *Population, Technology, Lifestyle: The Transition to Sustainability*. Washington DC: Island Press, pp. 38-51.

Hardin, G. 1968. 'The tragedy of the commons', *Science*, 162, 1243-8.

Hardin, G. 1993. *Living Within Limits: Ecology, Economics and Population Taboos*. New York: Oxford University Press, 339 pp.

Hicks, J.R. 1946. *Value and Capital*. Oxford: Clarendon Press, 446 pp.

Hueting, R. 1980. *New Scarcity and Economic Growth: More Welfare Through Less Production?* Amsterdam: North-Holland, 269 pp.

Hueting, R. 1990. 'The Brundtland report: A matter of conflicting goals', *Ecological Economics*, 2, 109-17.

IIASA 1992. *Science and Sustainability*. Laxenburg, Vienna: International Institute of Applied Systems Analysis, 317 pp.

IUCN 1980. *The World Conservation Strategy*. Gland, IUCN, WWF.

Jansson, Å., Hammer, M., Folke, C. and Costanza, R. 1994. *Investing in Natural Capital: The Ecological Economics Approach to Sustainability*. Washington DC: Island Press, 504 pp.

Kellenberg, J. and Daly, H.E. 1994. 'User costs', Environment Working Paper, Washington DC: The World Bank.

Korten, D.C. 1991. 'Sustainable development', *World Policy Journal*, Winter, 156-90.

Lutz, E. (ed.) 1993. 'Toward improved accounting for the environment'. An UNSTAT-World Bank symposium. Washington DC: The World Bank, 329 pp.

Malthus, T.R. 1964 (1836). *Principles of Political Economy*. London: Kelley, 446 pp.

Malthus, T.R. 1970 (1798). *An Essay on the Principle of Population*. Harmondsworth: Penguin, 291 pp.

Meadows, D., Meadows, D., Randers, J. and Behrens W. 1972. *The Limits to Growth*. New York: Universe Books, 205 pp.

Meadows, D., Meadows, D. and Randers, J. 1992. *Beyond the Limits: Global Collapse or a Sustainable Future*. Post Mills, VT.: Chelsea Green Publishing, 300 pp.

Mill, J.S. 1900 (revised ed.) (1848). *Principles of Political Economy*. New York: Collier, 2 vols.

Mishan, E.J. 1967. *The Costs of Economic Growth*. London: Staples Press, 190 pp.

Mishan, E.J. 1977. *The Economic Growth Debate: An Assessment*. London: Allen and Unwin, 277 pp.

Netherlands 1994. *The Environment: Towards a Sustainable Future*. Dordrecht: Kluwer Academic Publishers, 608 pp.

Opschoor, J.B. (ed.) 1992. *Environment, Economy and Sustainable Development*. Groningen: Wolters-Noordhoff, 149 pp.

Opschoor, J.B. 1994. 'The environmental space and sustainable resource use', in *Sustainable Resource Management and Resource Use*. Publication RMNO 97, 3, 33-67. Netherlands: Advisory Council for Research on Nature and Environment.

Opschoor, J.B. and van der Straaten, J. 1993. 'Sustainable development: An institutional approach', *Ecological Economics*, 3, 203-22.

Orr, D.W. 1992. *Environmental Literacy: Education and the Transition to a Postmodern world*. Albany: State University of New York, 211 pp.

Panayotou, T. 1993. *Green Markets: The Economics of Sustainable Development*. San Francisco: International Center for Economic Growth, 169 pp.

Pearce, D.W. and Redclift, M. (eds) 1988. 'Sustainable development', *Futures*, 20.

Pearce, D.W., Markandya, A. and Barbier, E. 1989. *Blueprint for a Green Economy*. London: Earthscan, 192 pp.

Pearce, D.W., Barbier, E. and Markandya, A. 1990. *Sustainable Development: Economics and Environment in the Third World*. Aldershot: Edward Elgar, 217 pp.

Redclift, M.R. 1987. *Sustainable Development: Exploring the Contradictions*. London: Methuen, 221 pp.

Redclift, M.R. 1989. 'The meaning of sustainable development', *Geoforum*, 23, 395-403.

Redclift, M.R. 1994. 'Reflections on the "sustainable development" debate', *International Journal of Sustainable Development and World Ecology*, 1, 3-21.

Ricardo, D. 1973 (1817). *Principles of Political Economy and Taxation*. London: Dent, 300 pp.

Serageldin, I. 1993a. 'Making development sustainable', *Finance and Development*, 30(4), 6-10.

Serageldin, I. 1993b. 'Development partners: Aid and cooperation in the 1990s'. Stockholm: SIDA, 153 pp.

Serageldin, I., Daly, H.E. and Goodland, R. 1995. 'The concept of sustainability', in van Dieren, W. (ed.), *Taking Nature into Account*. New York: Springer Verlag, 332.

Simon, J.L. and Kahn, H. 1984. *The Resourceful Earth: A Response to Global 2000*. Oxford: Blackwell.

Simonis, U.E. 1990. *Beyond Growth: Elements of Sustainable Development*. Berlin: Edition Sigma, 151 pp.

Solow, R. 1974. 'The economics of resources or the resources of economics', *American Economic Review*, 15, 1-14.

Solow, R. 1993a. 'An almost practical step toward sustainability', *Resources Policy*, 19, 162-172.

Solow, R. 1993b. 'Sustainability: An economist's perspective', in Dorfman, R. and Dorfman, N.S. (eds), *Selected Readings in Environmental Economics*. New York: Norton, pp. 179-87.

Summers, L. 1992. 'Summers on sustainable growth', *The Economist*, 30 May, 91.

Tinbergen, J. and Hueting, R. 1992. 'GNP and market prices: Wrong signals for sustainable economic success that mask environmental destruction', in Goodland, R., Daly, H.E. and El Serafy, S. (eds), *Population, Technology, Lifestyle: The Transition to Sustainability*. Washington DC: Island Press, pp. 52-62.

Tisdell, C. 1992. *Environmental Economics: Policies for Environmental Management and Sustainable Development.* Aldershot: Edward Elgar, 259 pp.

Toman, M.A. 1994. 'Economics and "sustainability": Balancing trade-offs and imperatives', *Land Economics*, 70(4), 399-413.

Turner, R. (ed.) 1993. *Sustainable Environmental Economics and Management: Principles and Practice.* London: Belhaven Press, 389 pp.

van den Bergh, J.C.J.M. 1993. 'Economy-environment-development relationships based on dynamic carrying capacity and sustainable development feedback', *Environmental and Resource Economics*, 3, 395-412.

van den Bergh, J.C.J.M. and Nijkamp, P. 1991. 'Operationalizing sustainable development: Dynamic ecological economic models', *Ecological Economics*, 3, 395-412.

von Weizsacker, E.U. 1992. 'Sustainability: Why the North must act first'. Geneva: UN Academy for the Environment (June Workshop), 13 pp.

World Wide Fund for Nature 1993. 'Sustainable use of natural resources: Concepts, issues and criteria'. Gland, Switzerland, 32 pp.

World Commission on Environment and Development, WCED (The Brundtland Commission) 1987. *Our Common Future.* Oxford: Oxford University Press.

World Commission on Environment and Development (WCED) 1992. *Our Common Future Reconvened.* Geneva: Centre for Our Common Future, 32 pp.

World Bank 1990. *World Development Report.* Washington DC: The World Bank.

World Bank 1992. *World Development Report 1992: Development and the environment.* New York: Oxford University Press, 308 pp.

5. Agricultural Sustainability and Conservation of Biodiversity: Competing Policies and Paradigms

Clem Tisdell

INTRODUCTION

Sustainability issues and matters involving the conservation of biodiversity are no longer new subjects for environmental policy. Nevertheless, they are of continuing interest, there are always new dimensions to consider and unresolved questions remain. In fact, it may only be now that we are starting to have a satisfactory overview of these subjects which have been intensively considered for around two decades. This paper provides an overview of these subjects, paying particular attention to agriculture.

In it the following are considered:

1. Different broad approaches to policy making and implementation applied to environmental policies.
2. Different concepts of and views about sustainability and biodiversity and their dissimilar policy implications.
3. Agricultural sustainability as a concept and as a goal and policies to achieve agricultural sustainability.
4. Important relationships between agriculture and biodiversity.
5. Reasons for sustaining biodiversity, possible methods for doing so and their implications for agriculture.

Let us consider each of these matters in turn.

APPROACHES TO POLICY FORMATION AND IMPLEMENTATION AND THEIR APPLICATION TO ENVIRONMENTAL POLICIES

To a considerable extent mainstream approaches to economic policy, including development policies, have tended to be technocratic. To some extent, this is a natural consequence of econometric model building and the use of mathematical economic models of a relatively deterministic nature. Such models make no allowance for the unexpected and they implicitly suppose a high degree of knowledge on the part of the model builders. Such models can easily become the handmaiden of top down policies and generate mechanistic approaches to economic growth, economic development and environmental policy with unfortunate consequences. The economic literature is not lacking in examples (see Tisdell 1990, Ch. 3).

With growing interest in economics of sustainable development, in ecological economics and in evolutionary economics and with the progressive acceptance that individuals (organizations and groups) are bounded in their rationality (Tisdell 1996a), the limitations of the technocratic approach to policy making and implementation of policies have become more obvious. These considerations have highlighted irreversibility and hysteresis, uncertainty and learning, institutional arrangements, the degree of motivation of actors and several other factors as having an important bearing on successful policy formulation and implementation. Such factors, often overlooked in mainstream economic theory, frequently play an integral part in the success or failure of environmental policy and suggest the relevance of models of an organic rather than a mechanical type.

Those who produce and try to implement policy recommendations in a mechanical manner face serious shortcomings, especially in relation to environmental policy and development. This is clear from recent demands for greater participation of local people in devising environmental policies affecting them, especially if they are required to implement these policies in their local area. Demands for the increased political empowerment of local communities and groups affected by policy making have become commonplace in recent times and academics have become increasingly interested in communitarianism (Etzioni 1991).

Appropriate links between the local community and central policy makers may be important for several reasons. For example, such links may be required to improve the environmental knowledge set of both parties, be needed to motivate the carrying out of policies as planned and may be required to provide appropriate feedback of knowledge between the groups involved and to supply effective governance. These links between policy makers and those affected are important from a motivational and a networking point of view. At the same time, it must be realized that costs are involved in networking and in participatory approaches to policy creation and implementation. Consequently, from a restricted economic viewpoint, participatory policy approaches should only be carried to the point where the additional benefits from these equals the additional cost of such institutional arrangements (Baumol and Quandt 1964 and Coase 1937). From a slightly wider perspective, participation might however, be carried further, for example, when account is taken of factors such as self esteem, sense of belonging. There is still much to be learnt about this area of policy making.

In the development studies literature reference is sometimes made to 'top down' and to 'bottom up' approaches to policy with the latter being preferred by those desiring to empower local communities or other social groups. Another possibility is a 'side by side' approach which involves a joint effort by (central) government and local communities in the policy arena (Tisdell 1995b). These three types are, however, gross simplifications. Nevertheless, even if we keep to the possibility of only 'top down' or 'bottom up' governance, a number of different situations can be imagined once it is realized that a dichotomy is possible between policy formulation and its implementation. For example, policy may be formulated centrally but may be required to be implemented locally. Four possibilities are shown in Table 5.1.

Table 5.1. Central and local responsibility for policies affecting local communities: An initial classification of possibilities

Combination	Party responsible for policy formation	Party responsible for policy implementation
1	Central	Central
2	Central	Local
3	Local	Local
4	Local	Central

Possibility one shown in Table 5.1 is the most centralized one and may show little or no regard to the wishes of the local community. However, Table 5.1 should be extended by taking into account a side by side approach as an additional possibility. If this is done, the additional cases set out in Table 5.2 could arise. In this table, case 5 involves the greatest degree of joint participation by groups.

Table 5.2. Combinations to be added to those in Table 5.1 to allow for side by side approaches to policy

Combination	Responsibility for policy formation	Responsibility for policy implementation
1	Side by side	Central
2	Side by side	Local
3	Central	Side by side
4	Local	Side by side
5	Side by side	Side by side

It should be noted that this classificatory system glosses over a whole range of complexities, many of which should be taken into account in refined analysis of the issues involved. Nevertheless, it makes it clear that even at a relatively superficial level, we need to go beyond the 'top down' and 'bottom up' classification in order to assess the desirability of alternative systems of government and policy creation.

Both for sustainable development, sustainability of land use and conservation of biodiversity, involvement in and empowerment of local communities in policy matters is seen as very important by conservation groups. They believe that such involvement will promote sustainability and be a positive force in conserving biodiversity. In reality, however, the empirical evidence is mixed. For example, with the devolution of control over protected areas from central to local authorities with the demise of the Soviet Union, economic exploitation of these areas has been commenced by some local authorities. Some 'protected' areas are being used for the grazing of livestock and timber is being extracted from others for example. Decentralization of government has proceeded quickly in the Philippines. There is fear that some local politicians will use their enhanced political power to exploit (to their advantage) local natural resources unsustainably. On the other hand, the CAMPFIRE programme has been a success in some parts of Zimbabwe as far as the conservation of elephants are concerned. This programme involves controlled devolution of power and provision of economic rewards to local communities for nature conservation. Loss of local political power has undermined conservation in some countries. Mishra (1982) for example, reports that the replacement of village control over forests by central control exercised by the Forestry Department in Katmandu undermined forest conservation in Nepal. Therefore, it is clear from the conflicting empirical evidence that centralization versus decentralization is only one factor influencing the likelihood of policies being adopted which favour sustainable development and the conservation of nature. Yet it is an important consideration from a conservation point of view. Consider another environmental example.

There is growing interest in social forestry in a number of developing countries and the possibility of harmoniously combining forestry, agriculture and even aquaculture in an integrated system designed to enhance sustainability of land use and counteract unfavourable externalities from agriculture, such as soil erosion. This is especially important on sloping lands. It is of considerable policy significance in many parts of Asia, for example, Northern India and Southwest China.

In China, as in many other countries, afforestation has often been a centralist initiative involving top down decisions and implementation. Plans to afforest hilly areas above the planned Three Gorges Dam on the Yangtze

River are of this nature. Such schemes may have little support at the local village level because they are seen as imposed and they may not be designed with local benefits in mind or may be drawn up without adequate assessment of methods to maximize these benefits. In the longer term, social forestry and agriculture schemes are likely to be more sustainable and effective in achieving the conservation goals being sought than state-imposed forestry. This will be especially so if local people have economic incentives to sustain social forestry and agro-forestry projects.

China appears to be moving towards a less centralist (top down) position in designing and implementing environmental conservation projects. For example, with World Bank support, China has undertaken rapid rural appraisal in Xishuangbanna Prefecture, Yunnan, to identify development projects that may be valued by villagers living near Xishuangbanna State Nature Reserve (Xiang 1995). It is proposed to use this appraisal to identify projects likely to be welcomed by villagers and to offer government aid for these. It is hoped that in return for such aid that villagers will agree to refrain from illegal exploitation of the Nature Reserve. Furthermore, assuming that the projects are an economic success, they will increase village incomes and thus reduce the economic need of villagers to use the Reserve illegally.

One cannot be certain yet whether this new policy will be a success. However, the discussion has raised holistic dimensions of environmental policy which are normally not given much attention in conventional economics. In the final analysis, all policy proposals need to be assessed on a holistic basis.

SUSTAINABILITY AND BIODIVERSITY: ALTERNATIVE CONCEPTS AND THEIR POLICY IMPLICATIONS

Many concepts of sustainability relevant to economic theory and environmental policy exist in the literature and the majority require a holistic approach to policy making. Furthermore, even the concept of biodiversity is not cut and dried. Depending on the measures chosen and on the dimensions of biodiversity stressed, different policy consequences may follow. The same is true of sustainability.

For some, the wide range of concepts of sustainability present in the literature have become a source of confusion and have led to doubts about the value of such concepts. Indeed, some use the term 'sustainability' in a value laden way and propagate the idea that things which are sustainable are desirable. This is clearly unsatisfactory because there are evil or unsavoury things such as poverty and disease which few would believe it desirable to sustain. On the other hand, there are characteristics the sustainability of which might be welcomed such as sustainability of levels of income or of biodiversity. The concept of sustainability gains meaning when it is related to an object such as income, level of returns, biodiversity or community.

Sustainability relates to the ability of a characteristic to maintain itself, that is not to decline with the passage of time. An unsustainable characteristic or variable may decline in varied ways or for varied reasons and the difference between these can be policy relevant.

The decline might for example be due to endogenous factors and might be regular, for example, a regular decline in crop yield due to falling soil fertility because of nutrient mining as a result of the type of cropping engaged in. Or, it might only occur after an exogenous shock. For example as suggested by Conway (1985 and 1987) as a result of ecological stress or an environmental shock, the yield from an agricultural system may be depressed and fail to recover fully once the shock has passed. Such systems are said to lack *resilience*. However, resilience is clearly not the only factor to be taken into account when assessing the sustainability of a system, such as yield or returns from an agricultural system.

An equally important characteristic may be the *robustness* of the system, that is the ability of a system to withstand a shock without being deflected from its path or being significantly deflected from its path (Tisdell 1994a). Some systems require larger minimum sizes of shocks to be deflected than others, deflect differently and so on. It is possible for a system to be robust and not to be resilient or to be resilient but not to be robust. If one has to choose between such systems, how will one choose from a sustainability point of view? The point is that in comparing the desirability of techniques or systems sustainability characteristics additional to resilience should be taken into account. For emphasis, Table 5.3 sets out the four possibilities as far as the resilience and robustness of systems are concerned. However, additional complications can emerge, some of which are mentioned in Tisdell (1994a).

Table 5.3. Resilience and robustness of a characteristic of a system

Possibility	Resilient	Robust
1	Yes	Yes
2	Yes	No
3	No	Yes
4	No	No

Knowledge of the sustainability or otherwise of welfare, or value significant variables can be of practical policy importance from several viewpoints. If, for example, sustainability of such a variable is of positive value and if the variable is predicted to decline, this information may allow;

1. defensive measures to be searched for and taken to avert the decline, or
2. if no such measures can be found and lack of sustainability is inevitable, the information may allow planned adjustment to the decline.

In some cases, both responses may be activated by the knowledge of sustainability problems. Methods may be sought which moderate the decline in a target variable and forward planning may occur to adjust to unavoidable decline.

Again, biodiversity, like sustainability of a variable, is not a straightforward concept and is multidimensional. It may refer to genetic diversity, species diversity, or ecosystem variation and there is far from complete agreement about how biodiversity is best measured (Pearce and Moran 1994, Ch. 1). Again the concepts have varying policy consequences. For example, if a tradeoff is required between ecosystem and species diversity, which should be preferred? Depending upon the type of measurement of biodiversity selected, the focus of policy for biodiversity conservation is likely to be different. If, for instance, genetic variability (within species) is stressed more than that variety of species, species may be more likely to be sacrificed (if necessary) to conserve genetic variability within surviving species. Methods of measurement by directing the focus of attention of researchers to particular characteristics often coincidently bias their policy prescriptions.

The concept of sustainable development and the related concept of ecologically sustainable development continues to be an important backdrop to environmental policy making. For some individuals, conservation of biodiversity is a prerequisite for sustainable development. However, even if we take the most common definition of sustainable development used in economics (namely that it is development ensuring that the incomes, or more generally living standards, of future generations are no less than those of current generations), the concept needs to be fully comprehended if it is to result in appropriate policies. This is so even leaving aside some philosophical difficulties involved in the concept and inadequate attention to the population variable by its exponents (Tisdell 1993, Ch. 10).

Taking the economic concept of sustainable development as given, much of the policy debate has become centred on determining the types of capital stock that might allow sustainable development to be achieved. Man-made capital stock can include physical capital, knowledge, human capital and institutional capital. All of these involve an investment which may be 'funded' by reducing the natural capital stock. In addition, physical capital normally embodies a part of the natural environmental stock. The following question is important: To what extent can man-made capital be substituted for the natural environmental stock and sustainable development still be achieved?

As is well known, a spectrum of views exist about this matter. On the one hand, some believe that the process of substitution of man-made capital for the natural environmental stock can continue without any significant threat to sustainable development. Supporters of this view place relatively *weak conditions* on conservation of the environment but often include the prescription that environmental externalities or spillovers should be taken into account. Indeed, it is possible that some on this side of the spectrum see continuing conversion of natural environmental resource stocks to man-made capital as essential for sustainable development.

On the other side of the spectrum are those who see continuing conversion of the natural environmental resource stock to man-made capital as a serious threat to sustainable development. They point out that the life of man-made capital is relatively short, for example, physical capital, compared to the natural environmental resource stock.[1] Furthermore, the natural resource stock itself provides productive services and in many cases consumptive ones. The destruction of natural capital will inevitably lead to loss of these services and undermine incomes both;

1. directly because fewer environmental services are available for direct consumption and
2. indirectly because the productivity of man-made capital is likely to be reduced once the relative size of the natural environmental resource stock is significantly reduced. In other words, increasing imbalance between factor proportions (an increase in man-made capital *relative* to natural environmental capital) will eventually result in reduced productivity and income.

Some supporters of the above view claim that already the substitution process has reached this critical stage and believe that *strong sustainability* conditions should be imposed to conserve the remaining natural environmental stock. They argue that it is not sufficient to make sure that environmental externalities are fully taken into account. They would favour externalities being taken into account in project evaluation but, in addition, usually want environmental *offset* policies to be implemented so as to keep the environmental resource stock constant.

Pearce (1993) describes those who favour weak sustainability conditions as growth optimists and those who favour strong sustainability conditions as 'dark greens'. However, this does not effectively distinguish between different types of 'dark greens'.

---

[1] In addition, note that the natural environmental resource stock is to a large extent self-reproducing or sustainable but this is not true of man-made capital in the same way. It lacks the degree of autonomy of natural capital in perpetuating itself.

Strong sustainability conditions may be supported for one or both of the following reasons:

1. They are believed to be necessary to ensure that the incomes of future generations do not fall below those of the present. This is a *positive* basis given that the intergenerational equity objective is accepted and that only human beings are to account.
2. Strong sustainability conditions may be supported for a *normative* reason. Some individuals believe that mankind has an obligation to help conserve God's natural creation, especially the living environment. Those holding this view usually support strong sustainability conditions. They are increasingly likely to do so as the availability of natural environments is reduced.

There are a number of variants on the capital substitutability theme. In one simplified version, no serious problem occurs until environmental resources are reduced to a core. However, once the core is reached serious problems arise for sustainability. If the theory is correct, the problem is to identify the core. To what extent for example is biodiversity in the core? To what extent can biodiversity be foregone and incomes be sustained? What is the nature of the core? Is it fuzzy or not, changeable or not? Are there regional cores and a global core? Can they be identified?

As will be noticed, the type of problem being raised here is the nature of the functional relationships involved when man-made capital is substituted for the natural resource stock. For instance are the effects on the sustainability of income continuous or discontinuous, positive, positive up to a point and then negative and so on? The nature of the relationship is of considerable importance from the viewpoint of policy. Furthermore, the fact that the relationship itself is uncertain can have policy implications. Consider for example the precautionary principle. If one believes that preservation of an environmental core is necessary for economic sustainability, but cannot determine the core exactly, one may be inclined to adopt the minimax loss strategy of conserving the environmental stock to a greater extent than is strictly necessary so as to make sure that it contains the core. As time goes on, greater knowledge may be obtained about what constitutes the core. This strategy retains flexibility which is likely to be optimal if irreversibility is present and if learning is expected to take place.

Turning to a slightly different matter, much has been made of the total economic valuation concept. In some respects possibly too much, even though it is a considerable advance on earlier narrower economic practice in relation to valuation. The main problem, as I see it, is the naive belief that it is imbued with superior moral standing. In reality, however, it is limited in its moral dimensions. It is essentially man based and the measuring rod of money used is subject to distortions. It does not satisfy those 'dark greens' who believe that mankind has a moral obligation, at least to some extent, to conserve nature independently of man centred wishes. This group also presumably believes that economic sustainability is not a supreme virtue and in fact, if necessary, would be willing to sacrifice economic sustainability to some extent for conservation of nature. In other words, restrictions on satisfaction of man centred economic welfare are favoured on moral grounds to preserve nature if a tradeoff is required, as some believe is necessary.

The total economic valuation concept encounters difficulties also when individuals possess dual or multiple utility or preference functions (Margolis 1982, Kohn 1993). For example, it is conceivable for an individual to have a self centred preference function and another incorporating a wider moral dimension(s) (Etzioni 1991). In relation to valuation, which of these should be afforded primacy? They could have very different policy implications. An interesting side issue is which of these multiple utility functions will politicians try to satisfy? The different utility functions of individuals change with time and circumstances. What factors determine the formation of such functions and their changing importance over time?[2] What is the consequence of different political arrangements and institutional setups for the influence on policy of these moral dimensions? If it is accepted that multiple utility or preference functions exist for the same individual based on different moralities, then it is clear that it is necessary to go beyond the total economic valuation concept.

AGRICULTURAL SUSTAINABILITY

Considerable discussion of agricultural sustainability and of sustainability of rural communities has occurred in the literature. However, whether sustainability of agricultural activities (or those of any particular industry) is desirable is a moot point. If sustainable development is adopted as the main goal (in the sense that the incomes of future generations should not be less than those of present generations), agricultural activities or other activities will only be considered desirable from a social point of view if they contribute to the main goal. Nevertheless, they could be important from the viewpoint of agricultural communities and could be policy relevant in practice. Politically,

---

[2] It is recognized that institutions may mould preferences to some extent (Kelso 1977). What exactly is their role in this regard? Do they help to establish 'extra' preference functions for individuals or change the degree of dominance or prominence of particular sets of preference functions which an individual may have?

policy makers may be forced to give special attention to the situation of agriculturalists, for example, because of the nature of the voting system.

Sustainability of agricultural characteristics may be of relevance to policy makers from at least two points of view:

1. If lack of sustainability of an agricultural characteristic, such as yields or incomes, is predicted it may be possible to adopt measures to avoid these, for instance commence research to discover ways to avoid the problem.
2. If agricultural sustainability cannot be achieved, then knowledge of this may enable suitable adjustment policies to be devised.

In other words, 'to be forewarned is to be forearmed'. Thus agricultural sustainability, in various forms, is relevant for policy purposes.

Several attempts have been made to specify agricultural sustainability with precision, provide criteria for its evaluation and suggest measures for it. The results have been mixed. There has been a tendency for writers to concentrate on the sustainability of different characteristics. Those chosen in many cases seemingly reflect the values of the individuals involved in choosing them. Given that sustainability often involves a variety of characteristics, simple measures of it usually fail to receive widespread support.

Lynam and Herdt (1989), for example, attempt to measure the sustainability of an agricultural system by the trend in the ratio of the value of agricultural output from the system divided by the value of inputs used by it. If the trend is non-declining, the system is said to be sustainable. This indicator will be non-declining if the value of output minus the value of input is not declining, that is if net income from the system is not declining.

This measure has a number of limitations (Tisdell 1996b). Firstly, past trends cannot necessarily be extrapolated. Second, economic viability depends upon biophysical and market factors. It is possible for yields to be declining and for profitability to be improving for market reasons. For some, this might not be regarded as a sustainable system.[3] In any case, in this circumstance the system would most likely violate strong conditions for sustainable development. Third, it is unclear from the Lynam and Herdt (1989) formula how opportunity cost and opportunity return are taken into account. For example, the net income from use of a technique may be non-declining but it may be relatively unprofitable to continue with its use because an alternative technique gives a higher net income or rate of return. Use of the former technique fails to be sustained for economic reasons.

It is useful to consider the Framework for the Evaluation of Sustainable Land Management (FESLM) suggested by the Food and Agricultural

---

[3] This is true for the Framework for Evaluation of Sustainable Land Management outlined below.

Organization (FAO) and the International Board for Soil Research and Management (IBSRAM).

The FELSM Working Party declared that:

> Sustainable land management combines technologies, policies and activities aimed at integrating socio-economic principles with environmental concerns so as to simultaneously:
> - maintain or enhance production/services (productivity)
> - reduce the level of production risk (security)
> - protect the potential of natural resources and prevent degradation of soil and water quality (protection)
> - be economically viable (viability)
> - and socially acceptable (acceptability).
> (quoted in Smyth *et al.* 1993, p. 7).

As indicated above, it would be possible for Lynam and Herdt's (1989) criterion to be satisfied and for FESLM not to be. It is *possible* for productivity to decline and economic viability not to decrease; or for natural resources to deteriorate and economic viability to be sustained. On the other hand, such deterioration could lead to lack of economic viability of an agricultural system. It all depends!

A common claim is that if an agricultural technique is to be sustainable, it must be simultaneously sustainable from a biophysical, economic and social viewpoint. In reality, however, agricultural techniques may remain economically sustainable for a very long period at the same time as biophysical characteristics are declining. Furthermore, a technique that is not entirely socially acceptable may be economically viable and in some cases, as time passes, may become more acceptable socially (social transformation occurs). This is not to suggest that holistic dimensions involved in agricultural sustainability should be ignored. Not at all. Nevertheless, one should be careful about drawing conclusions about what is needed for sustainability.

There has been considerable debate about the sustainability of different categories of agricultural techniques and their environmental impacts. It is worthwhile considering briefly some of the issues. Categorizations include:

1. Modern versus traditional techniques.
2. Conservation farming versus conventional farming.
3. High external input agriculture (HEIA) versus low external input agriculture (LEIA).
4. Organic agriculture versus non-organic.
5. Extensive versus intensive use of land for agriculture.

These classifications overlap to some extent but not entirely.

In order to place the discussion of these alternative agricultural systems in context, note that agricultural activities may prove to be economically (and in some cases, biophysically) unsustainable because of the type of techniques used or because of the nature of activities engaged in on a property (that is because of *internal* effects) or because of *external* effects. External impacts can include waterlogging and salinization of land from irrigation schemes, reduced water availability to particular properties due to demands by competing users and lack of appropriate methods for allocation of the water and so on. A large number of examples could be catalogued but I shall not do that here. Agricultural practices on particular properties may affect other agriculturalists, those engaged in other industries, or impact on consumers directly as a result of environmental spillovers. And other industries and consumers (individuals) can have adverse environmental consequences for agriculture. Overall economic efficiency in satisfying human wants and long term sustainable development requires that external effects be accounted for in policy making. (However, because of the scale factor, this is not sufficient.) I shall not on this occasion discuss the type of policies which might be adopted to cope with externalities because they have been the subject of a major part of economic research on environmental policy design.

Returning to alternative agricultural methods categorized above, consider the following matters:

1. Conway (1987) argues that modern agricultural systems are less sustainable than traditional ones. While this may be broadly so, there are exceptions. Minimum till and no-till systems for example are a modern type of technique and may be more sustainable than some tillage systems especially those which leave ploughed land to fallow, thereby exposing the soil to the elements. Trickle irrigation systems and irrigation systems using moisture sensors (modern techniques) add to conservation of water and may promote sustainability of yields. Furthermore, it is quite possible that 'modern' techniques will be discovered which greatly reduce non-point pollution from fertilizer. Already slow release pelletized fertilizers help do this. In any case, traditional agricultural systems are sometimes not sustainable or become unsustainable with changing socioeconomic conditions. Schultz (1974) has identified some modern agriculture systems which seem more environmentally sustainable than traditional ones. In reality, the sustainability of a technique does not depend solely on whether it is modern or traditional.

2. Many traditional agricultural systems are typified by a low level of external inputs (LEIA) whereas many modern ones exhibit a high degree of reliance on inputs external to the farm or village (HEIA). At first sight, some may believe that LEIA is very sustainable (Reijntjes *et al.* 1992). However

this is not necessarily the case. With growing population LEIA can intensify and result in an expanding area of land being cultivated. For example, swidden or shifting agricultural systems (called *jhum* in Northeast India) involve a low level of external inputs. However, as population increases and the need for providing greater economic needs makes itself felt, cycles of shifting agriculture become shorter and larger land areas are exposed to the elements as a result of this form of cultivation. The consequence is rapidly declining soil fertility, severe soil erosion and escalating loss of biodiversity. Such systems eventually become uneconomic and are unable to maintain the incomes of a rising population.[4] The dynamics of overall social change cause them to become unsustainable.

3.   Agricultural conservation techniques, such as the use of hedgerows with alley cropping on steep slopes, can add sustainability to agricultural yields and reduce adverse externalities. However, they are often not as economic as other methods and frequently involve an initial capital investment which farmers in less developed countries find difficult to make. There are traditional conservation methods using integrated methods and crop rotation but some conservation methods have been or are being developed in modern times. These modern conservation techniques do not necessarily rely on organic methods and need not involve low external inputs. Nevertheless they can be the source of considerable environmental improvement.

4.   Interest in organic agriculture has grown, especially in Germany mainly because of its perceived health benefits for humans (Lampkin and Padel 1994). In some quarters, there also appears to be a presumption that organic agriculture is environmentally benign or favourable. However, it is possible for organic agriculture to be intensive and not favourable to nature conservation. Furthermore, if organic agriculture results in reduced yields (which it need not do in the longer term), then for the same output it will require a larger land area to be used for agriculture so the environmental impact of agriculture will be more widely felt.

5.   It is true that most modern agriculture is intensive and reliant on a high level of external inputs, several of which are non-renewable. Several advocates of increased nature conservation support a return to more extensive systems

---

[4] Ramakrishnan (1992) has shown that for *jhum* cycles of 20-25 years, slash-and-burn agriculture in Northeast India is both very economic and sustainable. However, because of pressures, mainly as a result of rising population, the length of these cycles have in many cases fallen to 4-5 years. The method is now relatively uneconomic, biophysically unsustainable, a source of very serious adverse externalities and a major source of biodiversity loss.

of agriculture, especially in Europe (Hampicke 1996). In some countries, however, reliance on extensive systems would result in agriculture spreading over a larger land area. Even extensive agriculture can cause serious disruption to natural ecosystems. Extensive grazing by cattle and sheep in many parts of Australia has substantially changed natural ecosystems and has been implicated in the disappearance of at least one native species, a small marsupial or wallaby.[5] When extensive systems of agriculture replace intensive ones in a given area, biodiversity may increase and greater conservation of nature can occur. However, extensive systems often spread onto marginal lands with very adverse environmental consequences. Furthermore, if the choice is between (1) a small area under intensive agriculture with the remaining area not used for agriculture but left in a relatively natural state and (2) extensive agriculture over the whole area, which is best? In Australia for instance, some conservationists have supported the establishment of plantation forests on the grounds that this will reduce harvesting pressure on natural forests. It may do so but the economic benefits from increased economic productivity are not always utilized for greater conservation of nature (cf. Tisdell 1994b). They are often used to raise exploitation of nature even more.

I am sorry if the above makes simple suggestions for environmental improvements in agriculture appear to be problem ridden. However, it seems short sighted to ignore the type of issues raised above. Nevertheless, I accept that much of modern agriculture is over dependent on high external inputs, too intensive, gives less attention to conservation methods than is desirable and could make greater use of organic materials. However, there appears to be a strong argument for some use of artificial fertilizers but on a smaller scale than hitherto and in a way which reduces their leaching from the soil. Nevertheless, it is of concern when less developed countries like China try to indicate their agricultural progress by their rate of use of artificial fertilizer.

China is now using artificial fertilizer at one of the highest rates in the world and appears not to be recycling organic wastes including human excreta to the same extent as in the past. The latter is partly a result of increased urbanisation of China. For this and other reasons, water supplies in China have become nutrient rich; high in nitrates, phosphorous and organic matter. The increasing frequency of 'red tides' in the China Sea is partly blamed on discharge of such water. Many other adverse environmental effects are also being generated by this problem. It is surprising that a country which traditionally emphasized balanced agricultural systems and polyculture should

---

[5] Possibly a more dramatic example of the biodiversity loss due to extensive agriculture is the clearing of the tropical rainforest of the Amazonian Basin for cattle ranching; the so-called hamburger connection.

have allowed this modern trend to proceed so far. In the end (even now) it endangers its very large aquaculture industry (the largest in the world); a significant source of animal protein for its people.

AGRICULTURE AND THE CONSERVATION OF BIODIVERSITY

There are at least three angles from which we might be interested in agriculture and the conservation of biodiversity. These are:

1. The impact of agriculture on biodiversity conservation.
2. The benefits to agriculture from conservation of biodiversity.
3. The constraints placed on agriculture by decisions and policy measures to conserve biodiversity.

Let us consider each.

The intensification and spread of agriculture has been a major source (probably the prime source) of loss of biodiversity. This has mainly occurred because of destruction of wildlife habitat as a result of the conversion of wildlands to agricultural use and the increasing intensity of use of lands already used to some extent for agriculture. Where wild species of animals and plants compete with domesticated ones, they are seen as pests by the farmer and destroyed where possible.

Sometimes biologists see farming as a way of saving endangered species, for example, farming of turtles and of giant clams. If a commercially viable industry can be established, farming is an effective possible means of saving a species. However, profitable farming, depending upon its nature, may result in increasing displacement of the farmed species from the wild. Areas suited to farming the species concerned may also be the habitats favoured by the wild species. These may consequently be appropriated for farming displacing wild members of the species and in some cases thereby endangering their continued existence in the wild. There may also be other mechanisms which result in farming of species endangering wild stocks of the same species (Tisdell 1991). Furthermore, many of those who favour the retention of biodiversity do not consider domesticated stocks of a species to be an adequate substitute for wild stocks.

Just as the development of innovations and techniques used in economic production involve evolutionary aspects (Tisdell 1996a) and introduce inflexibility and hysteresis into systems, so can the development of the farming of species. Those species which have begun to be farmed early in the history of mankind tend to be increasingly advantaged for commercial purposes over others (Swanson 1994). This is because considerable learning and accumulation of knowledge about the capacities of such species in a domesticated situation takes place, which is reinforced today by formal research. Furthermore, the farmed species are selectively bred over a long period of time to become fitter for the tasks which human beings have assigned to them. In addition, their products become well known to consumers who discover an increasing range of ways to use them, such as varied recipes, find their use increasingly to be socially acceptable and develop personal tastes in their favour. All of these factors make it very difficult to develop economically the farming of a species not previously farmed, for example, kangaroo farming, giant clam farming or the growing of a new food crop. At the same time, the fact that one species is used commercially at an earlier stage than another may be to a large extent a matter of chance. The selection of species and techniques for use being in part myopic is often not the optimal from a long term viewpoint. This occurs for many innovations (Tisdell 1996a).

While agriculture has been and in many parts of the world continues to be, a major force destroying biodiversity, it can also be an economic beneficiary from the conservation of biodiversity. It is claimed that genetic diversity within species can provide a valuable bank to be drawn on to conserve the viability of cultivated plants and domesticated animals. Many cultivated crops depend on a narrow genetic base and from time to time, due to occurrence of diseases and other factors, lose their vigour and economic viability. By drawing on a wide gene bank, new varieties of a species can often be developed which at least for a time, show resistance to the problem.

Nature conservation can widen the scope for agriculture, sometimes species and their varieties with no apparent use now turn out to be useful in the future and profitable to cultivate or to husband. In so doing, they extend the range of agricultural possibilities or future options for agriculture.

It is, however, very difficult or impossible to place an exact value or even possibly a reasonable approximation, on the economic value of conserving biodiversity.[6] Nevertheless, we do know that if for genetic reasons, one of our major crops such as wheat or rice should fail to survive, or fail to survive productively from an economic viewpoint, that the economic costs would be

---

[6] Pearce and Moran (1994, Ch. 6) provide some monetary estimates for the value of conservation of diversity of medicinal plants in rainforests. The estimates, however, are very uncertain and problematic. This is especially true of those forecasts involving value of human lives saved or income loss avoided. Value is dominated by the needs of those in high income countries; OECD countries. In effect the lives of those in higher income countries are more valued than those in lower income countries. The effect could be to save the genetic pool which most favours higher income earners. This type of ethics disturbs me. It appears inequitable and unjust. It would for example violate Rawls's principle of justice (Rawls 1971) and would not appear to accord with the Christian principle that all are basically equal in the sight of God.

phenomenal. It is of course possible to give estimates *ex post* of the benefits of certain species having survived. Rubber for instance could be taken as an example. Rubber plays a very important role in modern transportation and although synthetic rubber exists, natural rubber is an essential component of radial tyres and has many other uses. I understand that the rubber plantations of Southeast Asia were only saved from a disastrous disease by drawing on genetic reserves present in the rainforests of Brazil.

Given that there are demands from the public for the conservation of biodiversity and rare species, agriculture activity is being increasingly constrained to help accommodate their demands. For example, in many countries agricultural properties are more frequently subject to preservation orders. The clearing of land or of habitat suitable for particular species is more and more restricted. In Australia, grazing of livestock on protected or relatively natural areas is increasingly banned or severely restricted. Furthermore, land use on many agricultural properties is subject to mounting limitations. Therefore, growing environmental concerns are imposing extra costs on at least some sections of the agricultural community. Agriculturalists are finding it necessary to adjust to this changing social climate.

SOCIOECONOMIC METHODS FOR SUSTAINING BIODIVERSITY AND THEIR AGRICULTURAL IMPLICATIONS

With the general increase of interest in the state of the environment, there has been growing interest in how economic and social mechanisms can be used to sustain biodiversity and attain environmental goals.

Substantial attention is being given to the possibilities for using economic incentives, to extending property rights and to harnessing markets to conserve biodiversity and natural resources. Indeed, in some quarters there is a state of euphoria about the likely effectiveness of these policies.

However, in relation to biodiversity, market related systems are liable to be very selective in the saving of species (Tisdell 1995a). Those species that can favourably be used for economic purposes in the relatively short run are liable to be favoured. Often this is at the expense of other species and as in agriculture, this can result in a reduction in biodiversity.

Maximization of economic benefit can lead to the rational elimination of some species. Discounting of economic gains, for instance favours the elimination of species which increase in value at a slower rate of growth than the interest rate (Clark 1976). Other things equal, these are slower growing or slower reproducing species. Observe however that opportunity rates of return provide another economic rational for extinguishing selected species. Where for example, two species are in competition for the use of the same resources and both are of commercial value, the one with the highest rate of return will be favoured. This will be so even if the internal rate of return from both is well in excess of the rate of interest. Elimination can occur in many ways, for example, by directly destroying the population of the economically less favoured species or by altering habitats to favour the economically more profitable species. In practice, the latter has had the greatest impact in reducing biodiversity.

It might be thought that the above failure of the market mechanism to conserve a species is a consequence of there not being total economic evaluation of a species. However, even if total economic valuation takes place and discounting of the estimated monetary flow occurs *both* of the above types of situation can occur within the extended framework. Economics can support the elimination of species of relatively low total economic value. Such a recommendation is anathema to many conservationists. I personally do not accept the total economic valuation test as a final arbiter of whether a species should survive. Its ethical foundations are too narrow. It does not sit well with strong (or even relatively strong) conditions for sustainability and is being increasingly challenged in terms of community values.

Transaction costs are likely to hamper the creation of property rights and the effective operation of market systems in conserving biodiversity and uncertainty further adds to market failures. Even methods which reward local communities according to economic use of species, such as rewards for use of elephants locally for trophy hunting, can lead to selective conservation of species. Whether such methods truly conserve biodiversity is therefore arguable. My own view is that considering the situation overall, they reduce biodiversity.

There is no guarantee that increased commercial use of wildlife or the greater commercial appropriation of total economic value will foster biodiversity. In my view the opposite is more likely as those species come to be favoured for which the largest total of economic value can be appropriated. However, the situation is complex. Nevertheless, I want to make it quite clear that I dissent from the blanket view that greater economic appropriation of total economic value of species and of their varied forms should be encouraged from a policy point of view in order to conserve biodiversity; it can lead to the opposite result.

A further observation may be in order. Some economists (Hampicke 1996) suggest that species conservation might be a non-economic decision but that economists can nevertheless be involved in terms of cost effectiveness analysis. While this may be so up to a point, the cost of saving some species may be the disappearance of others. So it is not clear that cost minimization can be divorced from evaluation after all.

If biodiversity is at least considered in part to be a type of merit good (or to some extent a type of public good) then there is a role for the state in financing its provision and/or in helping to supply protected areas and services supporting conservation of biodiversity. Furthermore, if biodiversity conservation is the goal, efforts to make *multiple use* of protected areas need to be resisted if the likely consequence of such multiple use would be to make for more uniformity of environments. In general, diversity of environments is needed to support biodiversity.

There is increasing pressure to establish biosphere reserves. These can assist in the conservation of biodiversity provided that they are not used as a means to reduce the size of core protected areas. Biosphere reserves do, however, place increasing restrictions on land use, for example, by agriculturalists. Furthermore, both the presence of protected areas and the use of biosphere reserves can result in increased populations of species regarded by many farmers as pests. This is a serious problem for farmers when these species are protected and farmers are either not compensated for the damage caused or are inadequately compensated, as is often the case.

CONCLUDING COMMENTS

New approaches to environmental policy making are needed which are less mechanical and more organic than some neoclassical approaches appear to be. Concepts of sustainability and of biodiversity are complex but useful. It was observed that sustainable agricultural systems need not promote sustainable development as such. Low external input agricultural systems, as well as traditional ones, are not necessarily sustainable, especially when dynamic exogenous changes, such as rising human population, occur. Extensive agricultural systems are not necessarily favourable for biodiversity conservation although on the same land type, such systems can result in greater preservation of biodiversity than intensive agricultural systems.

While agriculture is in some respects a beneficiary of biodiversity conservation it is also disadvantaged by it in a number of ways pointed out above. Consequently, many equity or income distribution problems are raised by biodiversity conservation.

That use of policies involving market mechanisms, economic incentives and property rights for protection of nature has significant limitations for conservation of biodiversity. This is not to say that advantage should not be taken of such mechanisms but state intervention to conserve biodiversity by direct means is still required given merit good and public good arguments, the presence of fundamental uncertainties and the occurrence of unavoidable market failures.

REFERENCES

Baumol, W. and Quandt, R. 1964. 'Rules of thumb and optimally imperfect decisions', *American Economic Review*, 54, 23-46.

Clark, C.W. 1976. *Mathematical Bioeconomics*. New York: Wiley.

Coase, R.H. 1937. 'The nature of the firm', *Economica*, New Series 4, 386-405.

Conway, G.R. 1985. 'Agroecosystem analysis', *Agricultural Administration*, 20, 31-55.

Conway, G.R. 1987. 'The properties of agroecosystems', *Agricultural Systems*, 24, 95-117.

Etzioni, A. 1991. 'Contemporary liberals, communitarians and individual choices', in Etzioni, A. and Lawrence, P.R. (eds), *Socio-economics: Towards a New Synthesis*. New York: M.E. Sharpe.

Hampicke, U. 1996. 'Opportunity costs of conservation in Germany'. Paper presented at the OECD International Conference on Incentive Measures for Sustainable Use, Cairns, March, 1996.

Kelso, M.M. 1977. 'Natural resource economics: The upsetting discipline', *American Journal of Agricultural Economics*, 59, 814-23.

Kohn, R.E. 1993. 'Measuring the existence value of wildlife: Comment', *Land Economics*, 69, 304-08.

Lampkin, N.H. and Padel, S. 1994. *The Economics of Organic Farming: An International Prospective*. Wallingford, UK: CAB International.

Lynam, J.F. and Herdt, R.W. 1989. 'Sense and sustainability: Sustainability as an objective in international agricultural research', *Agricultural Economics*, 3, 381-98.

Margolis, H. 1982. *Selfishness, Altruism and Rationality*. Cambridge: Cambridge University Press.

Mishra, H.R. 1982. 'Balancing human needs and conservation in Nepal's Royal Chitwan National Park', *Ambio*, 11, 246-51.

Pearce, D. 1993. *Blueprint 3: Measuring Sustainable Development*. London: Earthscan.

Pearce, D. and Moran, D. 1994. *The Economic Value of Biodiversity*. London: Earthscan.

Ramakrishnan, P.S. 1992. *Shifting Agriculture and Sustainable Development: An Interdisciplinary Study for North-Eastern India*. Carnforth, UK: Parthenon and Paris.

Rawls, J. 1971. *A Theory of Justice*. Cambridge, MA: Harvard University Press.

Reijntjes, C., Havekort, B. and Waters-Bayer, A. 1992. *Farming for the Future: An Introduction to Low-External-Input and Sustainable Agriculture*. London: Macmillan.

Schultz, T.W. 1974. 'Is modern agriculture consistent with a stable environment?', International Association of Agricultural Economics, *The Future of Agriculture: Technology, Policies and Adjustment*. Oxford: Agricultural Economics Institute.

Smyth, A.J., Dumanski, J.K., Spendjian, G., Swift, M.J. and Thorton, P.K. 1993. *FESLM: An International Framework for Evaluating Sustainable Land Management*. World Soil Resources Reports No. 73. Rome: Land and Water Development Division, Food and Agriculture Organisation of the United Nations.

Swanson, T.M. 1994. 'The economics of extinction revisited and revised: A generalised framework for the analysis of the problems of endangered species and biodiversity loss', *Oxford Economic Papers*, 46, 800-21.

Tisdell, C.A. 1990. *Natural Resources, Growth and Development*. New York: Praeger.

Tisdell, C.A. 1991. *Economics of Environmental Conservation*. Amsterdam: Elsevier.

Tisdell, C.A. 1993. *Environmental Economics*. Aldershot, UK: Edward Elgar.

Tisdell, C.A. 1994a. 'Biodiversity, sustainability and stability: An economist's discussion of some ecological views', Economics Discussion Paper, No. 139, Department of Economics, The University of Queensland, Brisbane, Australia.

Tisdell, C.A. 1994b. 'Conservation, protected areas and the global economic system: How debt, trade, exchange rates, inflation and macroeconomic policy affect biological diversity', *Biodiversity and Conservation*, 3, 419-36.

Tisdell, C.A. 1995a. 'Does the economic use of wildlife favour conservation and sustainability?' in Grigg, G.C., Hale, P.T. and Lunney, D. (eds), *Conservation Through the Sustainable Use of Wildlife*. Brisbane: Centre for Conservation Biology, The University of Queensland.

Tisdell, C.A. 1995b. 'Issues in biodiversity conservation including the role of local communities', *Environmental Conservation*, 22, 216-27.

Tisdell, C.A. 1996a. *Bounded Rationality and Economic Evolution*. Aldershot, UK: Edward Elgar (in press).

Tisdell, C.A. 1996b. 'Economic indicators to assess the sustainability of conservation farming projects', *Agriculture Ecosystems and Environment*, 57, 117-31.

Xiang, Z. 1995. 'Rapid rural appraisal (RRA), participatory appraisal and their application in the Global Environmental Facility (G-EF-B) Program in China', Biodiversity Conservation Working Paper, No. 19, Department of Economics, The University of Queensland, Brisbane, Australia.

6. Energy Productivity and Sustainability in Swedish Agriculture - Some Evidence and Issues

Hans-Erik Uhlin

INTRODUCTION

Using non-renewable resources inevitably means an increase in entropy. The entropy thermodynamic and systems aspects on economic life have been addressed by Georgescu-Roegen (1971), Odum (1971) and, lately, Ruth (1993). They have pointed at agriculture as an illustrative example of a shift towards an entropy destructive strategy (Figure 6.1, from Ruth (1993) p 88).

Modern agriculture has increasingly become dependent on fossil fuel. Some authors have argued for a different strategy, that agriculture should turn to low level inputs and practices that make agriculture more self dependent on energy.

Oil price shocks in the beginning of the 1970s and 1980s resulted in a number of studies on the increasing dependence of energy use in agriculture. Some pioneering studies were presented by Chapman (1973), Herendeen and Bullard (1974), Hirst (1974), Leach and Slesser (1973), Leach (1976), Steinhardt and Steinhardt (1974) and Pimentel et al. (1973) which all focused on the increasing use of fossil fuels. The standard conclusion in most of these studies is that energy productivity (index of output divided by index of man-made inputs all measured in energy terms) is decreasing, which makes agriculture vulnerable to increasing oil prices.

More recent studies have illustrated a possible shift during the 1980s from a decreasing to an increasing energy productivity in agriculture (Balwinder and Fluck 1993, Bonny 1993 and Cleveland 1994, 1995). During the 1980s energy issues were broadened to cover environmental and health risks as well as concerns about oil prices (Daberkow and Reichelderfer 1988). Lately relations between energy use, environment and sustainability have been a focus. The sustainability aspects of agriculture have been addressed in many articles (Cleveland 1994, Crosson 1991, Fox 1990, Henning et al. 1991, Ruttan 1991, Schoney and Culver 1991, Tweeten 1992, Van Kooten and Kennedy 1990).

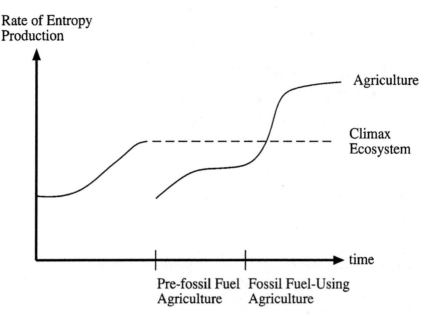

Figure 6.1   *Rate of entropy production in a pristine, stable ecosystem and in a human managed ecosystem on a unit of land area*

Although energy intensity in agriculture has been a big issue since the oil crisis in the early 1970s the discussions are still not settled with a common basis and an agreed strategy for agriculture. Nor are there shared grounds for policy formulation and directions of research for technological changes.

A survey of studies of energy use in agriculture gives an impression of almost two parallel and separate lines of perspectives. One group of approaches has the productivity aspects of the use of fossil or man-made energy as a main target. If choices are to be made for increasing productivity, these studies are looking at crop-animal relations, substitutes between labour, land, real capital, energy, fertilisers, scale and management measures. Most of these studies focus on measures to decrease energy input.

Another group of approaches has environment and ecological based arguments for energy use as a main target. These studies usually look for alternatives within agriculture to offset the current use of external supply of fossil energy and nutrients.

Three recurring themes seem to dominate these energy studies. First, an increasing dependence on fossil fuel and fossil fuel-based inputs in agriculture should be handled by measures to reduce energy intensive inputs. Energy intensive inputs should be replaced with land, labour, biotechnology and management. This is believed to increase energy productivity in agriculture (Lopez and Tung 1982, Gopalakrishnan *et al.* 1989, Debertin *et al.* 1990 and Balwinder and Fluck 1993. Second, animal production should be replaced with crops and ruminants should replace non-ruminants because the latter use crop products in competition with humans. Third, agriculture should turn to ecologically and biologically based systems for internal supply of energy and nutrients.

These themes are tested and analysed with the help of results from a study of Swedish agriculture. A common problem for most energy studies is lack of relevant in-depth data for all kinds of inputs and continuous time serial data. Here the underlying data originates from a complete and in-depth study of Swedish agriculture for three situations represented as 1956, 1972 and 1993.[1] These situations represent agriculture in the beginning of a phase of rapid mechanisation and specialisation (1956), just before the start of the oil crisis (1972) and a more stabilised mature fertiliser-based agriculture (1993).

The discussion concludes with the formulation of research issues and hypotheses of strategic choices to be made for future agriculture.

ENERGY FLOWS IN SWEDISH AGRICULTURE

Some results from an analysis of energy flows in Swedish agriculture concerning the situations of 1956, 1972 and 1993 (Uhlin *et al.* 1975, Uhlin and Hoffman 1995) have been used for this study. All flows of inputs, internal turnovers and outputs have been estimated from a combination of published data and in-depth complementary analyses. Energy requirements for each input are based on a wide range of other studies and own estimates relevant for each period. Thus technical and structural changes among supply sectors and agriculture are accounted for.

Energy values are based on careful estimates where all direct and indirect uses of energy are traced back to the original source of energy. This means, for example, that electricity based on nuclear power has been traced from the outlet back through the energy cost of distribution, transformation and mining. Thus the outlet measure has been transformed to a gross energy cost that is equivalent to the lost of energy content in the original uranium, following the principle meaning of entropy loss.

---

[1] The underlying data are taken as three year averages around the stated years and checked for normality regarding weather and yields.

The Use of Man-Made Energy Through Inputs

Table 6.1 is a summation of energy use from a number of details.[2] It can be concluded that the productivity of man-made energy (mainly based on exhaustible energy resources) decreased between 1956 and 1972 but then increased considerably (compare row 7 with row 1). These results are in line with findings from other international studies as mentioned above.

Table 6.1. Energy flows in agriculture measured in gross energy. Million MJ

Row OUTPUTS 10⁶ MJ	1993	1972	1956
1 Total (calorific content)	72,720	60,480	48,240
2 INPUTS 10⁶ MJ			
3 Direct energy	28,440	19,080	15,840
4 Real capital	16,920	24,480	16,920
5 Commodities	16,200	32,760	21,240
6 Services	2,410	3,780	1,980
7 Subtotal	63,970	80,100	55,980
8 Land/solar energy	83*10⁶	91*10⁶	115*10⁶
9 Labour input (million man hours)	90*10⁶	345*10⁶	510*10⁶

It should be noted that direct energy takes a larger and larger part of man-made energy inputs, from 28 per cent in 1956 to 44 per cent in 1993. These results support the arguments that energy studies based solely on direct energy are insufficient (Dovring 1985). More important though is the fact that other inputs such as real capital, commodities (dominated by fertilisers in energy terms) and services are constant or decreasing compared to 1956. It can be concluded that energy productivity has increased even when all indirect energy costs are included, a result that contradicts the concerns and preliminary suggestions otherwise put forward by Dovring (1985) and Pimentel and Dazhong (1990).

Comparing 1956 with 1993, it can be seen that an almost equal total input of man-made energy has given a remarkable increase in total export of products from agriculture to other sectors. The recognition of technical change is crucial for explaining this change in energy productivity. One part of this is the increase in energy productivity among manufacturers of inputs. The remarkable development in the production of nitrogen is illustrated in Table 6.2. The effects of both a change of energy source and technical change can

---

[2] In total energy values of 29 input groups have been estimated.

be seen. The nitrogen case is illustrative for similar developments regarding machinery, feed processing and transport. Even though the inputs, measured in physical terms, have increased, this is offset by large increases in energy productivity.

Table 6.2. Fertiliser input in agriculture measured in gross energy. Million MJ

	Gross energy MJ/kg	Quantity used 10^6 kg	Total gross energy 10^6 MJ	Main basis of energy in process
1993 Nitrogen	39.6	186	7,366	fossil gas
1972 Nitrogen	83.6	218	18,234	oil
1956 Nitrogen	152	90	13,673	coal

A comparison of nitrogen energy costs for 1956 and a total input of 90 million kg nitrogen, with those of 1993 and a total input of 186 million kg nitrogen, shows that a physical increase of 100 per cent has been paralleled with a decrease in total energy cost of almost 50 per cent. From this a general understanding of the total impact of technical and structural change can be gained. These results also give absolute figures that support the criticism by Smil *et al.* (1983) and Bonny (1993) of suggestions made by Pimentel *et al.* (1973) and Pimentel and Dazhong (1990), that either technology or energy cost for fertilisers is constant.

Internal Energy Flows in Agriculture

Internal energy flows in agriculture are mainly of three types: Non-exported biomass back to cropping, feed to animals and manure from animals to cropping. Recycled biomass has steadily increased from 55,000 million MJ in 1956 to 125,000 MJ in 1993, indicating a large decrease in the share of exported harvest of biomass. For the same period total feed (calorific value) to animals has decreased from 180,000 million MJ to 144,000 million MJ including imports from abroad.

In 1956 manure from animals was an important input to plant production considering both nutrients and energy. Measured by its calorific value the total volume of manure has been rather constant, about 72,000 million MJ. Following the opportunity cost principle of economics, manure has been valued by the amount of needed man-made energy for providing the same amount of nutrients through fertilisers. Measured in 1956 technology this gave an internal flow from animals to plants of 5,470 million MJ. Due to technical change this flow has shrunk to 1,590 million MJ which means that *if* manure is replaced by fertilisers the total input of man-made energy in 1993 will increase by 3 per cent.[3] It can thus be concluded that the importance and dependence of manure (especially nitrogen) in plant production measured in energy terms are almost negligible. This fact will be important for the discussion at the end of this chapter.

Solar Energy Inputs and Total Energy Productivity

It can be seen that solar radiation has decreased considerably (row 8 in Table 6.1). This is proportional to the decrease in land input in agriculture. From 1956 to 1993 the solar energy productivity has increased from 0.24 per cent to 0.42 per cent (Table 6.3). This fact will also be important for later discussions.

Table 6.3. Energy productivity, 1956, 1972 and 1993

	1993	1972	1956
Net delivery from agriculture/man-made energy (row 1/row 7 in Table 6.1).	1.14	0.76	0.86
Gross biomass in plant production/man-made energy.	6.75	4.79	4.34
Gross biomass in plant production as percentage of solar energy.	0.42%	0.36%	0.24%

Note: Output, or net delivery and biomass, measured in calorific values, man-made inputs as gross energy and solar energy as available energy in sunbeams reaching plants during the growing season (7,500 kWh/hectare).

NEW PERSPECTIVES ON ENERGY PRODUCTIVITY IN AGRICULTURE

The discussion so far has identified a number of central issues and for which opinions and facts still give an impression of divergence. This discussion starts with some concrete lessons from the Swedish case which are then related to other studies. After that, some more general aspects on energy relations and

---

[3] One major explanation for this besides technical change is that large parts of nitrogen in manure are lost to the air and water due to handling problems.

sustainability of agricultural systems are considered. Man-made energy productivity in Swedish agriculture has changed drastically over the studied period. This is contradictory to the common wisdom that may be explained by differences in recognition of technical and structural change.

A knowledge of an increasing productivity is not enough. Several studies show that energy related technical changes are biased and sensitive to changing price relations (Lopez and Tung 1982, Gopalakrishnan *et al.* 1989, Debertin *et al.* 1990 and Balwinder and Fluck 1993). More detailed analyses of input-output energy relations for different agricultural products are needed. A technique suggested by Herendeen and Bullard (1974) and an application to agroecosystems as done by Zucchetto and Bickle (1984) may be helpful.

More detailed analysis of input output relations will be of assistance in settling debates about not only the energy productivity of different inputs but also energy productivity relations for crop-animal and ruminants-non-ruminants. Traditional cost and production function approaches (Lopez and Tung 1982, Gopalakrishnan *et al.* 1989 and Debertin *et al.* 1990) depend much on good estimates of energy values of inputs. Typical results are that energy savings can be made by substituting energy intensive inputs with land, labour and capital. Derived policy suggestions are measures to improve land, labour markets and management but also to avoid price ceilings on energy. Ecologists and biologists seem to support these kinds of solutions by looking for low input production systems. In their world this should be combined with better use of biologically based techniques.

Revisiting the Swedish experience with an unprejudiced mind gives reasons to doubt the relevance of not only traditional economic and biological approaches but also their derived policy suggestions. A majority of cited energy studies have focused on man-made energy. It seems as if this focus on man-made energy has missed the central issue and thus missed the target of true energy productivity. What is needed is a deeper look into the importance of solar energy, land, land use and the opportunity cost aspects of alternatives.

A Case for an Assertive Strategy for Sustainability of Swedish Agriculture

As can be seen in Table 6.1, solar energy is 1000 times larger per hectare than the input of man-made energy. A strategy of increasing the 'use' of solar energy thus seems promising or, said even more firmly, necessary.

So, most approaches seem to suggest agricultural systems with low levels of man-made inputs from other sectors combined with a solar energy based internal supply of production means and closed material cycles. Such systems could be interpreted as slow contributors to entropy increases but their capacity of feeding a large population can be questioned.

Agricultural practices and land use are means to capture solar radiation into biomass which in principle can be considered as a way of storing renewable energy (Pimentel and Hall 1984). Agriculture has a potential to use natural and biological resources in ways that increase the binding of solar radiation into biomass. A possible direction of future agriculture can be imagined where technical change and exhaustible resources are means to create a capacity for using renewable energy resources (solar radiation) through investing in reproducible resources (knowledge, soil quality, genetics). This strategy would be in compliance with suggestions of a sustainability strategy made by Solow (1986).

Using new technology, high level inputs and allowing for intensive exchanges with other sectors, gives a possibility to transfer large quantities of solar radiation to biomass. The potentials are illustrated in Table 6.3. But, are not these suggestions incompatible with sustainability?

Most actions by humans increase entropy which seems to suggest a contradiction to natural science based sustainability definitions (Georgescu-Roegen 1971, Odum 1971 and Ruth 1993). But solar radiation violates the assumption of closed thermodynamic systems (Jaeger 1995). Careful use of solar radiation for biomass can be seen as lowering entropy. This fact makes the recognition of the systems level crucial. All the above cited studies relate energy productivity to actual input and output. They do not take account of 'freed' land through fertiliser-based agriculture in later energy comparisons. This is a violation of strict evaluations by not looking at comparable systems. In such cases it feels natural for an economist to apply the principle of opportunity cost.

Biologists suggest that it should be possible to develop systems that transfer about one per cent of solar radiation to biomass. This can be compared with the current transfer of 0.42 per cent in Sweden (Table 6.3). An increase of 0.1 per cent unit will give an increase in biomass that is equal to current total man- made energy input in plant production! Special energy crops like *Salix* constitute large potentials for binding solar energy. Put into this light some suggested energy saving and low input strategies for agriculture seem defensive or even unwise. What is needed is a careful applied strategy of using 'surplus' land, that has been made available through a fertiliser-based agriculture, plus technical and structural change, for harvesting the sun.[4]

Conservative calculations of a system where surplus land, comparing 1993

---

[4] We can observe the tremendous decrease in labour input (row 9, Table 6.1). Measuring labour input in energy terms has been a recurring issue in many energy studies. A meaningful measure seems difficult to define especially when a single sector is evaluated over time. To put an energy value on labour when man is the end consumer of final products will only become circular reasoning and thus double counting. Thus energy measures on labour seem relevant only when comparing marginal productivity of labour between different sectors.

with 1956, is put into energy forests (*Salix*) indicate a possible net delivery of more than 108,000 MJ.[5] This is a low estimate based on current technology. This exceeds the 64,800 MJ used in the current system. A surplus of available solar-based energy makes the system interesting from sustainability perspectives.

POLICY IMPLICATIONS

Recent studies strongly indicate that agriculture is reacting to price and technical change. This means that ordinary policy measures are enough in a narrow sense. The contradictory signals from research about energy relations may be a disturbance factor for society of a much higher importance. The analysis of Swedish agriculture indicates that quite different results and thus policy suggestions can be presented due to different recognitions of technical change and system definitions. This discussion has pointed at the fact that established concepts as opportunity costs are usually not used. Perhaps one explanation is that economists have not shown great interest in energy analysis.

More important though is the need for a total change of perspective. If energy matters, a totally new analysis on land use and its relation to technology is needed. In this chapter it is suggested that it is possible that modern fertiliser based agriculture may be seen as a transitional stage from a low-input self-dependent agriculture to a high-input society integrated and energy sustainable agriculture. The focus would be on binding as much as possible of solar radiation in a double strategy of both feeding an increasing population and contributing to the need for energy sources. If this is recognised by policy decision makers their input to support research, investments and institutional changes would be quite different from now. Van Arsdall's (1977) suggestions must be considered as an early warning in this direction where he particularly points at a possible breakthrough for biomass energy and photosynthesis. Economists have a possibility and a responsibility to further contribute with foundations to such policy considerations.

The biggest challenge seems to be to steer agricultural policy so that surplus land is used for energy crops and energy policy in a way that the energy sector switches to bioenergy. It seems necessary to settle the apparent contradiction between a low-input and self-dependent agriculture and an agriculture that delivers bioenergy to society on the same basis. For this to happen we need to clarify an assertive strategy as the one outlined above. This

---

[5] Gross energy value of dried chip-wood minus energy inputs for production, harvesting and chipping.

may take time, but, as argued above, current developments of a fertiliser-based agriculture may not be a hinderance. On the contrary, current changes may very well be seen as a part of and in line with the strategy for sustainability outlined by Solow (1986) and Goodland and Ledec (1987).

REFERENCES

Balwinder, S.P. and Fluck, R.C. 1993. 'Energy productivity of a production system: Analysis and measurement', *Agricultural Systems*, 43, 415-37.

Bonny, S. 1993. 'Is agriculture using more and more energy? A French case study', *Agricultural Systems*, 43, 51–66.

Chapman, P.F. 1973. 'The energy costs of delivered energy. UK 1968', Energy Research Group Open University Report ERG 003.

Cleveland, C.J. 1994. 'Resource degradation, technical change and the productivity of energy use in US agriculture', *Ecological Economics*, 13, 185–201.

Cleveland, C.J. 1995. 'The direct and indirect use of fossil fuels and electricity in USA agriculture, 1910-1990', *Agriculture, Ecosystems and Environment*, 55, 111-21.

Crosson, P. 1991. 'Sustainable agriculture in North America: Issues and challenges', *Canadian Journal of Agricultural Economics*, 39, 553-65.

Daberkow, S.G. and Reichelderfer, K.H. 1988. 'Low-input agriculture: Trends, goals and prospects for input use', *American Journal of Agricultural Economics*, 1159-66.

Debertin, D.L., Pagoulatos, A. and Aoun, A. 1990. 'Impacts of technological change on factor substitution between energy and other inputs within US agriculture, 1950-1979', *Energy Economics*, January.

Dovring, F. 1985. 'Energy use in United States agriculture: A critique of recent research', *Energy in Agriculture*, 4, 79-86.

Fox, G. 1990. 'The economics of the sustainable agriculture movement', *Canadian Journal of Agricultural Economics*, 38, 727-39.

Georgescu-Roegen, N. 1971. *The Entropy Law and the Economic Process*. Cambridge Mass: Harvard University Press.

Goodland, R. and Ledec, G. 1987. 'Neoclassical economics and principles of sustainable development', *Ecological Modelling*, 38, 19-46.

Gopalakrishnan, C., Khaleghi, G.H. and Shrestha, R.B. 1989. 'Energy - non-energy input substitution in US agriculture: Some findings', *Applied Economics*, 21, 673-79.

Henning, J., Baker, L. and Thomassin, P. 1991. 'Economics issues in organic agriculture', *Canadian Journal of Agricultural Economics*, 39, 877-89.

Herendeen, R.A. and Bullard, C.V. 1974. 'Energy costs of goods and services', CAC Document 140. Energy Research Group. University of Illinois, Urbana.

Hirst, E. 1974. 'Food-related energy requirements', *Science*, 12 April 1974.

Jaeger, W.K. 1995. 'Methodological and ideological options. Is sustainability optimal? Examining the differences between economists and environmentalists', *Ecological Economics*, 15, 43-57.

Leach, G. 1976. *Energy and Food Production*. Guildford: IPC Sci Tech Press.

Leach, G. and Slesser, M. 1973. 'Energy equivalents of network inputs to food producing processes', stencil, Glasgow.

Lopez, R.E. and Tung, F.L. 1982. 'Energy and non-energy input substitution possibilities and output scale effects in Canadian agriculture', *Canadian Journal of Agricultural Economics*, 115-32.

Odum, H.T. 1971. *Environment, Power and Society*. New York: Wiley.

Pimentel, D. and Dazhong, W. 1990. 'Technological changes in energy use in US agricultural production', in Caroll, C.R., Vandemeer, J.H. and Rosset, P.M., *Agroecology*. New York: MacGraw-Hill.

Pimentel, D. and Hall, C.W. (eds) 1984. *Food and Energy Resources*. Academic Press.

Pimentel, D. *et al.* 1973. 'Food production and the energy crisis', *Science*, 2, Nov.

Ruth, M. 1993. *Integrating Economics, Ecology and Thermodynamics*. Dordrecht, The Netherlands: Kluwer.

Ruttan, V.W. 1991. 'Constraints on sustainable growth in agricultural production: Into the 21st century', *Canadian Journal of Agricultural Economics*, 39, 567-80.

Schoney, R.A. and Culver, D. 1991. 'Economic analysis of sustainable production systems for Saskatchewan', *Canadian Journal of Agricultural Economics*, 39, 865-76.

Smil, V., Nachman, P. and Long, T.W. 1983. *Energy Analysis and Agriculture: An Application to U.S. Corn Production*. Boulder, Colorado: Westview Press.

Solow, R.M. 1986. 'On the intergenerational allocation of natural resources', *Scandinavian Journal of Economics*, 88, 141-9.

Tweeten, L. 1992. 'The economics of an environmentally sound agriculture (ESA)', *Research in Domestic and International Agribusiness Management*, 10, 39-83.

Uhlin, H.-E., Johansson, E., Lindstroem, I., Nilsson, P.-O., Myhrman, D., Moeller, G., Petre, H., Renborg, U., Wiktorsson, H. and Wunsche, U. 1975. 'Resource flows in Swedish agriculture and forestry with emphasis on energy flows', Report from Department of Economics and Statistics, No. 64 and 65, Uppsala (in Swedish).

Uhlin, H.-E. and Hoffman, R. 1995. 'Energy balance of agriculture - some perspectives on energy flows in agriculture 1956, 1972 and 1993', in KSLA's tidskrift 134 no. 6 (in Swedish).

Van Arsdall, R.T. 1977. 'Agriculture and energy use in the year 2000: Discussion of technological changes', *American Journal of Agricultural Economics*, 1071-72.

Van Kooten, G.C. and Kennedy, G. 1990. 'An economic perspective on sustainable agriculture in Western Canada', *Canadian Journal of Agricultural Economics*, 38, 741-56.

Zucchetto, J. and Bickle, G. 1984. 'Energy and nutrient analyses of a dairy farm in Central Pennsylvania', *Energy in Agriculture*, 29-47.

7. Technological Change, Ecological Sustainability and Industrial Competitiveness

Sylvie Faucheux

INTRODUCTION

Much work on sustainable development devotes attention to defining the technological necessities for sustainable development and the changes of life style or consumption patterns necessary to achieve this goal. At the same time, environmental regulations have tended to focus on control of end of pipe emissions. Given these particular emphases, public policies for industry development and environmental policies have actually been able to evolve largely independently of each other and, until recently, their interactions have attracted little attention. But there is now considerable discussion of the institutional arrangements and economic instruments needed to embody environmental concerns in industrial strategy. Analyses have suggested how it may be necessary to develop an ecological industrial policy, which uses several, combined instruments to bring about technological change and structural change of the economy.

There has, as yet, been relatively little discussion of the links between technological change, ecological sustainability and industrial competitiveness (Skea 1994 and other work cited there). We are interested in this chapter in the long term, environmentally motivated technological change involved in shifting from an end of pipe approach for capturing pollutants after they are generated to a focus on the prevention of environmental degradation. Indeed new fields such as the development of throughput minimising technologies, environmental management systems and new concepts of use and production, ecological restructuring of subsidy schemes are emerging.

Firms and sectors find themselves confronted by increasingly wide ranging environmental protection regulation and by the appearance of new markets for goods and services produced by 'clean' technologies, as well as the appearance of environmentally friendly consumer products. This can be an incitation to adopt commercial strategies that are 'environmentally friendly', but such an outcome is by no means sure. Leaving the initiative for technology trajectory choices up to industrial competitiveness could, equally plausibly, result in industry lock-in to unsustainable development choices. Lessons from evolutionary perspectives on technological change can here prove instructive and can help to provide insights into ways of promoting strategies that may reconcile competitiveness with sustainability norms.

The complicated relationships between the triad technological change, ecological sustainability and industrial competitiveness, thus demand analysis along several dimensions. To introduce our presentation, we recall the major role of technical change in the implementation of sustainable development. Subsequently, we deepen the discussion by considering the endogenous character of technical change in the possible dynamics of transition to sustainable development. This will allow us to introduce the evolutionary approach to technological change, placing emphasis on notions of strategy. Then we explain the fundamental roles that firms' strategies *vis-à-vis* the endogenisation of technological change can play for giving effect to norms of ecological sustainability, and we continue this theme by arguing that this apparently beneficial role of firms towards sustainability emerges only contingently, out of new challenges for commercial viability. Finally, to conclude, we mention some of the institutional factors that will have a bearing on technological change trajectories at local, national and international levels.

TECHNICAL CHANGE: A MAJOR ROLE FOR THE IMPLEMENTATION OF SUSTAINABLE DEVELOPMENT

The conflict between advocates of weak sustainability and of strong sustainability is founded, in large part, on a divergence in the confidence placed in technical change. Studies adopting the weak sustainability perspective extend the conclusions of neoclassical growth and capital theories to natural resources (now called natural capital). Since the 1970s, the range of analysis has been broadened through studies integrating pollution into the growth models including or excluding natural capital. While the models are fairly disparate in their details, in general a definition of conditions is sought in which per capita consumption does not decrease; we may refer to this criterion as 'neoclassical sustainability'.

This preoccupation remains more or less in line with the results produced by Stiglitz's (1974) pioneering model. In brief, a constant per capita consumption path can be permanently maintained as long as the positive effects of technical progress and/or capital accumulation are sufficient to offset the negative effects of the exhaustion of natural resources, of pollution, of population growth and of the discount rate (which plays the role of an intertemporal distribution parameter). In this theoretical perspective, sustainability is generally assured by assuming the existence of a back stop technology or by assumptions about improvements in factor productivity (high elasticities of substitutability and/or improved average productivity through time).

Conversely, those adopting the strong sustainability approach are distinctly pessimistic about the beneficial effects of technical change. In some cases this pessimism becomes the basis for a strongly prescriptive vision of the requirements for sustainability. For Daly (1991), for example, technological change can at best delay, but cannot prevent, the need for a transition to an ecologically limited stationary state. The reasoning given for this inevitability is the absolute nature of the ecological constraints imposed by the second law of thermodynamics, which precludes indefinite productivity improvements and substitutability.

Thus, whereas the weak sustainability protagonists place confidence in technological change as the vehicle for economic sustainability, Daly with his pessimistic vision of technical change deduces the obligation of a zero growth steady state respecting ecologically imposed constraints. In both cases, the view of technological change potentialities determines the vision of sustainability and of how to attain it. Each vision thus makes potential for technical change determinant. Correspondingly, both schools propose that measures of technical change and of production levels can be key indicators of success or not in the implementation of sustainability policies. However, neither of these perspectives offers the basis for an in-depth analysis of the real processes of technological change.

The reason for this common limitation can be seen in the similarity of the conception of economic production and of technological change in the two approaches. In effect, the question of production is reduced, at the aggregate level, to a problem of growth (or non-growth); and technology change is correspondingly reduced to a single dimension, a rate, whose maximum is presumed to be exogenously determined. The divergence between the two schools then concerns the value of this rate. A rate of technical progress for all the planet's economies of approximately 2 to 3 per cent per year has been posited by some economists. With the world population growth rate currently standing at 1.6 per cent per year, it could be deduced that by and large there should be no sustainability problem. Advocates of strong sustainability are, by contrast, less optimistic about the possible improvements to be obtained in marginal and average productivities and more worried about the disruptive effects of production and consumption byproducts.

This unidimensional conception means that neither party is able to incorporate the multidimensional nature of technological changes, bearing in qualitatively different ways on (inter alia) prospects for economic production, natural resource availability, waste production, mitigation or augmentation of the adverse environmental impacts of pollution, species viability, ecosystem conservation and biosphere life support functions. Moreover, even if the rate of technical change is considered, in some sense, as an economic variable, not much insight is given into the institutional, political or other determinants of the actual changes that do or might take place.

We therefore suggest that policy oriented analysis of prospects for sustainable development requires a more sophisticated treatment of both the sources and the effects of technological change (Faucheux 1993). In part this means developing a more sophisticated representation of the links between economic production and changes in the natural environment, for example viewing technological change as a dialectical phenomenon involving interaction of a productive system with its (changing) environment (O'Connor 1989, 1993, 1994a and 1994b). In this chapter, we will be concerned primarily with the sources and dynamics of technological innovation taking place within an economic system, not with the external processes of ecological change. We do, however, take it as self-evident that one of the major stimuli to economic and technical change is changed social perceptions (including accumulating scientific evidence and hypotheses) about ecological and health impacts of economic activity. The question we pose is how these social perceptions come to be reflected in choices at firm and industry level.

We will develop this theme through an appraisal of two approaches to the analysis of technical change as an endogenous process and its roles in relation to sustainability: Endogenous growth theory and evolutionary theories of technological change.

1. The first approach emerges from the idea that an explanation of long-term economic growth cannot be defended that is based on an exogenous parameter whose nature is unknown. Its advocates propose giving the growth theory a layer of theoretical underpinning through incorporating an analysis of its presumed driving force, viz., technical change.

2. The second perspective combines notions of complex systems inter-dependence with a dynamic framework for analysis. It considers the economic process as an open evolution, where the structure of economic activity is transformed over time by the cumulative causation of technological innovations, political choices and the opportunities and constraints presented by changing ecological and social conditions.

We proceed therefore to examine the insights that can be drawn from these two approaches for analysing the links between technical change and sustainable development.

IMPLICATIONS OF ENDOGENISATION OF TECHNICAL CHANGE FOR SUSTAINABLE DEVELOPMENT

There is no point in going back over the well-known limits of the standard growth theory based on the Solow model (1956). Suffice is to say that a problem is raised by the fact that standard growth theory provides no easy way of estimating technical progress and thus evaluating the past or possible future contribution of the technical progress to the acceleration (or slowdown) of the scarcity of natural capital. One consequence, important in the context of this chapter, is that there is no easy way of evaluating the contribution of technical progress to ecological sustainability (Faucheux and O'Connor 1997).

Recognition of this limitation has naturally triggered interest in possibilities of further developments in the growth theories that might give more clarity on such points (Rebelo 1991, Michel and Rotillon 1993, Gastaldo and Ragot 1996). (It should be noted that these models are highly abstract and do not cover natural capital in its entirety. Rebelo addresses purely natural resources whereas Rotillon and Michel merely consider pollution.) One of the aims of recent work in this domain is to provide indirect ways of measuring technical progress. Yet the fact remains that the resulting endogenous growth models tend only to offer a theoretical account of the origins of the technical progress (such as apprenticeship phenomena, human capital) rather than any estimate of its actual or possible future rate (Benhaïm and Schembri 1996).

Moreover, it should be noted that in these models the sources of technical change are ultimately reduced to economic type variables (appropriability, patents, educational expenditure and so on) presumed to conform to a market logic of 'rationality'. This means that the endogenisation is achieved by the reduction of technical change to purely economic phenomena. Although the attempt is now made to explain what was, in the past, an axiomatic conjecture concerning technical progress, the basic analytical structure has remained the same. Technical change is generally considered to be a simple accumulable good with characteristics distinctly similar to those of a public good. The Marshallian concept of industry level externality is used to solve the incompatibility between the dynamics of technical change generating increasing returns and the competitive equilibrium. Moreover, the endogenous growth theory preserves the equilibrium framework of analysis and thus the balanced growth logic, simply extending it to encompass a notion of technical change that it continues to class as a simple rate. There is an inherent presumption that all the coordination problems will be solved in the long run - and thus that the equilibrium concept has explanatory pertinence.

The endogenous growth models remain first and foremost equilibrium models, unable to take into account the complex nature of technical change and the discontinuities in time and perception that it implies. Technical change is given a purely quantitative significance. It is reflected by an increase in the activity level of the production structure whose characteristics, previously defined by the nature of the equilibrium, remain unchanged. Non-linearities are introduced within the models in order to open up the possibility of multiple equilibrium paths for the economy. The suitable choice of conditions, guaranteed by perfect expectations, then makes the spontaneous transition to a constant growth rate path possible.

The adequacy of this treatment is open to doubt. It does not take into account the problems connected with transition dynamics and in effect assumes that the technical change is automatically 'assimilated' by the economic system and the social collectivity. In reality, technical change causes ruptures, such as under-utilisation of capital (and of human capital, in so-called technological unemployment). In fact, the problem posed by persisting disequilibria influencing the growth path (or non-growth, or non-balanced uneven growth) means that we can no longer reason uniquely in terms of comparative stationary states. For this, a logic would need to be developed for describing processes of transition whereby the long term and the short term are addressed together.

The evolutionary theory of technical change breaks with the equilibrium framework found in both growth models (endogenous or otherwise) and zero growth models. This school of economics gives central place to processes of disequilibrium in which the concept of transition and properties of non-linearity have important roles to play. The evolutionary approach concentrates on observing economic reality without trying to find a normative reference situation such as an equilibrium. This is why, for example, the concept of the production function no longer has an axiomatic place here. The approach looks more at the conflicting relations and their development over time (the role of strategy in its different forms), whereas previous analyses nullified conflicts by using optimisation.

The notion of technological change such as it is addressed from an evolutionary standpoint, far surpasses the previously mentioned reductionist interpretations. The presumption is that an understanding of the workings of technological path selection and the nature of technological societal economic interrelations can only be gleaned when technical elements are represented as a complex dynamic system (Saviotti 1986 and Perrin 1991).

STRATEGY AND ENVIRONMENTALLY MOTIVATED TECHNOLOGICAL PATHS

The evolutionary approach posits that each technical system should be understood as an emergent whole rather than merely in terms of relations with its components. In other words, the structure of such a system has a specific nature that transcends the characteristics of its component parts. Change is explained by the system's ability to generate adaptation variables through its structure. The dynamic content of recurrent interactions between technical, socioeconomic and ecological systems demonstrates the uncertain and multidimensional nature of the causes directing the shape of technical systems. By providing an understanding of the selection methods for technological paths, it lays down the prerequisites for choice problematics to aid the decision on the direction in which to steer technological change.

The evolutionary approach provides a better understanding of how technological innovation influences long-term economic fluctuations. Moreover, it emphasizes a special selection mechanism derived from the interdependence of choices. Certain authors (for example, David 1985 and Arthur 1989) posit that technological diffusion does not depend on selection as asserted by Darwin, but on luck. Here the irreversibility of technical change is reflected by the lock-in phenomena developed by Arthur (1989). The lock-in phenomenon can be observed for a given technology when a combination of positive feedback effects, or dynamic increasing returns, give a competitive edge to the technological option first adopted. Once a few technological options start to be diffused, the sequential choice of technical options by the adopters is likely to lead to the supremacy of one option, even though this option may ultimately turn out to be inferior. It can prove to be impossible, or at least extremely difficult, to exit from the adopted technological path. If two technological systems start at the same time, market shares may fluctuate as external circumstances and luck change. If the self-reinforcing mechanism is strong enough, one of the two technologies may eventually accumulate enough to take one hundred per cent of the market.

Three properties can be expressed here: Multiple equilibria resulting from ex ante uncertainty over the multitude of possible solutions, possible inefficiency and lock-in. (Inefficiency here relates primarily to production and has two sides: The reduction of economic viability that comes with high fixed costs; and the increase in dangers of ecological unsustainability that comes with natural resource depletion and/or polluting emissions.) If the self-reinforcement mechanism is not offset by counteracting forces, local positive feedbacks may be found. This implies that deviations from certain states are amplified and are therefore unstable. Self-reinforcement generally means that a particular outcome or equilibrium possesses or has accumulated an economic advantage. This represents a potential barrier, because the given equilibrium is locked into a state measurable by the minimum cost to effect changeover to an alternative equilibrium. Consequently, lock-in happens dynamically, as sequential decisions make it difficult for the system to escape this equilibrium.

The problem of lock-in is potentially very significant when considering the impact of technology choices on the evolution of the natural environment. Lock-in expresses certain aspects of the wider notion of irreversibility. In modelling terms, the exit from a particular equilibrium or stable time trajectory in an economic system depends to a great extent on the origin and nature of the self-reinforcing mechanism characterising that path. The strength of this mechanism depends, in part, on the extent to which the advantages accrued by the equilibrium are irreversible or are transferable to an alternative equilibrium. Where learning effects and specialized costs are at the origin of reinforcement, advantages are neither reversible nor transferable to an alternative equilibrium. It then becomes difficult to reposition the system.

This can be observed, for example, with the nuclear energy option in France (Schembri, Méral and Zyla 1994). In short, the French energy policy contains two potential threats: That of hasty lock-in on an ecologically hazardous and/or economically unviable fossil fuel replacement energy technology and that of the rapid obsolescence of current social institutions designed for the fossil fuel age. The threat of a social crisis arises from the incompatibility of current social institutions with a new technology. Yet, uncertainty over environmental problems imposes the adoption of preventive policies to limit the potential damage that our generation could afflict on future generations.

Given these circumstances, one conclusion is that any strategy set up to attenuate constraints imposed by changes in the natural environment should ideally be kept extremely flexible. In other words, it should keep the technological choice options open so as not to burden future generations with heavy costs of subsequent technical change. If this flexibility is to be guaranteed and lock-in phenomena avoided, we must foster exploration of a diversity of technological paths, but reject them as they prove to be inefficient for economic production (appraised over the longer term as well as in the short term) or incompatible with environmental requirements.

This then raises the question of the processes influencing the choice of technological directions and whether or not the choices made are likely to be sympathetic to sustainability norms, as we explore below.

The evolutionary analysis as sketched above is a promising theoretical approach to representing and endogenising technical change in analyses for sustainable development. Contrary to more traditional economic analyzes which are based on a hypothetical and deductive approach to technical change, the evolutionary theories use an inductive method based on observation of the complex reality of economic, institutional and ecological changes. This has the advantage of allowing representation of the essential role that technology change choices unfolding over time will have in possible 'transition paths' for sustainable development. This further suggests the importance of economic policy for 'steering' the economic system in the cumulative process of change.

The evolutionary approach places emphasis on understanding the structure of economic (and ecological) activity and its change through time, and, more particularly, on strategies of economic/political actors and the way that, cumulatively, they contribute to institutional, economic and ecological change. The evolutionary approach concentrates on observing the reality without necessarily trying to find a normative reference situation such as equilibrium. The approach looks more at the conflicting relations and their development over time, whereas neoclassical approaches neglect conflicts by adopting optimization as their rule of thumb. The focus is put on strategy as a response to uncertain and changeable circumstances (Faucheux and Schembri 1995).

With the notion of strategy, the emphasis is placed on the degrees of freedom that actors possess; on the constraints that they face, but also the freedom of movement that they may have and the range of opportunities that they may identify and, over time, create.

FIRMS AS INTERESTED PLAYERS ON THE 'ENDOGENISATION' OF TECHNICAL CHANGE

For the analysis of technology change in industrial economies, three key categories of players can be identified (Schot 1992):

1. Those whose work determines the content of the technical change, such as private and public research and development departments;
2. Those who indirectly influence the direction of the technical change, such as government regulatory institutions;
3. Those who take account of market conditions to reconcile the opportunities offered by the former with the constraints imposed by the latter, such as the 'environmental' departments of large firms.

Correspondingly, we may characterise the respective roles of the three types of player as: That of change generation; that of influencing technological path selection; and that of the concretisation of links between generation and selection. Our main interest at this point is in the strategies of the third family of players. Firms and corporate enterprises are, for example, involved daily and through long-term strategic decisions, with implementation of new technologies, many of which may be characterised as 'natural capital augmenting' in the sense either of improving productivity of given natural resources or reducing adverse impact of pollutants and waste flows from a given level of goods and services production. Such innovations would seem, *a priori*, favourable to the achievement of ecological sustainability norms. The question is, what might induce firms to make such innovations?

Since the 1970s, the view has widely been expressed that industrial enterprise and consumption patterns production need to be guided and circumscribed so as to respect ecological 'limits to growth'. The task of regulation has, traditionally, been confided to the public sector, although accompanied sometimes by doubts about the efficacy of the state apparatus. The promotion of the policy goal of sustainable development during the last decade represents an attempt at softening the dichotomy growth versus the environment. In effect, sustainability aims at reconciling the pursuit of goals traditionally associated with economic growth (such as material wealth and consumer satisfaction), with ecological constraints on economic activity. A related evolution has taken place in the private sector and in regulatory theory and practice. On the one hand, firms have come increasingly to consider the necessities of 'taking the environment into account' and of introducing 'environmentally friendly' technological change not just as exogenously imposed costs or constraints, but as strategic opportunities. Necessity is thus converted into a virtue. On the other hand, public authorities and theorists concerned with environmental regulation have given increased attention to the extent to which environmental goals might be 'internalised' in norms of good commercial practice.

Environmentally motivated technological change can be interpreted as a direct strategic opportunity. In the first instance, environmental concerns may be translated into new market opportunities, such as energy efficient or environmentally friendly products. Commercial success here depends on an amalgam of technical mastery (process and product innovation, life cycle analyses), consumer attitude (demand for 'green' products) and public relations. In some cases a marketing advantage can be obtained through participation in quality certification programmes (such as ISO 9000 internationally and also national programmes). The innovative firm does not merely respond to pre-existing niches, but seeks also to influence the evolution of consumer perceptions and demand (for example, product differentiation, product acceptance and behavioural changes).

Environmental regulation appears now as a domain of strategic action. Firms in all sectors of production and service provision (such as transport), are obliged to respond to increasingly wide ranging regulatory controls reflecting concern for health, safety, environmental quality and natural resource conservation. Environmental policies may be seen as simply imposing additional costs, inhibiting flexibility and thus impairing competitiveness. But the implementation of comprehensive environmental policy at local, national and international levels is accepted as a fact. More and more, the private sector is involving itself as a partner in the negotiation and implementation of environmental policies. In these conditions their role in the choice of technological trajectory as regards sustainability is fundamental. For example, in the chemical fertiliser production industry (as cited by Borde and Douguet

1995), one prominent French firm states:

> l'engagement de progrès de l'industrie chimique pour la protection de l'environnement ... (the commitment within the chemical industry to progress for the protection of the environment)

and another

> ... estime que la maîtrise de ces risques [industrielles] et la protection de l'environnement font partie intégrante des bonnes pratiques industrielles et doivent donc être placées parmis ses objectifs majeurs ... (considers that the control of industrial risks and environmental protection are part and parcel of good industrial practices and should be placed amongst their prime objectives).

This engagement is not just a passive adaptation to imposed constraints, rather it is strongly proactive at the regulatory level. The French fertiliser producer just cited engages itself to 'participate with all the appropriate authorities and agencies in the development and implementation of measures corresponding with this objective' (our translation).

In developing environmentally motivated technologies, the firms can benefit from commercial advantages through being seen as environmentally responsible. Corporates now speak readily about their responsibilities in relation to concerns about energy efficiency, natural resource scarcity, chemical spills, pollutant disposal, waste management, recycling and nature conservation.

In some European countries (for example, France, but less so in Germany or the UK) the cement industry has claimed for itself a 'green' image by virtue of safe disposal through incineration of certain volumes of solid wastes (Gramont and Setbon 1995). The French chemical fertiliser industry, under pressure due to problems of nitrification and eutrophication of rivers, lakes and underground water, promotes 'la fertilisation raisonnée (reasoned fertiliser application)' (Borde and Douguet 1995); many examples from other sectors may be given. Here, the industry seeks not only to maintain a respectable public image, but also to claim the role of contributing positively to environmental consciousness and responsibility amongst users and the wider public. A good public image can translate directly into commercial advantage through enlargements of market niche and brand loyalty and can also be advantageous in negotiation of regulatory accords with governing bodies.

These categories of response are interwoven. Their relative importance varies a lot from firm to firm and from one sector of activity to another. Cumulatively we can speak of *corporate environmental strategy* (CES), in the sense of conscious and systematic efforts at integrating environmental considerations into the gamut of strategic considerations for commercial success. This activity now represents a significant investment of company time and financial resources, including the recruitment and retention of multi-disciplinary expertise (policy analysis, legal advisors, technical studies on feasibility, strategic market studies, lobbying activity). The significant costs mean that the practices have tended to develop most at the level of large corporate enterprise and also of sectoral associations where firms perceive a common interest, notably with regard to regulatory measures. But equally, this signals that large firms and, notably, the big corporate groups, are in a position to influence significantly the directions of technological innovation as well as being able to mould aspects of public policy.

ACCOUNTING PLURALITY OF MOTIVES IN INNOVATION STRATEGIES TO AVOID THE TRAP OF 'LOCK-IN'

Firms tend, increasingly, to present their technological and marketing strategies as responding to the needs of ecological sustainability. It may, nonetheless, often be the case that the chosen product and process innovations are motivated more particularly in favour of their own commercial interests under the changing regulatory and competitive conditions that confront them. If this is so, then the seeming public spirited character of the enterprise strategies is fragile. The emergence of 'environmental strategies' at the enterprise and corporate level and of environmentally motivated technological change by firms does not necessarily coincide with the altruism of a sustainability oriented 'industrial ecology' (as rather optimistically suggested by Duchin, Lange and Kell 1995). Rather it reflects the many facets of requirements for continuing commercial success. Leaving the choice of pollution abatement, product line and other technology trajectory choices at the mercy of considerations of industrial competitiveness leaves the door wide open to 'lock-in' to production and consumption regimes that are antagonistic to sustainable development norms.

Environmentally motivated technological change by firms are adaptations under conditions of rapid economic changes. These changes include the 'globalisation' of economic and ecological contexts of decision making and the restructuring of trading patterns. Economic globalisation is expressed foremost in the circuits of capital and of information, as well as increased volumes of trade in goods. The globalisation of environmental issues is expressed in, for example, the environmental provisions juxtaposed with pro-free trade provisions of the GATT; international accords on atmospheric emissions (ozone, acid rain, greenhouse gases); property rights over intellectual property and biodiversity; toxic waste transportation and disposal (Chailloux 1995).

Firms of all sizes must respond to commercial opportunity and regulatory constraint simultaneously on three levels: International (such as EU Single Market norms and environmental directives), national and sub-national. As such, environmentally motivated technological change by firms integrates a conscious preoccupation with social legitimacy. Because environmental quality is a matter of public good, firms must establish their social legitimacy by defining their participation in a larger community of interest. The reference community (or communities) may be expressed at local, national and trans-national levels and may extend to humanity at large and posterity (*viz.*, future generations). For example, an industrial enterprise may validate its insertion in a particular region or canton in terms of economic benefits such as employment alongside a social guarantee of good practice (safety, health, environmental protection).

Corporate practice for environmentally motivated technological change is, however, inevitably parochial. While an expressed premise of environmentally motivated technological change by firms is that commercial and wider public interests can be reconciled, this is something needing to be demonstrated rather than presumed. At any rate, in most instances the commercial imperatives have primacy. In effect, what we are seeing is the articulation of a corporate version of now well-established discourses for 'sustainable development'. These discourses and the accompanying practices, are marked by a number of now familiar tensions:

1. On the one hand there is the requirement for profitability in terms of costs and product price and preoccupations with competitiveness, market share and product niche.
2. On the other hand there is a concern for social legitimacy, referring to a notion of 'public interest' that, increasingly, includes ecological concerns and the interests of future generations.

The scientific analysis of these tensions requires the appraisal of environmentally motivated technological change strategies by firms within a wider societal frame. A central requirement is to understand the limitations, alongside the strengths of these practices, due to their parochial goals. This may be undertaken by articulating the analysis of economic determinants of technological choices (such as costs, barriers to entry, returns to scale and advertising strategies) with an analysis of the different terms in which *social legitimacy* may be sought and contested and positioning different forms of CES in this framework. A clear understanding of the different forms of legitimacy and their social bases will constitute an improved knowledge base for public/private/communal partnership in the framing and implementation of technological trajectory implementing sustainable development.

We conclude, thus, that leaving it up to the good will of private enterprise to lead the way in technological change runs the risk of (a) leaving the economy 'locked-in' to non-sustainable technological trajectories, or (b) allowing economic activity to be driven in new directions that, while commercially viable and consumer satisfying in the short term, are antagonistic to ecological sustainability objectives. (The same may be said with regard to equity considerations for social justice within generations or over time.) In fact, efforts to keep down costs can mean that commercial enterprises focus only on the immediate and short term determinants of 'supply' of needed inputs and thus provoke a double crisis: The degradation or non-reproduction of needed 'conditions of production' (as reflected in increasing supply costs or difficulties of access to the needed materials, sources and sites); and the impairment or non-reproduction of the needed 'conditions of consumption' (such as viable living conditions and incomes so that people qua consumers can buy the products).

Therefore a range of considerations other than competitiveness, such as ethical notions of public interest extended to interests of future generations and to norms of species and ecosystem conservation, need also to be given weight. This means that private enterprise must be challenged to respect the communal basis of people's livelihoods and to accept that long-term commercial sustainability depends on the health of people and communities and habitats.

SOCIAL AND INSTITUTIONAL DIMENSIONS OF TECHNOLOGICAL CHANGE

The evolutionary theories of technological change, while at an early stage of application to sustainability concerns, nonetheless give some clues as to the complementary roles of public strategy alongside private/corporate enterprise.

Public institutions can directly finance the development of alternative technologies and even their large scale implementation. One example of this capability, arguably contrary to sustainability norms, is the development of the nuclear industry in France (even though the initial objective had nothing to do with environmental protection). Another example, perhaps more favourable to ecological sustainability and respectful of the 'precautionary principle,' is the Dutch government's funding of solar and wind powered electricity production units (Schot 1992). Governments can exert indirect control by guaranteeing research and development subsidies to promote certain types of technology.

Secondly, the regulatory authorities can try to influence technology and product line selection by establishing norms (such as eco-labelling) and/or by using economic tools (taxes, subsidies) in order to internalize the external costs of pollution. It needs to be noted that the adjustment strategies induced by imposition of economic (dis)incentives can often conflict with the implementation of clean technology. Ideally, action should be taken at the level of process selection taking account of the taxes (subsidies) that will be applied. The nature of the regulations should therefore be made to evolve in such a way as to encourage the firms to produce technical changes which will help protect the natural environment (for example, to replace fossil fuels and nuclear electricity with biological renewable energy). This implies, for example, gradually introducing more restrictive norms whose technical requirements extend beyond the current potential. Such a policy seeks to trigger an announcement effect among the companies, whereby they anticipate the next step in the regulations and thus choose proactively.

The third and last category of actions consists of using existing institutional relations or creating new relations to ensure that the technical change is diffused in line with the environmental constraint. This could involve using the positive externalities produced by institutional connections (Foray 1992): Network externalities, positive retrospective effects brought about by apprenticeship phenomena and increases in the quality and quantity of goods generated by pecuniary externalities (as defined by Scitovsky 1954).

Obviously, the most effective strategy may be expected to come from the joint use of these three series of measures.

Technological change cannot be divorced from public policy. In fact, given the strong interdependencies of costs and technological choices (the non-linear 'feedbacks' of the system dynamics), we would argue that overall production efficiency would probably be enhanced if the process of technical change regulation is managed by public institutions as a process of social partner negotiation. Beyond this, a negotiated evolution also allows 'public interests' to be expressed and debated. The possibilities of adapting the economic system depend on a range of scientific and political factors which may all be brought on stage by the regulatory authorities: Progress in the understanding of natural phenomena, the setting up of suitable negotiation processes, implementation of policy programmes including fiscal and social reforms and the placement and scale of new investments. Social or organizational changes should precede and anticipate major technical change, in such a way as to ensure an apprenticeship period to avoid crisis states arising from the transition.

We can speculate that new social alliances, new forms of social partnership and new processes of negotiation will need to be forged along lines that are 'communal' as much as industrial. Negotiation will need to extend not just to workplace solidarities on such matters as occupational health and safety, working conditions, hours of employment and wage levels (as in the post World War II Keynesian compromise of the mixed capitalist state), but also to the maintenance and enhancement of collective livelihood on such matters as toxic waste control and respect of habitat as a cultural as well as ecological milieu.

In principle, what might be sought are strategic partnerships between communities and commercial enterprise, where each respects the functional imperatives and requirements of the other. Ideally, enterprises might be encouraged to understand that, on the one hand they sustain communities through providing employment and on the other hand they have a debt to the districts and communities that sustain them. The honouring of this debt involves sustainability commitments far beyond the mere payment of workers' wages. Local and state governments can have key roles in helping to define the social responsibilities of enterprise to their host region and also to workers and their families employed in a region. Clear messages about these sorts of responsibilities, for example as embodied in EC Directives and in official regulations concerning health, risk management and communication, pollution abatement, can provide 'signals' to enterprise that will influence their technological choices.

Of course, such propositions of partnership are normative and optimistic. One factor working against their achievement is the inclination of corporate players, especially the trans-national enterprises, to search out new cost shifting opportunities elsewhere, such as lower wages, lesser social responsibilities, weaker or non-enforced environmental quality requirements. Thus different districts and nations may be played off against each other, with capital threatening to 'withdraw' and relocate elsewhere unless attractive conditions (meaning attractive to commercial investors, but exploitative of workers, communities and nature) are furnished. Any compromise will thus be unstable, a kind of duel or tug of war. For this sort of political partnership strategy to be effective, there are two crucial requirements.

1. First, people acting as workers and as citizens of their districts, must collectively and individually give a high weight to maintaining the 'communal conditions of life', habitat, local infrastructures, community, culture, solidarities of place (as well as workplace).

2. Second, the people must guard against the 'divide and rule' tactics habitually employed by firms under competitive pressure. A district, nation, region, or community being successful in negotiating a 'partnership' with capital to respect local ecological or social conditions of production, may achieve this success simply at the expense of other communities. One manifestation of politicking that may be compromised in this way, is myopic NIMBY politics (Not In My Back Yard) in relation to the siting of industrial complexes, motorways and other infrastructures of modern life and waste disposal sites and facilities.

Evolutionary theory, with its notions of non-linear feedbacks and multiple equilibria, can help to suggest ways that technological economic social futures are created by 'crucial' innovations and policy choices that come to be amplified in their effects through time. A bridge can thus be built between the tools and results of analytical economics and utopian intuitions about directions of social change. The ideals of social as well as economic and ecological sustainability entail pursuit of strategies of solidarity, refusing short term gains at others' long-term expense, refusing insularity and looking for opportunities to build a wealth in common through mutually affirming labours and reciprocation at many levels. One challenge for the evolutionary theories is to help discern technological and institutional choices that are 'constructive' in this normative sense.

REFERENCES

Arthur, W.B. 1989. 'Self-reinforcing mechanisms in economics', in Anderson P.W. *et al.* (eds), *The Economy as an Evolving Complex System*. Santa Fe Institute Studies in the Sciences of Complexity.

Benhaïm, J. and Schembri, P. 1996. 'Technical change: An essential variable in the choice of a sustainable development trajectory', in Faucheux, S., Pearce D.W., Proops J.L.R (eds), *Models of Sustainable Development*. Aldershot: Edward Elgar.

Borde, A. and Douguet, J.-M. (sous la direction de J.F. Noël) 1995. *Competitivité et Environnement: Le Cas de la Filière Engrais*, mémoire de DEA, C3ED/Université de Paris I, October.

Chailloux, N. (sous la direction de S. Faucheux) 1995. *Les Firmes Face à la Mondialisation Écologique*, mémoire de DEA, C3ED/Université de Paris I, October.

Daly, H.E. 1991. *Steady State Economics*. Washington DC: Island Press.

David, P. 1985. 'Clio and the economics of QWERTY', *American Economic Review*, 75(2).

Duchin F., Lange G.-M., Kell G. 1995. 'Technological change, trade and the environment, *Ecological Economics*, 14(3), 185-94.

Faucheux S. 1993. 'The role of energy in production functions', *International Journal of Global Energy Issues*, 5(1).

Faucheux, S. and Schembri, P. 1995. 'The implications of the "endognenization" of technical change in the implementation of sustainable development'. Working paper presented to Wuppertal Workshop on Socio-ecological Economics, 27-29 May.

Faucheux, S. and O'Connor, M. 1997. *Valuation for Sustainable Development: Methods and Policy Indicators*. Aldershot: Edward Elgar (forthcoming).

Foray D. 1992. 'Introduction générale', in Foray, D. and Freeman, C. (eds), *Technologie et Richesses des Nations*. Paris: Economica.

Gastaldo, S. and Ragot, L. 1996. 'Sustainable development through endogenous growth models', in Faucheux S., Pearce D.W. and Proops J.L.R (eds), *Models of Sustainable Development*. Aldershot: Edward Elgar.

Gramont, V. and Setbon, V. (sous la direction de S. Faucheux) 1995. *Analyse des Implications Stratégiques des Contraintes et Opportunités Environnementales: Une Comparaison France-Allemagne à Partir d'une Étude du Secteur Cimentier*. Rapport pour le Programme Environnement, Société, Entreprises: La Nouvelle Donne, Convention ADEME/CNRS, no. 92-233.

Michel, P. and Rotillon, G. 1993. 'Disutility of pollution and endogenous growth', *Environmental and Resource Economics*, 5.

O'Connor, M. 1989. 'Codependency and indeterminacy: A critique of the theory of production', *Capitalism, Nature, Socialism*, No.3, November, 33-57. Reprinted (with slight revisions) in O'Connor, M. (ed.) 1994, *Is Capitalism Sustainable? Political Economy and the Politics of Ecology*. New York: Guilford Publications, 53-75.

O'Connor, M. 1993. 'Entropic irreversibility and uncontrolled technological change in economy and environment', *Journal of Evolutionary Economics*, 3, 285-315.

O'Connor, M. 1994a. 'Entropy liberty and catastrophe: On the physics and metaphysics of waste disposal', in Burley, P. and Foster, J. (eds), *Economics and Thermodynamics: New Perspectives on Economic Analysis*, Dordrecht: Kluwer, pp. 119-82.

O'Connor, M. 1994b. 'Thermodynamique, complexité, et codépendance écologique: La science de la joie et du deuil', *Revue Internationale du Systémique* 8, No. 4-5 (December), 397-423.

Perrin, J. 1991. 'Analyse des systèmes techniques', in Boyer, R., Chavance, B. and Godard, O. (eds), *Les Figures de l'Irréversibilité en Économie*, éditions de l'École des Hautes Études en Sciences Sociales, Paris.

Rebelo S. 1991. 'Long run policy analysis and long run growth', *Journal of Political Economy*, 99(3).

Schembri, P., Méral, P. and Zyla, E. 1994. 'Technological lock-in and complex dynamics: Lessons from the French nuclear policy', *Revue Internationale de Systémique*, 8 (4-5).

Schot, J. 1992. 'The policy relevance of the quasi-evolutionary model: The case of stimulating clean technologies," in Combs, R., Savioti, P. and Walsh, G. (eds), *Technological Change and Company Strategies*. London: Academic Press.

Scitovsky, T. 1954. 'Two concepts of external economies', *Journal of Political Economy*, 62, 70-82.

Skea, J. 1994. 'Environmental issues and innovation', in Dodgson, M. and Rothwell, R. (eds), *The Handbook of Industrial Innovation*. Aldershot: Edward Elgar, pp. 421-31.

Solow, R.M. 1956. 'A contribution to the theory of economic growth', *Quarterly Journal of Economics*, 70.

Stiglitz, J.E. 1974. 'Growth with exhaustible natural resources: Efficient and optimal growth paths', *Review of Economic Studies: Symposium Volume*.

8. Environmental Valuation: From the Point of View of Sustainability

Martin O'Connor[1]

INTRODUCTION

The economics of the industrial age focussed on mechanisms of production and exchange of commodities (produced capital and consumption goods). This commodity production activity was represented as drawing upon an *external* (environmental) domain that furnished raw materials and waste disposal services. Subsequently, it was admitted that there were *environmental costs* associated with the economic commodity production and the question from an optimising point of view became to know whether the economic benefits outweighed the environmental costs.

On this basis, methods have been developed for trying to put money values on environmental assets through establishing tradeoffs between money valued goods and environmental amenities or damages. And in this way, through the enlargement of cost-benefit analysis to the environmental domain, it was hoped to reconcile economic output growth the concerns for quality of the environment. But this enlargement of physical spatial domain has a temporal corollary. The comparison of alternative uses of environmental assets and the assessment of risks and impairment of habitat conditions due to pollutants and ecosystem disruption, pose difficulties of high uncertainties, the irreversibility of many effects and (thus) long time scales. Concern with economic, ecological and social sustainability brings the long-term future into confrontation with the considerations of the present. How should we seek to reconcile preoccupations with the future with those of the present?

The response of established economic valuation methodology has been to extend conventional cost-benefit analysis also across time, through the attempted quantification of environmental damages and of economy

[1] The author acknowledges financial support from the DG-XII of the European Commission under contract ENV4-CT96-0226 for the project *Social Processes for Environmental Valuation: Procedures and Institutions for Social Valuations of Natural Capitals in Environmental Conservation and Sustainability Policy.*

environment tradeoffs through time through *discounting*; we may summarise this perspective in the aphorism of maximising net present value (NPV). But this practice does *not* reconcile future interests with the present, it simply discounts future values. Conversely, the less the future is discounted, the more weighty in the cost-benefit scales become the imponderables of uncertainties about longer term change. Given the distributional conflicts between present and future and the ethical and axiological disagreements between existing interested parties, the cost-benefit *optimising* approach becomes fairly useless as a guide for decision making.

If we want to provide decision support while we enlarge our scope of concern to the ecosystems of the planet and the long term, we should adopt a different perspective. One option is the representation of 'sustainable development' as a symbiosis between economic production and ecological (re)production. This implies an emphasis on *managing* and investing in the reproduction, transformation and renewal of the terrestrial habitats that are not just raw materials sources but veritable life support systems that underpin the overly analysed commodity production systems. These are also habitats in the sense of being the places of life, invested with social and community significance, or meanings. So valuation for sustainability cannot be separated from the idea of actions whose effect is to sustain this or that *form of life*, in the cultural as well as ecological economic sense.

The first part of this chapter recalls in a synthetic way the insurmountable difficulties encountered in attempts at the application of cost-benefit analysis as a decision aid for large scale and long-term environmental problems. In particular, we show how the habitual practice of time discounting simply gets in the way of intelligent analysis of long-term problems.

Part two of the chapter sketches the outline of a different approach to environmental valuation, centred around the notion of the *distribution* of sustainability. Policies for economic, ecological and social sustainability involve choices for the redistribution through time of economic opportunity and of access to services and benefits provided by the biophysical environment. Out of the range of possible economic and ecological trajectories, there are choices to be made about which environmental features and functions, which ecosystems and habitats and which spectra of economic opportunities, might be sustained - and for whom? Choices are also made about the distribution of hazards and environmental 'bads', the 'dis-services' deriving from poisoned or disrupted life support systems.

The third part illustrates how this understanding of valuation as action for and against sustainability may in practice be applied. The example concerns small forest pockets situated in an agricultural region of France; here it is a question of understanding whether and in what sense enough significance is attached to the forest to ensure that it is sustained. We outline a framework for analysis that places the emphasis on the forest *socio-eco-system* as an indivisible *unité de valeur*. A dynamic simulation model represents the evolving forest system through the interaction of human and ecological forces. We think of the value of the forest as embodied in the enduring socio-ecological system. The model shows, in a simplified way, how relatively small and imperceptible changes in human actors' behaviour can, in the long term, be critical for the robustness or diminution of the forest as a source of economic, wildlife, lifestyle and recreational values. The model also expresses, as a sort of metaphor, the way that social meaning is invested in the living whole and that the *value* of the forest is inseparable from this *collective* (shared or communal) investment.

The chapter concludes with some brief remarks suggesting how this approach to *valuation* for sustainability brings with it a distinctive epistemological perspective on *living in nature and living in time*.

SPLENDOUR AND MISERIES OF ENVIRONMENTAL VALUATION

The classical economists, in the 18th and 19th centuries, tended to take as given the primary environmental supports for economic production activity. They were either non-scarce (such as air) or non-depletable (such as arable land). From this point of view, a growth in the volume of economic output from one year to the next was a gain from the point of view of immediate consumption prospects and also a net improvement to the resource base upon which future economic output could be achieved. Success in the short term was thus synonymous with augmentation of potentials for consumption and capital accumulation in the long term. Two ideas grow out of this:

1. Sustainable (economic) growth was simply the continuation of short-term (economic) growth.
2. Material progress was synonymous with the augmentation of quality and quantity of economic output. Value in economics meant the value of economic (produced) goods and services.

The suggestion that there are binding 'ecological limits to growth' due to depletion of important natural resources or disruption of ecosystems and biosphere life support systems, due to soil and water contamination, salinisation, soil erosion, deforestation, climate change, changes all this. If natural resources are depletable and essential environmental services can be irreversibly impaired through pollution or ecosystem change, then present day economic activity can have very high inter-temporal opportunity costs. The existence of such irreversibilities ruptures the consonance between short run performance (GNP growth) and long run prospects for (a) economic output and hence consumption levels and (b) the sustaining of the cycles of resource renewal and the environmental life support functions that underpin economic activity. It is, thus, no longer possible to regard GDP growth as a signpost pointing in the direction of long-run economic progress. There are two dimensions to this.

> First, the short run and the long run may be in conflict: the pursuit of rapid (economic) output growth as a short term objective may impair durably the economic welfare prospects of future generations. Second, since economic value cannot increase without limit and even short term growth in value of economic output can have durable impact on environmental quality, it is no longer satisfactory to confine valuation attention to the produced goods and services alone, while ignoring ecological determinants of well being. (Brouwer *et al.* 1996)

A wide range of approaches have been devised with a view to ensuring that the various categories of environmental change - deterioration, depletion, damage and the like - are 'taken properly into account'. Often the demand for taking the environment into account is for valuation in monetary terms. This allows environmental impacts and protection questions to be formulated as optimal resource use problems through the extension of traditional cost-benefit analysis techniques. Alternatively, reasons such as uncertainty, distributional concerns and diversity of ethical positions may be given as reasons for the difficulty or inappropriateness of monetary valuation. In such cases there is a need for decision support techniques that do not depend exclusively on monetary valuation, such as multi-criteria and deliberative methods. At issue here are the advantages and disadvantages of having sacrificed commensurability of valuations, widely seen as one of the chief merits of CBA methods, in favour of more explicit political decision-making procedures. We argue that in application to long timescale and large spatial scale environmental problems, the cost-benefit calculus is largely illusory.

Monetary Valuation of Environmental Damage, Methods and Applications

The main reason for monetary valuation is to provide a common and understandable measure through which different objectives can be traded-off, so that the loss in relation to one objective can be evaluated against the gain in relation to another. Placing money figures on environmental damage gives a quantification of the scale of adverse effects and of the investment and adjustments needed to restore damaged environments and avoid further damages.

In conventional economic terms, the internalisation of the environment in evaluation practices requires; (a) developing ways of estimating in monetary terms the opportunity costs associated with alternative uses of economic and environmental resources, which means placing monetary values on environmental goods and services (and also environmental bads); and (b) choosing the course of action that is judged to be the 'best' for the society. This sort of approach depends on a combination of analytical and normative premises. First, the act of 'costing' environmental damage is taken to mean finding a way of comparing environmental with non-environmental goods in monetary terms. We refer to this as the assumption of *monetary commensurability*. Second, the monetisation of environmental costs and benefits provides the basis for maximising the balance of benefits over costs for the society, through applying the criterion of Pareto efficiency for policy and project selection decisions in the usual way.

The underlying principle for environmental cost-benefit analysis is that although we cannot introduce all ecological goods and services into actual markets, it is nevertheless possible to extrapolate in various ways from actual market transactions so as to get an estimate in money terms of the value of some environmental good, or the cost of some environmental harm. Environmental good or damage may be assessed in terms of its impact (direct or indirect) on other sectors of activity, for example the production of goods having a market price, or it may be assessed on the basis of substitute or complementary goods that do have a price (Hanley and Spash 1993).

There are a wide range of approaches to the pricing of environmental damage once it is identified. The methods are well documented in published literature and our purpose in mentioning some of them is simply to highlight their roles and limitations in policy applications.

1. Cost of response methods, look at actual expenditures incurred in environmental protection or in abating or repairing damage or for access to comparable amenities. There are two sorts of reasons for such expenditures. The first is that there is a benefit obtained directly by the person or agency taking the protection, abatement or repair action. The second is the existence of an obligation to pay in relation to damages for which the party is in some way held responsible; for example, versions of the polluter pays principle (PPP) imposing tax, restoration, or damage compensation payments.

2. Revealed preference methods, seek to value individuals' preferences for environmental goods through inference from their behaviour in actual markets. The two main categories of such methods are: (1) The travel cost method, which uses the costs that are incurred by visitors to a site as a proxy to calculate the recreation value they place upon that site. (2) The hedonic pricing method, which employs a proxy good in the market to estimate individuals' willingness to pay for environmental goods and to avoid environmental damage. The most widely used proxy good is property: Property values reflect many different attributes, both non-environmental (for example, room numbers and sizes, proximity to work and recreation) and environmental (such as noise levels from road and airports, the surrounding landscapes).

3. Expressed preference methods, notably contingent valuation (CVM), seek by means of questionnaire to present people with hypothetical situations, in the aim of eliciting statements about what they would be willing to pay for preserving a specified environmental feature or the compensation that they would find acceptable in the case of its loss.

All of these methods have distinctive limitations. The use of actual expenditure figures as proxies for the value of environmental damage is flawed for several reasons, including; 1. that people are not always in a position to spend money to remedy fully the harms or losses that they experience and 2. there may be many categories of harms felt, or likely to be felt, by human beings in the future and by other living beings, that are in no way provided for in the expenditures actually undertaken. The travel cost and hedonic pricing methods capture preferences as they are revealed in the behaviour of consumers in markets; and therefore are concerned only with use values. Use values refer to those that are incurred from the actual use of environmental goods, for example, for recreation. But there are also non-use values. Non-use values include, as general categories, the option values that express the preferences that individuals have for a good they might use; bequest values, preferences for the preserving an environmental good for others, including future generations; and finally, existence values, which signal preferences individuals have for some good they may never actually or potentially use for example, the preservation of some species, ecosystem, habitat and the like. One argument put forward for contingent valuation as a method of arriving at monetary values for environmental benefits, is that it is the only method that can capture both use and non-use values and hence the only measure that is capable of capturing the total value of an environmental good and hence the full cost of its loss or of damage to it. However, valuations that are defensible and robust in policy applications prove elusive. Practitioners of CVM have, over the years, constructed a long catalogue of difficulties of implementation and obstacles in the way of effective use of the results in decision making. Some of these difficulties relate to defining the object or service to be valued, others to the plausibility of the respondents' value statements and the adequacy of the sample used. Internal validity problems for CVM relate to its claims to being objective and systematic in the estimate of benefits and costs and being able to capture the 'true' price of a good - the persons' willingness to pay for the good at the margin given their budgetary constraints were it to be the case that a market exists. In the absence of real markets for the goods for which they are attempting to infer values, the economist attempts to establish validity by ensuring that different elicitation procedures converge on the same results or by eliminating sources of ambiguity or 'bias'. However, this search to eliminate bias may be an illusory goal. (For more extensive discussions see Jakobsson and Dragun 1996 and Holland *et al.* 1996).

The Quantification of Opportunity Costs

The conventional approach to costing environmental damage is to consider the physical environment as comprising stocks of natural capitals which furnish environmental goods and services - that is, primary energy and other natural resources, waste assimilation services, recreational amenity and life support functions. Natural capital is limited: There are constraints on availability and tradeoffs between different uses. Increasing attention is, correspondingly, being placed on prudent management of and investment in the maintenance, regeneration and enhancement of natural capital. So valuation of these natural capital stocks and the flows of benefits obtainable from them (or reductions in flows due to pollution or other degradation) may be attempted through making estimates of shadow prices reflecting opportunity costs, along much the same lines as produced commodities and economic capital goods bought and sold in markets.

Strictly speaking, these opportunity costs are quantifiable only within a tightly formalised modelling perspective - that of an inter-temporal general equilibrium.[2] The adoption of this analytical framework is often only implicit in applied valuation studies, yet it is important to understand the assumptions that underpin the habitual practices of searching for a *willingness to pay* or a tradeoff in monetary terms. The presumption usually is of a reference state with a Pareto efficient resource allocation. If given an explicit model

---

[2] This includes, for example, the neoclassical growth models extended to include categories of 'natural capital' as factors of production and/or environmental services as contributions to utility, which are the basis for theoretical investigations of *sustainability* (for example, Stiglitz 1974, Solow 1974, Dasgupta and Heal 1974) and for the definition of so-called *weak* indicators of sustainability (Faucheux, Muir and O'Connor 1997). Numerous model variants exist. On the economic side, a typical model may have economic capital (also called *built* or *produced* capital) and human capital (this latter being usually an exogenously specified population that provides labour as a productive input through time). On the 'natural' side it will have depletable and/or renewable resources, and/or an environmental stock that supplies amenity and/or a durable pollutant that reduces productivity or that reduces amenity. Utility or *welfare* depends positively on the level of consumption of the produced goods, and may also depend positively on the level of environmental amenity stocks or negatively on *bad* flows received from polluted nature.

representation, this would most often be an equilibrium satisfying the rule of maximum present value of *economic output* (henceforth NPVmax) or, as a variation along the same principle, maximum present value of *utility* (henceforth PVUmax). Such solutions are considered as proxies (or inter-temporal analogues) for 'perfect competition' general equilibrium. Under certain fairly standard - and highly unrealistic - analytical assumptions, one can establish that a PVUmax solution is characterised by a set of (shadow) equilibrium relative prices for all economic and environmental goods and services (present and future) - these prices including the interest rates from period to period - that correctly 'signal' the relative marginal productivities and the relative marginal utilities, hence the opportunity costs - including inter-temporal opportunity costs, on all margins.

The results obtained for economic output and hence potential for welfare delivery over time, depend strongly on the values of model parameters chosen, such as elasticities of substitution between different forms of capital, relative factor importance, consumer's preferences and social rules for inter-temporal distribution of purchasing power (or property rights). For example recent work has shown that, for the growth with natural capital models, at least four qualitatively different sorts of PVU maximising time paths are obtainable depending on initial stock levels and the specification of the social discount rate (Asheim 1994, Pezzey 1997, Pezzey and Withagen 1995 and Faucheux, Muir and O'Connor 1997). These are:

1. Monotonic decrease in utility over time: Non-sustained.
2. Increase of utility for a while, then a turning point with monotonic decline thereafter: Non-sustained.
3. Exactly constant utility through time: Sustained economic activity.
4. Monotonic increase in utility: More than sustainability.

The trouble as regards policy purposes is that nothing can reliably be inferred from measurements of current economic outputs and environmental changes as to which of these time path types best represents the 'business as usual' scenario for the economy in question; and nor can the potential for a sustainable economic output be reliably quantified. The problem becomes: Which model is the 'right' one for value estimation purposes? What functional forms and parameter settings are plausible? (Common 1993, Vanoli 1996 and Faucheux, Muir and O'Connor 1997). Even if the theoretical framework were agreed for response on these questions (which it is not - witness the debates over modelling of climate change and costs/benefits of remedial action), there are also practical measurement obstacles. These include the difficulty of achieving complete inventories of all significant environmental damages in the sort and long terms. All of this adds up to the impossibility of estimating in a meaningful way the inter-temporal opportunity costs associated with complex environmental functions. In theoretical terms, estimating the 'true' opportunity costs would depend on:

1. Knowing - or, at least, knowing within bounds - the inter-temporal production possibility frontier for economic production and environmental functions (and, ipso facto, the elasticities of substitution and the technological changes for the time span of analysis).
2. Knowing - or, at least, placing bounds on - the pattern of 'demand' for economic goods and environmental functions on the part of future generations; and this in turn depends on, inter alia, the distribution of purchasing power of future generations with unknowable preferences.

Given that there is no consensus on these matters, the use of any calculation results in a policy context will be controversial. The obstacles to applying the monetary valuation methods arise, in fact, directly from the attempt to transpose traditional economic valuation methodology into an arena for which it was not originally devised, namely:

1. Extension spatially and materially to the non-produced and largely non-commodified natural environment.
2. Extension temporally to the long term of ecological change and sustainability concerns.

The biophysical milieu evolves under the influence of forces that are largely independent of human action. On the other hand, this same milieu is subject to uncontrolled (and increasingly severe) perturbation as a 'side effect' of human economic activity. Mineral and hydrocarbon natural resources are, for all practical purposes, non-renewable (Peet 1992). The complex habitats that furnish life support functions for human and other species cannot be produced in factories. So restoration of ecosystems that are damaged or altered through economic activity or pollution, is often impossible. Ecosystem change and biosphere dynamics are not controllable by human intervention in the same way that commodity production processes are (Godard 1984, Norgaard 1994 and O'Connor 1989, 1994). For all these reasons, the provision of many environmental services and also of harmful effects, is characterised by time irreversibilities. Ecological harms include the risks and burdens falling on people as a result of pollution or exploitation - for example disturbed or degraded ecosystems, interruptions to ecological life support cycles, carcinogenic substances and toxic substances in workplaces and in homes and loss of food production capacity. The unplanned 'side effects' on ecological distribution will, in many cases, fully emerge only over long periods of time and across large distances. The interested parties may be extremely diffuse (for example people suffering from health problems induced by or aggravated by urban pollution or carcinogenic substances), or hypothetical in character (future generations that may be affected by climate change, accumulation of toxic wastes). These uncertainties are inherent in the complexity of ecosystem interactions and timescales of change. Climate change is an obvious case (Hourcade 1994 and Spash 1994a, 1994b); toxic waste disposal is another.

Apart from scientific uncertainties about economic and ecological evolutions, there are also irreducibly social obstacles to specification of opportunity costs in monetary terms - linked, for example, to notions of rights to life or property for other people or other species; to people's individual and collective senses of the sacred; or to natural or built features that are paramount matters of local identity. When people express, for example, a love of a particular scenery or preferences for a world with wolves and whales rather than one without wolves and whales, they are affirming the goodness of a certain order of things, which is quite different from their need to buy milk or bread. They are signalling a sort of affection or caring and probably also a desire that society as a whole should take more proper account of it.

Time and Value

The irreversibilities of ecological changes, often foreseen as adverse, bring the problems of the long term and of uncertainty into the mainstream of moral and political attention. In valuation terms, the question is how to give weight to long-term concerns at the same time as admitting the difficulties of quantification of the possible effects of actions taken in the present day.

The conventional monetisation techniques allied to optimisation and putative efficiency preoccupations, adopt the device of present value for comparing investment and resource use alternatives whose costs and benefits are distributed over time. Examples include the modelling of economic costs and benefits of different technological choices for energy supply and for the abatement of carbon dioxide (and other) emissions thought to be contributing to climate change. There is now quite a large literature (for critical appraisals of features of some typical models of optimal abatement of CO_2, see among others: Funtowicz and Ravetz 1994 and Howarth 1996). A typical feature is the reliance on mathematical constrained maximisation techniques to define an optimal abatement trajectory for the economy in question; in most cases this is net present value maximisation with a positive time discount rate.

This practice of time discounting involves several layers of assumptions. First, there is the premise of the commensurability of present costs/benefits with future costs/benefits, which permits aggregation over time to measure a best result for society for the horizon in time. Second, CBA normally weights costs and benefits differently depending on the time at which they occur. By applying a social discount rate, future benefits and costs are converted to present values when aggregating costs and benefits. With a positive discount rate, there is the result that a contribution to production or damage (a good or a bad) in the future counts less than the same output (good or bad) in the present.[3]

In the same spirit, the device of *expected value* is used to permit the extension of the CBA optimisation approach to situations of uncertainty. Put briefly, within the logic of traditional CBA, elements of uncertainty may be internalised if predicted outcomes are replaced by probability distributions (for all outcomes imagined as possible) and the values associated with outcomes are replaced by expected values (for example, expected utility maximisation). Two main variants exist:

1. The first arrives at the expected value of some action or effect (good or bad) by taking people's estimates for each conceivable outcome as if it were certain to materialise, then weights this value by the (alleged) actual probability of its occurring.

2. The second admits that defining actual ('objective') probability distributions is often open to doubt and arrives at the expected value by taking people's own subjective estimates of the probabilities, whether or not these appear justified from some 'expert's' point of view.

While the mathematical formalism lends an aura of precise quantification to the evaluation procedure, these are situations where precise quantification is quite impossible. First, it is impossible to quantify all the roles played by the environment as a source of livelihood and as a site for waste disposal. Second, long-term ecological effects of many economic decisions are unquantifiable and in any case will depend on actions subsequently taken, interwoven with side effects of other past actions. So 'probability distributions' for future outcomes do not really exist (which is different from not knowing them). As such, the approach is unlikely to produce decision support information which commands scientific or political consensus. Underlying disagreements on scientific, political and ethical matters may end up reframed

---

[3] If a preference to avoid some damage is n ecus, the annual discount rate is r, then the preferences in t years time is $n/(1+r)t$. Thus, for example, if we assume a preference to avoid toxic damage expressed today at willingness to pay value of 1000 ecus, then applying a discount rate of 5 per cent, the *present value* of the same toxic damage occurring in 50 years time would be $1000/(1.05)^{50}$ ecus = 87.2 ecus. The further into the future, the lower the value.

in the arcane language of modelling, but without being resolved at all.[4]

The NPV optimisation and expected value procedures are grounded on the hypothesis of making tradeoffs between, *inter alia*, the present generation's economic welfare and the possible exposure of future generations to unlivable damages. This substitutability assumption is not only difficult to quantify, it is furthermore open to ethical objection. In effect, discounting combined with NPV optimising appears to provide a rationale for displacing environmental damage into the future, since the value placed upon damage felt in the future will be smaller then the same dollar value of current consumption. As many commentators have pointed out, it is one thing to be impatient yourself, that is, have a preference for consumption desires to be satisfied now rather than later. This relates to what is optimal for me or you a consumer making choices with a given budget constraint. It does not resolve the question of what is or might be fair or unfair between generations.

In the context of model solutions obtained with PVU/NPV maximisation as the social optimum criterion, the inter-temporal distribution of output or purchasing power is interdependent with the interest rate used for aggregating the output across time or with the social discount rate used for weighting the relative significance of consumption across generations (Howarth 1996 and Faucheux, Muir and O'Connor 1997). In general terms, if environmental resources are scarce and depletable or degradable, then a shift of the inter-temporal distribution of output (and hence the relative purchasing power in models where the focus is also on consumption) from present to future is, under standard assumptions, associated with a lowering of the rate of value or utility discounting over time. That is, the selection of discount rate in this sort of modelling, just as in project cost-benefit analysis, involves implicitly or explicitly the making of inter temporal distributional choices.

The problem of the long term is at the heart of sustainability concerns. It is true that, in this context, decisions must be formulated with a view to keeping options open for the future. Yet while there are benefits and burdens

---

[4] In a similar way, the criterion of maximum present value of economic output, with a positive time-discount rate, may be applied in order to identify an optimal sequencing of investments in new energy supply capacity (photovoltaics, nuclear, wind alongside hydrocarbons). The results obtained are very sensitive to assumptions about the future unit costs of technology options, about the dynamics of learning (as reflected in the downward responsiveness of unit cost to research and development investment and learning-by-doing), and about the discount rate to be applied. In short, these models illuminate rather well the significance of technological as well as ecological uncertainties, but - precisely for this reason - they cannot have the traditional role of helping the policy maker to identify the *best* technological strategies. Rather, the models function as parables or heuristic devices that can help to bring to attention the significance that such features as *endogenous learning* may have on output paths and that 'no regrets' might have on a preferred abatement policy.

to be assessed, little is gained from complicated discussions about public and market interest rates, social and private preferences, risks and portfolio choices. In the context of sustainability goals, the best way out of these analytical convolutions is simply to emphasise that the basic issues refer not to criteria for optimisation but rather to the inter-temporal distribution of benefits and costs including exposure to different sorts of environmental changes and hazards. In practice the best way to deal with 'discounting' questions is to formulate explicitly the intertemporal performance goals (for example, social and economic distribution, ecosystem protection, biodiversity and the like) and then to assess the compatibility of policy alternatives with these goals.

THE DISTRIBUTION OF SUSTAINABILITY

For many categories of environmental change, estimations of the impacts (harmful or otherwise) in monetary terms can only be incomplete and extremely speculative. Attempts to put money values on stocks of natural capital, on environmental life support functions and on damages that are spread over time and whose significance is sometimes as much ethical as biophysical, is often quite an artificial process. Monetary valuation of damages to environmental functions cannot, therefore, be a general objective.

But this is not the end of the road. It is not, in fact, necessary to base valuation studies on speculative calculations about the money value of environmental assets and damages. On the contrary, a more modest (and hence also more robust) approach is to confine monetary aspects of valuation to the question of economic resources that must be committed in order to specified hazards or categories of damage or to ensure the maintenance of specified dimensions of environmental quality. The logic of valuation would then be: First make the proposition to sustain/conserve the forms of life or environmental features in question (that is, avoid the production of toxic wastes, preserve a designated forest system, or the biological diversity, or other feature of nature) and then investigate what commitments this entails.

The crucial matter here is to appreciate the variety of forms that these commitments may and indeed would have to take. Consider any given sustainability objective, say a lake or a community or a bird rich ecosystem. The question *how much* it is worth may first be answered in terms of other opportunities foregone - that is, by making explicit the nature of the choices as to what forms of life are sustained and what other sustainability possibilities are foregone.

Framed in this way, it is easy to acknowledge that the identification of a commercial or tangible economic interest does not exhaust the enquiry into value. People in their different cultural settings articulate their sense of value about nature in multi-layered ways. The significance of nature and of built environments, is embodied in a person's or a community's way of life, in their institutions and taboos, in their principles and precepts of right conduct, their habits and forms of cooperation. Very often, explicit value statements about the environment emerge only when these principles are compromised or ways of life are threatened: *Value* then is associated with social processes of controversy and conflict. So *valuation* should be taken broadly to refer to people's notions of *what matters for the future and why*. Moreover, the persons or collectivities involved are faced not only with decisions between protection and damage, but with the distribution of different kinds of damage and benefits and with conflicts between the avoidance of environmental damage and various other social, economic and cultural objectives. Many of the adverse consequences of current environmental activity will also fall upon future generations and this raises ethical issues about our responsibilities.

These choices for the *distribution of sustainability* often cannot be quantified, or can only partly be quantified (often only in non-monetary and somewhat speculative terms). Nonetheless, we emphasise, these arbitrations over survival, expansion and disappearance of different forms of life, economies, ethical and aesthetic sensibilities, constitute real resource management choices. As such they can quite properly be seen as embodying statements of relative valuation. This is not the same valuation logic as is conveyed in, for example, the notion of ecologically right prices or in the proposals for creating legal rights to carbon dioxide emissions or to biological diversity and then organising a market in these rights so as to encourage an optimal use of these resources. The first of these notions abstracts away from the question: Sustaining of what and for whom? The second is related to the ideology of 'wealth maximisation', meaning maximisation of present value based on some existing structure of market power, purchasing power and control, which has nothing in particular to do with sustainability.

Sustainability in Ecological Economics Perspective

In ecological economics, sustainability conveys the requirement of maintenance and renewal, where the legacy of the past is transformed into the welfare base furnished towards the future (see, for example, Faucheux and O'Connor 1997). From this point of view, economic resource management must fulfil two complementary functions:

1.   The delivery of an ecological welfare base through assuring maintenance of critical environmental functions.

2. The delivery of an economic welfare base through production of economic goods and services.

We can start to give analytical form to this perspective by introducing a postulate of value incommensurability between economic and ecological domains, as follows. Ecological goods and services (natural resources, amenities, waste reception, environmental life support functions) are considered as broadly complementary with economic goods and services, but money valuations are not applied to the environmental functions as such. That is, while the two sets of goods/services both contribute to human welfare, they are not considered incommensurate.

Environmental quality is thus considered as a primary or 'basic' requirement for human welfare and for sustainable economic activity. Economic resources must be committed (directly or indirectly, in ways that we will discuss) in order to maintain the desirable level of environmental functions. This corresponds to the 'social demand' for maintenance of environmental functions. In this regard:

1. There is no way that this 'demand' - which in principle includes some provision for future generations and which includes demand for protection from environmental harms - can be expressed in a market like institution, because most of the interested parties cannot be present and many of the benefits in question are 'public' (and largely indivisible) in character. The best operational specification will be in non-monetary terms, through defining environmental standards, or norms, which represent a society's objectives for the delivery of the *ecological welfare base* to present and future generations.

2. Establishing priorities in environmental norm setting is a political process which involves an integration of scientific, economic and social considerations. Because of uncertainties and differences of opinion within a society, it is more appropriate to adopt a multiple criteria decision support framework and to speak of *satisfying* (contentment) rather than optimising (better and best). Furthermore, environmental priorities and policies will undergo continual revision as a social adaptation and negotiation process (Faucheux and Froger 1994, Faucheux and O'Connor 1997 and Brouwer *et al.* 1996).

3. Within the economic system, tradeoffs will exist between economic output and environmental maintenance and enhancement goals. In this respect, it is possible to apply the principle of cost effectiveness or *least economic cost* for achievement of environmental objectives (cf. Baumol and Oates 1971).

4. However, application of this principle for sustainability policy requires

careful problem framing and analysis. The economic efficiency (cost effectiveness) criterion may not be separable from distributional considerations and other social criteria (Martinez-Alier and O'Connor 1996 and Holland *et al.* 1996). Policy makers must compare options across the different values and objectives that inform our choices - economic, aesthetic, social justice, cultural, recreational and so on. Many of these considerations cannot be made commensurate with each other (O'Neill 1993 and Munda 1995). Resource requirements and effects of alternative course of action may be comparable in a number of different ways, but often this information cannot easily be brought into a single unit of measure and even where a common unit is possible (energy flow units) this may not be decisive for judging between alternatives. An overall 'optimising' calculation is therefore not possible. Rather, an evaluative procedure can structure the problem for the decision maker in the sense of presenting the information about the different objectives and the various bases for comparisons in a systematic way.

Valuation as Choices Amongst Different Possibilities of Solidarity

We have introduced the idea of complementarity between economic and ecological sources of wellbeing, but this certainly does not mean separateness of the two domains. Representation of 'sustainable development' as a symbiosis between economic production and ecological (re)production implies emphasis on managing and investing in the reproduction, transformation and renewal of the terrestrial habitats that are not just raw materials sources but veritable life support systems that underpin commodity production systems. These are also habitats in the sense of being the places of life, invested with social and community significance, or meanings. So valuation for sustainability cannot be separated from the idea of actions whose effect is to sustain this or that form of life, way of life - in the cultural and ecological economic sense.

The view of sustainable development as a process based on cycles of renewal and regeneration, a symbiosis of ecological and economic reproduction, is already found in the concept of *eco-development* expounded in the early 1970s by some international agencies, at first with reference mainly to rural development projects in the Third World. At that time it joined a large array of concepts and terminologies proposing an 'alternative' development, whose common feature was rejection of the dominant views of development couched in terms of rapid GNP growth, throughput of resources and technological modernisation. More specifically, as Ignacy Sachs wrote;

Ecodevelopment is a development of peoples through themselves utilising to the best the natural resources, adapting to an environment which they transform without destroying it. ... Development in its entirety has to be impregnated, motivated, underpinned by the research of a dynamic equilibrium between the life process and the collective activities of human groups planted in their particular place and time. (1980, p. 37)

Emphasis is on 'the cultural contributions of the peoples concerned' in the effort to 'transform the various elements of their environment into useful resources' (Sachs 1984, pp. 28-30). In effect, systems concepts from ecology, such as cycles and functional harmonisation, were transposed to the social and organisational domain. In biophysical terms ecodevelopment aims at achieving a lasting symbiosis between humanity and the earth; at the social level the search is for a harmonisation of relationships based on cooperation at local and inter-national levels to achieve economic equity.

This picture is good as far as it goes. But in order to allow resource management decisions to be framed incisively we must add a further dimension, that of conflict resolution or choices of which sustainability and for whom? The simple invocation of *symbiosis* or *sustainability* as a reference concept does not serve as a decision criterion. It does not, for example, guarantee the conservation of specified productive or reproductive potentialities of any particular society or ecosystem! Nor does it assure the sustaining of all the particular interests, communities, or ecologies thus given hope. So we must introduce explicitly the idea of human actions and policy choices as involving decisions about the distribution of sustainability: Which interests and forms of life will be sustained and which ones left behind, relinquished, destroyed or left to rot?

Let us, for a moment, consider abstractly the requirements for distributed sustainability (another term would be disaggregated sustainability; see O'Connor and Martinez-Alier 1996) in the following terms: The simultaneous maintenance of the stock levels of a set of interdependent communities' respective 'capitals'. The capitals in question will be ecological and produced, material, cultural, human and so on. (The category becomes very broad.) Suppose we have a set of interdependent 'sectors', such as manufacturing, households, forests, marine ecosystems and so on. Each sector may be presumed to have its characteristic 'capitals,' and each sector provides useful services or produced surpluses (as well as possible dis-services) to other sectors, while receiving inputs from others in its turn. It is convenient to assume that every economic and ecological capital has a human proprietor (a society or social group) and that this human proprietor group is sustained along with the capital(s) that they 'own'.

We will say that an ensemble of capitals is sustained in a material sense, as long as sectors give to each other and receive from each other, exactly what each needs for self-maintenance. This would mean a cyclical dynamism - a symbiosis where each sector gives to the others (as a group) what they need in order to be able, in turn, to furnish the inputs required by the first.

But alternatively, there might be 'imbalance'. One possible sort of imbalance is a 'supply crisis' which could arise for any part of the symbiosis if the required inputs are physically not available, or if the costs associated with obtaining needed inputs (through trades with other proprietors) is higher than the sector proprietors can afford, or if the needed inputs are withheld by the action of other proprietors. The consequence of an enduring supply crisis is the diminution or cessation of activity of the sectors thus deprived. The symbiosis is broken. Another aspect of possible imbalance is a demand crisis which could occur if no other economic or ecological sector has a 'use' for the outputs in question, or the sectors having a use for them cannot afford to pay for them. An enduring demand side crisis may mean a buildup of unwanted surpluses (including various categories of toxins and wastes) and may also mean that the sector's proprietors are not able to obtain through trades the inputs needed for their own sustenance.

Take the example of flowing water resources, as in a river. The watershed defines a *natural* unit of ecosystem analysis; the flow patterns are woven into the habitats of hillside, swamp, riverbank and aquatic species; but the water may also be considered as a valuable input for industrial, agricultural and urban consumptions. Who owns the water? If water flow is diverted for irrigation, for factory use, for power plant cooling or for urban drinking supply purposes (for example), or if the continuity of flow is interrupted through dams, reservoirs and other forms of storage, these natural forms of life may be put at risk.

Conversely, water that has been used for economic purposes may be allowed to flow back into natural systems in a dirtied or polluted condition; this also can menace the viability of life forms and can pose problems for human health. Finally, rivers are not always docile systems and (for example) floods can damage or destroy the natural habitats as well as the built human habitats that have been constructed over time. The decisions for management of flowing water systems can thus be understood as a problem of the distribution of sustainability; and the regulation of access to water and the control of water quality can be posed in terms of distinct (yet often interdependent) needs for sustainability and of the vulnerabilities of the different habitats and forms of life to changes - controlled or uncontrolled - in the terms of access and quality.

Sustainability of the set of sectors and proprietors making up the watershed together (and also, by extension, linked further afield) means that the sectors that are mutually interdependent for their water flows must operate (de facto or by design) in solidarity with each other. If some users accumulate water stocks or flow volumes at the expense of others, or some users maintain their activity while dumping their toxic wastes and unwanted refuse into waters flowing on to other populations and habitats, we could speak of an uneven distribution of the conditions for sustainability. So lived sustainability implies a logic of reciprocation expressed on material and social planes. Distributed sustainability means affirming the richness of diversity and accepting the obligations and inconveniences alongside the pleasures of coexistence with others considered as friends and members of extended community (human and non-human life).

How may the various candidates for sustainability - for example terrestrial and aquatic ecosystems in natural or human modified form, agricultural systems, rural and urban communities in their physical settings - be assessed in relation to each other? We are forced to acknowledge incommensurabilities. In a typical watershed management situation the maintenance of (say) bird populations and riverbank rural economies through flood management assuring year round flows, would serve different communities of interest from (say) damming and piping the water for urban supply.

From a decision making and policy assessment point of view there are both advantages and disadvantages of sacrificing the ideal of full commensurability of valuations. The approach being suggested here emphasises the need to present information for discussion and decision making procedures in ways that will not yield a unique ranking of options but that make explicit the sorts of social choices and ecological and economic tradeoffs that might be involved. The disadvantage is the greater complexity in the way of framing decision problems. The advantage is the richer appreciation of the significance to different communities of interest of the choices to be made.

Choices about sustainability goals and priorities are unavoidable. The way they are made can vary from acts of straight violence to patient efforts at accommodation of distinct interests. Where compromise or reconciliation is sought after, the decision has to involve an iterative collective process of analysis, debates, negotiations, tradeoffs and compromises with the aim of ending up with a solution that is satisfactory in terms of economic, social and ecological imperatives. Thus the selection of spaces and species to be protected, pollutants to be curbed and more generally the *social demand* for this or that level of environmental functions to be 'sustained' emerges from a choice process that is essentially collective and socio-political rather than technical in nature.

LIVING SUSTAINABILITY: THE EMBODIED SOCIAL VALUE OF FOREST ISLANDS IN FRANCE

As an example of this perspective on valuation for sustainability, we now consider the case of small forest pockets in agricultural France, in the Gâtinais region some 100 kilometres south of Paris. The analysis reported here is in relatively early stages and our theoretical tools and frameworks are being developed interactively with empirical studies. There are many small such forest islands *(îlots boisés)*, which have been the object of several recent studies (carried out by several different research teams) looking at various ecological, economic and social dimensions (see Dubien 1993, de la Gorce 1994). We do not detail the findings of this background literature here; rather we report simply on one part of our own methodological work which is designed to frame subsequent phases of our own empirical investigation (see also O'Connor and Heron 1996).

We first identify our scale of analysis. As Richard Norgaard (1988, 1994) suggests in his coevolutionary perspective on sustainability, the questions of coexistence and coevolution can usefully be considered along several different spatial, as well as temporal scales - from specific 'local' communities and territories, through nation states, regions and trade blocs, to the global level. At each scale, one can consider the community or system for itself and also its exchanges and coevolution with other systems and communities, asking: 'Will the resource base, environment, technologies and culture evolve over time in a mutually reinforcing manner? ... Will [the resource users] destroy the local resource base and environment or, just as bad, the local people and their cultural system?' (Norgaard 1988, p. 607).

These characterisations address the sustainability of the interactions between people and their environments over time. They refer particularly to 'the sustainability of the interactions between regions and cultural systems' (ibid., p. 607), that is, to exchange and reciprocal transformation as a cultural as well as material process. A coevolution, if it occurs, is a biophysical symbiosis; but it is not simply the biophysical coexistence. The crucial questions of autonomy and vitality are located on the symbolic planes as well as the biophysical planes. Economic autonomy refers not just to indigenous sources of natural wealth, it also means, in cultural terms, the experience and action of being part of a meaningful and creative social process. This raises the question: In what ways does a person feel part of a community, in what ways do their choices and actions depend on their sense of being part of a community?

We refer for illustration to a particular ecosystem, the Bouchereau woodland. This is about 40 hectares in area. We want to look into the ways in which the different classes of owners and users of the forests attach significance (value?) to the forest. Our approach is one that places the emphasis on a whole socio-ecological system as a *unité de valeur*. The emphasis is on obtaining a picture of the local economy community ecosystem features, but implicitly this *unit of analysis* is embedded in the larger fabric of French society, agricultural practice and patrimony. We do not, in this very incomplete presentation, discuss these larger scale linkages, though obviously their analysis is necessary for a full diagnosis of the prospects and vulnerabilities of the local values.

As an heuristic tool, a quite simple dynamic simulation model has been developed which represents the evolving forest system through the interaction of human and ecological forces (Heron 1996). We think of the value of the forest as embodied in the enduring system. Using the model, we can explore possible evolutions of the forest unit which are slow and quasi-irreversible. The future of the forest (in the model) is determined by the cumulative effect of many different classes of interactions. The influence diagram of the model is shown in Figure 8.1.

In effect, the influence diagram serves as a way of organising the description of the woodland. There is not space to detail all the components and relationships here and we will concentrate on only a few key points. First it is necessary to note the variety of actors (or stakeholders?) who contribute to the forest system's behaviour over time. Second, we discuss the variety of values attributed to the forest system and in particular the question of what constitutes biodiversity value in such a woodland. Third, we consider the relationship between community viability and forest value.

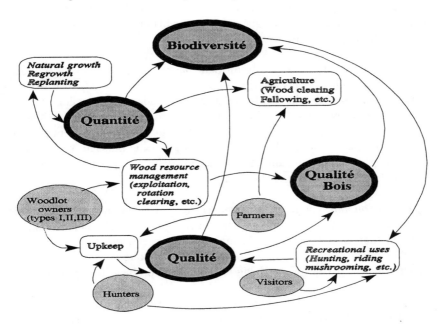

Figure 8.1   *The woodland model*

The Human Actors

(a) The owners: As of 1991 (the most recent year of collected statistics), the woodland was fragmented into 289 lots, distributed across 116 separate owners most of whom live in the nearby farming communities - though hereditary transmission means a growing proportion of distant owners. This is *private property* to some extent. The wood is exploited by owners, primarily as a source of fuel, with a smaller amount harvested for timber or woodworking. For the model we define three classes of proprietor: Type 1 does not carry out any maintenance of their woodland lots. Type 2 carries out periodic clear felling (rotation period of around 30-45 years). Type 3 undertakes continual maintenance and selective harvesting.

(b) The farmers: Whose lands adjoin the forest. There are about 20 such farmers, the majority being around 60 years old. There are pressures on these farmers to leave some lands fallow (European agricultural policy directives) and at present the tendency is to let areas adjacent to the forest lie 'unproductive' so that they become a sort of scrubland which is a good habitat for some forms of wildlife.

(c) The hunters: Hunting is a traditional pastime and the woodlands are privileged domains for this activity. In the district of the Bouchereau woods there is a hunting club with nearly 100 members, made up of woodlot owners, farmers and a few outsiders. Since the 1970s, the game populations have diminished markedly, due in part to isolation of the woodland and in part to illicit hunting by outsiders. Various measures are being pursued by the (also diminishing) hunting community to enhance the wildlife populations while still preserving the spontaneity of the hunt.

(d) Visitors on foot: The forest is valued as a recreational opportunity and also for its contributions to the local cuisine: Berries, mushrooms, snails and other items in their seasons. These are mostly local users, but there are some outsiders. In some instances there is inconsiderate picking or over exploitation which impairs renewal of the living resource: The problem of free riders.

(e) Those acting for the community: There are numerous groups and authorities which represent in differing ways a common interest for the district. These include the local commune which undertakes maintenance of the public walkways and roads, including some replanting in consultation with the hunting club and an environmental organisation *Les Mains Vertes du Gâtinais* whose preoccupation is preservation of the *patrimony naturel*. The national hunting authority and the regional council both also play important

roles in defining conservation perspectives, priorities and measures for implementation.

The various categories of human actors can be understood as agents of ecosystem stability and of change, their significance not being defined externally but rather depending on the overall state of *balance* - or imbalance - in the woodland system dynamics. We give some indications of these interactive dynamics below. Note that we do not represent the commune, regional, or national level organisations explicitly in the model, but their influence directly and indirectly on the other actors needs to be understood.

The Non Market Forest Values

The description of the various classes of actors already suggests the variety of values attributed to the forest system. There are direct economic values of the wood as fuel and (to a lesser degree) as timber and of the food items to be found in the forest; these are non-market values and are inseparable from a *customary* way of life. Similarly the hunt may be said to constitute a recreational value, but it is also inseparable from the tissues of local social life. In the model, we summarise the evolution of the woodland values through four aggregate indicator values. These are woodland size (*Quantité*), woodland aesthetic quality (*Qualité*), the timber quality (*Qualité bois*) and an indicator of biological richness (*Biodiversité*).

(a) The *Quantité* is measured by the estimated volume of wood and the surface area of the forest. As it happens, there are no immediately visible pressures for the reduction of the woodland area and our scenarios suggest that it is conceivable that, through replanting and reversion of adjacent fallow land, the Quantity could slightly increase over the decades to come.

(b) The woodland *Qualité* is a positive function of the amount of maintenance effort and a negative function of the volume of hunting and walking activity; note that hunting and walking levels are themselves sensitive to the aesthetic quality and biodiversity of the forest.

(c) The timber quality (*Qualité bois*) depends on the amount of maintenance and the patterns of wood cutting, the selective harvesting being the most advantageous.

(d) The *Biodiversité* is assumed to be an increasing function of the two sorts of woodland quality and the quantity; in this sense it is a variable presumed to express the *state* of the forest. Obviously this is a very simplistic representation and very much open to discussion. It nonetheless has a quite good heuristic value.

In brief, the forest considered as an ecological system is open to several outside influences, notably human ones, which may assure its reproduction or, alternatively, bring about its decay or disappearance. The model shows how relatively small changes in the human actors' behaviour, or in the relative and absolute size of different user populations, can in the long term be critical for the robustness or diminution of the forest as a source of economic, wildlife, lifestyle and recreational values. For didactic purposes, we developed two scenarios for evolutions over 50 years of the model forest (see Heron 1996):

1. In Scenario One it was hypothesised that Type 1 owners come to predominate, meaning that there is less and less maintenance of the woodland.
2. In Scenario Two it was hypothesised that owners Type 2 and 3 predominate, so that the wood resource is closely managed.

In Scenario One the forest *Quantité* increases but the aesthetic value *Qualité* and the timber quality *Qualité bois* both decline. The result is that the *Biodiversité* also declines. In Scenario Two, the *Quantité* decreases slightly over 50 years, the aesthetic *Qualité* is stable, the timber *Qualité bois* improves and the *Biodiversité* indicator rises significantly. The closely tended forest has a higher value according to the model indicators.

Value From Within: The Relationship Between Community Viability and Forest Value

What insights can we obtain from this sort of modelling activity? It is important to note that this model is not predictive. It is extremely simplistic and has didactic utility. What it does is bring together, as shown in the influence diagram, a set of propositions derived from empirical investigation about key categories and effects of human interaction with the forest. In this way the model helps us to sharpen some questions (while no doubt neglecting many others). For example, what can we learn from the result in Scenario One that, when the woodland area increases and, due to neglect, it becomes more wild, at the same time the *Biodiversité* indicator diminishes? And conversely, in Scenario Two, the *Biodiversité* indicator rises when the proprietors are attending more closely the wood resource?

First, we can answer by mentioning that, worldwide, the quantification of biodiversity is a fairly cloudy business anyway, so the excessive simplicity and rather arbitrary derivation of our *Biodiversité* indicator draws attention to the fact that the object and basis for measurement is far from clear. Second, we may bring back to mind that this little forest is extremely *anthropomorphised*, that is, its current state is the product of a long history of human tending and utilisation. It is therefore quite possible (though in reality we cannot say for sure either way) that the biological diversity (including flowering species, mushrooms, butterflies, birds, game animals and various species of trees) might indeed fall off if the woodland is generally neglected over a long period of time. In any case it is fairly sure that the existing distribution of biological diversity is very strongly a function of past and present human activity. Third, therefore, we are reminded that the values of this forest associated with just this diversity are inseparable from the customary ways of life of the people involved.

We are not dealing with intrinsic value here as if it were independent of human perception; rather we are documenting the human appreciation of the richness of the forest life forms. No doubt there is an economic value of the wood as fuel and (to a lesser degree) as timber and perhaps also of the food items to be found in the forest; no doubt the hunt may be said to be a recreational value (perhaps quantifiable in terms of other opportunities foregone and the travel costs involved). Yet all these non-market values and the labours of woodlot tending and other maintenance are inseparable from the tissue of a customary way of life. The men, women and children who search for the mushrooms and berries probably do not make a rational use of their time: They talk and they play. The investments of time, thought and effort in woodlot maintenance, trail clearing and replanting would be unlikely to take place on an individualistic basis: They depend for the meaning and justification on the membership (*appartenance*) of each person to the social groups and networks that constitute this *way of life*. So notwithstanding the apparent private dimensions of the woodlot property as an exploitable resource, we are presented with a wealth held in common: This is the significance (value) of the forest to the members of the community. It is a *value as a whole* and it is not easy to see how it could be made divisible. The tending of the forest is a sort of metaphor for the maintaining of human community; and the one and the other are vulnerable to decline, death or decay.

Valuation of Sustainability

As already mentioned, the representation of sustainability dynamics and vulnerability given here is very preliminary and incomplete. It will be necessary to embed the investigation of the local socio-ecosystem features in the larger contexts of commercial and non-commercial agricultural practice and the institutional as well as cultural framing of French management of patrimony. Nonetheless there are already some insights we can claim with some direct policy relevance.

First, let us ask: Do the investments of time and money and of meaning, made by the owners/users of the forest make sense in terms of economic cost-benefit analysis? The answer would have to be: Quite possibly not (although this is a question that we want to investigate in ongoing research). If the questions of woodland value are posed in monetary terms, then we should not expect profitability, because these are largely traditional practices that, for the most part, have been based on a *communal logic of reproduction and renewal* rather than a logic of profit.

On the other hand, this tradition may be dying and the forest value with it. In view of the aging and diminishing economic vigour of the community of interested local users and owners, the *organic* maintenance of the woodland may be at risk. Suppose a demand is expressed to have an external agency assume responsibility for maintaining the woodland as an amenity value. Can it be expected that a new generation of users, not having the same sorts of communal roots, would be willing to pay money (through, for example, local or national taxes, or access fees) in scale equivalent to the embodied time willingness to pay of the traditional communal owners? Quite possibly not. The economists' standard explanation might then be that the population's tastes would have changed (and in fact, it would also be that the population itself has changed). This explanation could be true, yet is it the most useful one? Another form of explanation would be that the forest community symbiosis as a structure of lived and shared meaning (and a form of local economic life) has not been sustained. This second form of explanation is possibly not any more true than the first, but it may be a more useful one for helping to decide about rural and regional development and nature conservation policies.

CONCLUDING REMARKS

The concepts and arguments presented briefly here can, we would suggest, fruitfully be applied as a framework for identifying the dimensions of choice for many sorts of renewable natural capital management problems. For any ecosystem, environmental function or category of natural resource, the process of identification of alternative uses and their benefits and costs is inseparable from the question of the distinct (but often interdependent) communities of interest to be, or not to be, sustained.[5]

To avoid the accusation that this is merely a tarted up descriptive (resource inventory) analysis, we conclude by attempting to explain what is distinctive about the *normative* as well as *positive* dimensions of our notions of valuation for sustainability. In part the argument of this chapter is a version of the old quarrel of welfare economics, concerning the inseparability of allocative (efficiency) and distributional (equity) goals. But we give a particular slant and meaning to this debate. First, we insist that the further that concerns of environmental policy extend to the long-term future, the more will inter-temporal distributional considerations need to predominate over allocative efficiency in policy appraisal. Second, we insist that the further that concerns for environmental values extend into the domains of aesthetic and cultural as well as economic appreciation of natural cycles and systems, the more difficult it becomes to apply (or justify) the assumptions of value commensurability and substitutability that underlie conventional economic valuation methodology. For both these reasons, it is necessary to frame decision making ideals in terms such as compromise and fairness, distinguishing this sharply from the more familiar optimisation and its close cousin best balance.

The nature of the choices inherent in the setting of ecological, social and economic sustainability goals cannot be expressed satisfactorily in such terms as optimal choice, nor can the pursuit of sustainability goals be guided by market based valuations. The reasons for this are simple. Optimal choice requires, at some level or other, the application of a single principle for ordering, judging and ranking what is right and best. But sustainability in its general social economic ecological acceptance signals a desire to accommodate a multiplicity of different ordering principles and involves cherishing the richness of living with and living in nature with its great variety of life forms. Market type valuations are based on a logic of rational exploitation of an external domain (the free gifts and services of nature) and on a similarly utilitarian attitude towards others as fellow economic agents (producers, traders and consumers and police, reconciled contractually in a general equilibrium). But valuation for sustainability starts from and seeks to affirm, an experience of symbiosis, deeper and more complex than a rational contractual form.

Decision making for sustainability has to be based on a spirit of willingness to share the riches of this planet - meaning economic and ecological solidarity in reciprocal exchanges and also inter-temporal solidarity. As members of ecological and human communities, we are each others' guests. Receiving

---

[5] At present a number of research studies are in progress, which seek to apply this perspective on valuation and decision support to different renewable natural capital domains, including (among others) water resources and wild and agricultural biodiversity - and the associated cultural variety and richness of knowledge.

from others and from the past, we may affirm our place in the living world in the ways we seek in turn to provide for the future. In this way the gifts of nature are renewed and we acknowledge gratitude or appreciation for the gifts received by making counter gifts. This is a different logic of valuation from what 'the market' can provide.

The fundamental normative orientations are established along two axes. First, when a sustainability goal is first expressed, from which point of view feasibility and opportunity costs can be explored. Second, when attention is given to the question of how to reconcile this goal to the diverse sustainability concerns expressed by others. In short, a sustainability commitment even if affirmed individually, must find collective expression and be accommodated with other parties' concerns. In situations of indeterminacy and conflict (which are most often the case), many different sustainability commitments might be identified and explored. Difficult choices and compromises will have to be made. This is the matter of the distribution of sustainability; these are not the sorts of choices that may be determined on allocative efficiency grounds. If there is to be any alternative to endemic war on various scales of a small planet, these are choices that must be made on a basis of purposefulness and compassion, acknowledging the grief of those whose principles, sentiments and interests are not respected and sharing empathically in this pain.

REFERENCES

Asheim, G.B. 1994. 'Net national product as an indicator of sustainability', *Scandinavian Journal of Economics*, 96, 257-65.

Baumol, W. and Oates, W. 1971. 'The use of standards and prices for the protection of the environment', *Swedish Journal of Economics*, 73, 42-54.

Brouwer, R., O'Connor, M. and Radermacher, W. 1996. 'Defining cost effective responses to environmental deterioration in a periodic accounting system', paper for the London Group Meeting, Stockholm, 28-31 May 1996.

Common, M.S. 1993. 'A cost-effective environmentally adjusted performance indicator', Discussion Papers in Environmental Economics and Environmental Management 9307, Department of Environmental Economics and Environmental Management, University of York, UK.

Dasgupta, P. and Heal, G. 1974. 'The optimal depletion of exhaustible resources', *Review of Economic Studies*, 41, 1-23.

Dubien, I. 1993. 'Devenir des Ilots Boisés du Gâtinais Nord Occidental', research essay *mémoire de DEA*. UFR d'Economie, Université de Paris I, France.

de la Gorce, L. 1994. 'Homme/biodiversité: l'impact des coupes forestières sur la richesse floristique d'un îlot boisé en plaine de grande culture', research essay *maîtrise*. UFR de Géographie, Université de Paris I, France.

Faucheux S. and Froger G. 1994. 'Le "revenue national soutenable", est-il un indicateur de soutenabilité?', *Revue Française d'Economie*, 92, 3-37.

Faucheux, S. and O'Connor, M. (eds) 1997. *Valuation for Sustainable Development: Methods and Policy Indicators*. Aldershot: Edward Elgar, in press.

Faucheux, S., Muir, E. and O'Connor, M. 1997. 'Neoclassical theory of natural capital and "weak" indicators for sustainability', *Land Economics* (forthcoming).

Funtowicz, S. and Ravetz, J. 1994. 'The worth of a songbird: Ecological economics as a post-normal science', *Ecological Economics*, 10, 197-207.

Godard, O. 1984. 'Autonomie socio-économique et externalisation de l'environnement: La théorie néoclassique mise en perspective', *Economie Appliquée*, 37(2), 315-45.

Hanley, N. and Spash, C.L. 1993. *Cost-Benefit Analysis and the Environment*. Aldershot: Edward Elgar.

Heron, C. 1996. 'La représentation systémique de l'îlot boisé: Vers une mise en evidence de la valeur sociale', *Cahiers du C3ED*, Université de Versailles, France.

Holland, A., O'Connor, M. and O'Neill J. 1996. 'Costing environmental damage: A critical survey of current theory and practice and recommendations for policy implementations', Report for the Directorate General for Research, STOA programme, European Parliament, April 1996.

Hourcade, J.-C. 1994. 'Analyse économique et gestion des risques climatiques', *Natures, Sciences, Sociétés*, 23, July, 202-11.

Howarth, R.B. 1996. 'An overlapping generations model of climate-economy interactions', paper presented to the 4th Conference of the ISEE, Boston 4-7 August.

Jakobsson, K.M. and Dragun, A.K. 1996. *Contingent Valuation and Endangered Species: Methodological Issues and Applications*. Cheltenham: Edward Elgar.

Martinez-Alier, J. and O'Connor, M. 1996. 'Economic and ecological distribution conflicts, in Costanza, R., Segura, O. and Martinez-Alier, J. (eds), *Getting Down to Earth: Practical Applications of Ecological Economics*. Washington DC: Island Press, pp. 153-84.

Munda, G. 1995. *Multicriteria Evaluation in a Fuzzy Environment. Theory and Applications in Ecological Economics*. Berlin: Physica-Verlag.

Norgaard, R.B. 1988. 'Sustainable development: A co-evolutionary view', *Futures*, 20, 606-20.

Norgaard, R.B. 1994. *Development Betrayed: The End of Progress and a Coevolutionary Revisioning of the Future*. London: Routledge.

O'Connor, M. 1989. 'Codependency and indeterminacy: A critique of the theory of production', *Capitalism, Nature, Socialism*, 3, 33-57.

O'Connor, M. (ed.) 1994. *Is Capitalism Sustainable? Political Economy and the Politics of Ecology*. New York: Guilford Publications.

O'Connor, M. and Heron, C. 1996. 'Forest value and the distribution of sustainability: Valuation concepts and methodology in application to forest islands in agricultural zones in France', paper prepared for the International Symposium on The Non-Market Benefits of Forestry sponsored by the Forestry Commission of the United Kingdom, held at Edinburgh, Scotland, 24-28 June 1996.

O'Connor, M. and Martinez-Alier, J. 1996. 'Ecological distribution and distributed sustainability', in Faucheux, S., O'Connor, M. and van der Straaten, J. (eds), *Sustainable Development: Concepts, Rationalities and Strategies*. Dordrecht: Kluwer.

O'Neill J. 1993. *Ecology, Policy and Politics. Human Well-being and the Natural World*. London: Routledge.

Peet, J. 1992. *Energy and the Ecological Economics of Sustainability*. Washington DC: Island Press.

Pezzey, J. 1997. 'Sustainability constraints, present value maximisation and intergenerational welfare', *Land Economics* (forthcoming).

Pezzey, J. and Withagen C. 1995. 'Single-peakedness and initial sustainability in capital-resource economies', Discussion Paper No. 95-09, Department of Economics, University College London.

Sachs, I. 1980. *Stratégies de l'écodéveloppement*. Paris: Les Editions Ouvrières.

Sachs, I. 1984. *Développer les Champs de Planification*. UCI. English translation by Fawcett, P. 1987. *Development and Planning*. Maison des Sciences de l'Homme, Paris and Cambridge University Press, Cambridge.

Solow, R.M. 1974. 'Intergenerational equity and exhaustible resources', *Review of Economic Studies*, 41, 29-46.

Spash, C.L. 1994a. 'Trying to find the right approach to greenhouse economics: Some reflections upon the role of CBA', *Analyse and Kritik: Zeitschrift für Socialwissenschafen* 16(2), 186-99.

Spash, C.L. 1994b. 'Double CO_2 and beyond: Benefits, costs and compensation', *Ecological Economics*, 10(1), 27-36.

Stiglitz, J.E. 1974. 'Growth with exhaustible natural resources: Efficient and optimal growth paths', *Review of Economic Studies*, 41, 123-37.

Vanoli, A. 1996. 'Modelling and accounting work in national accounts', paper for the special IARIW conference on integrated environmental and economic accounting in theory and practice, Tokyo, March 5-8 1996.

9. Environment, Equity and Welfare Economics

Andrew Dragun and Kristin Jakobsson[1]

INTRODUCTION

Environmental conservation and quality are among the most pressing social issues confronting modern society. Given that most human activities are priced in some way or other, there is a temptation to down play or ignore environmental conservation and quality values as a function of the non-existence of prices for environmental considerations.

Modern welfare economic theory does not handle the problem of the environmental very well. The orthodox Pigovian approach tends to focus on valuation issues in relation to the 'non-priced' benefits and costs of the environment generally within which a range of indirect valuation approaches have been innovated. But most of the indirect valuation approaches are plagued with methodological problems in the first instance and more substantively they do not escape basic welfare economic difficulties, particularly relating to consistency, equity and distribution.

The Public Choice alternative, which portends to avert the difficulties of conventional welfare economics, yields quite different policy suggestions and results to the Pigovian approach, but they can be quite perverse in environmental application.

Ultimately, the various welfare economic approaches are found to be deficient on the issue of environmental management in terms of an inability to deal with the questions of equity and distribution which seem to be inherent and unavoidable to most environmental problems.

PIGOVIAN VALUATION

In the setting of market failure in the environment, the absence of prices for valuable environmental considerations is interpreted to mean that there are too

[1] Both of the Swedish University of Agricultural Sciences.

179

few of such things as against other things that humans use. Here, the Pigovian welfare economic approach attempts to deal with the apparent market misallocation of resources by determining some form of *proxy price* to include in the social welfare calculus which determines the optimal allocation of resources.[2]

A range of methods are available by which the benefits and costs of environmental goods may be evaluated. A key issue when considering these methods is the ability to capture non-use values, which are crucial to environmental conservation issues because for many environmental attributes non-use values are the primary (or even only) source of value. Considerable progress has been made in the past 20 to 30 years in developing techniques for placing monetary values on benefits which are not exchanged in markets.

There are a number of main approaches, including;

Opportunity Cost Based Approaches

With cost based approaches no attempt is made to estimate the benefits. The actual or potential costs of a proposed conservation activity are estimated using market prices and a judgement is made as to whether the benefits could be expected to be greater than the costs.

Physical Linkage or Dose Response

Physical linkage or dose response methods are also known as indirect valuation. These methods attempt to link physical information with some kind of market information.

Revealed Preference Techniques

In some circumstances, individuals' preferences for environmental goods can be revealed or estimated from market data for private goods and services that are either produced or consumed in conjunction with that good (Barrett 1988 and Bateman 1993).

For example, contributions to private conservation organisations, media coverage of a environmental conservation issues or protest action may give some indication that particular environments or habitats have a positive value. However, the techniques used most widely for evaluation of environmental goods are the travel cost method and hedonic (or implicit) pricing. A review of both these methods is given in Bateman (1993).

---

[2] For an overview of the theoretical comparisons of the Pigovian and Public Choice approaches see Dragun and O'Connor 1993.

Survey Methods

A further approach to determining the values that individuals place on improvements in environmental quality, such as improving the probability of environmental conservation, is simply to ask people through surveys and direct questioning (Freeman 1979). The most commonly used method is known as the contingent valuation method. The contingent valuation approach uses survey methods to measure benefits directly, rather than to infer them from a demand curve. The underlying idea of this technique is that individuals have true, hidden preferences for environmental goods, which they will reveal if they are asked the appropriate, specific questions. These methods are the only ones capable of estimating non-use values.

There appear to be a range of particular methodological issues compromising the application of each of the indirect methods and the literature in each case is quite specific and detailed (for example, Arrow *et al.* 1993, Bateman 1993, Jakobsson and Dragun 1996, and Mitchell and Carson 1989). In the scope of this analysis, focus will be directed to the crucial issues of welfare economics in general.

PROBLEMS WITH PREFERENCES

The dilemma in considering management issues in relation to many environmental circumstances is that it is, by definition, not possible to observe the welfare consequences of people's behaviour with respect to the environment because the necessary markets for individuals to express their values do not exist. Consequently, there is a difficulty in measuring the welfare of individuals here and the need is to take the individual preferences with respect to environmental conservation to be an indicator of their actual welfare. In practice however, there are a wide range of reasons why preferences might not be an indicator of welfare, as explored by Sagoff (1994).

Probably most importantly here, individual preferences may not only be affected by an individual's own welfare for the conservation of the environment, but may also be influenced by the welfare of other persons. Thus, a person when confronted with an issue of environmental conservation might prefer an alternative situation which yields less direct individual welfare because the welfare of other persons is greater in that situation.

In the setting of environmental conservation, where a good many persons respond to survey questions expressing concern that their children might enjoy the environment in the future, the possibility here is not hard to see. This consideration relates to the broader issue of intergenerational equity which seems to be irremovable from the analysis and discussion of environmental management over time. Additionally, given the complex technical settings of many environmental issues it could be the case that individuals are ignorant of certain of the possibilities or otherwise their perspective is incorrect. For example, in terms of some recent controversy on the nature and meaning of the extinction of species by many eminent and learned biologists (Lawton and May 1995), it would not be unreasonable to expect that most citizens would have considerable difficulty in identifying all the scientific information relevant for the conservation of a particular environment and then actually coming to some meaningful analytical assessment of such information. Consequently, it would be reasonable to expect that the preferences that individuals might have on environmental conservation issues could be based on ignorance and imperfect consideration and foresight.

It is notable that the environmental conservation issue has ignited deep fundamental passions from some individuals, special interest groups and communities. As a function of certain customs, habits, traditions and principles certain individuals appear to take particular positions on environmental issues generally, which seem to run counter to their own welfare. Thus, preferences for certain environmental outcomes could include an element of irrationality. Further, given the great temptations of wealth and pleasure, which might often be associated with the frontier lands where many sensitive ecosystems might be found, there is again the basis that individual preferences for environmental conservation (or development) might be irrational as a function of the great temptations of imaginary gains in such circumstances (Xanadu).

In conclusion, as Sagoff (1994) has observed, there is a good deal of reason to suggest that the preferences that individuals might express on a particular issue, could actually mean a multitude of other things. Of course the actual values derived in this setting could be construed in either direction according to the weight of the other things. However, if it is considered that preferences are acceptable, the need is then to consider some fundamental issues of ordinal welfare functions.

ORDINAL WELFARE FUNCTIONS

The evidence of a great many empirical studies on environmental issues has demonstrated a strong link between willingness to pay for environmental considerations and ability to pay. At the same time there is little evidence to suggest that the marginal utility of environmental considerations is the same for all persons in a community (Kanninen and Kriström 1992).

As a function of the inability to make interpersonal comparisons of utility, it is generally accepted that there is very little justification for using other social welfare forms (such as a cardinal social welfare function) other than the traditional ordinal form, known as the Samuelson-Bergson ordinal social welfare function. However, the application of the Samuelson-Bergson form of social welfare function raises several classes of issues. The first considered here, relates to the actual application of the social welfare function, while the second focuses on the consistency of the results obtained from the application.

COMPENSATION CRITERIA

Even if the social welfare function is well defined in relation to individual utilities, it is not clear that such a function will be well defined in connection with different social states (Little 1949 and 1957). Where it emerged that some persons might be made better off whilst others were rendered worse off, the only recourse seemed to be the unsatisfactory one of adopting some form of cardinal welfare function where a direct comparison of utilities could be made. In this setting Kaldor raised the possibility of conceiving of compensation to establish a socially desirable outcome (Kaldor 1939).

Kaldor, contrasting the Paretian insight where 'everybody could be made better off without making anybody worse off', with a reality that some persons were going to suffer, suggested that if 'all those who suffer as a result are fully compensated for their loss, the rest of the community will still be better than before' (1939, p. 550). The result here is that a social improvement would occur if the beneficiaries of some alternative could remain better off even if they fully compensated the losers. This criterion was strengthened by Hicks (1939) who added the dimension that the losers in turn could not bribe the beneficiaries to oppose the change.

If the compensation in the Kaldor-Hicks criterion were real there would in fact be little need for the criteria and reference to the Pareto criterion would be sufficient to establish the desired alternative. This hypothetical character of compensation in the Kaldor-Hicks setting, led to Scitovsky (1954) identifying a contradiction where a reverse change might be possible which was also permissable on the grounds of the original Kaldor criterion. Extending his analysis Scitovsky proposed a compensation criterion which in effect satisfied both the Kaldor and the Hicks criterion (the Scitovsky reversal test) to achieve apparent unambiguous results. However, cyclicity still seems to remain with this criterion, as with the precursors, after repeated application.

Little proposed an additional criterion which focused on the distributional implications explicit in rendering someone worse off whilst others are made better off - and where the criterion should deal with actual improvements rather than the potential improvements suggested by the previous criteria (Little 1949 and 1957). Little's criterion incorporates the Kaldor and Scitovsky criterion with an additional consideration establishing if any redistribution was good so that an improvement could occur if the Paretian consideration was achieved as the income distribution was improved. But again the Little criterion has been found to suffer reversal contradictions, which led Samuelson (1950) to respecify a criterion which is effectively the original social welfare function - the Samuelson-Bergson social welfare function. And of course we have begun this discussion by considering the limited applicability of this alternative, so the cycle is complete. The Samuelson-Bergson social welfare function does not handle states of Paretian non-comparability and the compensation tests devised to avoid this lacuna inevitably lead us back to the original as a function of their own contradictions.

This indecisiveness on social welfare rules is especially important in the setting of environment issues where it is fundamentally clear that any social change will make some persons worse off whilst others are made better off. Here, as Little (1957) has observed, the intractable issue is how to deal with or incorporate the distributional consequences of the social policy into a meaningful social welfare statement. For example, in that the contingent valuation methodology relies on improvement which seem to be based on the Kaldor-Hicks criterion, it cannot be considered that distributional issues have been avoided. Although there is considerable evidence that absolute willingness to pay for environmental considerations increases with income, it is the case that the relative willingness to pay seems to diminish so that the overall distributional affect of a social change which conserves environment is indecisive. Irrespective of the issue of the ambiguity of the compensation criteria, the ordinal social welfare function suffers a more consequential dilemma in terms of consistency as demonstrated by Arrow (1950).

IMPOSSIBILITY PROBLEMS

Once we have established that some structure of social choice is necessary for individuals to realise their interests (say with respect to environmental amenity), the need is to establish *which* structure of social choice provides the best results. Unfortunately, we can establish that no social choice mechanism, including those involving the various social welfare functional forms, can provide us with a consistent result. The circumstances are portrayed by the Arrow impossibility theorem.

Considering the process of passing from individual preferences to a social choice, Arrow observes that no mechanism exists which does not impose or is not dictatorial. Thus from Arrow:

If we exclude the possibility of interpersonal comparisons of utility, then the only methods of passing from individual tastes to social preferences which will be satisfactory and which will be defined for a wide range of sets of individual orderings are either imposed or dictatorial. (1950 p. 342)

Given certain reasonable conditions of social choice, the implication is drawn that it is possible to identify circumstances where social decisions are inconsistent with the individual preferences that were instrumental in generating the social decision in the first place. The insight of the impossibility theorem is that such individual freedom is compromised relative to reasonable conditions of social choice. Another way of expressing this result is that social welfare functions are inconsistent and incapable of aggregating individual preferences to social choices. The key to this statement is that the inconsistency of social welfare functions is usually perceived as a loss of individual freedom.

The traditional interpretation of the impossibility theorem is that the Samuelson-Bergson type social welfare function, which is generally assumed in the contingent valuation methodological setting, is inconsistent in aggregating individual preferences to social choice. Other forms of social welfare function which are relevant to social choice are the market mechanism as well as majoritarian democracy. The implication of the impossibility theorem can easily be seen with reference to democracy. With individual freedom articulated as the significant social principle, a good many economists have been forward in observing the tyranny of majoritarian decisions (Buchanan and Tullock 1962 and Mishan 1969).

PARETIANISM AND SOCIAL CHOICE

Given the intractability of social welfare functions on social choice, the range of options is observed to be decidedly small. While a good deal of economic attention has been directed to circumventing the impossibility theorem - with little apparent success - the more positive alternatives include deriving social choice rules from the conditions of the impossibility theorem or discarding the theorem altogether. Both possibilities will be considered in turn.

In terms of the current debate on social choice the most crucial condition of the impossibility theorem is possibly the weak Pareto principle. This condition specifies that if all individuals rank one alternative higher than another, then that alternative would rank higher in the social ordering. If it is expected that individuals will not prefer alternatives which render themselves worse-off, it would appear that Pareto safety remains the only non-imposing criterion of social choice (Buchanan 1959). Consequently, if social choice situations can be recognised which do render some persons better-off, whilst no other individual is made worse-off, it is clear that a social choice rule in

Pareto safety can be invoked which does not impose on the freedom of individuals in the society. Otherwise it would appear that the process of social choice is hamstrung. Subsequently, the resultant question for practical social choice is to establish the relative importance of social decisions which, while making some persons better-off, do cause some other persons to be worse-off.

THE IMPOSSIBILITY OF A PARETIAN LIBERAL

That the Paretian approach is not inviolable to the very principles which provide its strongest justification has not gone unobserved (Sen 1970). In essence Sen has established that Pareto safety can be inconsistent with minimal conditions of liberalism. The strength of Sen's analysis is that the arbitrariness of individual freedom relative to various status-quo rights distributions can be readily observed.

The implication is that whilst the Arrow impossibility theorem finds social welfare functions inconsistent as social choice mechanisms - with the recourse seen to lie with the Paretian criterion - that Paretian criterion is itself found to be inconsistent in terms of the value of freedom, which was originally considered to be its virtue. Despite this, a substantive alternative to orthodox welfare economic theory has been developed in the setting of Public Choice theory and the implications of this approach for policy on environmental conservation will be briefly considered.

PUBLIC CHOICE AND PURE PARETIANISM

Relative to the problems of inconsistency and interpersonal comparisons of utility, the Public Choice approach is a fundamental change in direction from the traditional welfare economic perspectives. The Public Choice approach emphasises the pure Paretian interpretation and then focuses on the process implied by a free market, rather than being constrained by the results of some process (Sen 1995).

The general inspiration for Public Choice theory, besides the difficulty of ordinal social welfare functions evident in the orthodox neoclassical method, appears to have arisen in connection with what is perceived as the failure of the neoclassical orthodoxy to confront or even recognise certain institutional issues that seemed to be irremovable from the application of economic theory to a range of problem situations. Two crucial issues emerge in this institutional context. The first, being a fear that government interference in certain economic inter-relationships could impede free and mutually beneficial trades and in some cases generate inefficiency, and the second, involving the recognition that an inadequate property rights could be seen as the root of a range of economic problems.

In that the explicit consideration of property rights is a precondition for recognising particular economic breakdowns, such as in an externality situation, the focus of Public Choice theory then turns to the activity of government in resolving such breakdowns. This view is highlighted by Buchanan's (1959) concern that too much government involvement in society will impede genuine trades that would normally lead to mutual gains for all parties. Subsequently, the Public Choice perspective on such issues as environmental conservation is that such problems are only relevant when the benefited (damaged) parties have a desire to modify the behaviour of the parties that might be causing a threat to the environment (Buchanan and Stubblebine 1962). The crux here is that where gains from trade are recognised in the Paretian sense, it is expected that individuals who value environmental conservation can and will initiate genuine trades of mutual benefit and establish the economy at a Pareto optimum. Paretian gains from trade are realised in an externality situation where affected parties can be made better off without others being made worse off (Buchanan and Stubblebine 1962, p. 480).

In this setting the trades are realised within the existing economic institutional structure without any direct government direction or involvement. Fundamentally, if individuals do not have an incentive to bargain to a mutually beneficial Pareto optimum, then the issue is irrelevant. It follows that government involvement in such a context, must necessarily conduce a loss of utility as well as generating further inefficiency as a result of the transaction costs of government (Buchanan and Stubblebine 1962 p. 480).

PUBLIC CHOICE AND ENVIRONMENTAL POLICY

The essence of the Public Choice theory on environmental problems would be that a range of problems might exist due to a breakdown in the property rights structure. A combination of factors including the notions of transactions costs and government interference contribute to the general malaise. In this setting a Pigovian approach which utilises the valuations obtained from contingent valuation for a policy which favours environmental conservation would be seen as arbitrary in terms of both the transaction costs of government intervention and the implicit assignment of right implied by the Kaldor-Hicks criterion. An additional concern would be that the property rights structure created by government would not necessarily be conducive to negotiation and change if some more beneficial reallocation was possible.

However, despite the characterisation of externality situations according to a breakdown of the property rights structure and recognising that property rights might be created with a Pigovian policy solution, a pervading theme exists in the Public Choice literature that some individuals do in fact have rights to act even in externality situations. Such a perspective is exemplified in an externality situation where government interference is recognised as initiating an attenuation of rights or more generally a taking of property rights. In a similar vein requirements for the payment of compensation to individuals restricted in externality circumstances appears to imply a right taken.

The conclusions here are then twofold, either a normative bias is introduced in favour of certain types of individual behaviour with clear and obvious distributional implications for *status quo* interests, or alternatively the class of economic inter-relationships which have generally been referred to as externalities in the Public Choice literature are misconceived and are in fact institutionally analogous to formal market transactions in that property rights must always exist for this methodology to be consistent. The consequence in an economic policy setting is that Public Choice prescriptions on externality must either introduce normative bias according to an arbitrary description of individualist behaviour or otherwise propose remedial action to an existing problem by assuming that the problem doesn't exist in the first instance.

In addition, in the context of resolving existing externality problems the Public Choice rationale requires that the involved individuals, realising the mutual gains from trade, would bargain amongst themselves as to the conditions of inter-relationship of the particular externality activity. It follows here that the Pareto-Wicksellian bargaining procedure would conduce to a final property rights assignment which is purportedly Pareto preferable and also consistent with Wicksellian unanimity - it would also be expected that such a bargained agreement would finally be the subject of a binding legal contract that resolves the pre-legal state to one of *de jure* economic transactions. Whilst questions of efficiency have been raised in this context previously - especially in the setting of common property problems and large group affects (Mishan 1971) - the crucial issue here appears to revolve around the use of the Pareto criterion and purported efficiency improvements to decide straightforward distributional questions.

The Public Choice blending of efficiency and distributional criteria is exemplified in the application of the standard Coasian dictum. According to Coase (1960) we are led to believe that from the perspective of economic efficiency the initial allocation of property rights is irrelevant. The usual interpretation of Coase's major contribution to economic irrelevance is that irrespective of the initial assignment of property rights, the final distribution of property rights will always be such that the value of social product will be maximised, since individuals perceiving a greater value to specific rights will always be prepared to bargain for such rights provided that a suitable medium of transactions is available.

However, if economic efficiency can be achieved from all of a range of initial property rights assignments, as Coase suggests, then preoccupation with economic efficiency is in fact irrelevant, since it can be expected that economic efficiency will always be established from all the possible initial property rights assignments. What is of course most relevant to social welfare in this context then is the actual interpersonal assignment of the involved property rights and the inevitable consequences for such an assignment for the distribution of income and wealth, the distribution of economic power in society, market structure and also environmental quality.

To neglect the explicit issues of property rights assignment in this setting is to presume a sanctity in the *status quo* distribution of property rights - a position which even Buchanan does not see fit to justify (Buchanan and Samuels 1975, p. 27). The implicit issue on the other hand is that the medium of transaction is indeed satisfactory and socially acceptable. Of course, the core of the consideration of the actual assignment of property rights revolves around the questions of how the property rights are to be assigned and to whom the property rights are to be assigned and it is here that the inherent and irremovable normative content of Public Choice becomes manifest.

The conclusion here is that Public Choice does highlight that the *distribution* of property rights is fundamental to such issues as environmental conservation and this is also a natural conclusion from a consideration of compensation criteria in conventional welfare economic theory. The issue now is to contemplate how contingent valuation and the propositions of welfare economic theory can better determine economic policy for environmental conservation and the distribution of property rights and wealth that are inherent to such policy.

ENVIRONMENTAL POLICY AND EQUITY

Fundamentally, the various economic social choice processes considered here, from the various Pigovian indirect valuation approaches and their implicit ordinal social welfare foundations to Public Choice, reduce the social issue of environmental conservation to one of the distribution of the property rights to the environment. If a society were egalitarian and the distribution was even, it would appear that the benefits of environmental conservation could be distributed along all segments of the community and any negative impact on the basic distribution of income might not be that great.

But in practice the problem of income distribution inherent in conserving the environment is very great as a function of the income disparities in most societies and the non-existence in entitlements or property rights in most environmental situations. Thus, public decisions on environmental conservation will create a new structure of entitlement and income and the distributional consequences could be quite marked. This is especially the case at an international level where most of the willingness to pay for environmental conservation will be seen to originate from the more developed countries, whilst most of the environment at risk is actually located in less developed countries. Also there is a need to consider the question of the distribution over time (Norgaard and Howarth 1991).

Thus, according to the Kaldor-Hicks criteria the more wealthy individuals residing in the developed world would obtain the entitlements to environmental amenity existing in the less developed nations, according to principles of potential compensation - because they appear to be willing to pay more - while the poor citizens could be deprived of the basic sustenance for their day to day survival. Ironically, the Public Choice approach could have the poor people of the less developed countries actually pay the wealthier citizens of the developed world for not taking environmental amenity away.

In the case of environmental issues occurring at the national level, it is not clear that many citizens in most nations would support some form of auction of environmental amenity rights to the highest bidder, especially if the high bidder was subsequently excused payment. Alternatively, the prospect of compensating the presumptive rights of all persons negatively affected by environmental conservation, would probably attract even less support. But at a national level, entitlements will be created and income will be distributed as part of the accepted political process.

But probably the more substantive issues of environmental conservation occur with an international dimension, where the willingness to pay for environmental conservation resides in the wealthier developed nations while much of the environment at risk resides in the poorer less developed nations. Here, the possibilities for redistributions are not so obvious.

Overall, it is clear that while the values derived by indirect valuation methods may not actually enable the description of the optimum use of environmental resources, the values at the same time will provide valuable input and information on an indelibly complex social issue and should provide the font of explicit social discussion and deliberation.

REFERENCES

Arrow, K.J. 1950. 'A difficulty in the concept of social welfare', *Journal of Political Economy*, 58, 328-46.
Arrow, K.J., Solow, R., Portney, P.P., Leamer, E.E., Radner, R. and Schuman, H. 1993. 'Report of the National Oceanic and Atmospheric Administration Panel on Contingent Valuation', *Federal Register*, 58(10), January 15, 4602-14, US.

Barrett, S. 1988. 'Economic guidelines for the conservation of biological diversity', Paper prepared for Economics Workshop at IUCN General Assembly, San Jose, Costa Rica, Feb.

Bateman, I.J. 1993. 'Evaluation of the environment: A survey of revealed preference techniques', GEC Working Paper 93-06. Centre for Social and Economic Research on the Global Environment, University of East Anglia and University College London.

Buchanan, J.M. 1959. 'Positive economics, welfare economics and political economy', *Journal of Law and Economics*, 124.

Buchanan, J.M. and Samuels, W.J. 1975. 'On some fundamental issues in political economy: An exchange of correspondence', *Journal of Economic Issues*, 9, 15-38.

Buchanan, J.M. and Stubblebine, W.C. 1962. 'Externality', *Economica*, 29, 371-84.

Buchanan, J.M. and Tullock, G. 1962. *The Calculus of Consent*. Ann Arbor: University of Michigan Press.

Coase, R.H. 1960. 'The Problem of Social Cost', *Journal of Law and Economics*. Vol III, Oct, 368-91.

Dragun, A.K. and O'Connor, M.P. 1993. 'Property rights, Public Choice and Pigovianism', *Journal of Post Keynesian Economics*, 16(1), 127-52.

Freeman, A.M. 1979. *The Benefits of Environmental Improvement: Theory and Practice*. Baltimore: Johns Hopkins University Press.

Hicks, J.R. 1939. 'Foundations of welfare economics', *Economic Journal*, 49, 696-712.

Jakobsson, K.M. and Dragun, A.K. 1996. *Contingent valuation and endangered species: Methodological issues and application*, Cheltenham: Edward Elgar.

Kaldor, N. 1939. 'Welfare propositions of economics and interpersonal comparisons of utility', *Economic Journal*, 49, 549-52.

Kanninen, B.J. and Kriström, B. 1992. 'Welfare benefit estimation and the income distribution', Beijer Discussion Paper Series No. 20. Beijer International Institute of Ecological Economics, The Royal Swedish Academy of Sciences.

Lawton, J.H. and May, R.M. 1995. *Extinction Rates*. Oxford: Oxford University Press.

Little, I.M.D. 1957. *A Critique of Welfare Economics*. London: Oxford University Press.

Little, I.M.D. 1949. 'The foundations of welfare economics', *Oxford Economic Papers*, 1, 227-46.

Mishan, E.J. 1969. *Welfare Economics: An Assessment*. Amsterdam: North Holland.

Mishan, E.J. 1971. 'The postwar literature on externalities: An interpretative essay', *Journal of Economic Literature*, 9, 1-28.

Mitchell, R.C. and Carson, R.T. 1984. 'A contingent valuation estimate of national freshwater benefits', Technical report to the US Environmental Protection Agency. Washington DC: Resources for the Future. Cited in Mitchell, R.C. and Carson, R.T. 1989.

Mitchell, R.C. and Carson, R.T. 1989. *Using Surveys to Value Public Goods. The Contingent Valuation Method*. Washington DC: Resources for the Future.

Norgaard, R.B. and Howarth, R.B. 1991. 'Sustainability and discounting the future', in Costanza, R. (ed.), *Ecological Economics*. New York: Columbia University Press.

Sagoff, M. 1994. 'Should preferences count', *Land Economics*, 70(2), 127-44.

Samuelson, P.A. 1950. 'Evaluation of real national income', *Oxford Economic Papers*, 2, 1-29.

Scitovsky, T. 1954 'Two concepts of external economies', *Journal of Political Economy*, 17, 143-51.

Sen, A.K. 1970. 'The impossibility of a Paretian liberal', *Journal of Political Economy*, 78, 152-7.

Sen, A.K. 1995. 'Rationality and social choice', *American Economic Review*, 85(1), 1-24.

10. Evaluation and Environmental Policies: Recent Behavioural Findings and Further Implications

Jack L. Knetsch[1]

INTRODUCTION

The growing recognition of the economic value of the amenities and productivity of natural environments has greatly increased demands to take such values into account in the design of environmental policies. At least implicit weightings of pecuniary and non-pecuniary environmental and resource values are now quite commonly used in allocating resources among competing uses, in justifying expenditures and dedications of lands for parks and reserves, in determining damage awards for environmental harms, in setting prices for the use of resources, in determining appropriate levels of mitigation activities, in setting pollution standards and in guiding investments which have impacts on levels of natural resource productivity. The urgings of most economists has been overwhelmingly for ever greater use of environmental valuations in such matters.

While the particulars of individual applications vary, the main prescriptions for the use and determination of environmental values have remained relatively constant. On these, recent textbooks in environmental economics read very much like the texts of earlier decades, for example. Many of these working rules, of course, continue to provide useful guidance: Comparing gains and losses, favouring more valuable over less valuable, taking account of the temporal nature of outcomes, recognizing risks and lining up marginal values, remain socially constructive valuation notions.

Many long held valuation principles, however, involve various assertions of people's behaviour that may not be sustainable. The results from many surveys, experiments and other behavioural studies suggest that many common

[1] This research was, in part, supported by the Social Sciences and Humanities Research Council of Canada and has benefited from the comments of Bernhard Borges.

assertions provide neither a very good description of people's preferences nor very useful predictions of their reactions to real choices.[2] One implication of these findings is that some environmental valuation prescriptions that continue to appear in even recent texts and continue to provide the basis for current practice, may be seriously in error. Although the substantial and growing empirical evidence has been widely reported in leading journals, curiously, there remains little reckoning, or even acknowledgment, of these findings and even less attention given to exploiting them to improve environmental policies.

RISK PERCEPTIONS TIME PREFERENCES AND DISCOUNTING

As with other cases of disparities between traditional assumptions and observations of people's behaviour, some of those related to environmental valuation issues are more pervasive and more thoroughly tested and documented than others. Differences in the areas of risk perceptions and time preferences are perhaps illustrative of these.

Risk Perceptions

Many environmental policies are related to risks to individuals and to the environment. The extent to which people view risks as important and particular risks as being more serious or worrisome than others are usually important issues addressed in designing controls and policies to discourage more serious risks, in justifying expenditures to reduce risks and mitigate losses and in creating incentives to encourage choices more consistent with the full costs of risky activities. Environmental risk assessments are often difficult and contentious because of such factors as the limited knowledge of ecological relationships, the lack of actuarial experience with many risks, the prominence given to particular events or episodes by media attention and the often long delay of consequences and the confounding impacts of other factors.

There is also, however, the well-documented difference between assessments of experts, which are based primarily on expected loss calculations and those of the affected general population, which are based on a much wider array of risk characteristics (Slovic 1987). The differences may, in part, result from different information, or interpretations of facts; from

---

[2] An extensive and useful set of examples was provided by Richard Thaler in the set of papers published in *The Journal of Economic Perspectives*, and later brought together in book form (Thaler 1992). Camerer and Kunreuther (1989) compiled another survey of policy implications of people's reactions to low probability events.

different subjective calculations, especially given the propensity of many people to give more than proportional weight to extremely low probability events; and different levels of trust that cleanup can be as thorough as proclaimed (Gregory *et al.* 1996).

In some cases individuals may be confused or base their valuations on erroneous facts or interpretations. However, the evidence suggests that, quite apart from confusion and the like, people value risks differently because various characteristics of activities or events are important to them in addition to the narrower calculations of probabilities and expected losses. Most people, for instance, react far more negatively to a risk imposed on them by others than to an otherwise identical risk that they assume voluntarily. Further, people are willing to sacrifice much less to avoid a risk over which they feel they have some control than they are to avoid risks with equal expected value over which they feel a lack of influence. They are also much more averse to risks that have unknown effects, are less familiar and have delayed outcomes, than they are to ones they are more used to and have more immediate results. The differing weighing of these attributes has fairly direct impact on many environmental valuations and consequences for risk management decisions and mitigation of risky activities.

Time Preferences

The accounting of intertemporal preferences is another area in which behavioural findings are seemingly at variance with common assumptions guiding valuations and environmental policy analyses. The major valuation issue involves the appropriate discounting of the value of future outcomes. The well known standard practice calls for weighing all future costs and benefits with the same positive discount rate, even though the specific rate is often in dispute, the convention is not.

Rather than a single rate of discount to reflect all dimensions of time preferences, inherent in common valuation practice, there is increasing evidence that people have widely different time preferences that vary depending on the characteristics of particular cases. Not only do people often make purchases with borrowed money while at the same time retaining saving accounts paying a much lower rate of interest, but they have been found to use different rates to discount outcomes over shorter and longer periods. A fixed time delay is less important the further into the future these times are moved, a delay in the incidence of costs or benefits from the present to a year from now is typically far more important to individuals than a delay of the same outcome from 15 to 16 years in the future, for example.

This common difference effect has been found to give rise to a near doubling of discount rates for short periods over those for time spans of a year

(Benzion *et al.* 1989) for instance, and is clearly inconsistent with valuation prescriptions calling for constant discount rates (Harvey 1994). Further inconsistencies are apparent with observations that time preferences vary with the size of the stake and the findings that future losses are usually discounted at significantly lower rates than future gains (Thaler 1981, Loewenstein and Prelec 1992).

It may be, as some contend, that people do not appreciate the low rates and inconsistencies implied by their choices, but rather than such innumeracy it may also be that, analogous to characteristics beyond expected loss being important in the case of risks, various attributes of particular future consequences may be important in people's preferences involving timing. To the extent that this is the case it can have a major impact on the valuation of environmental changes and on the rationalization of environmental policies and actions. The apparent lack of easy economic justification of efforts to deal with global climate change, long-term storage of hazardous materials and unsustainable development, may well be a function of a failure to account for discount rates that decline over longer periods of time for such actions. To the extent that people's time preferences are not well reflected in the use of constant and invariant discount rates, their continued use can only distort environmental policy design and choice.

While the available evidence appears to confirm preference patterns having varied time preferences which imply the use of varied discount rates, there seems yet to be a lack of replication and confirmation of many of the specifics of these relationships. Although rates decline with more distant futures, relatively little is yet known about the nature of the decrease or factors that might influence the falling off of rates. And though future gains are weighed less than otherwise commensurate future losses, the role of dread and anticipation as contributors to this difference remains largely unknown. Similarly, the observations of near zero and even negative time preferences are largely unexplained.

There may also be some variations among observations that are due in part, and perhaps in large part, to the nature of the tests and demonstrations of varied time preferences. Most of the reported observations are based on responses to hypothetical questions and one of the major conclusions stemming from the extensive research on contingent valuation methods is that the specifics of the information provided to respondents and the question format can have a major influence on the replies. In a recent survey carried out among Simon Fraser University students, for example, the answers to an open ended question implied discount rates of about half those indicated by answers to an almost identical question using a multiple comparison format, with still a third very different estimate derived from a single question closed ended format.

There may be similar differences stemming from comparisons of outcomes occurring with those at some other time, possibly implying a lower risk, or whatever, as well as a specific time, somewhat analogous to the certainty effect in risk assessments. There may also be differences due to the nature of the outcomes, as well as their temporal spacing. On present evidence, it seems unlikely that time preferences are well modeled by the standard assertion of invariant rates, but further confirmations and estimates of various parameters would no doubt yield more useful guidance.

DISPARITY BETWEEN VALUES OF GAINS AND LOSSES

A further and likely more pervasive and certainly more well known and more conclusively tested behavioural finding that is seriously inconsistent with nearly all current environmental policy analyses, is that people commonly value losses much more than they do commensurate gains. As essentially all analyses continue to rely on willingness to pay measures to assess losses as well as gains, the valuation disparity has very significant practical importance.

Environmental evaluations are intended to assess losses, or gains, in terms of changes in the economic well being, or economic welfare, of individuals affected by an action or activity, to determine, for example, if the welfare gain to those benefiting from a change outweigh the loss in welfare of those adversely affected. The convention, which is not disputed, is that the economic value of gains and losses in well being is measured by individuals' willingness to sacrifice, what they are willing to give up to acquire something or willing to give up to keep it.

> Benefits are measured by the total number of dollars which prospective gainers would be willing to pay to secure adoption and losses are measured by the total number of dollars which prospective losers would insist on as the price of agreeing to adoption. (Michaelman 1967, p. 1214)

The long-standing conventional assumption is that for essentially all evaluations the compensation measure, the minimum sum people are willing to accept (WTA), and the payment measure, the maximum sum they are willing to pay (WTP), will lead to fully equivalent values except for a trivial difference due to possible income or wealth effects: 'we shall normally expect the results to be so close together that it would not matter which we choose' (Henderson 1941, p. 121). This remains the presumption of choice, as confirmed, for example, in the recent widely discussed review of damage assessment methods: 'This [WTP] is the conservative choice because willingness to accept compensation should exceed willingness to pay, *if only trivially*' (US NOAA Panel 1993, p. 4603, emphasis added).

The equivalence assertion provides a working justification for the current near universal practice of using the WTP measure to value losses as well as gains, as the choice of the more appropriate WTA measure would presumably result in only a trivial difference in any actual estimate of value. While the equivalence assertion continues to be repeated in texts and policy manuals and is used to justify present valuation practice, it has little empirical support. Instead, the empirical evidence overwhelmingly shows that losses matter much more to people and consequently are far more valuable, than commensurate gains; and reductions in losses are worth far more than foregone gains. On present evidence, losses may be valued from two to five or more times more than gains and the use of the WTP measure to assess losses and reductions in losses when it is inappropriate may be expected to distort valuations accordingly.

The now widely reported results of survey studies and more persuasive real exchange experiments show large and systematic valuation disparities which are independent of transactions costs, repetition of trade offers, income effects or wealth constraints (for example, Knetsch and Sinden 1984, Kahneman *et al.* 1990, Boyce *et al.* 1992, Kachelmeier and Shehata 1992). In one example, participants were willing to pay an average of $0.96 to acquire a lottery ticket, but these *same individuals* demanded an average of $2.42 to give up exactly the same entitlement (Borges 1995).

The results of some studies have indicated that the disparity may decrease, or even disappear, over repeated trials (for example, Shogren *et al.* 1994). However, it now appears on the basis of further tests, that such results may be attributable to the failure of the Vickrey auction design, used in these studies, to accurately reveal people's valuations (Kahneman *et al.* 1995).[3]

Similar larger valuation of losses relative to gains which is evident in people's actual behaviour in making ordinary real choices have been documented as well (Kahneman *et al.* 1991). Frey and Pommerehne (1987), for instance, note that collective endowment effects clearly motivate the asymmetric treatment accorded the acquisition and retention of national art treasures. The valuation disparity and the consequent reluctance to sell at a loss, has also been evident in the greater volume of house sales when prices are rising, over the number when they are falling and in the similar smaller volume of sales of securities that have declined in price relative to those for

---

[3] Hanemann's demonstration that large variations may also occur given particular substitute and income effects, of course does nothing to eliminate the possibility of large disparities. This possibility, however, is one which is in addition to the likely far more pervasive presence of an endowment effect, or loss aversion, cause of the observed differences, as is made clear in the last footnote of the Hanemann paper, 'This [loss aversion] is a different phenomenon from that involved in the Randall-Stoll bounds' (1991, p. 645).

which prices have increased (Shefrin and Statman 1985). Consistent with these findings, the greater sensitivity of investors to losses than to gains has been found to be associated with the historical profit premium they give up to invest in bonds rather than more volatile equities (Benarzi and Thaler 1995).

The strong reluctance to give up a default automobile insurance option when an otherwise more attractive choice is readily available (Johnson *et al.* 1993); the typically greater demands for regulation of new environmental risks than of equivalent old risks (Sunstein 1993); and the greater legal protection accorded losses over foregone gains in judicial choices (Cohen and Knetsch 1992) are further examples of the difference in valuations of gains and losses.

Differences are also observed in comments in the financial press, which are presumably written by and for reasonably sophisticated individuals: 'When the market is up, people don't get overly price sensitive. However, when the arrow starts to point down, investors will begin to kick up a fuss [and] will begin shifting investments to look for more competitive MERs' (Gammal 1993, p. C12); 'Fees are not a great concern when returns are good, but can be devastating if returns are below average' (Kane 1996); 'As the investment banker puts it, Wall Street greatly prefers a dollar of cost saving to a dollar of extra revenue' (Jackson 1996).

The evidence does not indicate equivalence, it strongly indicates that over a wide range of circumstances people weigh changes in entitlement levels in terms of an initial reference point and a kinked value function which is much steeper in the domain of losses than in the domain of gains. As Bromley suggests, 'It is now well established that individuals value possible gains much differently than they value possible losses' (1995, p. 133). A good will commonly have one value to a person in terms of how much this individual is willing to sacrifice in order to obtain it, the identical entitlement will have a different value in terms of how much this same person would sacrifice not to accept its loss.[4]

Continued assertions of valuation equivalence in texts notwithstanding, the more interesting questions may no longer be ones of the pervasiveness of the valuation disparity, but ones instead of the implications of the observed difference. As Sunstein aptly suggests, 'If all this is correct, large consequences follow' (1993, p. 30).

---

[4] In instances where the same individual is observed to be willing to pay a relatively low price for an entitlement and then almost immediately demands a high price to give it up - or to display the same behaviour in reverse order - (Kachelmeier and Shehata 1992, Borges 1995), it is very unlikely that the individual is not aware of the real worth of the entitlement. It is instead simply that the entitlement is worth one value when acquiring it and a greater value when giving it up.

IMPLICATIONS OF DISPARITY FOR ECONOMIC ANALYSIS AND PRACTICE

Some of the consequences of the disparity are ones directly related to fairly standard assumptions of economic principles and economic analyses that are based on them. These include the following, which have at least indirect implications for environmental policies and also provide further evidence of the pervasiveness of the valuation asymmetry.

Gains from Trade and Trade Volumes

If people's WTA values were equal to their WTP values, if buy prices were equal to sell prices for each individual, then costless market exchanges would be expected to exhaust all gains from trade and shift entitlements to those individuals willing to pay the most for them. However, a consequence of the valuation disparity is that sell prices will generally be much higher than buy prices of individuals thereby reducing the possible gains available from voluntary exchanges. The smaller gains from trade will decrease the number of Pareto efficient trades that would take place even in costless markets and depending on the initial distribution of entitlements, market exchanges will likely not shift goods to those willing to pay the most for them.

Two tests of such possibilities has been conducted using two sets of actual buy and sell valuations of individuals (Borges and Knetsch 1997a). Two sets of market simulations were carried out for each data set. The first was run assuming that each individual's selling price was equal to that person's actually observed buying price, the conventional assumption of valuation equivalence, or of values being independent of entitlement. The second was run using each individual's actual selling as well as their actual buying price. Each simulation was conducted assuming that all Pareto efficient trades would take place without any transactions costs.

The results show that when actual preferences and real buy and sell valuations are taken into account not only will final allocations vary depending on initial assignments of entitlements, but the magnitude of possible gains that can be realized from voluntary exchanges are perhaps less than half the gains that are assumed to be available with the traditional assumption of valuation equivalence, actual numbers of trades that will take place in such markets are less than half the number that would normally be expected and completion of all possible Pareto efficient exchanges fail by a wide margin to shift entitlements to those willing to pay the most for them. Costless voluntary exchanges will exhaust all gains from trade even with the disparity, but these gains will be much smaller than normally assumed; and final outcomes will be Pareto efficient, but they will usually not maximize the value of final holdings as some individuals willing to pay more for an entitlement will be unable to secure one from others willing to pay less.

These findings suggest that the disparity may be a significant cause of market stickiness, which is independent of transactions costs. They also indicate that the shortfalls from traditionally assumed trade numbers and gains may not be trivial. They should also provide further pause to assertions of the irrelevance of initial distributions of tradable pollution permits and resource entitlements and to predictions of the numbers of expected trades and the likely gains from their exchange.

Indifference Curves

Another implication of the disparity, which among other things is of particular interest in deriving criteria for choosing an appropriate measure of a welfare change (Knetsch in press), is that indifference curves will not be independent of the initial reference point and direction of exchange offers (Knetsch 1989 and 1992). People will commonly demand more of a good A to give up another good B, than they are willing to pay of A to obtain B. This produces a discontinuity, or kink, in the indifference curve at the reference position and differing slopes over the same range of quality depending on how individuals perceive the change relative to the reference state.

Preference Order Axioms

To the extent that people demand more to give up an entitlement than they are willing to pay to acquire or keep an identical one suggests that common preference order assumptions such as transitivity, completeness, dominance and independence, may not usefully describe actual preferences. A test of this involving voluntary exchanges of three entitlements - two simple goods and money - demonstrated that this was the case (Knetsch 1995). Individuals were first given either a mug, a pen, or $2 and then given the opportunity to exchange this initial random allocation for one of the others. The results showed strong violations of the axioms. In the case of transitivity, for example, when first given a mug 97 per cent of the participants preferred a mug to the money, when first given money 86 per cent preferred money to a pen, but yet when first given a pen 90 per cent preferred a pen to a mug.

Here again, people indicated a much greater reluctance to give up entitlements than allowed for in traditional analyses. There appears to be no evidence that they might be any less reluctant to accept environmental losses.

The Coase Theorem

The usual Coase Theorem prediction that final entitlements will be independent of initial allocations, originally proposed as a demonstration of the importance of transactions costs, is often used in the analysis of legal rules and the design of policy reforms, prominently including those related to environmental issues. However, the predictions and policy prescriptions based on them, are critically dependent on not only people's willingness to pursue all gains regardless of fairness or other worries, but on the assumption that their valuations of rights and consequent motives for exchange are independent of entitlements, that having or not having an initial entitlement, or having or not having injunctive relief from an environmental loss, does not influence parties' valuations of gains and losses.

The extent to which the valuation disparity undermines the usual prediction of costless exchanges was demonstrated in a simple experiment that mirrored the essentials of a Coase world (Kahneman *et al.* 1990). Even though an initial distribution of money to potential buyers encouraged participants to conclude presumably mutually advantageous trades, the actual number of exchanges was less than half the number predicted by the usual application of the Theorem. Environmental and other policies designed on the basis of the Coase Theorem may or may not be desirable, but their justification will likely need to be on other grounds.

Distribution and the Veil of Ignorance

Policy prescriptions that involve redistribution issues, which is often the case with ones dealing with the environment, are often influenced by the presumption that individuals behind a 'veil of ignorance', in which they do not know their place among those to be affected by the policy, will choose rules that lead to greater equality of outcomes. However, to the extent that people weigh losses more than gains and that initial distributions are seen to be deserved or warranted, many people may not choose to impose losses on some individuals to confer benefits on others.

A series of empirical tests in which respondents chose between alternative distribution rules under circumstances approximating a veil of ignorance showed large differences in redistributional preferences depending on the reference positions from which gains and losses were valued (Bukszar and Knetsch 1997). They clearly discriminated on the basis of assigning greater value to losses from what they viewed as warranted positions relative to gains beyond them.

Fairness

Judgments of what actions and policies people regard as fair and acceptable or as unfair and unacceptable are also far more in keeping with the findings of valuation asymmetries than they are with traditional assertions of gain and loss valuation equivalence. For example, survey and experimental studies have found that actions that impose losses on parties or groups are widely regarded as being more onerous and therefore more unfair than ones that result in forgoing gains (Kahneman *et al.* 1986, Shiller *et al.* 1991; Frey and Pommerehne 1993). Cutting wages is widely viewed as imposing a loss and is generally considered unfair, reducing a bonus by the same amount is seen as reducing a gain and judged to be far more acceptable. Similarly, raising prices to reflect market shifts was much less justifiable than raising them to cover cost increases.

Negotiation and Conflict Resolution

The disparate views of losses and foregone gains has also been found to influence the acceptability of alternative negotiation and conflict resolution proposals. Results from tests of acceptances suggest that people are far more willing to concede allowances to cover direct costs than they are to accept proposals of concessions to cover foregone opportunities (Borges and Knetsch 1997b). These and other findings offer encouraging promise of greater understandings of which characteristics make proposals for resolving conflicts more acceptable and which discourage settlement.

Investments and the Payback Period

Financial advisors and texts regularly point out the advantages of choosing investments on the basis of criteria such as maximum net present value rather than one having the shortest period over which the original investment is paid back. The need for this advice and the apparent propensity to ignore it, may well be due to people giving greater weight to the potential loss of any part of their invested capital relative to the value of gains net of their investment. Early findings suggest that this may influence people's investment choices.

IMPLICATIONS OF DISPARITY FOR ENVIRONMENTAL POLICY

The difference in the value of gains and losses has direct implications for environmental valuation and policy issues, especially given the near universal use of the WTP measure to assess losses and reductions in losses, as well as to assess the value of gains. This practice will likely result in systematic understatements of values. Consequently, activities with negative environmental impacts will be unduly encouraged, as the real value of losses will be underestimated; compensation and damage awards will be too small to provide proper deterrence and restitution; inappropriately lax standards of protection against injuries will be set, as assessments of the added costs of further harm will be heavily biased; too few resources will be devoted to avoiding environmental degradation; choices of legal entitlements well be biased because comparisons between the efficiency of alternative allocations will be based on incorrect measures; and full accounting and appropriate pricing of environmental resources will be frustrated (Knetsch 1990).

Mitigation and Compensation Remedies

A further illustrative example of a likely bias toward inefficient policies resulting from a failure to take a more realistic account of people's preferences is the frequently recommended choice of compensation payments over mitigation measures as a preferred remedy for harms. This preference stems from the usual economic critique that presumes people should favour money compensation over efforts to mitigate the injury because a money award permits injured parties to substitute other goods for the loss, whereas mitigation measures restrict their remedy to reducing the particular injury. The reasoning turns on the well known economics textbook presumption that a monetary award will yield greater welfare gains than an equal sum in the form of a particular good, the usual demonstration allegedly shows the superiority of money over housing allowances or food vouchers.

The findings of losses being valued more than gains point to the possibility that, rather than an inferior choice, mitigation may be a preferred option. This arises because mitigation actions might be valued more as they reduce losses and compensation awards might be heavily discounted by people as they fall in the domain of gains. Further, the findings of what people regard as fair and unfair suggest that tying a relief action to the injury, as with the acceptance of passing on directly related costs, increases the acceptability of a remedy.

The limited available empirical evidence is consistent with this view of preferences for mitigation measures (Knetsch 1990). A further example is provided by the results of a random survey of Vancouver, Canada, households in which people were presented with a choice between a compensation and a mitigation remedy for a particular harm. The questionnaire was intentionally designed to suggest a minor injury, 'sediment in a local stream that reduces fish populations by 10 per cent' and mitigation efforts that could only 'reduce the loss by half' and could not eliminate the harm completely. Four attractive alternative compensation remedies were provided to four sub-samples of respondents. In the first, 85 per cent chose the mitigation alternative over putting the same amount of money in 'the general fund of the Province', an option which is clearly consistent with the standard public finance dictate. In the second, 81 per cent chose mitigation rather than put a like sum in the general fund of the local municipality, a choice that would appear to yield fairly apparent benefit to the individuals questioned. In the third, 68 per cent chose mitigation over giving the same money to the local authority to spend on 'parks and recreation facilities', a seemingly attractive alternative having some similar environmental characteristics as the fish loss. In the fourth, two thirds still selected mitigation rather than spending the money 'to increase other fish populations', a good if not perfect substitute for the loss of fish.

Dedicated Funds

In much the same way that people often prefer mitigation measures to monetary compensation for an injury, they also commonly want funds collected from user fees or other special purpose levies used for a purpose related to the levy, rather than have such monies put into general or consolidated revenue accounts. The use of such dedicated funds, or 'earmarking' of funds, is widely criticized by public finance economists and is frequently discouraged by official policies on roughly the same grounds as favouring compensation over mitigation, the alleged greater efficiency.

The valuation disparity can, again, result in net gains from the use of some forms of dedicated funds. Feelings of loss may well be reduced if the funds are seen to be spent for actions related to the purpose for which the money was taken. Park entry fees, for example, are usually far more acceptable to users if they know the money will go towards the maintenance and improvement of the park rather than to general government revenue accounts. Similarly, pollution charges and probably even carbon taxes might be more acceptable if resulting revenues were allocated to environmental purposes rather than to government support or even international redistributional efforts.

Sustainability Policies

The behavioural findings raise further questions about policies that might be pursued to further sustainability. One concerns the discount rate. To the extent that non-constant rates and particularly rates declining with longer time periods, better reflect people's real time preferences this will likely favour different policies than those chosen on the basis of constant positive rates.

A second concerns the reference state and what negative impacts are considered to be losses rather than foregone gains, or reductions of losses rather than gains. Much of the current orthodoxy appears to take current productivity levels as the reference, so that any decrease is censured as a loss of productivity. There is, however, little to suggest that current levels are in any other way optimal or more desirable than any other, other than the greater weight attributed to losses by the valuation disparity.

A third turns on the acceptance of substituting one form of natural (or even human) capital for another, thereby maintaining the present level of total productivity. Thus, if forests are harvested in one area, total productivity might be maintained by planting an alternative species in another region or by enhancing soil fertility or fish and wildlife habitat. However, for reasons analogous to those giving greater weight to mitigation measures and consistent with the survey results noted above, people's willingness to accept one resource gain as a substitute for loss of another resource may be more constrained than usually presumed on the basis of valuation equivalence.

Choice of Measures

Because the WTA measure will normally be far larger than the WTP measure, the choice of which measure is used in a particular assessment of an environmental quality increase or decrease has very significant practical importance. Given the likely magnitude of the difference, an inappropriate choice will seriously compromise the intent of the valuation, allocation and deterrence incentives will be distorted, damages will be improperly assessed and confidence in the resolution of disputes will be undermined.

Current practice routinely assesses environmental losses and reductions in losses, as well as environmental gains, in terms of the smaller WTP sums, measuring losses by how much people are willing to pay to avoid such impacts. The continued use of the WTP measure to assess environmental losses, as well as gains, is at least in part due to a combination of the widely acknowledged inability to elicit meaningful answers to WTA questions in contingent valuation surveys and the growing demands to produce a number. A typical justification to use the WTP measure rather than the more appropriate WTA measure in such studies is:

> Respondents will be far less familiar with the notion of receiving compensation for losing something ... This is likely to cause far greater uncertainty and variability in answers to WTA questions than occurs with WTP questions. Therefore, the former are to be avoided in favour of the latter. (Turner, Pearce and Bateman 1993, p. 123)

This appears to give empirical convenience a heavy weighting, with no apparent empirical justification.

The choice of WTP to value both losses and gains in contingent valuation studies and in nearly all discussions of environmental damages, is commonly further justified, or rationalized, by two widely held assertions: (1) That despite evidence to the contrary, there is no practical difference between the WTP and WTA measures, as economists have long maintained, and that either measure will result in equivalent assessments; and (2) the appropriate measure to use in particular circumstances is prescribed by legal entitlements.

Neither assertion appears correct: Instead of equivalence, essentially all of the many tests show large disparities and rather than serving as a useful guide, appeals to extant legal rights will often dictate improper choices.

Rather than legal rights, which are about whether or not an injured party has a cause of action against a neighbour, the choice of measure which best reflects people's real changes in wellbeing seems more appropriately based on the reference state from which individuals judge positive changes to be either gains or reductions of losses and negative changes as either losses or foregone gains. The position of people's reference state, on which these distinctions are based, seems to turn largely on expectation of normalcy and what people regard as fair. An otherwise commensurate change will have a greater or lesser impact on the welfare of an individual depending on whether it is viewed by the individual as being in the losses or in the gains: An increase in quality will be worth more if seen to reduce a loss than to provide a gain, a decrease more if perceived to impose a loss than forego a benefit.

Four individual evaluations can be distinguished that depend on the combinations of the direction of change, of having more or less of the good, and the initial level relative to the reference state: (1) Gain, a positive change beyond the reference measured by the maximum sum the individual is willing to pay (WTP) for this increase; (2) Loss, a negative change from the reference measured by the minimum compensation that the individual will demand to accept the loss and maintain the present level of well being, the WTA measure; (3) Foregone Gain, a reduction from an initial point back to the reference measured by the sum which the individual would pay to avoid foregoing the quantity above the reference; and (4) Reduction of a Loss, a positive change from below the reference state in the direction of the reference measured by the compensation that would be necessary for the individual to forego this reduction of an existing loss, the WTA measure.

The impacts of the two positive and two negative changes on welfare appear to be best assessed by either the WTP or the WTA measure depending on the change being below or above the reference level. Many reductions in losses, which call for the WTA measure, are misconstrued by defining the change of eliminating the harm as being a gain, or benefit, for which the WTP would be the correct measure, as is implied in the suggestion to assess the damages from oil spills that have already occurred by using the answers to contingent valuation questions asking people how much they would pay to prevent future spills.[5] Assessing reductions in losses as gains, can result in serious understatements of the value of such changes.

Income Elasticity of Environmental Goods

It appears to be the conventional view that nearly all environmental values are highly income elastic, that is, that people's concerns for environmental matters are ones that accompany attainment of higher incomes. The policy response is to more or less resolve competing demands and allocate support to protect and enhance environmental resources accordingly, countries and communities with poorer people end up with fewer amenities and more degraded environments relative to ones with better off individuals because demands and environmental values are thought to be highly correlated with incomes.

The empirical estimates suggesting this relationship are based largely on spending patterns of people with different levels of income and wealth. The observed pattern is, not surprisingly, that poor people spend a smaller amount of money on skis and other outdoor equipment than the rich, and similarly, they spend less on gaining access to cleaner and more pleasant environments than people of greater monetary means. The result is that for any percentage difference in income or wealth, the percent difference in the sums spent for these purposes is substantially larger. Hence, the estimate of a large income elasticity.

There may, however, be another view of the matter and an alternative calculation that might yield a substantially different estimate. Individual's expenditures on environmental goods are, as they are for other goods, constrained by incomes and the poor are restrained by very limited wealth and the necessity to provide minimal sustenance. Environmental changes in large part, though not entirely, involve losses or reductions in losses - decreases in air and water quality or reducing pollution levels. As indicated earlier, for these changes the non-income constrained WTA measure of value may be more appropriate than the WTP, or expenditure, measure. In such cases the income elasticity estimate might be more appropriately based, not on expenditures, but on the sums people would be willing to accept to put up with greater losses or to accept the lack of improvement. It is by no means clear that the resulting estimates of income elasticities would indicate the

---

[5] An example of such a use of answers to one question to imply answers to a very different one is the use of valuations from the question: 'What is the most your household would be willing to pay in total over the next five years in higher prices for programs that prevent oil spills, like those described above, along the West Coast over the next five years?', to provide 'a measure of the damage of the Nestucca oil spill' - a spill that had already occurred (RCG/Hagler, Bailly, Inc. 1991, p.6-3).

degree of dependence of environmental valuation on income or wealth that is suggested by expenditure observations - a suspicion that is further encouraged by the very limited, but consistent, evidence suggesting that people's WTA and WTP valuations of the same asset is only weakly correlated (Borges and Knetsch 1997a).

A different reading, and estimate, of income elasticity of the demand for environmental quality, if this should be the case, would call for quite different policy priorities than one based on the current presumption of very high coefficients. It would suggest, for example, more environmentally sensitive development activities in areas of poorer individuals, than might now be the case.

CONCLUSIONS

As the illustrative sampling of implications makes fairly clear, the consequences of the behavioural findings may well be significant as well as pervasive. And while considerable effort has been expended to refute these findings, as Camerer suggests, 'Not a single major recent (post 1970) anomaly has been 'destroyed' by hostile replication of this sort' (1995, p. 647).

In view of the evidence, the seemingly quite deliberate avoidance of any accounting of these findings in the design of environmental policy or in debates over environmental values, does not appear to be the most productive means to improvement. On this score the wider community may not be particularly well served by texts that continue to avoid any acknowledgment of the possible significance, implication, or even the existence, of these behavioural findings and therefore fail to exploit the potential for improving understanding of people's reactions and improving prescriptions to deal more effectively with environmental issues.

However, the shortfall of texts and the seeming lack of interest by policy analysts may be more symptomatic than cause. So too may be the disinclination of environmental economists, who generally have a major preoccupation with market failure and means to overcome them, to have much interest in this instance of a seeming divergence of social and private interest in taking more account of these findings. Aside from the usual litany of explanations, the present structure of rewards and incentives may be a major contributor to the continuing disinterest. The criteria provided to book publishers to gain course adoptions, for economists to gain employment and promotion, and for analysts to gain grants and contracts, may not all be congruent with the larger public interest. Intransigence may have social if not private costs, but given present incentives there may be some margin for poor science as well as poorer policy to survive.

REFERENCES

Benarzi, S. and Thaler, R.H. 1995. 'Myopic loss aversion and the equity premium puzzle', *The Quarterly Journal of Economics*, 110, 73-92.

Benzion, U., Rapoport, A. and Yagil, J. 1989. 'Discount rates inferred from decisions: An experimental study', *Management Science*, 35, 270-84.

Borges, B.F.J. 1995. 'The prevalence of valuation disparities: Within- and between-subject evidence for close substitute goods', Simon Fraser University Working Paper.

Borges, B.F.J. and Knetsch, J.L. 1997a. 'Tests of market outcomes with asymmetric valuations of gains and losses: Smaller gains, fewer trades and less value', *Journal of Economic Behavior and Organization* (forthcoming).

Borges, B.F.J. and Knetsch, J.L. 1997b. 'Valuation of gains and losses, fairness and negotiating outcomes', *International Journal of Social Economics* (forthcoming).

Boyce, R.R., Brown, T.C., McClelland, G.H., Peterson, G.L. and Schulze, W.D. 1992. 'An experimental examination of intrinsic values as a source of the WTA-WTP disparity', *The American Economic Review*, 82, 1366-73.

Bromley, D.W. 1995. 'Property rights and natural resource damage assessments', *Ecological Economics*, 14, 129-35.

Bukszar, E. and Knetsch, J.L. 1997. 'Redistribution and the valuation of gains and losses: Choices behind the veil of ignorance', *Journal of Risk and Uncertainty* (forthcoming).

Camerer, C. 1995. 'Individual decision making', in Kagel, J.H. and Roth, A.E. (eds), *The Handbook of Experimental Economics*, Princeton, New Jersey: Princeton University Press.

Camerer, C. and Kunreuther, H. 1989. 'Decision processes for low probability events: Policy implications', *Journal of Policy Analysis and Management*, 8, 565-592.

Cohen, D. and Knetsch, J.L. 1992. 'Judicial choice and disparities between measures of economic values', *Osgoode Hall Law Journal*, 30, 737-70.

Frey, B. and Pommerehne, W.W. 1987. 'International trade in art: Attitudes and behaviour', *Rivista Internazionale de Scienze Economiche a Commerciali*, 34, 465-86.

Frey, B. and Pommerehne, W.W. 1993. 'On the fairness of pricing - an empirical survey among the general population', *Journal of Economic Behavior and Organization*, 20, 295-307.

Gammal, P. 1993. 'Manager's fees may be getting out of hand', *Toronto Globe and Mail*, 18 November, p. C12.

Gregory, R., Brown, T.C. and Knetsch, J.L. 1996. 'Valuing risks to the environment', *Annals of the American Academy of Political and Social Sciences*.

Hanemann, M. 1991. 'Willingness to pay and willingness to accept: How much can they differ?', *The American Economic Review*, 81, 635-47.

Harvey, C.M. 1994. 'The reasonableness of non-constant discounting', *Journal of Public Economics*, 53, 31-51.

Henderson, A.M. 1941. 'Consumer's surplus and the compensation variation', *Review of Economic Studies*, 8, 117.

Jackson, T. 1996. 'Corporate America is dumbsizing', *The Financial Post*, 25 May, p. 87.

Johnson, E.J., Hershey, J., Meszaros, J. and Kunreuther, H. 1993. 'Framing probability distortions and insurance decisions', *Journal of Risk and Uncertainty*, 7, 728-41.

Kachelmeier, S.J. and Shehata, M. 1992. 'Examining risk preferences under high monetary incentives: Experimental evidence from the People's Republic of China', *The American Economic Review*, 82, 1120-41.

Kahneman, D., Knetsch, J.L. and Thaler, R.H. 1986. 'Fairness as a constraint on profit seeking: Entitlements in the market', *The American Economic Review*, 76, 728-41.

Kahneman, D., Knetsch, J. and Thaler, R. 1990. 'Experimental tests of the endowment effect and the Coase Theorem', *Journal of Political Economy*, 98, 1325-48.

Kahneman, D., Knetsch, J.L. and Thaler, R.H. 1991. 'The endowment effect, loss aversion and status quo bias', *Journal of Economic Perspectives*, 5, 193-206.

Kahneman, D., Knetsch, J.L. and Thaler, R.H. 1995. 'The endowment effect and the Vickrey auction', University of Chicago Working Paper.

Kane, M. 1996. 'Time to shatter the myths', *The Vancouver Sun*, 3 February, p. 5.

Knetsch, J.L. 1989. 'The endowment effect and evidence of nonreversible indifference curves', *The American Economic Review*, 79, 1277-84.

Knetsch, J.L. 1990. 'Environmental policy implications of disparities between willingness to pay and compensation demanded measure of values', *Journal of Environmental Economics and Management*, 18, 227-37.

Knetsch, J.L. 1992. 'Preferences and nonreversibility of indifference curves', *Journal of Economic Behavior and Organization*, 17, 131-39.

Knetsch, J.L. 1995. 'Asymmetric valuation of gains and losses and preference order assumptions', *Economic Inquiry*, 33, 134-41.

Knetsch, J.L. in press. 'Reference states, fairness and choice of measure to value environmental changes', in Bazerman, M., Messick, D., Tenbrunsel, A. and Wade-Bensoni, K. (eds), *Psychological Perspectives to Environment and Ethics in Management*, San Francisco, California: Jossey-Bass.

Knetsch, J.L. and Sinden, J.A. 1984. 'Willingness to pay and compensation demanded: Experimental evidence of an unexpected disparity in measures of value', *The Quarterly Journal of Economics*, 99, 507-21.

Loewenstein, G. and Prelec, D. 1992. 'Anomalies in intertemporal choice: Evidence and an interpretation', *The Quarterly Journal of Economics*, 107, 573-97.

Michaelman, F.I. 1967. 'Property, utility and fairness: Comments on the ethical foundation of "Just compensation" Law', *Harvard Law Review*, 80, 1165-258.

Prelec, D. and Loewenstein, G. 1991. 'Decision making over time and under uncertainty: A common approach', *Management Science*, 37, 770-86.

RCG/Hagler, Bailly, Inc. 1991. *Contingent Valuation of Natural Resource Damage due to the Nestucca Oil Spill: Final Report*. Boulder, Colorado.

Shefrin, H. and Statman, M. 1985. 'The disposition to sell winners too early and ride losers too long: Theory and evidence', *Journal of Finance*, 40, 777-90.

Shiller, R.J., Boycko, M. and Korobov, V. 1991. 'Popular attitudes towards free markets: The Soviet Union and the United States compared', *The American Economic Review*, 81, 385-400.

Shogren, J.F., Shin, S.Y., Hayes, D.J. and Kliebenstein, J.B. 1994. 'Resolving differences in willingness to pay and willingness to accept', *The American Economic Review*, 84, 255-70.

Slovic, P. 1987. 'Perceptions of risk', *Science*, 236, 280-5.

Sunstein, C.R. 1993. 'Endogenous preferences, environmental law', *Journal of Legal Studies*, 22, 217-54.

Thaler, R.H. 1981. 'Some empirical evidence on dynamic inconsistency', *Economic Letters*, 8, 201-7.

Thaler, R.H. 1992. *The Winner's Curse: Paradoxes and Anomalies of Economic Life*. New York: The Free Press.

Turner, R.K., Pearce, D. and Bateman, I. 1993. *Environmental Economics*. Baltimore, Maryland: Johns Hopkins Press.

US NOAA Panel 1993. Report of the NOAA Panel on Contingent Valuation. *US Federal Register*, 58(10), 4602-14, January 15.

11. Tournament Incentives in Environmental Policy

Jason Shogren and Terrance Hurley[1]

INTRODUCTION

Economic prescriptions for environmental problems usually presume that absolute payoffs motivate individual behaviour. Even if there is a trivial difference between measurable performance and the associated payoffs from optimal and suboptimal behaviour an individual is still purposeful if she finds it worthwhile to capture the extra unit of satisfaction. But evidence from the lab suggests that people are not so exact in their ability to discern and react to trivial differences in payoffs. An individual's likelihood for misbehaviour increases the smaller the gap between optimal and suboptimal payoffs (Harrison 1989). Trivial payoff differences do not really punish deviations from optimal behaviour, regardless of whether utility is assumed ordinal or cardinal. At this point, one comes to the crossroads where one can either reformulate the model of behaviour to included factors that may lead to suboptimal choices given absolute payoffs matter (altruism, envy, errors) or one can impose an institutional incentive that provides sufficiently high rewards for trivial differences in measurable performance (for example, parts per billion) such that relative payoffs matter, that is, a tournament.

This chapter takes the second path and considers how tournament incentives affect behaviour and the implications for environmental policy. Identifying oneself as a high ability individual who deserves the higher reward requires some signal of type that is based on relative performance, not absolute. In the wild economy, tournament incentives have evolved as an exchange institution that increases the incentive for high ability behaviour when the difference between winning and losing is measured in fractions of seconds or points. Tournaments where payoffs increase at an increasing rate are designed to reward a trivial numerical deviation between optimal and suboptimal behaviour by a substantial difference in payoffs (Lazear and Rosen 1981, Drago *et al.*

---

[1] This paper draws on work with Kyung Hwan Baik.

213

1996). Many sports like track and field, tennis, or golf reward players using a non-linearly increasing reward system where the winner's payoff is often twice the runner up's (Ehrenberg and Bognanno 1990); performance pay in top management positions uses a similar reward structure (Jensen and Murphy 1990). A tournament incentive scheme with non-linearly increasing payoffs mimics a hierarchy of exchange institutions that reward rational self interest by driving out players who are not at the top of their form.

If individuals differ in their ability to discern and select optimal strategies, it is well known in the mechanism design literature that high ability individuals can gain an information rent by mimicking the behaviour of low ability individuals. With flat payoff structures high ability individuals see no reason to exert the extra effort needed for optimal play when they are mixed in with low ability individuals who are more likely to make errors. As such the high ability individuals can save their mental energy and gain information rents by simply copying the suboptimal effort by low ability players. Optimal payoff contracts given information rents require a non-linear payoff schedule that rewards the high ability individuals for their extra effort (Lewis 1996). An accurate understanding of the behaviour underlying environmental policy requires capturing the institutional structure in which incentives and information work to induce individual rationality presumed by theory (Smith 1989, Nau and McCardle 1991). With this in mind, individual behaviour is examined in both a standard design and a tournament design for four experimental settings: Coasian bargaining, environmental conflicts with endogenous timing, the centipede game and conflicts with asymmetric information.

COASIAN BARGAINING

Coase (1960) advanced the idea that with low transactions costs two disputing parties should be able to bargain to an efficient and mutually advantageous agreement. Experiments designed to test the Coase Bargaining have often observed highly efficient but equitable agreements (Hoffman and Spitzer 1982). This pattern of equitable splits of expected wealth has led some to argue that a bargainer acts more like a fair person rather than a games person theory predicts. As such, these fair persons must have something more than expected wealth in their preferences, something like altruism (Roth 1995). Evidence of equal splits or self interest constrained by equity belies the presumption of rationality and provides a challenge to both theorists and experimentalists to refine their notions of rationality.

Shogren (1997) designed a Coasian bargaining tournament with a nonlinear payoff structure to understand the relationship between the institutional environment and rational self interest in face to face bargains. Face to face bargains have been pointed to as the instigator of equitable splits in that uncontrollable social cues are passed from one bargainer to another. The implication is that anonymous pairings of bilateral bargainers reduce social constraints on rational self interest. But is the face to face structure really the reason for equal splits or is it the context free environment of previous Coasian bargaining experiments? Putting bargainers in an explicitly defined institution that rewards competition rather than punishes it, we should not observe equitable splits with the same high frequency.

Standard Design

Three elements root the standard design: The *Lottery Schedule*, the *Controller* and the *Number* and *Transfer contracts*. The lottery schedule presents the arrangement of the 100 lottery tickets. Table 11.1 shows an example lottery schedule. The schedule has seven numbers representing alternative distributions of the 100 lottery tickets. For example, number 3 implies that player *A* has 15 out of 100 lottery tickets implying a 15 per cent chance to win the session, player *B* has 65 tickets implying a 65 per cent chance and there is a 20 per cent chance neither subject will win, that is, the house wins. Number 5 is the efficient allocation as the bargainers leave no surplus lottery tickets on the table. A player wins a session by possessing the lottery ticket selected at random by the monitor.

Table 11.1. Example lottery schedule

Number	*A*'s chance to win (%)	*B*'s chance to win (%)	Joint chance[c]
1	0	80[b]	80
2	10	70	80
3	15	65	80
4	30	55	85
5	65	35	100
6	70	10	80
7	80[a]	0	80

[a] Subject *A*'s outside option if controller.
[b] Subject *B*'s outside option if controller.
[c] Joint chance was not included on any Lottery Sheet used in the experiment.

At the start of each round, each bargaining pair determines the Controller, the subject with unilateral property rights over the lottery schedule. The Controller can exercise his or her *outside option* or threat point by unilaterally selecting a number from the lottery schedule and informing the monitor, who then ends the session and determines the winner. For example, if player A is the Controller, his or her outside option is number 7 with 80 lottery tickets. The other subject, the Non-controller, attempts to reach a mutually acceptable agreement by offering to give some of his or her lottery tickets to the Controller. Each pair use a *matching game* to determine the Controller: The subject with the most matches from eleven face-down cards is the Controller.

Each session involves two contracts; the number contract requiring the bargaining pair to select one number from a Lottery Schedule and the transfer contract that redistributes the lottery tickets. If number 3 is chosen, if B agrees to give A 55 tickets, A's chance of winning increases to 70 per cent, while B's chance falls to 10 per cent.

After the monitor read the instructions out loud, each subject answered a set of written questions to test their understanding. After the monitor answered all relevant verbal questions, the bargaining pairs were matched up. Bargains are face to face, physical threats are not allowed and there is a ten minute time limit. Bargains are unstructured in that the sequencing of offers and counter offers is endogenous. After a bargaining pair reaches an agreement or the Controller unilaterally selects a number, the monitor determines who wins the bargaining session.

Tournament Design

The tournament design uses the same design elements and procedures as the standard experiment except it introduces an explicit non-linear payoff scheme. A 32 player *first to four victories* elimination tournament is used to provide incentive for self-interested behaviour in a face to face setting. The five round tournament has the following features: Round 1 the monitor matches subjects into sixteen pairs where the first subject in a pair to win four sessions advances; Round 2 the remaining sixteen players match up and begin bargaining again until one player in each pair has four wins; Rounds 3 and 4 the remaining eight and four players pair off, again winners advance; and finally, Round 5 pairs the two finalists who bargain until one secures four wins and is declared the tournament winner; the loser is the runner up. The bargaining tournament uses a non-linearly increasing payoff scheme - $250 to the winner, $125 to the runner up, $70 to the two subjects eliminated in Round 4, $25 to the four subjects eliminated in Round 3, $10 to the eight subjects eliminated in Round 2 and $5 to the sixteen subjects eliminated in Round 1, for a total purse of $775. Again the matching game determines the

Controller. For example, if player *A* had the most matches, the sequence of the Controller would be *A - A - B - B - A - B - A - B - A* - and so on, until one of the pair secures four wins.

Results

Consider both efficiency and the distribution of wealth. A self interested bargain occurs when the Controller receives at least the value of his or her outside option; an equitable bargain is when the pair split the lottery tickets down the middle such that both players have an equal chance of winning the session; and constrained self interest is a distribution of tickets such that the Controller has a greater expected payoff than the Non-controller, but not as great as would be dictated by his or her outside option (for example, a 60-40 or 70-20 split).

Table 11.2. Summary statistics of Coasian bargaining tournament

Round	N	Outside option or better	Constrained self interest	Equal split of lottery tickets	Split of outside option surplus =( )[a]	Unilateral outside option	Maximum joint chance
1	112	89	19	4	12(28)	59	50
2	55	46	4	5	2(9)	34	21
3	30	30	0	0	6(10)	20	10
4	13	12	1	0	1(2)	9	4
5	6	5	1	0	3(4)	1	5
Total	216	182	25	9	24(53)	123	90

[a] '=' implies a 50/50 split of the surplus above the outside option, while '( )' implies a 50/50 split or better for the non-controller.

When comparing the results from the tournament to the standard designs, more self-interested bargains, fewer equitable splits and lower efficiency should be observed. The results support this. Table 11.2 shows that rational self interest was observed in 84 per cent (182 of 216) of the tournament bargains, while equitable and constrained self interest splits fell to 4 per cent (9 of 216) and 12 per cent (25 of 216). In contrast, Shogren's (1992) standard design observed less than 10 per cent self-interested and over 80 per cent equitable bargains. The bargaining tournament matched more closely with

Shogren's (1989) team treatments which had 80 per cent self-interested and under 10 per cent equitable bargains. The cost of achieving more self-interested bargains, however, is more inefficiency, only 42 per cent (90 of 216) of all bargaining agreements were efficient as compared to Shogren's (1992) high of nearly 90 per cent efficiency. The tournament incentives pushed rational self interest to the forefront at the expense of efficiency. The Coase theorem appears extremely sensitive to institutional incentives.

ENVIRONMENTAL CONFLICT AND ENDOGENOUS TIMING

Environmental policy abets environmental conflict by promoting technological solutions that simply transfer risk through time or space. Taller stacks transfer risk to other geographic regions, storage sites transfer risk to future generations (Shogren *et al.* 1991). One aspect of the theory of environmental conflict is the behaviour of mismatched opponents, favourites and underdogs. A favourite is the player with more than a 50 per cent chance of victory at the Nash equilibrium, an underdog implies the opposite (Dixit 1987). The behaviour of mismatched opponents is a meaningful aspect of conflict theory given wealth disparities across countries.

Consider a conflict where two risk neutral players, A and B, compete to win a fixed environmental reward, G. Let x_A and x_B represent the observable and irreversible effort expended by players A and B to influence their probabilities of winning the contest, $p_A = p_A(x_A, x_B, \alpha)$ and $p_B = 1 - p_A$, where α is a parameter of relative ability. Player i selects a level of effort, x_i, to maximize his or her expected payoff, $E\pi_i = p_i(x_A, x_B, \alpha)G - x_i$. Suppose the players face an endogenous timing game that has the following structure: First the players announce simultaneously and independently when they will expend their effort, either in the first or second period; then knowing who will move when, the players choose their effort levels in the period they selected in the announcement stage. Given asymmetric ability and a logit form probability of winning function, Baik and Shogren (1992) demonstrate that in the subgame perfect equilibrium the underdog expends her effort before the favourite does.

While subgame perfection is the most popular solution concept for multi-stage games of complete information, experimental support is mixed. Harrison and Hirshleifer (1989) observed a reasonable correspondence with actual and predicted behaviour in a two stage public good contribution game, but McKelvey and Palfrey (1992) and Ochs and Roth (1989) did not. Now consider how behaviour in a standard and tournament design with non-linear payoffs matches with the theoretical predictions of the conflict with endogenous timing.

Standard Design

Figure 11.1 shows the basic 5*5 matrix used in the experiments, where $p_A(x_A, x_B, \alpha) = x_A/(x_A + \alpha x_B)$, $\alpha = 2$ and $G = 1440$. Player A is the underdog and B is the favourite. Each player is allowed to choose from 5 effort levels. Player A chooses from rows R1-R5, player B chooses from columns C1-C5, where R1 = C1 = 0, R2 = C2 = 180, R3 = C3 = 270, R4 = C4 = 320 and R5 = C5 = 720. Player A's payoff is the first number in each cell and player B's is the second. For example, if A selects R2 and B selects C2, A's and B's expected payoffs are 700 and 1180 tokens.

	C1	C2	C3	C4	C5
R1	400, 400	400, 1660	400, 1570	400, 1520	400, 1120
R2	1660, 400	700, 1180	580, 1210	536, 1204	380, 960
R3	1570, 400	747, 1043	610, 1090	557, 1093	357, 893
R4	1520, 400	758, 982	616, 1034	560, 1040	342, 858
R5	1120, 400	640, 700	503, 747	442, 758	160, 640

Figure 11.1   *5 x 5 expected payoff table. Player* B *across the columns, player* A *down the rows*

There are three potential equilibria in Figure 11.1. First, the equilibrium in the simultaneous move subgame is (R4, C4) = (560, 1040) - neither player has an unilateral incentive to deviate from his or her strategy, given the supposed strategy of the other player. Second, the equilibrium in the favourite leads subgame is (R1, C5) = (400, 1120). Third, the equilibrium in the underdog leads subgame is (R2, C3) = (580, 1210). Since both players' expected payoffs in the underdog leads subgame exceed those in the other two subgames (favourite - 1210 > 1120 > 1040; underdog - 580 > 560 > 400), the subgame perfect equilibrium is for the underdog to move first and select R2 and for the favourite to follow and select C3.

In the standard design, each token in the 5*5 matrix lists is worth $0.01 each. For example, if the underdog selects row R2 and the favourite selects column C3, the underdog's expected payoff is 580 tokens - $5.80, while the favourite expects to earn 1210 tokens - $12.10. Twenty trials are run, each player faces a different opponent for each trial and there is no time limit to make a choice. One trial is selected at random to determine take home pay.

Examining the 5*5 matrix, players lose between 6 and 30 tokens by a one row or column deviation from the subgame perfect equilibrium (R2, C3), a small amount if a token is worth $0.01. Therefore, Figure 11.2 presents a 3*3 matrix also used to examine behaviour given more distinct payoff differences between cells, each token was worth $1.00. The subgame perfect equilibrium is (R2, C1) = (9,12). All other design features are identical to those for the 5*5 matrix.

	C1	C2	C3
R1	6, 14	6, 13	6, 10
R2	9, 12	7, 11	5, 7
R3	10, 8	8, 9	4, 6

Figure 11.2　　　*3 x 3 expected payoff table. Player* B *across the columns, player* A *down the rows*

Tournament Design

The high point elimination tournament was designed as follows. First, players were randomly assigned as either an *A* or *B* player. Each player independently fills out a *Strategy Sheet*, or a set of best actions, based on the 5*5 matrix. Players knew their strategy would be played against the strategies of all opposing type players and would determine how far she would advance in the tournament and her take home pay. A Strategy Sheet had two parts, best action and timing, presented in a backward inductive structure.

The tournament had five rounds. Round 1 was a qualifying round that accommodated all who wanted to play. Round 2 cut the field down to the top sixteen players, eight *A* and *B* players. Rounds 3 and 4 cut the field down to eight and four players. Finally, Round 5 matched the top *A* and *B* player. *Top players* were the subjects with the greatest average scores at the end of a round. Ties were resolved by a random draw.

The value of a token increased at an increasing rate by round: $0.005 in Round 1; $0.02 in Round 2; $0.04 in Round 3; $0.08 in Round 4; and $0.15 in Round 5. For example, if an *A* player was bounced after Round 3 and if her average score was 700 tokens for Round 3, her payoff was $28 (700 tokens @ $0.04). If she advanced to Round 5 and if her score was 700 tokens, her payoff was $105 (700 tokens @ $0.15).

Results

The results from the standard design do not support the subgame perfect equilibrium, either for the 5*5 or 3*3 matrix. The underdogs do not always prefer to lead (35-58 per cent in all trials) and favourites do not always follow (55-77 per cent). Underdogs who lead overinvest in effort, while favourites underinvest. Total dissipation of the reward is also greater than predicted; a result more consistent with the argument that number 2 tries harder. Figures 11.3 and 11.4 show the breakdown of the results.

	C1	C2	C3	C4	C5
R1	1	6	0	1	0
R2	2	3	9*	2	1
R3	1	1	1	8	0
R4	1	2	4	27	0
R5	0	0	1	1	0

	C1	C2	C3	C4	C5
R1	0	1	4	0	20*
R2	2	1	0	0	2
R3	1	5	6	4	0
R4	0	10	16	26	3
R5	1	3	1	2	1

	C1	C2	C3	C4	C5
R1	1	3	2	9	0
R2	2	10	9	16	2
R3	1	6	21	21	2
R4	3	11	25	32*	3
R5	1	1	10	8	0

Note: * = equilibrium cell.

Figure 11.3   *Cell frequency by subgame (5 x 5 matrix - standard design - all trials). Underdog subgame (left), favourite subgame (centre) and simultaneous move subgame (right)*

	C1	C2	C3
R1	5	0	0
R2	73*	4	3
R3	6	14	1

	C1	C2	C3
R1	0	1	6*
R2	1	0	1
R3	7	9	0

	C1	C2	C3
R1	4	6	0
R2	6	18	1
R3	29	46*	9

Note: * = equilibrium cell.

Figure 11.4   *Cell frequency by subgame (3 x 3 matrix - standard design - all trials). Underdog subgame (left), favourite subgame (centre) and simultaneous move subgame (right)*

The results from the tournament design, however, provide support for subgame perfection as a reasonable predictor of behaviour. In Round 1, subjects made 170 theoretically predicted choices in best actions out of 208 decisions (82 per cent). The majority of mistakes were timing decisions by the players who did not survive the cut to Round 2; and after these players were eliminated, the remaining players made 111 theoretically predicted choices out of 112 decisions in the final three rounds, with players capturing 100 per cent of the potential rewards. Figure 11.5 illustrates the breakdown of results in round 1.

The potential reasons why the tournament format did better is that tourney players specified a complete strategy, had more time to think about that strategy, had a monetary incentive to use that time wisely and were eliminated if they made several mistakes in strategy. This provided more incentive to take

Round 1 seriously rather than use it as an opportunity to explore the consequences of unpredicted behaviour as is often the case in standard design with multiple trials. The players who survived to Round 2 only received the strategies of the opposing type players who also survived, thereby reinforcing rationality in the later rounds. In contrast, the standard design did not eliminate 'bad' players who altered the nature of the equilibrium throughout the remaining trials. In the standard design, if a player was sloppy in her choice of strategy, he or she could contaminate the entire experiment regardless of how many trials were run. If opponents did not believe the sloppy player would make rational choices, they had to make rational deviations from what theory would otherwise predict. In the tournament, however, a player had less incentive to make sloppy decisions because it increased the likelihood that she would not make the cut. By shifting attention to relative performance measures, choices were much more in line with theoretical predictions, but mistakes on-the-equilibrium path lead to uneven performance.

	C1	C2	C3	C4	C5
R1					
R2		4	24*		
R3					
R4					
R5					

	C1	C2	C3	C4	C5
R1					27*
R2					
R3					
R4				14	
R5				2	4

	C1	C2	C3	C4	C5
R1					
R2			4	5	
R3			4	5	
R4			27	45	
R5					

Note: * = equilibrium cell.

Figure 11.5   *Cell frequency by subgame (5 x 5 matrix - tournament design - round 1). Underdog subgame (left), favourite subgame (centre) and simultaneous move subgame (right)*

THE CENTIPEDE GAME

Another test of the power of subgame perfection in an environmental conflict is the centipede game. Introduced by Rosenthal (1982), the centipede game has two players who alternative moves over a finite horizon. Figure 11.6 illustrates a six stage centipede game. Player A moves first; she can either terminate the game by 'taking', T, or she can pass, P, the decision on to the other player. If A passes, player B then decides to take or pass. This continues until one the players terminates the game or we hit the final stage. The centipede game reflects the noncooperative element involved in open access property disputes where individuals are hypnotized by myopic over harvesting of a resource.

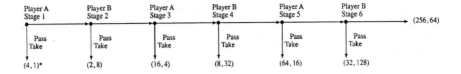

*(Player 1's payoff, Player 2's payoff)

Figure 11.6   Six stage centipede game

The subgame perfect equilibrium of the centipede game is for player *A* to take in stage 1. While stage 6 has the highest payoff, if player *A* uses backward inductive reasoning, she will see that stage 6 should never be seen because player *B* can always do better by taking in stage 6, 128 > 64. Knowing this *A* should take in stage 5, 64 > 32. But knowing this *B* should take in stage 4 and so on until the game unravels back to stage 1.

Standard Design

The standard design follows McKelvey and Palfrey (1992). Figure 11.6 is given to each subject. The subject then fills out a strategy sheet which asks her to: (i) select a number from 1 to 99 that will be compared to a randomly drawn number to determine whether she is an *A* or *B* player, that is, who gets the first mover advantage; (ii) specify when she would end the game if she was the *A* player (Stage 1, 3, 5, or not at all); and (iii) specify when she would end the game if she was the *B* player (Stage 2, 4, 6, or not at all). All strategy sheets were collected and then randomly matched by the monitor. Subjects did not know their opponent. After the monitors calculated the results, each subject received feedback on how many tokens she earned given her and her 'opponent' choices.

Each subject participated in 3 practice games and 10 binding games. Each subject earned the sum of the tokens in the 10 binding games times the token value (1 token = $0.01) plus a $5/hour participation fee. Fourteen subjects participated in the standard design.

Tournament Design

The tournament design was identical to the standard design except for the tournament incentives. Now subjects played 6 practice games identical to the games in the standard design; they then moved into a 4 round single elimination tournament. Two 16 player tournaments were run as follows. Subjects again filled out the three question strategy sheet. Players were randomly matched and then the *A* and *B* players were determined by the numbers selected compared to the 'monitor' number. The *A* 'player' strategy sheet was compared to the *B* players strategy sheet such that whichever player had more tokens advanced to the next round. For example, if an *A* player ended the game in stage 1 such that she has 4 tokens and *B* has 1 token, *A* advances and *B* does not.

Tournament payoffs increased non-linearly such that Round 1: V = number of tokens times $0.01 plus $5; Round 2: V plus $10; Round 3: V plus $25; Round 4 runner up: V plus $45; and Round 4 winner: V plus $75.

Results

The results from the standard and tournament designs are summarized in Table 11.3. The results from the standard design match up with the findings of McKelvey and Palfrey (1992) where the majority of games ended after stage 4. Not one subject ended the game in stage 1, either in the practice or binding games. Subgame perfection did not organize behaviour as predicted.

Table 11.3. Proportion of time a game ended on a particular stage

Design	1	2	3	4	5	6	7
Standard							
Practice	0	0.095	0.381	0.095	0.381	0.048	0
Binding	0	0	0.143	0.286	0.343	0.171	0.057
*Tournament**							
Practice	0.555	0.277	0.126	0.031	0.021	0	0
Round 1	0.688	0.250	0.063	0	0	0	0
Rounds 2-4	1.00	0	0	0	0	0	0
*McKelvey and Palfrey (1992)**							
Actual	0.007	0.064	0.199	0.384	0.253	0.078	0.014
Predicted	0.031	0.076	0.108	0.433	0.274	0.069	0.009

Note: * = Mean values.

The tournament design, however, imposed such a heavy hand on the shoulder of each player that now the majority took the opportunity to terminate the game immediately in stage 1. Nearly 56 per cent of the games ended in stage 1 in 6 practice games, while 69 and 100 per cent ended in stage 1 in Round 1 and Rounds 2-4 of the tournament. The difference between behaviour in the standard and tournament designs was significantly different ($F = 162.7$).

Simply introducing the idea that each players would eventually compete in a tournament was sufficient to alter behaviour toward rationality in the initial practice rounds even though no tournament took place and no money was exchanged. Rational behaviour in the tournament practice round increased to 60 per cent from 0 per cent observed in the standard design. The opportunity cost of not advancing in the tournament was sufficiently great to induce players to adopt the noncooperative self-interested behaviour presumed by the subgame perfect solution concept.

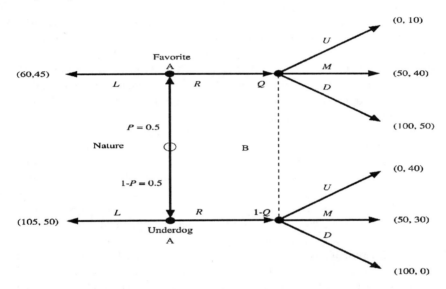

Figure 11.7   *Environmental conflict with asymmetric information*

CONFLICT WITH ASYMMETRIC INFORMATION

One aspect of environmental conflict that has been insufficiently examined is asymmetric information. Asymmetric information permeates environmental conflict. The value of an environmental asset that could be used for either development or conservation generates an informational asymmetry where tangible market prices strongly signal development value while intangible nonmarket preferences weakly signal preservation value. For example, suppose a Northern country wants to preserve a Southern 'country' forest for its biodiversity, while the South wants to develop the forest to increase its per capita income. Given observable market prices for the timber products from development and unobservable nonmarket values for biodiversity, the North knows the value of both preservation and development, the South knows only its value of development and not the 'North' value of preservation.

Figure 11.7 illustrates an environmental conflict between two players, A and B. The game begins by Nature choosing between favourite and underdog with equal probabilities, $P = 0.5$ and $(1 - P) = 0.5$. 'Natures' choice is revealed to A but not to B. Player A begins by either signalling its willingness to challenge B without revealing effort, R, or by explicitly revealing its level of effort, L. If the favourite, A's expected payoff given L is 60, while B's is 45; if the underdog, A's expected payoff given L is 105; B's is 50.

Let Q and $(1 - Q)$ represent B's updated probabilities that A is a favourite or underdog. Player B selects from three levels of effort given its updated beliefs: U, M, or D. Effort expended is ranked: $U > M > D$. If B thinks A is the underdog, B prefers U. But if B believes A is the favourite B prefers D. If B is relatively uncertain as to whether A is a favourite or underdog, B prefers M hedging its bets by over-investing effort against a favourite and underinvesting against an underdog.

The game in Figure 11.7 can be solved using the perfect Bayesian equilibrium concept. There are two distinct equilibrium behaviours, a unique separating equilibrium and a pooling equilibria. Perfect Bayesian equilibrium refinements derive a unique equilibrium by arguing that B should concentrate its off-the-equilibrium path beliefs on types of opponents that are most likely to deviate from their equilibrium actions. Using Cho and Kreps's (1987) intuitive refinement, the pooling equilibria can be eliminated. The deviation set of player A as underdog is empty because its equilibrium payoff, 105, exceeds any possible payoff from deviating: 0, 50 or 100. Therefore, B should suspect that a deviation came from a favourite, not an underdog and B should update its priors such that $Q = 1$, then B chooses D. The multiple pooling equilibria are eliminated and the remaining unique separating equilibrium is equivalent to an intuitive equilibrium (also see Brandts and Holt 1992).

Standard Design

In the standard design, 15 subjects were recruited for a treatment. The monitor assigned subjects randomly to one of three groups, $A1$ (favourite), $A2$ (underdog) and B, each with five players. The three groups played the game in Figure 11.7 where the $A1$s and $A2$s chose between L and R and the Bs chose between U, M and D.

Each treatment had five periods, 1 practice and 4 binding. For each period, a subject completed a strategy sheet with two sets of questions that elicited: (i) a subject's beliefs about how he or she thought the three representative players would play the game (defined below) where subjects were paid $0.25 for each correct prediction (Banks *et al.* 1994) and (ii) the subject's choices on how he or she wanted to play five games against the representative player.

A common history was created throughout the five periods by constructing three representative players Rep-A1, Rep-A2 and Rep-B, such that all *A1* and *A2* players were matched against the Rep-B, while all *B* players were matched against the Rep-A1 and Rep-A2. A representative player is a combination of the choices made in a period by all five subjects of that type. For example, the Rep-A1 in period 1 is constructed from an equally proportioned random sample of the strategy choices made by all five *A1* players in period 1. Each *B* subject played against both the representative *A1* and *A2* player to maintain a risk neutral player's incentives.

After all subjects completed their strategy sheets, the monitor determined the representative players choices for each group and calculated the results of each game. The resulting earnings (the sum of the earnings for the five games plus a reward for correctly guessing how the representative player in each group played) were returned to the subjects on a round earnings sheet. The round earnings sheet also revealed the strategy choices of the three representative players. A subject's earnings equalled the sum of his or her earnings in the four binding periods multiplied by one cent plus a ten dollar participation fee.

Tournament Design

In the tournament session, 24 subjects were divided into 8 *A1*, *A2* and *B* players. For Round 1, the subjects were randomly ordered and assigned to one of the four games. After Round 1 removed four subjects of each type, the strategies of the remaining subjects were randomly assigned to one of the games in Round 2. After Round 2 eliminated two subjects of each type, the strategies for the remaining subjects were randomly assigned to two of the games in Round 3. Round 3 eliminated one subject of each type. The strategies of the remaining three subjects (one of each type) were played for each of the four games in Round 4.

Subjects were paid a $5.00 participation fee plus the value of their tokens in the round that they were eliminated. If a subject was eliminated in Rounds 1, 2 or 3, she earned $0.01, $0.05 or $0.10 per token earned in that round. A subject earned $0.25 per token earned in the Round 4. Subjects advanced in the tournament by earning more tokens in the round than a randomly selected subject of their same type. Ties were broken by comparing the accuracy of a subjects beliefs about the opponents actions. If two subjects had identical beliefs, a coin toss was the second tie breaker.

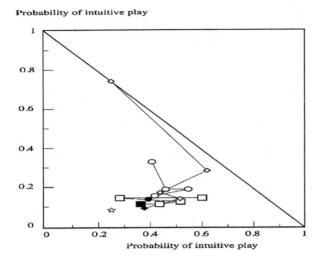

Figure 11.8   *Probability of equilibrium play*

Results

The likelihood that the subjects played the intuitive equilibrium equals the probability that the $A1$s chose R, the $A2$s chose L and the Bs chose D. The likelihood that the subjects played the unintuitive equilibrium equals the probability that the $A1$s chose L and the $A2$s chose L. First, consider the behaviour of $A1$ subjects. No explicit preference for any particular action with either the standard or experimental design seems to have developed. On average, 60.3 per cent of the $A1$s chose R with a probability between 0.40 and 0.60. In the standard design, pure strategy play in session 1 was evenly dispersed across rounds 1, 2, 3 and 5 with 75 per cent of pure strategy play being unintuitive, while in session 2 pure strategy play occurred exclusively in rounds 3 and 4 with 75 per cent of pure strategy play being intuitive. Within the tournament design, no pure strategy was chosen in any round.

Second, the $A2$s appear to be playing the equilibrium strategy regardless of the design. On average, 74 per cent of the $A2$s chose to play a pure equilibrium strategy in each round, a percentage non-decreasing by round. Third, the Bs appear to move towards the refined equilibrium strategy and away from mixing strategies. On average, 56.2 per cent of the Bs played either an intuitive or an unintuitive strategy. Within the standard design, 62.5 and 20 per cent of pure strategy play was intuitive in sessions 1 and 2. Within the tournament design, 40 per cent of pure strategy play was intuitive.

Figure 11.8, from Hurley and Shogren (1997), shows the dynamic time path of the probability that the subjects played the intuitive and the unintuitive equilibria: Points (0,1.0) and (1.0,0) represent intuitive and unintuitive play with probability 1.0, the origin represents non-Nash play. The solid star within the simplex denotes purely random play, solid markers show the probability of intuitive and unintuitive play for Round 1 and the sequence of open markers denote the likelihood of intuitive and unintuitive play for Rounds 2-5. The trend within the standard design was that session 1 play moved toward the intuitive equilibrium, while session 2 play moved toward the unintuitive equilibrium. Tournament play also moved toward the unintuitive equilibrium. The tournament incentive failed to induce clear cut rational behaviour in the environmental conflict with asymmetric information.

CONCLUDING OBSERVATIONS

Tournaments are real world institutions that reward competition over seemingly trivial differences in measurable performance. The economic relevance of a tournament structure comes from an explicit or implicit design that rewards a small numerical deviation between the optimal and second best responses by a sizable difference in monetary rewards. Many incentive systems use a non-linearly increasing reward system where the winner's payoff is often twice the runner up's, such as sporting events and performance pay in top management positions. Granted a tournament shifts the players' emphasis to distributional from efficiency concerns, it is noteworthy that this refocus on relative rather than absolute payoffs generates the behaviour we normally presume in standard game theoretic models of environmental policy.

Plott's (1996) discovered preference hypothesis posits that subjects progress through three stages of rationality when confronted with a new or unfamiliar task in an experimental setting. In stage 1, a subject's choices seem myopic and random as she gropes for profitable behaviour. With experience, a subject's behaviour becomes more purposeful in stage 2, but it is still naive in that she fails to account for other players' behaviour. Finally in stage 3, a subject's behaviour becomes sophisticated and her actions reveal well developed preferences and an anticipation for other subjects' actions. Not all subjects make it through all three stages in any given experiment. Some players begin in stage 1 and never leave, other agents start in later stages or move quickly through all three stages.

In three of the four experiments we have examined in the chapter, the tournament incentives seems to encourage the climb through the three stages of rationality quicker than the standard design. Tournament incentives focus the subject's mind on the key parameters presumed to drive the models of economic behaviour used in environmental policy.

Govindasamy *et al.* (1994) have examined how environmental policy could use a tournament incentive structure based on readily available information on input use or pollution control effort to construct an ordinal ranking of the set of producers. The advantage of the environmental tournament is that the ordinal relative ranking of producers by some proxy of actual pollution control provides information that is typically less costly to obtain than the cardinal rankings required by most emission and ambient charges and it ranks producers by actions rather than a random assignment of blame required by a random penalty scheme. In the case of nonpoint source pollution, for example, a regulator would monitor say surface water contamination for the entire area, rank producers based on their input use or pollution control effort and then penalize one or more of the lowest ranking producers if the ambient concentrations for the area exceed the prescribed standard.

Alternatively, the regulator might reward the highest ranking producers if the ambient concentration is better than the prescribed standard. Rewards or penalties depend on the relative rank of the producers, not on the absolute level of pollution emissions. The key is knowing how large to make the spread between the large and small penalties or rewards. Experimental markets provide a tool to further understand this spiral of logic entwining tournament incentives and behaviour around environmental policy.

REFERENCES

Baik, K.H. and Shogren, J. 1992. 'Strategic behaviour in contests: Comment', *American Economic Review*, 82, 359-62.

Banks, J., Camerer, C. and Porter, D. 1994. 'An experimental analysis of Nash refinements in signalling games', *Games and Economic Behaviour*, 6, 1-31.

Brandts, J. and Holt, C.A. 1992. 'An experimental test of equilibrium dominance in signalling games', *American Economic Review*, 82, 1350-65.

Cho, I-K. and Kreps, D. 1987. 'Signalling games and stable equilibria', *Quarterly Journal of Economics*, 102, 179-221.

Coase, R. 1960. 'The problem of social costs', *Journal of Law and Economics*, 3, 1-44.

Drago, R., Garvey, G. and Turnbull, G. 1996. 'A collective tournament', *Economics Letters*, 50, 223-7.

Dixit, A. 1987. 'Strategic behaviour in contests', *American Economic Review*, 77, 891-8.

Ehrenberg, R. and Bognanno, M. 1990. 'Do tournaments have incentive effects?', *Journal of Political Economy*, 98, 1307-24.

Govindasamy, R., Herriges, J. and Shogren, J. 1994. 'Nonpoint tournaments', in Dosi, C. and Tomasi, T. (eds), *Nonpoint Source Pollution Regulation: Issues and Analysis*. Amsterdam: Kluwer Academic Publishers, pp. 87-105.

Harrison, G. 1989. 'Theory and misbehaviour of first-price auctions', *American Economic Review*, 79, 749-62.

Harrison, G. and Hirshleifer, J. 1989. 'An experimental evaluation of weakest link/best shot models of public goods', *Journal of Political Economy*, 97, 201-25.

Hoffman, E. and Spitzer, M. 1982. 'The Coase Theorem: Some experimental results', *Journal of Law and Economics*, 25, 73-98.

Hurley, T. and J. Shogren, J. 1997. 'Environmental conflicts with asymmetric information: Theory and behaviour', in Hanley, N. and Folmer, H. (eds), *Game theory and the global environment*. Aldershot: Edgar Elgar (forthcoming).

Jensen, M. and Murphy, K.J. 1990. 'Performance pay and top-management incentives', *Journal of Political Economy*, 98, 225-64.

Lazear, E. and Rosen, S. 1981. 'Rank order tournaments as optimal labor contracts', *Journal of Political Economy*, 89, 841-64.

Lewis, T. 1996. 'Protecting the environment when costs and benefits are privately known', *Rand Journal of Economics*, winter, 27(4) pp 819-847.

McKelvey, R. and Palfrey, T. 1992. 'An experimental study of the centipede game', *Econometrica*, 60, 803-36.

Nau, R. and McCardle, K. 1991. 'Arbitrage, rationality and equilibrium', *Theory and Decision*, 31, 199-240.

Ochs, J. and Roth, A. 1989. 'An experimental study of sequential bargaining', *American Economic Review*, 79, 355-84.

Plott, C. 1996. 'Rational individual behaviour in markets and social choice processes', in Arrow, K.J., Colombatto, E., Perlman, M. and Schmidt, C. (eds), *The Rational Foundations of Economic Behavior*. New York: St. Martin's Press.

Rosenthal, R. 1982. 'Games of perfect information, predatory pricing and the chain store paradox', *Journal of Economic Theory*, 25, 92-100.

Roth, A. 1995. 'Bargaining Experiments,' in Kagel, J. and Roth, A. (eds), *Handbook of Experimental Economics*. Princeton, New Jersey: Princeton University Press, pp. 253-348.

Shogren, J. 1989. 'Fairness in bargaining requires a context: An experimental examination of loyalty', *Economics Letters*, 31, 319-23.

Shogren, J. 1992. 'An experiment on Coasian bargaining over ex ante lotteries and ex post rewards', *Journal of Economic Behaviour and Organization*, 17, 153-69.

Shogren, J. 1997. 'Self-interest and equity in a bargaining tournament with non-linear payoffs', *Journal of Economic Behaviour and Organization* (forthcoming).

Shogren, J., Baik, K.H. and Crocker, T. 1991. 'Environmental conflicts and strategic commitment', in Pethig, R. (ed.), *Conflicts and Cooperation in Managing Environmental Resources*. Berlin: Springer-Verlag, pp. 85-106.

Smith, V.L. 1991. 'Rational choice: The contrast between economics and psychology', *Journal of Political Economy*, 99, 877-97.

12. The Production of Biodiversity: Institutions and the Control of Land

Ian Hodge

PRESSURES ON THE LAND

Human development is causing increasing pressures on the land to provide resources for agriculture, forestry, mineral extraction and waste disposal. The development of land for commodity production competes with alternative extensive land uses and reduces the space available for plant and wildlife populations (Swanson 1995). Biodiversity is defined in the Biodiversity Convention as 'the variability among living organisms from all sources including, *inter alia*, terrestrial, marine and other aquatic ecosystems and the ecological complexities of which they are a part; this includes diversity within species, between species and of ecosystems'. It is generally reduced by development pressures, as is represented in the destruction of rainforests, in threats to charismatic species in Africa or India, or in the loss of wetland or moorland habitats in the United Kingdom.

The effects of biodiversity decline are uncertain. In some circumstances species become extinct, permanently closing options that may have been a source of future human welfare. The true extent of species loss is unknown. Some have argued that we are currently experiencing a period of mass extinctions comparable to any others experienced within geological time periods (Wilson 1993), although the evidence and the implications are the subject of dispute (Budiansky 1995). Any estimates of the numbers of species becoming extinct that are made are fraught with difficulty and, without doubt many species are lost before they have been documented and classified.

Decline in biodiversity is also commonly associated with other forms of environmental degradation, including damage to ecosystem functions, such as soil erosion and siltation of waterways or salinity, damage to the productive capacity of renewable resources and a loss of aesthetic and recreational values. There may also be a loss of human cultural values. Longstanding patterns of land use develop their own characteristic habitats and these systems may be valued both for the plant and animal species supported by them and for the human cultural values embodied within them. The balance between the relative

233

significance of these impacts varies greatly between different types of physical and human environment. For many, the specific concerns may not be clearly thought out and expressed; biodiversity may itself stand as a proxy for a much wider range of fears and concerns for environmental change. There is thus often no single variable that represents the output of biodiversity. It may also be regarded as a non-point source benefit, with further implications for the design of effective policy mechanisms.

Monetary valuation of these impacts probably presents an impossible task. Even in circumstances where the physical impacts of environmental change are well documented, the lack of information about future human possibilities, environmental relationships and the controversy surrounding the ethical issues raised (Randall 1994) almost certainly rule out any widely acceptable valuations. In contingent valuation studies, individuals sometimes appear unwilling to tradeoff biodiversity against other goods (Spash and Hanley 1995). What is apparent is that there is widely expressed concern about the decline in biodiversity, that the impacts are at least regarded as potentially large relative to many other human values and that significant causes and impacts operate at a global scale, either as a result of implications for the global climate or in terms of the opportunities foregone.

The problem of biodiversity decline has much in common with other concerns for environmental quality: Externalities, diffuse impacts, uncertainty about environmental relationships and problems of valuation. However, it is different in that in contrast to pollution, there is no general presumption that land users have a duty to protect the environment. Rather biodiversity is often regarded as a public good and positive policies are directed towards its provision. We may then be looking for a 'beneficiary pays' or a 'provider gets' principle rather than a 'polluter pays principle' (Brown 1994, Blöchliger 1994). This implies the need for mechanisms for the transfer of funds to providers (the PGP), consistent with the underlying distribution of property rights. These may be generated from the beneficiaries (the BPP) or else they may be allocated from general taxation. However BPP mechanisms may have merit in contributing towards the revelation of demand in an area where valuation is so difficult. There may be other circumstances where the 'polluter pays principle' would be deemed to apply, but they are not considered here.

EXPLAINING SPECIES DECLINE

Economic analysis of species loss has commonly been founded in the economics of open access and species growth rates and harvest costs, particularly drawing on the model of the fishery (Gordon 1954, Clark 1973). Extinction is explained in relation to three factors: Open access to the resource, relative price to cost of harvesting the resource and the relative growth rate of the resource. Low growth rates combined with relatively high price cost ratios push towards the extinction of the species. The situation may be compounded in the context of an open access property regime.

Swanson (1994) has extended the model in order to bring it 'on-shore', most significantly to recognise the opportunity costs of the land resources on which land based species depend. He widens the analysis in two ways: To take account of the allocation of base resources; the land, water, foods that provide the biological service flows upon which species depend and of the management services, the development of appropriate institutions for the allocation of resources. In this, attention is helpfully focused on land and institutions.

While marine species can exist largely independently from other human pressures, the great majority of threatened species are land based where humans have competing uses for the habitats that support them. In effect, the assumption of the marine model is that the opportunity cost of the biological services upon which species depend is zero. This is clearly not a plausible assumption for land based species. Swanson argues that the amount of habitat available to a given species is probably the single most important factor determining species viability in the short and medium run. The cost of foregoing the returns from alternative land uses must be incorporated into the model of determining the feasibility of species survival.

The second extension of the conventional model takes account of the institutional context and particularly the property regime over the species in question and the base resources on which they depend. In the traditional model, species decline is seen to be caused by the presence of open access. However, in contrast, Swanson argues that open access should be regarded as itself a consequence of the failure to invest in management services which arises from the low returns. The lack of perceived benefits from the resource leads to a lack of investment in institution building. Open access is a consequence rather than a cause of low returns. The open access regime is not an exogenous 'state of nature', but an endogenous 'notion of the state'.

But the logic here is less straightforward. It is not clear to what the determination of institutions is endogenous. The institutional arrangements determine whose values are relevant to the decision making problem and what priorities are placed on those values. It must therefore be incomplete to argue that low values are the cause of the open access regime. Even low values under open access serve certain interests in respect of the exploitation of the resource and these interests will resist changes to property rights arrangements. The problem is that certain values are not given expression through available institutional structures and are therefore excluded from consideration.

ALLOCATING FOREST BENEFITS

The importance of property rights can be illustrated through the values that can be generated in tropical forests. Some studies have indicated that the value of non-timber forest products can be substantial in relation to the potential value of logging and/or conversion to non-sustainable agricultural use. A detailed study of one hectare of rainforest in Peru (Peters *et al.* 1989) valued the fruit and latex which it could provide. In the area, 72 species yield products with a market value. By estimating production rates and collecting information on prices from the local market and sawmills it was possible to estimate the total value of products from the site. The study found that the area produces annually fruit and rubber worth some $422, after allowing for costs of collection and transport. Allowing that 25 per cent of the product should be left for regeneration and discounting at 5 per cent gives a present value of sustainable fruit and latex harvests of $6,330 per hectare.

Alternatively, the area could be felled for timber. If taken in one felling, the timber would generate a net revenue of $1,000. Periodic selective felling every 20 years would generate a net present value of $490. Sustainable timber harvest together with fruit and latex harvest would generate a net present value of $6,820. Given the apparent considerable financial superiority of sustainable use, we may wonder why timber felling is so prevalent in practice.

We should note some qualifications to this comparison. It does neglect any potential value from the land once the timber has been cleared. It is difficult to know what value this might have and it would vary greatly from place to place. For a very rough comparison, pasture and arable land in Brazilian Amazonia was recorded as selling for about $140/ha in 1984 (Katzman and Cale 1990). However, adding this to the value of logging would still leave the sustainable use as the clearly more valuable option. There is too considerable danger in extrapolating from a single site, which may not be representative of other areas. Prices and production levels will change and not every hectare of rainforest will have this market value. Further, if a large volume of rainforest products were to be harvested in this way, the supply to local markets would no doubt quickly exceed demand, forcing prices down.

But none of this perhaps fully answers the question as to why such an apparently valuable option appears to be so neglected. A more complete explanation would need to recognise the importance of property rights. There are several aspects to property rights allocation that can lead to less sustainable uses. These local values are often not considered by those who take over the land for clearance. Local interests often do not have secure property rights over the forest area, even though their peoples may have used it for generations and so the loss of value to them is an external cost of land clearance by loggers and settlers. Further Mendelson (1994) argues that even relatively low probabilities of losing control over land can discourage uses that are sustainable in the long term in favour of short run exploitative uses such as a destructive agriculture with declining physical product. He also develops a model that demonstrates the way in which poorly defined property rights can lead colonists to dissipate a large fraction of the value of the natural resources on wasteful defensive expenditures.

THE WIDER INTERESTS IN BIODIVERSITY

It will be apparent that very many people are affected in one way or another by the decisions taken on how to manage land resources. In particular, those who stand to gain from the logging or from the agricultural use of rainforest land are generally different people from those who stand to lose from clearance. The gains from clearance are experienced locally, while the gains from conservation are experienced globally. Table 12.1 compares the benefits and costs of protecting areas of rainforest at three different spatial scales. The local scale represents the effects of the protected area itself and on the local communities. The regional/national scale represents the wider region of the country and the nation as a whole, through environmental effects, impacts on the economy and effects arising from the involvement of regional and national governments. The transnational or global scale, represents effects outside the country.

The most immediate effects of the impact on land use from establishing protected areas for forests are experienced at the local level. The gains take the form of the consumptive benefits of the forest: Hunting, fishing, collection of edible and medicinal plants. The extent to which these benefits are possible within a protected area, or at least the extent to which they are permitted, will depend upon the sensitivity of the local ecology. These benefits should be gained on a sustainable basis. The protection of the area can also provide opportunities for recreation and tourism, which offer an alternative source of local income. Future values are those benefits which are expected to arise, but which have not yet been identified. At a local level there may be new consumptive benefits. But the extent to which the benefits will go to local people is uncertain. The rosy periwinkle was discovered in Madagascar, but the country receives no royalties from its exploitation. Creation of a protected area also causes costs. The most common indirect cost is damage caused by wildlife. Substantial damage to property and injury and even loss of life can be caused in communities surrounding protected areas from elephants, wild pigs, tigers, bears and rhinos. The opportunity costs are the gains foregone, the lost profits, from the land uses which are prevented by protection.

Table 12.1. Comparing the distribution of the costs and benefits of protecting rainforest at three spatial scales

Potentially Most Significant Benefits	Potentially Most Significant Costs
LOCAL SCALE	
Consumptive benefits	Indirect costs
Recreation/tourism	Opportunity costs
Future values	
REGIONAL/NATIONAL SCALE	
Recreation/tourism	Direct costs
Watershed values	Opportunity costs
Future values	
TRANSNATIONAL/GLOBAL	
Biological diversity	(Costs have been minimal)
Non consumptive benefits	
Ecological processes	
Education and research	
Future values	

Source: Wells (1992)

At the regional/national scale the major gains are due to recreation and tourism. Rainforests have the potential to attract significant numbers of visitors to the area. But the avoided environmental damage which would be caused by deforestation is also important. The direct costs here refer to the direct budget outlays by government for the acquisition and operation of the protected area; the purchase of land, the costs of wardens, planning, research and so on. Again, future values and opportunity costs are experienced at this wider level.

The gains in terms of biodiversity, through the protection of the earth's ecological processes and non-consumptive benefits, the aesthetic and cultural benefit from the presence of the rainforests, are enjoyed at a global scale. The gains from the discovery of new drugs are enjoyed worldwide. At this level, the costs of protecting areas are minimal. These different distributions inevitably mean that different groups of people in different places will take different view of the appropriate uses for the rainforest.

INSTITUTIONAL ARRANGEMENTS TO REPRESENT WIDER VALUES: ARTICULATION

Many interests are thus affected by the level of biodiversity, interests widely separated by space, culture and wealth. Many of the values have significant public good attributes. For reasons of transactions costs and power relationships, few of them are reflected in conventional market transactions. The aim must be to establish institutional arrangements that give all interests an appropriate opportunity to have an influence on resource allocation decisions and to establish mechanisms whereby funds may be transferred from beneficiaries, to those directly bearing the opportunity costs.

The implication is that we need to establish new institutions that can stand in for the functions of a market. This is *inter alia* to transmit the preferences and values of potential consumers to those decision makers controlling the relevant resources and to establish incentives for resource managers to act entrepreneurially to seek out opportunities to move their resources to higher value uses either individually or in co-operation with others. In what follows, the approach is simply to separate out the various functions of a market system and to rethink the mechanisms that may be appropriate to represent the values of biodiversity under alternative circumstances.

We summarise these elements through alternative models of articulation. This concerns the vertical relationships through various intermediaries between producers and consumers. We may interpret articulation both as a form of expression of the potential benefits involved and in terms of the linkages between the individual elements involved. There is also an issue of coordination between decision makers at a horizontal level, but this is not dealt with here. See Hodge (1995) for some discussion of this in a UK land use context.

There are several stages between the identification of demand and the response in terms of practical changes in land use. The aim is to consider policy and market mechanisms that can support conditions favourable for the conservation of biodiversity.

Expressing Values

The first stage is to generate evidence of the extent of demand for a good. In conventional market terms, this would provide evidence of willingness to pay. In some circumstances in the absence of a market, this may be demonstrated through the analysis of revealed or expressed preferences, although the problems have already been indicated.

Alternatively there may be opportunities for making donations towards the costs of provision, although this is likely to remain incomplete due to free riding. Failing this, demand may be revealed through the political process of lobbying and voting and reflected in the objectives of national and local governments and international organisations.

Legitimating Interests

An associated question relates to the rights and responsibilities that those affected by land use may have in respect of the values in question. In essence this requires a definition of the property rights held by those with some claim to the values arising from land uses. In order to have value a right must be defined and enforced by the state on behalf of the claimant. This requires an adjudication on the customary rights of local communities and on the rights of recent colonists into an area. It requires a clear definition of the reference level of environmental quality, which landowners will be treated as having a duty to maintain (Hodge 1989). It will require a comprehensive treatment of the rights and duties of individuals and organisations extracting benefits from an area and will establish the framework within which new market or policy mechanisms can be developed.

Establishing Linkage Mechanisms

Those landholders who control relevant areas of land will need to be given incentives to make the necessary adjustments to their land management. The expression of value needs to be articulated towards the decision makers who control resources. This may either be through the implementation of policy mechanisms, such as management agreements, or may be by establishing the conditions under which a market can operate.

Controlling Land

Land managers need to have access to the appropriate resources and information. In many circumstances, as is almost invariably the case in respect of conventional environmental policy, this involves ensuring that those who currently have control over the land also have the necessary information so that they are able to respond to the incentives. In other cases, the aim may be to establish new, alternative owners with particular objectives or skills.

MARKET MODELS OF ARTICULATION

There is clearly a vast array of alternative ways in which these issues may be treated and it is not possible to consider them all. In practice there will be numerous stages, each of considerable complexity. The aim here is to illustrate some basic characteristics of some alternative models. These involve different degrees of individual, collective and government action and will be relevant in different circumstances.

The Attenuated Market Model

At present the dominant model is one driven primarily by market forces. Markets capture some of the potential values from land, but as we have noted many values are not captured by the available institutions. The attenuated market model is illustrated in Figure 12.1.

Expressing values	demand for marketed commodities
	⇓
Legitimating interests	poorly defined property rights
	⇓
Establishing linkage mechanisms	market
	⇓
Controlling land	land leasing or acquisition

Figure 12.1.   Attenuated market model

Incentives are driven primarily by markets, but these are incomplete in a variety of ways, many of which have already been referred to. The most important markets tend to be for timber and agricultural products. Property rights may be incomplete and uncertain such that significant values have little influence on the choice of land use.

In practice the problem of incentives may be exacerbated by government policies that give support for commercial primary sector land uses. These have been documented in respect of tropical forestry (Biswanger 1991) and in respect of agricultural policy within Europe (Bowers and Cheshire 1983).

An Extended Market Model

An extended market model (Figure 12.2) might begin by introducing more secure property rights. Mendelson (1994) for instance suggests that property rights to well defined parcels of land could be sold in financial markets or alternatively land could be given to citizens without requiring improvements. But beyond this positive market incentives may be established through commoditisation, especially for products that are jointly supplied with biodiversity. New arrangements might also be used to secure resource rents for the commercial use of genetic material (Sedjo and Simpson 1995). This may be possible by extending patent rights to cover newly discovered genetic material or through individual contracts in which countries agree to permit the collection of material in return for a share in the value arising from the commercial developments based on the material. It is necessary to ensure that the extension of rights in these ways does establish incentives for the conservation of habitat and countries will only benefit if the genetic resources are truly scarce and access to them is limited.

Expressing values	Identification of values and potential products
	⇓
Legitimating interests	definition and enforcement of property rights; reduction of transactions costs
	⇓
Establishing linkage mechanisms	commoditisation
	⇓
Controlling land	incentives to rights holders

Figure 12.2.   An extended market model

More careful definition of products and the provision of further information to consumers can enhance the return to production practices that are more consistent with the goals of conservation. Perhaps the most obvious example is labelling timber harvested on a sustained yield basis or the products of organic agricultural systems. Consumers may be willing to pay a premium for these, either through a belief that the products are better or safer for the consumer than the alternatives or for less direct personal benefit as a contribution to environmental conservation.

Similar arguments may be applied to the development of commercial tourism based on the biodiversity of the local area. This may be supported by giving rights to operate tourist enterprises to local communities so that decisions on land use are made by the beneficiaries of tourist activities. It may be appropriate to establish rights over public access and vest them in a local community so as to translate an open access regime into some form of private or collective regime.

Generally this approach will still fail to provide full market incentives for the production of biodiversity, rather it establishes markets for products with varying degrees of jointness in supply with biodiversity. The scope in any particular situation will depend considerably on particular local circumstances.

ALTERNATIVE MODELS OF ARTICULATION

The limits of market models suggest a role for alternatives that involve a greater role for collective organisations, within either the public or the private sectors. Three possibilities are outlined in Figure 12.3.

The Management Agreement Model

The dominant form of rural environmental policy to have been adopted in the UK in recent years is centred around management agreements between a government agency and an individual landholder. The typical pattern is that a goal is established by a central government department and an area is designated within which individual landholders are offered environmental contracts under which payments are made for undertaking (or not undertaking) certain actions. While the approach was formally introduced into legislation in 1949 and 1968, it has only come into widespread use since the 1981 Wildlife and Countryside Act, in particular in relation to the protection of Sites of Special Scientific Interest. Since then it has formed the basis for Environmentally Sensitive Areas, Nitrate Sensitive Areas and the Countryside Premium and Stewardship Schemes. Similar arrangements have been used in other countries, such as the Conservation Reserve Program in the United States.

	Management agreement model	CART model	Hypothecated fund model
Expressing values	lobbying and political opportunities	membership, donations and government grants	local taxes, charges and donations
	⇓	⇓	⇓
Legitimating interests	landholders rights to determine environmental quality	charitable and/or trust status	rights to raise local taxes and charges
	⇓	⇓	⇓
Establishing linkage mechanisms	agency powers to enter into environmental contracts	CART strategy	local trust fund and environmental contracts
	⇓	⇓	⇓
Controlling land	landholder participation	CART management	landholder participation

Figure 12.3.   Alternative models of articulation

The approach has been implemented in various formats. Some agreements are individually negotiated between agency and individual landholder, others are applied on a standardised basis within designated areas. All are essentially voluntary, although in some cases the government has reserve powers of compulsory purchase in case of a failure to reach agreement. In practice these powers have been extremely rarely applied. Contracts can define quite detailed management requirements in order to achieve specific nature conservation objectives within particular locations.

While representing a significant policy development, this model would seem to have certain limitations as a means of promoting varied habitat and attractive landscapes in the long term. While flexible, the landholder requirements have to be capable of being defined in written contracts and subject to some level of enforcement. Ideally, the scheme would purchase environmental outputs from landholders, leaving them free to select least cost methods of provision. In practice because of problems of definition, measurement and enforcement, the contracts tend to specify the inputs and activities that should or should not be used. Agreements operate over a defined period with no guarantee that any conservation benefits will be maintained beyond that period. But, perhaps most critical is simply the costs of operating this type of scheme, both in terms of the payments made from the exchequer to landholders and in terms of the transactions costs, which can represent a substantial proportion of the total cost.

A CART Model

A number of private sector organisations have objectives which match quite closely those of the state. This is clearly the case in respect of most charities and includes a variety of conservation bodies, several of which have the provision of conservation goods by means of direct management of land among their objectives. Such organisations are referred to as Conservation, Amenity and Recreation Trusts (CARTs) (Dwyer and Hodge 1996). These are non profit-making organisations with the aim of generating wide public benefit through nature conservation and environmental improvement, provision of amenity and opportunities for public recreation and conservation of landscape.

While most such organisations operate at a local or national level, some, notably the Nature Conservancy from the United States' have international involvement. It has for example 14 data centres in Latin America but works with partner organisations within each country. Thus the model might operate in specific cases with more than one particular organisation.

The achievement of conservation goals can often require detailed information both about the ecology of the habitat being managed and about the agricultural system which is operated within it. In some circumstances, guidelines for management can provide sufficient information for a farmer without a detailed understanding of the ecosystem involved. However, in other circumstances, for instance where habitat is being recreated or where a rare habitat is being protected against external pressures, then a more proactive form of environmental management may be necessary. This would involve a more regular monitoring of the ecosystem and review of the appropriate management responses. This may require a range of skills which are not always available to the particular landholders who happen to be owners of the conservation sites and may be difficult to write into contractual agreements.

While the Management Agreement model involves agreements with existing owners, the CART model implies some change in the character of property owners. An alternative approach is therefore for the state to promote the actions of organisations which have objectives in common with those of the state. This may be done in terms of grants for the purchase of land, contributions towards labour costs and the tax relief generally available to non-profit organisations.

Where such an organisation owns land which is being managed for landscape or wildlife conservation, it will be the residual claimant. As such, it will seek to maximise the value to it of the residual which is left after all costs have been paid. In this case, the value will include the non-monetary value of the conservation goods. The conservation organisation will have an incentive to seek out least cost ways of generating and protecting the conservation values under its particular circumstances. It will be prepared to trade off costs against conservation gains.

In this, the implied price of conservation goods may not be different from that implied in government actions. Therefore such organisations will tend to act entrepreneurially, seeking new products and new methods of achieving conservation goals. It will respond to changes in relative prices and technology. This suggests that the conservation organisation will require less detailed monitoring than a conventional landholder and that in the longer term it would be likely to develop more cost effective methods of conservation management.

Conservation organisations may also be more flexible and less bureaucratic than many government agencies given their generally smaller size and the lack of democratic accountability. They may be able to respond more rapidly to opportunities which arise, such as in purchasing significant conservation sites when they become available on the market. Such organisations often specialise in particular types of conservation, such as the protection of birds, or may focus their efforts within a particular area. In this way, although they be relatively small organisations, they can build up a level of expertise within their own particular speciality.

Hypothecated Fund Model

The final example operates around a fund established to support local action for conservation. There are three main elements: Fundraising, fund consolidation and disbursement, and some arrangement for the control of land. Expenditure from the fund is restricted to activities that advance the conservation objective.

Funds may be raised in various ways, depending on circumstances and objectives. In some cases there may be opportunities for user charges. Charges may be more or less directly related to the benefit which the payer gets from the natural resources of the area and opportunities for this will depend on the nature of the benefits and the existence of property rights. In such cases the fund will be needed where those who are able to extract charges from visitors are not the same as those who would bear the opportunity costs of conservation. Thus there is a need for some sort of redistributive mechanism.

As an alternative to a user charge it may be possible to raise a tax that is in some way linked to the benefit from amenity. In practice, the distinction between a user charge and a tax may not be clear, particularly as the item charged for becomes more remote from the direct consumption of the natural resource. Examples of taxes would be a bed tax charged on tourists staying in an area or airport taxes. There have, for instance, been suggestions for a tax on walking boots to help pay for the maintenance of footpaths. Two difficulties here are that the level of tax paid may not be closely related to the extent of the benefit which is gained from the amenity and secondly, in the United Kingdom at least, that the Treasury is generally unwilling to accept hypothecation; that is, restricting the expenditure of revenue from a tax to specific purposes. In practice taxes may have an additional objective of limiting the impacts of tourism or recreation to limit the external costs of these activities, although there is no reason to believe that a single rate could meet fund raising and internalisation objectives simultaneously.

Finally, donations may be solicited from those benefiting from the quality of the local environment on a voluntary basis, from the users directly, from firms whose business depends upon it in some way, or from people who have no direct connection with the area. Collection methods may range from simple collection boxes to more complex schemes such as linking payments to the use of particular credit cards. A few business chains have instituted a 'voluntary dollar' scheme, whereby customers are encouraged to make a voluntary donation that will be matched by the firm. Given the probable limits of voluntary donations, particularly because of the public good nature of the benefits, more rigorous approaches are likely to be desirable.

The fund may be administered and used in many ways to promote local conservation. It may be operated by a local government or some nongovernmental body. It may be used to finance environmental contracts or be directed through CARTs.

CONCLUSIONS

The production of biodiversity has some particular characteristics. Typical assumptions about property rights imply that incentives for landholders should be based on payments rather than penalties. Benefits are shared widely, even globally, while costs are generally borne locally. The aim of the mechanisms are to generate heterogeneity rather than homogeneity. While the immediate objectives in terms of land use vary considerably in different parts of the world, the principles are similar in countries at differing stages of development: Assessing and capturing demand, establishing linkages between demand and conservation actions and implementing mechanisms to influence the use of land.

None of this guarantees a particular outcome. We are still likely to find situations where biodiversity continues to decline and species continue to become extinct. The aim of institutional development can only be to give preferences for conservation the maximum opportunity to influence choices for land uses through a relatively low cost institutional arrangement. The public good characteristics of biodiversity means that this may always be incomplete.

Various models have been suggested, but there are without doubt many other elements and combinations that might be suggested. There is no single solution to the problem. Alternative models will be appropriate to different contexts and indeed it must be expected that they will operate in parallel. The outcome of diversity may only be possible through a diversity of institutions. We may generally seek the combinations that promote the desired outcomes with the minimum transactions costs, but inevitably any evaluation is confounded by the fact that the institutions determine the characteristics of the outcome that is desired. Some institutional development will undoubtedly be stimulated by opportunities to gain. CARTs have been established by private groups even though they provide public goods. But we cannot expect that such forces will take us very far towards our likely goal. The state will need to be active in institution building and support.

REFERENCES

Biswanger, H. 1991. 'Brazilian policies that encourage deforestation in the Amazon', *World Development*, 19(7), 821-9.
Blöchliger, H.-J. 1994. 'Main results of the study', Chapter 5 in OECD, *The Contribution of Amenities to Rural Development*. Paris: OECD.

Bowers, J. and Cheshire, P. 1983. *Agriculture, the Countryside and Land Use.* London: Methuen.

Brown, G. 1994. 'Rural amenities and the beneficiaries-pay-principle', Chapter 4 in OECD, *The Contribution of Amenities to Rural Development.* Paris: OECD.

Budiansky, S. 1995. *Nature's Keepers: The New Science of Nature Management.* London: Weidenfeld and Nicholson.

Clark, C. 1973. 'Profit maximisation and the extinction of animal species', *Journal of Political Economy*, 81, 950-61.

Dwyer, J. and Hodge, I. 1996. *Countryside in Trust: Land Management by Conservation, Amenity and Recreation Organisations.* Chichester: John Wiley and Sons.

Gordon, H.S. 1954. 'The economic theory of a common-property resource: The fishery', *Journal of Political Economy*, 62, 124-42.

Hodge, I.D. 1989. 'Compensation for nature conservation', *Environment and Planning A*, 27(7), 1027-36.

Hodge, I.D. 1995. 'Institutions for co-ordinating the supply of countryside goods', *Agricultural Policy and the Countryside*, Proceedings from the Holmenkollen Park Workshop, Agricultural University of Norway.

Katzman, M.T. and Cale, W.G. 1990. 'Tropical forest preservation using economic incentives', *Bioscience*, 40(11), 827-32.

Mendelson, R. 1994. 'Property rights and tropical deforestation', *Oxford Economic Papers*, 46, Supplementary Issue, 750-6.

Peters, C., Gentry, A. and Mendelson, R. 1989. 'Valuation of an Amazon rainforest', *Nature*, 339(6227), 655-6.

Randall, A. 1994. 'Thinking about the value of biodiversity', Chapter 14 in Kim, K.C. and Weaver, R.D. (eds), *Biodiversity and Landscapes: A Paradox of Humanity.* Cambridge: Cambridge University Press.

Sedjo, R.A. and Simpson, R.D. 1995. 'Property rights, externalities and biodiversity', Chapter 7 in Swanson, T.M. (ed.), *The Economics and Ecology of Biodiversity Decline: The Forces Driving Global Change.* Cambridge: Cambridge University Press.

Spash, C.L. and Hanley, N. 1995. 'Preferences, information and biodiversity preservation', *Ecological Economics*, 12, 191-208.

Swanson, T. 1994. 'The economics of extinction revisited and revised: A generalised framework for the analysis of the problems of endangered species and biodiversity losses', *Oxford Economic Papers*, 46, Supplementary Issue, 800-21.

Swanson, T. 1995. 'Uniformity in development and the decline of biological diversity', Chapter 4 in Swanson, T.M. (ed.), *The Economics and Ecology of Biodiversity Decline: The Forces Driving Global Change.* Cambridge: Cambridge University Press.

Wells, M. 1992. 'Biodiversity conservation, affluence and poverty: Mismatched costs and benefits and efforts to remedy them', *Ambio*, 21(3), 237-43.

Wilson, E.O. 1993. *The Diversity of Life.* London: Allen Lane.

13. Development and Global Finance: The Case for an International Bank for Environmental Settlements

Graciela Chichilnisky[1]

INTRODUCTION

The Bretton Woods institutions show their age. Creatures of the postwar reconstruction, they served us well for half a century. Since World War II, a newly introduced system of national accounts has supported the activities of the World Bank, the IMF and the GATT, institutions that have led the world economy into an unprecedented pattern of industrialization, material expansion and global commerce. During this period economic progress has come to mean doing more with more. But as the century turns, industrial society's voracious use of the earth's resources has reached its logical limits. For the first time in recorded history, human activity has reached levels at which it can alter the atmosphere of the planet and change irreversibly the complex web of species that constitutes life on earth. Humans have the ability to destroy in a few years the massive infrastructure that supports the human species on the planet, the global habitat to which humans have adapted optimally throughout the ages. Industrial society's runaway and uneven use of the planet's resources is now under close scrutiny.

To help redress the environmental imbalance which developed substantially during the last fifty years, this chapter proposes the creation of a new global institution: An international bank for environmental settlements (Chichilnisky 1996a). The aim is to develop innovative financial institutions and instruments to obtain market value from environmental resources without destroying them. Global finance is an ideal complement for the international organizations of the future. Emissions trading, the global reinsurance of environmental risks

---

[1] This paper was also presented as a keynote address to the Third Annual World Bank Conference on Effective Financing of Environmentally Sustainable Development, Washington DC, October 1995. The author would like to thank the participants of a UNDP Meeting in June 1996 for their comments, as well as Dr. Jorge Werthein of UNESCO, Inge Kaul of UNDP and Patricia de Mowbray of UNDP for valuable suggestions.

and the securitisation of the earth's biodiversity resources are natural financial instruments that merge the interests of private financial markets with international development policy. These instruments and institutions should help to redefine economic progress in a way that is compatible with the harmonious use of the world's resources.[2]

The time is ripe for change. Industrial society is in the process of transforming itself into a knowledge society. It is not a service economy as was previously thought. Humans can now achieve a new form of economic organization where the most important input of production is no longer machines, as in an industrialized society, but rather human knowledge. Instead of burning fossil fuels to power machines, we burn information technology to power knowledge. Information is a much cleaner fuel than coal and petroleum and one that puts humans rather than machines at the center of economic progress. I propose that economic progress must be knowledge-intensive rather than resource-intensive and must mean achieving more with less material input.

The principles discussed in this chapter apply very widely to the use of all environmental assets, such as biodiversity, soil and forests. However to fix ideas, the examples and the data used here concentrate on the use of the atmosphere of the planet through the emission of greenhouse gases, mostly derived from the burning of fossil fuels, such as coal and petroleum, to generate energy.

This chapter discusses how the IBES could impact developing countries. I show that, contrary to common wisdom, achieving a more even distribution of property rights on environmental assets involves more than equity issues. Property rights matter a great deal for market efficiency. Indeed, I will show that a precondition for market efficiency is that more property rights on the global commons should be given to those regions that own fewer private goods. As a result, developing countries should be assigned proportionately more property rights on global environmental use in order to ensure efficient market solutions.

A fundamental new fact presented in this chapter, that is behind the proposal for the creation of the IBES, is that standard competitive markets,

---

[2] During the May 1994 Seminar on Joint Implementation organized with the support of GEF and the FCCC at Columbia University, New York, by the author and by Professor Geoffrey Heal of Columbia Business School, and in various FCCC meetings, I have benefited from discussions with several members of the INC/FCCC, who provided important insights: Minister Raul Estrada Oyuela, Chair of the INC/FCCC; Mr. Ismail Razali, Ambassador, Permanent Mission of Malaysia to the UN; Mr. Xialong Wang, Third Secretary, Chinese Permanent Mission to the UN: Mr. James Baba, Deputy Permanent Representative of Uganda to the UN; Dr. John Ashe, Councillor, Permanent Mission of Antigua and Barbuda to the UN; and Mr. Carlos Sersale di Cerisano, adviser to Gustav Speth at UNDP.

such as stock exchanges, are not efficient institutions for the trading of property rights on the use of public goods. This fact is established below on the basis of economic principles and substantiated with data. It means that conventional markets for trading emissions rights on greenhouse gases, such as stock exchanges, are not efficient in general and that new institutions, such as the proposed IBES, are needed to complement the market and achieve economic efficiency in the trading of emission rights.

The atmosphere of the planet is a public good because it is one and the same for all. It cannot be chosen in different quantities of qualities by different people as private goods are. I explain below why a new institution may be required to complement the Bretton Woods institutions, how the IBES will work in practice and why the role of the IBES complements markets but goes much further than anything that unaided markets can achieve. An appendix presents the results within a model of an international market trading goods and emissions permits, as well as numerical simulations using the PIR-OECD Green model of international trade which confirm the results.

THE GLOBAL ENVIRONMENT

Widespread concern about the problems of ozone depletion and global climate change led to the 1992 Earth Summit in Rio de Janeiro. One hundred nations agreed to consider a treaty to reduce the threat of global warming by rolling back industrialized countries' emissions of greenhouse gases to the 1990 level by the year 2000. The Summit emphasized the importance of achieving sustainable development. For this purpose, United Nations Agenda 21, adopted in 1992 by one hundred and fifty nations, has as an explicit objective pattern of consumption oriented towards the satisfaction of *basic needs*.[3]

Despite the interest generated by the Rio Summit, the implementation of its goals has been slow. Part of the problem comes from scientific uncertainty about the impact of the emission of greenhouse gases into the planet's atmosphere. Science increasingly supports the view that human activity is causing climate change, according to the 1996 IPCC report; therefore this justification for inertia is being removed.

A second and more difficult factor hindering the negotiations is the

---

[3] The concept of *development oriented towards the satisfaction of basic needs* was created and developed empirically by this author in 1974, in the context of empirical studies of sustainable development in five continents (see for example, Chichilnisky 1977). The Brundtland Report's definition of sustainable development is also anchored to basic needs: Sustainable development satisfies the needs of the present without compromising the needs of the future, (Brundtland 1987, Chapter 2, para. 1).

divergence in the perceptions of the industrialized and developing countries. Most emissions have originated in and continue to originate from the industrialized countries and many developing countries take the position that only changes to this pattern can have an impact on the problem. Many industrialized countries, on the other hand, take the position that the biggest threat is the harm that developing countries can produce in the future. This divergence of views between industrialized and developing countries has slowed the progress of the negotiations since Rio.

Rio Targets and Berlin Mandate

The next most important international meeting on climate change was the Berlin Conference of the Parties. It concluded on 7 April, 1995 by adopting a call for action. It found that the Rio Articles were not adequate. A mandate adopted in Berlin, called here the Berlin Mandate, requires the negotiation of an emissions-reduction protocol. This requires to set hard, quantified, limitations on the greenhouse gas emissions by developed countries in 2005, 2010 and 2020.

Another major decision in Berlin was to establish a pilot phase for joint implementation.[4] Many developing countries had seen joint implementation as a mechanism for transferring responsibility for reducing emissions away from industrialized countries, which account for most of the emissions of the planet. To address this concern, industrialized countries may not take credit for any reduction on their emissions during the pilot phase, towards their commitments of reducing emission to 1990 levels by 2000. The results of this pilot phase will be reviewed before the turn of the century.

Geneva 1996 and the IBES

Following Berlin, the United Nations Framework Convention on Climate Change (FCCC) met in Geneva in July 1996. In this meeting, the US adopted a new position, one which supports for the first time the developing countries' concerns for hard targets on industrialized nations' greenhouse gas emissions. Taking a leading position, the US advocated a market approach, which followed the approach originally proposed in this chapter, as presented at the Annual World Bank Meetings in Washington DC, October 1995, for the trading of rights to emit greenhouse gases among the industrialized nations. The US approach did not, however, include the creation of an International

---

[4] *Joint implementation* refers to one or more parties taking actions - or financial actions - in the territory of other parties, and it is seen as a prelude to emissions trading by a number of government and observers.

Bank for Environmental Settlements, which is a natural next step, as argued here.

Below I set out policies that can help implement the Rio targets and the Berlin Protocol resulting from the Berlin Mandate. I will focus on the Berlin decision towards joint implementation and the US proposal in Geneva, both of which are a prelude to the multilateral trading of emission rights. In this context, I will explain the need for an addition to the Bretton Woods institutions: An *International Bank on Environmental Settlements* (IBES). This Bank will use as collateral the environmental assets of the planet, perhaps the most valuable of all assets known to humankind, and will facilitate the execution and settlement of the trading of global environmental assets and related financial instruments within the global emission ceilings stipulated by the protocol. It has been established that at present most forests are destroyed in order to produce minerals or to grow agricultural products for sale in the international market.[5] The IBES will help developing countries, who own most of the forests and biodiversity in the planet, to obtain economic value from their value without destroying them. This may include securitization of commercial applications of biodiversity, such as the Merck-INBIO deal in Costa Rica (Chichilnisky 1993a). The Bank will help to organize, execute and monitor the trading of emission permits, loans on these and of derivative instruments associated with them. The IBES can also serve to ensure the integrity of markets for emissions trading and their efficiency.

The approach proposed here was discussed with members of the INC/FCCC, of the US Council of Economic Advisors, the Global Environment Facility and the Organization for Economic Cooperation and Development. The responsibility for the ideas and conclusions presented here rests solely with the author.

North-South Issues

It is useful to start with a brief summary of the issues involved in the climate negotiations. Developing countries fear the imposition of limits to their growth in the form of restrictions on emissions and on the use of their own resources. They observe that most environmental damage currently originates and originated historically in the industrialized countries, whose patterns of development are at the root of the environmental dilemmas we face today. OPEC countries are particularly concerned with the changes that the protocol's

---

[5] For example, in Ecuador the Amazon forest is destroyed currently for the exploration and extraction of petroleum by international corporations, petroleum that is destined for sale to the USA. A similar situation prevails in Africa's korup forest, which at 60 million years of age is one of the oldest in the world.

decisions could precipitate in their export markets if petroleum prices increase. A similar position is taken by other resource-intensive exporters such as Australia.

Industrialized countries have a different set of concerns: They fear excessive population growth in developing countries and the environmental damage that this could bring. While recognizing their historical responsibility for excessive environmental use, they focus on a long-term future in which global environmental problems could originate mostly in the developing countries.

As a result of these differences, the Berlin Conference of the Parties was not able to reach an agreement on rules of procedure. Geneva moved the debate a step forward, but the road ahead is long and steep. International agreements are customarily adopted by consensus. How to achieve this?

THE ECONOMICS OF THE GLOBAL ENVIRONMENT

The implementation of the Rio targets, the FCCC Berlin Mandate and Geneva's goals require a measure of consensus about the policy instruments to be utilized. The instruments available are new: Joint implementation and emissions trading involve the trading of rights to use the planet's atmosphere. These instruments share a novel and unusual characteristic. They trade rights to use the atmosphere of the planet, which are rights to use a public good: The quality of the earth's atmosphere is the same for all and cannot be chosen in different quantities for different people. Although different regions are affected differently, the concentration of greenhouse gases in the atmosphere is fairly even and stable and is the same worldwide. This puts environmental markets in a class of their own and requires that we complement these markets with more sophisticated financial institutions. As explained below, this means that unaided markets to trade emissions permits cannot reach efficient solutions and more sophisticated backup institutions are needed, such as those proposed.

It is worth examining the issue closely. Private goods, such as apples and cars, are rival in consumption, while public goods are not. Public goods are typically provided by governments, as are roads and armies and their use is not usually traded in markets, as is proposed here. The quality of the atmosphere a public good. Why? Because individuals cannot choose different atmosphere qualities independently from each other. Since the quality of the atmosphere of the planet is one and the same the world over, this is a public good. Therefore, trading rights to use the atmosphere is trading a public good. Another new aspect of the environmental problem is that emissions, although producing a public good, the atmosphere quality, are *not* centrally produced by a government, as roads or armies are. In contrast with the classic case examined by Lindahl, Bowen and Samuelson, the public good that interests us here is privately produced. Indeed every person on the planet emits greenhouse gases through driving cars, heating homes, or releasing energy by burning fossil fuels. Emission markets are therefore markets to trade *privately produced public goods*. Such markets are quite different from classical markets. More on this below.

To understand the issues and develop policy, conceptual advances in economics are needed. The economics of climate change is new and involves challenging issues. The following are examined in this chapter:

1. Which policy instruments or combination of instruments - carbon taxes, joint implementation or tradeable emissions permits for CO_2 - are preferable for controlling emissions?
2. What institutional structures for trading carbon emissions - such as property rights regimes and market structures - will lead to efficient allocations?
3. How can an acceptable degree of equity in the use of the global commons be ensured?
4. How would the notions in this chapter impact developing countries? Should developing countries have more property rights on the global commons and if so, why?
5. Which institutions may be needed to support and regulate the trading, clearing and settlement of emissions rights and related assets and to ensure the efficiency and integrity of the market?
6. What type of environmental accounts will help record and monitor the successes or failures of taxes, joint implementation schemes or emission markets?
7. When do market prices accurately reflect the value of resources and when should new institutions be created?
8. What is the scope for applying the proposals in this chapter beyond the greenhouse effect to tackle other cross-border problems, such as soil erosion and deforestation?

Below I discuss the issues and offer practical policy recommendations grounded in economic theory and on empirical observations. A main recommendation is the creation of an International Bank for Environmental Settlements, which will use as collateral the wealth of environmental assets of the planet. These assets include the world's forests and bodies of water, its minerals and biodiversity. Today most forests are destroyed to produce minerals or agricultural products for sale in the international market (Chichilnisky 1994, 1997); the IBES will help to realize their value without destroying them.

The Bank will help to organize, execute and monitor the trading of emissions permits, loans on these and of derivative instruments associated with them. I show below:

1. Why a new institution may be required to complement the Bretton Woods institutions.
2. How the IBES will work in practice.
3. Why the role of the IBES complements markets but goes much further than anything that unaided financial markets for trading emissions rights can achieve.

In Appendix 1, I present a general equilibrium model of North-South trade which includes trade on environmental assets. Appendix 2 reports on simulations using the PIR-OECD Green general equilibrium model of international trade. This model was developed by OECD and was adapted at the Program on Information and Resources (PIR) of Columbia University for the purposes of this article.

Common Interests

Implementing the Rio targets and the Berlin Mandate requires a substantial and concerted effort on the part of all parties to communicate and to understand each other's concerns, to address in-depth the problems and the possible solutions and to reach consensus. A better understanding of the economic issues is valuable because, as shown below, it can foster consensus.

In developing consensus, it helps to concentrate on and to build from, common interests. While the main concerns are ecological and environmental, the main stumbling blocks in reaching solutions are of an economic nature. To abate carbon emissions means, in the short term, burning less fossil fuels and producing less energy. This means less economic output. Who should abate? (Chichilnisky 1993b, Chichilnisky and Heal 1994).

Both industrialized and developing countries face significant abatement costs in the short run, since current patterns of development are resource intensive and it is costly to change them. Although the outcome of our policies is uncertain because we know relatively little about the impact of human activity on the environment of the planet, the risks we face are nevertheless sufficient to make it compelling that precautionary steps be taken now. How much is it worth to improve our environment and who should pay?

The main findings and policy recommendations of this chapter address these questions. I will discuss who should abate and why and I will seek to explain from this answer how to arrive at a cooperative solution that can help bring about consensus.

Resource-intensive and Knowledge-intensive Growth

The most dynamic sectors in the world economy today are not resource-intensive; they are, rather, knowledge-intensive, such as software and hardware, biotechnology, communications and financial markets (Chichilnisky 1994 and 1996b). These sectors are friendly to the environment. They use relatively few resources and emit relatively little CO_2. They are the high-growth sectors in most industrialized countries.

Parts of the most dynamic developing countries are making a transition from traditional societies to knowledge-intensive societies. Mexico produces computer chips, India is rapidly becoming a large exporter of software and Barbados has recently unveiled a plan to become an information society within a generation. There is nothing new about such policies. These were precisely the policies followed by the Asian Tigers, Hong Kong, Republic of Korea, Singapore and Taiwan Province of China, who have achieved extraordinarily successful performance over the last twenty years by relying not on resource exports but rather on knowledge intensive products such as consumer electronics. By contrast, Africa and Latin America emphasized resource exports and lost ground (Chichilnisky 1995 and 1996b).

The lessons of history are clear: Not to rely on resource exports as the foundation of economic development. Africa and Latin America must update their economic focus. Indeed, the whole world must shift away from resource-intensive economic processes and products. In so doing, fewer minerals and other environmental resources will be extracted and their price will rise. This is as it should be because today's low resource prices are a symptom of overproduction and inevitably lead to overconsumption.

Not surprisingly, from an environmental perspective one arrives at exactly the same answer: Higher resource prices are needed to curtail consumption. Producers will sell less, but at higher prices. This is not to say that all will gain in the process. If the world's demand for petroleum drops, most petroleum producers will lose unless they have diversified into other products that involve fewer resources and higher value. Most international oil companies are investigating this strategy. The main point is that nations do not develop on the basis of resource exports. As the trend is inevitable, the sooner one makes the transition, the better. Economic development means achieving more with less. It does not mean doing more with more.

MARKET INSTRUMENTS FOR INTERNATIONAL POLICY

Following the Berlin protocol, the international community will set up emission ceilings. Once the targets on emissions levels have been agreed upon by the FCCC Protocol, a wide variety of instruments are available for their implementation. Some are simple command and control instruments, which establish bounds on economic behaviour. They command how much petroleum to consume or how much energy to use. These are typically cumbersome as they involve restrictions on trading and other economic practices which can lead to inefficiencies.

Taxes and Emissions Markets

Other economic instruments are based not on command and control but on prices. The idea is that higher prices deter consumption and induce appropriate use of resources. Examples are taxes, joint implementation and markets for emission permits. These are discussed in more detail below. In a nutshell, taxes deter resource use by imposing costs on resource use. Joint implementation and markets do the same in a different way. In all cases, one has to pay for emissions, but with markets one pays by buying permits. Taxes and emission permits are therefore very similar. Taxes, however, penalize emissions in a manner prescribed by a central authority. Emissions permits penalize emissions but the effective *rate* is not set. Rather this rate is flexible, depending on market forces and therefore changes through time with supply and demand conditions.

How do Emissions Markets Work?

The simplest forms of emissions markets restrict total quantities for each agent and allow free economic agents to make choices about how to implement these limits and within these limits to trade quotas among themselves. A country will buy permits if it wishes to emit more than its quota and will sell them otherwise. Prices on permits are flexible: They are determined by supply and demand. The total emissions in the world remains unchanged. Such practices are often called market instruments because in a way they mimic market solutions. For example, a limit is placed on one or more agent's emissions (such as the Rio targets, which aim at rolling back the industrialized countries' emissions to 1990 levels by the year 2000). Within this overall target, however, industrialized countries could be allowed to adopt their own economic policies to comply. They are also allowed to trade among themselves if this is desirable for achieving their targets.

Who Should Abate?

Underlying the policy issue is the question: Who should abate? Who should contribute most to the improvement of the atmosphere, to the recovery of the global commons? One answer that is often heard is: The developing countries, because they have lower abatement costs. Never mind the fact that industrialized countries contribute most of the carbon dioxide; if anyone must sacrifice consumption, it is the developing countries. OECD has argued for this because it would equate marginal costs of abatement across countries and therefore bring about efficiency.[6] The idea was simple: It was based on the belief that abatement of carbon emissions costs less in developing countries. In this view, abatement would be carried out in developing countries where the cost of achieving the same goal is lower in dollar terms: This would ensure efficiency. Is this argument valid?

This argument is certainly true in markets for private goods. Here efficiency can be obtained by equating marginal costs. However, this argument fails in markets with privately produced public goods. This failure shows an important difference between standard markets and environmental markets.

In markets with privately produced public goods, it is not the dollar value of the abatement that counts for efficiency but rather the opportunity cost of that dollar value in terms of the utility that it can provide. The point is that the same dollar brings about very different utility gains in a rich country than in a poor country. It is marginal utility gains that determine efficiency. For example, suppose that abatement of an extra ton of carbon costs $1.00 of output in India and $2.00 in the US. Abatement of an extra ton of carbon costs less in India. Who should abate?

In this example, the real loss of utility from abatement in India can be much higher than in the US because the $1.00 of goods can have a major impact on the average citizen in India while a $2.00 loss in the US has only a marginal impact for the average citizen of the US. The point is simple: The marginal utility of income decreases with income. The more income we have, the less our utility increases with the additional dollar. These matters do not count in economies with private goods because everyone chooses independently and traders can adjust their consumption to equate the marginal gains they derive from all markets.[7] However, with privately produced public goods, they do. In these cases, the condition of equal marginal costs is not appropriate for efficiency.[8] It is appropriate only when all countries have the same marginal utility of income.

---

[6] See Coppell (1993) and the response in Chichilnisky (1993b) as well as Chichilnisky and Heal (1994).

[7] In an efficient market equilibrium with private goods, marginal rates of substitution must all be equal across markets, and must equal also the marginal rates of transformation in those markets.

[8] See Atkinson and Stiglitz (1980). The rule is typically that the sum of marginal rates of substitution equals the marginal rate of transformation when the government produces the public good. Privately produced public goods have yet another rule; see Chichilnisky, Heal and Starrett (1993).

Only when (free) transfers are made between countries so as to equate their marginal valuations of private consumption does efficiency require that marginal abatement costs be equal. Such transfers are not realistic.[9] In general, efficiency implies that abatement will come proportionately more from those countries that have higher income, because these countries have a lower marginal utility from increased consumption than poorer countries. Under general conditions, the proportion of income dedicated to abatement should increase with the level of income (Chichilnisky and Heal 1994). Who then should abate? First of all, the industrial countries (Chichilniksy and Heal 1994). This has been the position of the developing countries for many years. As reported, even the US agreed with this position in Geneva in July 1996.

Requiring abatement from the developing countries first would be a regressive measure, like taxing the poor the most. There are other concerns about regressive measures. They can cause problems because environmental degradation and poverty are closely connected. Anything that worsens poverty is likely to lead to further environmental degradation and to increased rates of population growth (World Bank 1992 and Chichilnisky 1994). In other words: A policy that lowers the price of wood and therefore the income of harvesters can lead to more rather than less extraction of wood. Since the purpose of taxing the price of wood is to discourage extraction of wood, by decreasing the income of the harvesters the tax could achieve exactly the opposite effect than what it is meant to achieve. Therefore the tax is unreliable; it could defeat its purpose.

Joint Implementation

Article 4 of the Rio Convention allowed for cooperative solutions, in which an industrialized country could satisfy its target of decreasing emissions to 1990 levels either within its territory or in the territory of a cooperating country. A major decision of the 1995 Conference of the Parties in Berlin was to establish a pilot phase for joint implementation. An industrialized country can barter with another with the final aim of reducing carbon emissions, in financial terms or in kind. Projects of this nature have already been executed in Mexico and Poland on an experimental basis. To ensure that the pilot does not discourage the industrialized countries' shift to a more sustainable use of resources, there will be no credit assigned to the industrialized countries for their reduction of emissions during the pilot phase towards the existing commitments of industrial countries to return emissions to 1990 levels by 2000. The results of the pilot phase are to be reviewed before the turn of the

---

[9] Through paid transfers, such as those which occur within international markets, markets may not reach the same solutions.

century and the issue of credit will be revisited at that time, if not earlier, in combination with the adoption of a reductions protocol.

Joint implementation schemes are in the nature of bilateral trade agreements and represent a natural extension of the economic practice of barter trading, a practice which can hardly be restricted. However, bilateral trading is typically inferior to multilateral trading since, in the latter case, all parties have access to all possible deals and could in principle reach substantially more favourable trades and better terms of trade (Chichilnisky and Heal 1995).

Multilateral Agreements

Bilateral trading usually leads to multilateral trading. Yet a widely expressed concern is that during the development of a multilateral market, the prices may turn against the developing countries involved. Developing countries will typically be sellers of permits initially, when prices are lower. If they buy permits later in order to industrialize, they may be paying much more for the same permits they initially sold. Selling a country's rights to emit is the same as selling its rights to industrialize. There is a chance that the first buyers will reap unfair rents or bargains over later buyers.

A response to this is a proposal for leapfrogging into multilateral trading sooner rather than later and attempting to assure fair trading practices, such as uniformly distributed price information and other practices that are widely adopted in the most successful markets in order to ensure equal access to information and trading opportunities, efficiency, market integrity and depth.

One problem still remains: In contrast with other markets, here one would be trading a public good that we all must consume in the same quantities. How to ensure efficiency and integrity of such a market? What additional steps must be taken to achieve the Rio goals and the goals of the protocol mandated in Berlin within a trading based strategy?

How to Distribute the Rights to Emit

Emission trading has as a goal an efficient allocation of emissions within the global limit. However, in order to trade one must know who owns what. This simply means that property rights must be established, to establish who has the right to emit and how much. This is not necessary for taxes, but it is for markets.

Until now the issue of property rights on emissions has been left to the political arena, with the understanding that it involved exclusively a transfer of wealth between countries. An implicit assumption was that markets themselves always function efficiently; the matter to be decided was the distribution. The two issues, efficiency and distribution, were seen as separate.

The latter, distribution, was a major political hurdle and a divisive issue that complicated matters and interfered with the development of consensus.

However, recent advances in the economics of climate change have disclosed a somewhat unexpected source of common interests among industrialized and developing countries.[10] The appropriate equitable distribution is needed for markets to function efficiently. Somewhat surprisingly, a measure of equity is needed to reach efficient allocations.[11]

THE ECONOMICS OF CLIMATE CHANGE

The new source of common interest between industrialized and developing countries originated in a recently discovered link between the *efficiency* of an emission market and *equity* in the allocation of property rights on emissions traded in this market. Efficiency is a property often favoured by industrialized countries that have the most developed markets, while equity is an issue that concerns the developing countries most. The close connection between two issues that are typically taken as independent from one another, indicates that a new source of common interests may be developed. What is the origin of this somewhat unexpected source of common interest?

The unexpected link between efficiency and equity emerges from an idiosyncratic economic property of markets for public goods. These are goods whose consumption is not rival (see Appendix 1).

Emission trading is the trading of the rights on a public good: The rights to use the atmosphere as a sink to absorb emissions. Public goods are typical of environmental problems; examples are the total biodiversity of the planet and the quality of the planet's climate. These are different from standard private goods because they are available to everyone in the same quantity. Private goods, on the other hand, allow more choice: One person can consume quite independently of others. Not so with public goods, for which everyone's consumption is connected.

Markets in which private and public goods are traded simultaneously can achieve efficiency. However, recent advances in economics show that markets cannot achieve this goal unaided. It turns out that for efficiency, global emissions markets require relatively egalitarian distributions of emission rights. The reason is that efficiency in a competitive market requires that the total amount emitted across the globe, which determines the quality of the

---

[10] See Appendix 1 and Chichilnisky (1993b), Chichilnisky and Heal (1994), Chichilnisky Heal and Starrett (1993).

[11] A distribution is efficient (i.e. Pareto efficient) if it cannot be improved so as to make everyone better off, or some people better off and no one else worse off.

atmosphere for all, be precisely the choice that individual traders themselves would make independently, given their other holding of private goods.

The connection between distribution and efficient operation of the world economy stands in sharp contrast with markets for private goods, where the issues of efficiency and of distribution are largely divorced from each other. With private goods, no matter what the distribution of property rights, a Pareto efficient allocation is always reached by a competitive market. When markets trade private and public goods simultaneously, then only certain allocations of property rights are consistent with efficiency. To achieve efficiency, those traders who own fewer private goods should own more property rights on the environment than those who own more private goods. Market efficiency requires a somewhat flexible but inverse relation between property rights in private goods and property rights in public goods.

In practice this means that industrialized countries, which have a much larger initial allocation of property rights on private goods, should initially be given relatively smaller endowments of property rights on public goods as a precondition for market efficiency. This unique property of markets with privately produced public goods will be developed in the following section and in the appendix. It leads us to the main policy proposal of this chapter: The creation of an International Bank for Environmental Settlements.

Why Financial Markets do not Suffice?

The atmospheric concentration of gases (such as CO_2 or the other greenhouse gases contemplated by the Rio Convention) is a public good because of its physical characteristics. These gases diffuse uniformly across the world: Atmospheric concentration is the sum total of every country's emissions and is similar for all countries. This property is what differentiates the trading of emissions rights from the trading of standard private goods. In the latter, consumers may choose the quantities they wish to consume independently of each other while in the former this is impossible: Public goods are available in the same amount to all. In markets for private goods the problem of distribution of welfare is divorced from that of economic efficiency in the sense that no matter who owns what, a market solution is always efficient.

One may object to the welfare implications of a market solution. Indeed, in markets for private goods, a market allocation can be efficient even when one person has all and nobody else has anything. But whatever the market allocation is, there is no way to change a competitive market allocation for private goods so as to make everyone better off - or even some better off and nobody else worse off. However, when trading public goods, this is no longer the case. In markets with public goods, the standard notion of efficiency (Pareto efficiency) is connected with distribution. The situation is quite different: The two properties - efficiency and distribution - merge.

This property of markets for public goods appears to be an additional burden on the efficient functioning of the market. However, somewhat paradoxically, this additional burden presents an interesting opportunity for developing consensus on global environmental issues. Typically, developing countries raise distributive issues, while industrialized countries emphasize efficiency and market-oriented approaches. There is therefore little intersection between the interests of the two groups of countries in markets for private goods. But this is different in markets for public goods. As we already saw, unaided markets do not suffice to reach efficient solutions. To trade efficiently the rights to emit gas into the atmosphere requires a good distribution of property rights across countries. Only relatively egalitarian distributions will led to market efficiency. Efficiency and distribution are no longer divorced: They reinforce each other. Through this unique characteristic of markets for public goods, a common interest emerges between the two groups of countries.

Property Rights on Greenhouse Gas Emissions

A recent discovery is a property rights regime that leads to efficient allocations. This is similar to a system of licences to use intellectual property, for example, software. To see how this works, some background is needed.

The CO_2 concentration in the atmosphere is not a classic public good that is produced by a centralized agent (as are roads, the army bridges or broadcasting). Every individual and every firm in the world causes emissions of CO_2 through the consumption and production of goods that burn fossil fuels in production. Therefore, every individual and firm is engaged in the production of the atmosphere's carbon concentration, that is the public good. This is quite different from the classic case where the public good is produced in a centralized fashion. Typically individuals cannot produce bridges or an army. The quality of the atmosphere is a public good which is produced privately by consumers and producers in a manner which is concomitant with and impossible to disassociate from other economic actions. This changes the analysis of optimality with new insights and policy recommendations.

One insight is that the equalization of marginal costs of abatement across countries is no longer a sufficient condition for efficiency in these markets. Since competitive trading of permits leads to the equalization of marginal costs of abatement, it follows that competitive trading of carbon emissions will not by itself lead to efficient allocations and other forms of market allocations may be needed.

The policy implication is that a market for emissions trading must be complemented by other institutional arrangements to reach efficient solutions (Appendices 1 and 2).

In practical terms this means that of all possible ways of allocating a given total of emission rights across countries, only a small number of allocations will lead to efficient patterns of resource allocation. These property rights regimes are called *efficient property rights* and have points in common with licences in the realm of intellectual property rights.

ENVIRONMENTAL MARKETS AND GLOBAL FINANCE

The same principles and institutional mechanisms suggested here can be used to induce efficient limitations on the emissions of many other environmentally harmful substances. The IBES could provide the backbone of global environmental markets, extending existing institutions to the global level and ensuring their efficiency and integrity.

Indeed, some of these principles have been applied to sulphur dioxide (SO_2), nitrous oxides and various water pollutants.

In 1993 the Chicago Board of Trade (CBOT) introduced SO_2 markets for trading rights to emit SO_2, following the US Clean Air Act, which introduced ceilings and rights to emit for US utilities. These markets are less appropriate than CO_2 markets because, as opposed to CO_2, SO_2 does not mix uniformly in the atmosphere. As a result, trading between states can lead to violations of the US Clean Air Act; localized trading is necessary in some cases limiting market depth.

Water markets are emerging now in Southern California. Other environmental markets have emerged for trading weather risks, such as hurricanes, which have become more unpredictable and violent owing to global climate change, which is believed to be associated with an increasing concentration of greenhouse gases in the atmosphere.[12] In 1992, Chichilnisky and Heal (1993) proposed the creation of an instrument that is now traded on the Chicago Board of Trade under the name of Catastrophe (CAT) Futures. The creation of a more sophisticated instrument, which is obtained by bundling up contingent insurance contracts as well as securities, called Catastrophe Bundles, has also been suggested recently in Chichilnisky (1996c); see also related results in Cass, Chichilnisky and Wu (1996).

In Chichilnisky (1993a), I studied the use of profit sharing agreements to obtain value from biodiversity without destroying it, using the Merck-INBIO deal as an example and proposed deeper access to capital by securitising such deals. A Wall Street report on these novel instruments appeared in Bernandez (1996).

---

[12] The IPCC has recently agreed that there is a discernible effect of anthropogenic emissions of greenhouse gases on climate change.

Simulations of Emissions Trading

At the Program on Information and Resources of Columbia University we have carried out computer simulations of the OECD GREEN model modified to incorporate the possibility of trading emission permits between the countries. This has confirmed the results discussed above: The runs are reported at the end of this document. The most efficient runs, in terms of the size of the loss of economic growth which abatement induces, are those in which the distribution of permits favours the developing countries.

INTERNATIONAL BANK FOR ENVIRONMENTAL SETTLEMENTS

We already saw that financial markets for trading emissions may not by themselves reach efficient solutions because the atmosphere of the planet is a public good. Since more sophisticated market structures are required to trade emissions, one may wish to consider a bank with the role of regulating the market and ensuring its integrity. This bank could also fulfil the role of a clearing and settlement institution, such as the Bank for International Settlements. It could offer credit enhancements for the carbon emissions permits sold by adding creditworthiness to contracts sold and perhaps by ensuring that the counterpart to each contract is the bank rather than another country or corporation, as is the case in a commodities clearing house. The bank could also determine which types of instruments will be traded - for example, derivative securities (options, futures) and if so, how.

The bank could also serve as a forum for recording environmental accounts that could be used to monitor the success and failures of implementation. It could regulate the relationship between primary and secondary markets, a matter of great importance in ensuring market liquidity. It could run open market operations and, in general, have an impact on borrowing and lending conditions and rates. The name proposed here, the International Bank for Environmental Settlements, is suggestive of the type of institution envisioned.

The research that we have carried out at the Program on Information and Resources at Columbia University has led to some unique insights into the structure of the CO_2 emission abatement problem and has led to the preliminary policy conclusions and recommendations outlined below. These have been discussed with members of the FCCC, of the US Council of Economic Advisors, the GEF and with OECD members:

Recommendation 1.

A migration from joint implementation to a multilateral procedure involving global markets for emission rights. The emissions market would involve only industrialized countries initially. This recommendation was supported by the US in Geneva in July 1996.

Recommendation 2.

Emission rights could be *loaned*, rather than *sold*, with the lending and borrowing managed by the International Bank for Environmental Settlements. The key aspect of a loan rather than a sale of an emissions rights is that developing countries need not be concerned about unforeseen long-term consequences of an irreversible transfer of their emission rights to other countries, nor need they be concerned that they will make irreversible deals today at prices that will subsequently look unreasonable. Lending rather than selling these rights avoids many uncertainties faced by developing countries entering into an emission abatement agreement.

Recommendation 3.

Developing countries are likely to want to lend emission rights for limited periods until their needs for these are clear, whereas industrialized countries are likely to want to borrow for longer periods. The bank managing this market would match these positions by borrowing short and lending long in the traditional manner of financial intermediaries. In exchange for the risk involved, it would charge a borrow-lend spread. Commercial capital and international financial institutions, private or not, would undoubtedly be attracted to such an operation.

Recommendation 4.

In order to ensure fair prices to developing countries, it may be desirable for the bank to establish a market rate of interest on emission permits in a market open only to industrialized countries and then pay this rate on deposits from developing countries.

The securitization of the planet's biodiversity and global reinsurance of environmental risks that are associated to developing areas could be equally handled by the IBES. A similar treatment of the planet's airwaves would be desirable.

Implementing Rio Targets and the Berlin Mandate

The following policy issues will be part of the proposed IBES's mandate:

1. The trading of greenhouse gas emission rights should not compromise the future ability of developing countries to grow.
2. The trading of emissions rights should not conflict with humanitarian aid or other international flows.
3. The IBES should provide more access to capital for development. It will

not induce selling of emissions rights under less favourable prices.

4. The trading of emission rights will be initially between industrialized countries. It should not enforce ceilings on developing countries rights to emit which are neither required by the 1992 Rio Convention nor by the 1995 Berlin Conference of the Parties.
5. The IBES will have the role of ensuring fair markets, for example equal access to information and to trading; it will also ensure market integrity and depth.
6. Deals will be structured so that they can be reversed without undue penalty to the traders for countries which may revise their priorities in the future.
7. A system to monitor and account for the successes and the failures of the trading agreements will be developed.

APPENDIX 1.

International Trade and Permits Markets

This section presents a general equilibrium model of international trade in which the results of this chapter have been formally established. The next section reports on simulations using the PIR-OECD general equilibrium model of trade.[13]

The model presented in this section is a simplified version of the general equilibrium model in Chichilnisky (1993b), Chichilnisky and Heal (1994) and Chichilnisky, Heal and Starrett (1993), to which the reader is referred for the general form and for the proofs of the theorems reported below.

A General Equilibrium Model with Environmental Markets

There are two traders, North and South, denoted by the index $i=1,2$ respectively, each producing two goods: One private good (x) and another a privately produced public good (a) representing *total abatement* - the negative of emissions - of greenhouse gases. The production of x requires energy and thus the burning of fossil fuels. Therefore more production leads to more emissions and there is a trade-off between abatement and production - the more one produces, the more fossil fuels are burned and the more one emits.

---

[13] The OECD model is called GREEN.

This tradeoff is represented for each region i by a function with a negative slope:

$$x_i = g_i u_i(a_i), \dot{g}_i < 0$$

and

$$\dot{g}_i < 0$$

Each region has a utility function depending on its consumption of private goods, x_i and on the total quality of the atmosphere a. The utility increases on both variables:

$$u_i(x_i, a)$$

The quality of the atmosphere a depends on the total level of emissions, which is the sum of what both countries emit:

$$a = a_1 + a_2$$

A limit on the total amount of emissions originating from both regions is postulated and is denoted a^*. For example, this limit a^* could be given by the Rio target or by those limits to be reached pursuant to the Berlin Mandate.

Each trader is assigned property rights on the environmental asset, namely rights to emit gases into the planet's atmosphere. For each trader i, denote its property rights on the environmental asset by the expression a^*_i. Then;

$$\sum_1^2 a^*_i = a^*$$

International Markets with Emissions Trading

How does the market with emissions permits work? The regions trade in two markets: Those for private goods and those for rights to emit. Each region uses some of its permits to produce private goods and trades any left-over emission rights in the international market in exchange for private goods. A competitive market equilibrium determines the market prices; that is, the terms of trade between private goods and emission rights, the levels of emissions that maximize each region's utility and clear the markets, and the level of trade. Assuming that the private good is the *numeraire*, that is, $p_x = 1$, then the market equilibrium determines the (relative) price of the permits obtained by equating supply and demand in the international market, given by the letter Π.

Formally, a competitive equilibrium is defined as follows. Given the technologies g_i, the utilities $u_i(x_i, a)$ and the property rights on atmospheric use denoted by the expression a^*_i a competitive equilibrium is given by a price Π and a choice by each region i of how many permits to use for production, a_i and how many permits to trade internationally $(a_i - a^*_i)$, so as to maximize

utility subject to a budget constraint:
Maximise

$$u_i(x_i, a)$$

subject to

$$x_i = g_i(a_i) + \pi(a_i - a_i^*)$$

and simultaneously, markets clear:

$$\sum_1^2 a_i = \sum_1^2 a_i^*$$

Observe that a competitive equilibrium determines endogenously eleven relevant prices and quantities: The level of production and of consumption of private goods x_i by each country, the level of emissions of each, a_i and the level of trade of private and public goods between the two countries. The equilibrium determines also the terms of trade between the private and public good, Π which is the international price of the permits. This price Π can be thought of as a market determined *tax* on emissions, since it is a penalty that must be paid for emitting above the allowed level.

Equity and Efficiency Results

The main results are as follows (Chichilnisky 1993b, Chichilnisky and Heal 1994 and Chichilnisky, Heal and Starrett 1993):

Theorem 1. (Chichilnisky, Heal and Starrett.)
Given a total global level of emissions a^* there exist a finite number of ways to allocate property rights on emissions among the two regions. That is, there is a finite way of distributing emissions rights (or permits to emit) a_1, a_2^* with;

$$\sum_1^2 a_i^* = a^*$$

so that at the resulting competitive equilibrium, the allocation of resources in the world economy, a_1, a_2, x_1, x_2, is Pareto efficient. For distributions of permits other than these, the competitive market equilibrium is inefficient. When both traders have the same preferences, then the region with more private goods should be given fewer property rights on the public good.

Theorem 1 is illustrated in Figure 13.1. The figure shows a starting distribution of permits that gives proportionately more rights to emit to the North and computes the corresponding competitive market equilibrium allocation. In a second step, by redistributing the permits in favour of the

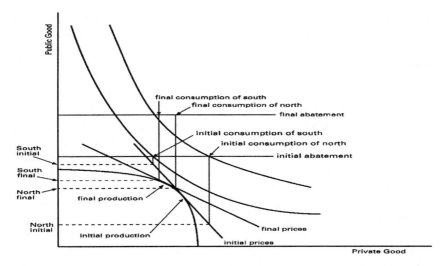

Figure 13.1   *Distribution of emission permits between the North and the South*

South and at the same time tightening the emission targets on the whole world, the competitive market achieves a new equilibrium allocation which increases simultaneously the welfare of the North and the South. This means that the first distribution was not Pareto efficient and illustrates the potential efficiency gains obtained by redistributing permits in favour of the poorer countries.

Theorem 2. (Chichilnisky.)

By allowing total world emissions a^* to vary, one obtains a one-dimensional manifold of property rights from which the competitive market with permits trading achieves a Pareto efficient allocation of the world's resources.

Theorem 2 identifies the set of all *efficient* allocations of property rights on the use of the global commons.

The intuition behind these results is simple. Competitive markets in which public goods are traded have more stringent criteria for efficiency than markets for private goods. In addition to the standard marginal conditions (that is; marginal rates of substitution must equal the marginal rates of transformation) the allocations must also satisfy the Lindahl-Bowen-Samuelson conditions for efficient levels of the public good, requiring that the sum of the marginal rates of substitution equals the (common) marginal rate of transformation between the private and the public good. Since more conditions are needed, the standard competitive allocations are not generally first best, that is; they are not generally Pareto efficient. In addition it can be shown that they are not second best efficient as well, where second best means that they are Pareto efficient conditional on a total level of world emissions which does not exceed the given target. Generally the total amount of the public good is lower in competitive markets than the first best or Pareto efficient level.

There is another way of looking at the same problem. Lindahl showed that efficiency in markets with public goods requires the use of so-called *personalized* prices, that is; ones that require as many market prices as the number of people times the number of goods. In our simple example, rather than two markets one would need four. If the population is large, the number of markets required by Lindahl would be unrealistically large and in addition would lead to arbitrage opportunities across traders. Traders with lower prices would buy on behalf of others, reselling to others at a profit or arbitrage. Because such prices would be unrealistic, the model and example presented above deal solely with competitive markets in which everyone pays the same prices. But according to Lindahl's theorem, this means that there are not enough markets to achieve efficiency. Lacking markets, in our case the solutions of competitive markets are typically inefficient, as pointed out above.

These results have proved surprising to those who interpret Coase's propositions as implying that allocating property rights always leads to efficient markets. However, nothing in Coase's work ensures such a result when one of the goods traded is a privately produced public good, as happens here. Coase's results, in addition, explain that Pareto efficient allocations are the rest point of trading activity when all possible Pareto improving positions are traded. There is nothing wrong with his result, but it is not applicable to markets in which all traders face the same prices and trade according to competitive market rules. Coase's proposition does not involve competitive market trading, in which by definition all trades trade simultaneously at the same prices, but rather all sort of bargaining between any subset of traders, at the same or at different prices. The framework proposed by Coase is therefore generally different than that of a competitive market. Nevertheless, with private goods the first welfare theorem does ensure that the competitive equilibrium is Pareto efficient. There is in this sense a consistency between competitive markets and Coase's propositions in this case. But not generally. In brief: Nothing in Coase's work ensures the Pareto efficiency of competitive equilibrium in markets which trade private goods and privately produced public goods, as those formalized here.

The results presented above have been surprising also to general equilibrium theorists, but for the opposite reasons. They establish that a judicious selection of property rights can recover first best efficiency in markets with public goods. In the general equilibrium literature it is well understood that markets with public goods are generally inefficient. Indeed our results show that one can replace personalized markets, which is Lindhal's solution, by the appropriate choice of property rights. This is an innovative result which can lead to more international cooperation.

APPENDIX 2.

Simulations with the PIR-OECD ('GREEN') General Equilibrium Model

The OECD Green model is a general equilibrium model of trade and economic growth with 12 regions (of which six represent developing regions) and eight sectors of production. Columbia University's Program on Information and Resources (PIR) adapted this model to the trading of emission permits on greenhouse gases across the regions. The specification is available from the author on request.

Notes on Simulation Results

In all figures the abbreviations for country names are: JPN = Japan, OOE = other OECD, EEX = energy exporters, CHN = China, FSU = former Soviet Union, IND = India, EET 0 Eastern European economies in transition, DAE = dynamic Asian economies, BRA = Brazil, ROW = rest of world.

World emissions shows total world emissions of CO_2, measured in millions of tons, under two alternative scenarios; 'business as usual' (BaU) and an agreement between the major emitters to stabilize emissions at their 1990 levels by the year 2000.

Decomposition of world emissions in the BaU scenario is self-explanatory: It shows how the total global emissions break down between countries under the business as usual scenario.

Real income loss over 2000-2050 shows the impact of alternative ways of stabilizing emissions at their 1990 levels on individual countries. Costs are measured in terms of the loss of real (constant price) consumer expenditure over the period 2000 to 2050 relative to the BaU scenario. Column 1 (indiv. stab) shows the welfare costs to each country of the use by that country of a carbon tax to cut back emissions to 1990 levels. In this scenario there is no policy coordination across countries; each country separately and independently cuts back its emissions to 1990 levels.

Column 2 shows the results of using a uniform tax across all countries at a level at which total global emissions are cut back to their 1990 levels, although on a country-by-country basis the cutbacks need not be to 1990 levels. Columns 3, 4 and 5 show the costs of cutting global emissions to 1990 levels by use of tradeable permits, with three different allocation rules, as discussed in the text.

As is to be expected on basic principles, the total costs are highest in column 1, where each country independently cuts emissions back to their 1990 levels. Of the three tradeable quota scenarios, it is of some interest that the most obviously egalitarian - a population-based allocation - is the least costly. As noted in the text, different quota allocations lead to very different income levels in the world's most populous countries, China and India.

Emission rights trade - these three figures show which countries are importers (negative) or exporters (positive) of emission permits under alternative permit allocation rules.

Table 13.1 Real income loss over 2000-2050 (in percentage deviation relative to BaU)

	Indiv. Stab	Uniform tax	Grandfathering	Pop. based	Mixed
USA	-0.79	-0.90	-0.76	-2.94	-1.84
JPN	-2.41	-1.24	-1.83	-2.84	-2.34
EEC	-1.23	-1.16	-1.22	-3.13	-2.19
OOE	-0.58	-0.55	-0.54	-1.53	-1.04
EEX	-3.39	-0.83	-0.78	0.09	-0.39
CHN	-3.88	-3.47	-4.14	6.02	1.04
FSU	-1.42	-2.66	1.08	-7.13	-2.92
IND	-2.61	-2.00	-2.94	14.62	7.00
EET	-0.33	-1.09	0.81	-5.94	-2.51
DAE	-0.29	0.16	0.20	-0.19	-0.05
BRA	-1.60	-1.78	-4.40	-0.55	-2.45
ROW	-0.40	-0.01	0.05	0.21	0.12
World	-1.65	-1.16	-1.17	-1.06	-1.07

Note: World emission stabilized at 1990 level after 2000.

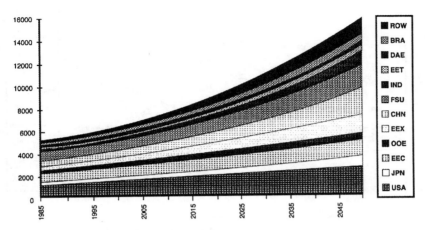

Figure 13.2   *Decomposition of world carbon emissions in the BaU scenario (millions of tons)*

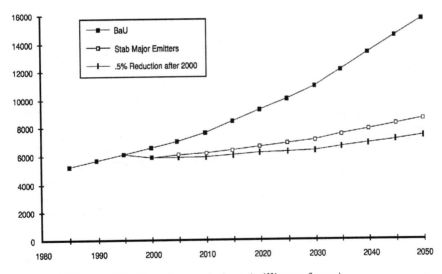

Figure 13.3   *World carbon emissions (millions of tons)*

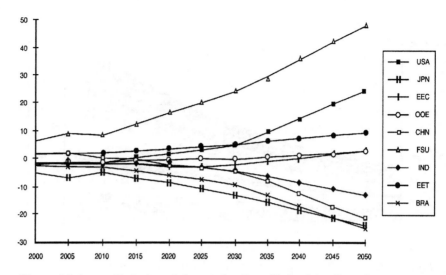

Figure 13.4   Emission rights trade, Grandfathering allocation

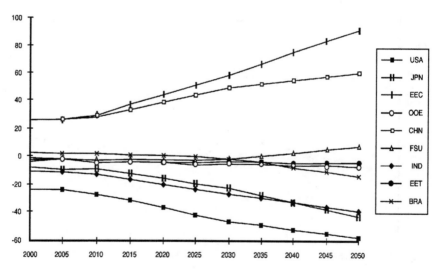

Figure 13.5   Emission rights trade under mixed allocation criterion

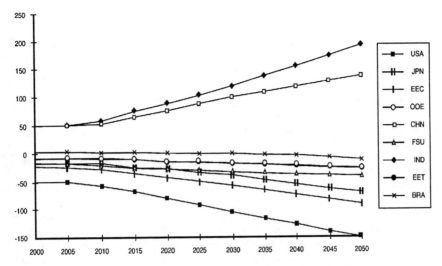

Figure 13.6   *Emission rights trade: Population based allocation*

REFERENCES

Atkinson, A. and Stiglitz, J.E. 1980. *Lectures on Public Economics*. Maidenhead, England: McGraw Hill.

Bernandez, C. 1996. 'Environmental assets and derivatives', *Derivatives Week*, June 3, Vol. V, No. 22.

Brundtland, G.H. 1987. *The UN World Commission on Environment and Development*, Oxford: Oxford University Press.

Cass, D., Chichilnisky, G. and Wu, H. 1996. 'Individual risk and mutual insurance', *Econometrica*, 64(2), 333-41.

Chichilnisky, G. 1977. 'Economic development and efficiency criteria in the satisfaction of basic needs', *Applied Mathematical Modelling*, 1(6), 290-7.

Chichilnisky, G. 1993a. 'Property rights on biodiversity and the pharmaceutical industry'. Case Study, Columbia Business School.

Chichilnisky, G. 1993b. 'Comment on: The abatement of CO_2 emission in industrial and developing countries', in Jones, T. (ed.), *OECD: The Economics of Climate Change*, Proceedings of OECD/IEA conference. Paris, June 1993, pp. 159-70.

Chichilnisky, G. 1994. 'North-South trade and the global environment', *American Economic Review*, 84(4), 427-34.

Chichilnisky, G. 1995. 'Strategies for trade liberalization in the Americas,' in *Trade liberalization in the Americas*, Inter-American Development Bank (IDB) and United Nations Commission for Latin America and the Caribbean (ECLAC), Washington DC.

Chichilnisky, G. 1996a. 'The economic value of the earth's resources'. Invited perspectives article, *Trends in Ecology and Evolution*, 11(3), 135-40.

Chichilnisky, G. 1996b. 'Trade regimes and GATT: Resource intensive vs. knowledge intensive growth', *Journal of International Comparative Economics*, 147-81.

Chichilnisky, G. 1996c. 'Catastrophe bundles can deal with unknown risk', *BEST's Review*, 1-3.

Chichilnisky, G. 1997. 'The economic value of the earth's resources', *Trends in Ecology and Evolution*, Elsevier (forthcoming).

Chichilnisky, G. and Heal, G.M. 1991. *Oil and the International Economy*. Clarendon Press, Oxford University Press.

Chichilnisky, G. and Heal, G.M. 1993. 'Global environmental risks', *Journal of Economic Perspectives*, Special Issue on the Environment, Fall, 65-86.

Chichilnisky, G. and Heal, G.M. 1994. 'Who should abate carbon emission? An international perspective', *Economic Letters*, Spring, 443-9.

Chichilnisky, G. and Heal, G.M. 1995. 'Markets for tradeable CO_2 emission quotas: Principles and practice. OECD Working Paper No. 153, Paris.

Chichilnisky, G., Heal, G.M. and Starrett, D. 1993. 'International markets with emission rights: Equity and efficiency'. Center for Economic Policy Research, Publication No. 81, Stanford University. Forthcoming in *Advances in Economics and Finance*, 1(1), Sept. 1997.

Coppel, J. 1993. 'Implementing a global abatement policy: Some selected issues', in Jones, T. (ed.), *OECD: The Economics of Climate Change*, Proceedings of OECD/IEA conference. Paris, June 1993.

14. Dynamic Systems Modelling for Scoping and Consensus Building

Robert Costanza and Matthias Ruth[1]

INTRODUCTION

This chapter assesses the changing role of dynamic systems modelling for the understanding and management of complex ecological economic systems. It discusses new modelling tools that can be used for initial problem scoping and consensus building among a broad range of stakeholders and describes several case studies in which this approach to dynamic modelling has been used to collect and organize data, synthesize knowledge and build consensus about the management of complex systems.

The case studies range from industrial systems (mining, smelting and refining of iron and steel and production of pulp and paper products in the United States) to ecosystems (Fynbos ecosystems in South Africa, Louisiana coastal wetlands and the Florida Everglades) to linked ecological economic systems (Banff National Park in Canada, the Patagonian Coastal Zone and Maryland's Patuxent River basin in the United States). Each of these case studies are briefly discussed to illustrate the use of dynamic systems modelling for scoping and consensus building as part of a three-stage modelling process which includes research and management models at the later stages.

TYPES AND USES OF MODELS

In environmental systems, non-linearities and spatial and temporal lags prevail. Traditional, reductionist science typically disregards these system features or treats them as anomalies. As a consequence, the presence of non-linearities and spatial and temporal lags significantly reduces the ability of traditional, reductionist science to provide the insights that are necessary to make proper

---

[1] Carl Folke and Marjan van den Belt provided helpful comments on earlier versions of this paper. The Pew Charitable Trusts and the Beijer International Institute for Ecological Economics provided support during preparation of this manuscript.

decisions about the management of complex ecological economic systems. New modelling approaches are required to effectively identify, collect and relate the information that is relevant for understanding those systems, to make consensus building an integral part of the modelling process and to guide management decisions.

Model building is an essential prerequisite for comprehension and for choosing among alternative actions. Humans build mental models in virtually all decision situations, by abstracting from observations that are deemed irrelevant for understanding that situation and by relating the relevant parts with each other. Language itself is a form of mental modelling and one could argue that without modelling there could be no rational thought at all. For many everyday decisions, mental models are sufficiently detailed and accurate to be reliably used. Our experiences with these models are passed on to others through verbal and written accounts that frequently generate a common group understanding of the workings of a system.

In building mental models, humans typically simplify systems in particular ways. We base most of our mental modelling on qualitative rather than quantitative relationships, we linearise the relationships among system components, disregard temporal and spatial lags, treat systems as isolated from their surroundings or limit our investigations to the system's equilibrium domain. When problems become more complex, however, and especially when quantitative relationships, non-linearities and time and space lags are important, our mental models need to be supplemented.

Statistical approaches based on historical or cross-sectional data often are used to quantify the relationships among system components. To be able to deal with multiple feedbacks among system components and with spatial and temporal lags requires the availability of rich data sets and elaborate statistical models. Recent advances in statistical methods have significantly improved the ability to test for the goodness of fit of alternative model specifications and have even attempted to test for causality in the statistical models (Granger 1969, 1993). Despite these attempts to use statistical models to arrive at a better understanding of the cause-effect relationships that lead to system change, the results are driven by data and a modeller's choice of functional specifications that is primarily based on convenience of estimation techniques and statistical criteria - none of which ensure that the fundamental drivers for system change are satisfactorily identified. By the same token, a statistical modelling exercise can only provide insight into the empirical relationships over a system's history or at a point in time, but are of limited use for analyses of a system's future development path under alternative management schemes. In many cases, those alternative management schemes include decisions that have not been chosen in the past and their effects are therefore not captured in the data of the system's history or present state.

Systems models are distinct from statistical models by building into the representation of a phenomenon those aspects of a system that we know actually exist, such as the physical laws of material and energy conservation that describe input-output relationships in industrial and biological processes. Our systems alternative therefore starts with an advantage over the purely statistical or empirical modelling schema. It does not rely on historic or cross sectional data to reveal those relationships or on a modellers' choice of functional specifications to capture them in their regression equations. This advantage also allows the systems model to be used in more related applications than the empirical model. The systems model is more transferable to new applications because the fundamental concepts on which they are built are present in many other systems.

Computers have come to play a large role in developing systems models for decision-making support in complex systems. Computer models can quantify relationships, including complex non-linear relationships, among system components and can deal with time and space lags and disequilibrium conditions in order to allow us to 'see' the dynamics of complex systems.

Models have sometimes been compared to maps. Like maps, they have many possible purposes and uses and no one map or model is right for the entire range of uses (Levins 1966, Robinson 1991, Ruth and Cleveland 1997). It is inappropriate to think of models or maps as anything but crude (but in many cases absolutely essential) abstract representations of complex territory, whose usefulness can best be judged by their ability to help solve the navigational problems faced (Ruth and Hannon, in press). Unlike maps, however, the *dynamic* models presented in this chapter are not static representations of systems but capture the processes that determine system change. They are interactive tools that reflect and respond to the choices made by a decision maker.

Models are essential for policy evaluation, but, unfortunately, they can also be misused since there is 'the tendency to use such models as a means of legitimizing rather than informing policy decisions. By cloaking a policy decision in the ostensibly neutral aura of scientific forecasting, policy makers can deflect attention from the normative nature of that decision' (Robinson 1997). The misguided quest for 'objective' model building has returned us to a point at which we need to recognize and more effectively deal with the inherent subjectivity of the model development process. In this chapter we wish to put computer modelling in its proper perspective; as an inherently 'subjective' (but absolutely essential) tool useful in supplementing our existing mental modelling capabilities in order to make better, more informed decisions, both individually and in groups.

In the case of modelling ecological and economic systems, purposes can range from developing simple conceptual models, in order to provide a general understanding of system behaviour, to detailed realistic applications aimed at evaluating specific policy proposals. It is inappropriate to judge this whole range of models by the same criteria. As a minimum, the three criteria of *realism* (simulating system behaviour in a qualitatively realistic way), *precision* (simulating behaviour in a quantitatively precise way) and *generality* (representing a broad range of systems' behaviours with the same model) are necessary. Holling (1964) first described the fundamental tradeoffs in modelling between these three criteria. Later Holling (1966) and Levins (1966) expanded and further applied this classification. No single model can maximize all three of these goals and the choice of which objectives to pursue depends on the fundamental purposes of the model.

In this chapter we propose a three-step process for developing computer models of a situation that begins with an initial scoping and consensus-building stage aimed at producing very simplified, high generality models and then moving to a more realistic research modelling stage and only then coming to a high precision management model stage. We elaborate this process further on.

USING MODELS TO BUILD CONSENSUS

Models of complex system behaviour are frequently used to support decisions on environmental investments and problems. To effectively use those models, that is, to foster consensus about the appropriateness of their assumptions and results and thus to promote a high degree of compliance with the policies derived from the models, it not enough for groups of academic experts to build integrated dynamic computer models. What is required is a new role for modelling as a tool in building a broad consensus not only across academic disciplines, but also between science and policy. More broadly, this process of stakeholder involvement is a key one to achieving sustainability. Ethicist John Rawls (Rawls 1971, 1987) has argued persuasively that policies that represent an 'overlapping consensus' of the interest groups involved in a problem will be fair and this will result in their also being effective and resilient. Thus, solutions to the problems of sustainability will only be robust (resilient) and effective if they are fair and equitable (the fair distribution criteria mentioned earlier) to all of the interest groups involved, including future generations and other species. How can we identify and promote such solutions?

Integrated modelling of large systems, from individual companies to industries to entire economies or from watersheds to continental scale systems and ultimately to the global scale, requires input from a very broad range of people. We need to see the modelling process as one that involves not only the technical aspects, but also the sociological aspects involved with using the process to help build consensus about the way the system works and which management options are most effective. This consensus needs to extend both across the gulf separating the relevant academic disciplines and across the even broader gulf separating the science and policy communities and the public. Appropriately designed and appropriately used integrated modelling exercises can help to bridge these gulfs.

The process of modelling can (and must) also serve this consensus-building function. It can help to build mutual understanding, solicit input from a broad range of stakeholder groups and maintain a substantive dialogue between members of these groups. In adaptive management, integrated modelling and consensus building are essential components (Gunderson *et al.* 1995).

MODELLING TOOLS FOR SCOPING AND CONSENSUS BUILDING

Various forms of computer models for scoping and consensus building have been developed for business management applications (Roberts 1978, Lyneis 1980, Morecroft *et al.* 1991, Vennix and Gubbels 1994, Morecroft and van der Heijden 1994, Westenholme 1990, 1994, Senge and Sterman 1994). While previous emphasis was placed on the provision of computer hardware and software to support group communication (Kraemer and King 1988), recent trends are to facilitate problem structuring methods and group decision support (Checkland 1989, Rosenhead 1989, Phillips 1990). The use of computers to structure problems and provide group decision support has been spurred by the recognition that in complex decision settings bounds on human rationality can create persistent judgmental biases and systematic errors (Simon 1956, 1979, Kahneman and Tversky 1974, Kahneman *et al.* 1982 and Hogarth 1987). To identify relevant information sources, assess relationships among decisions, actions and results and hence to facilitate learning requires that cause and effect are closely related in space and time. Dynamic systems modelling is increasingly promoted as a tool to close spatial and temporal gaps between decisions, actions and results.

Dynamic systems modelling has increasingly become a part of executive debate and dialogue to help avoid judgmental biases and systematic errors in business management decision making (Senge 1990, Morecroft 1994). It has also penetrated, albeit to a lesser extent, the discussion of environmental investments and problems. Both areas of application of dynamic systems modelling have significantly benefitted from the use of graphical programming languages. One of the main strengths of these programming languages is to enable scientists and decision makers to focus and clarify the mental model they have of a particular phenomenon, to augment this model, elaborate it and then to do something they cannot otherwise do: To run the model and let it yield the inevitable dynamic consequences hidden in their assumptions and their understanding of a system. With their relative ease of use, these graphical programming languages offer powerful tools for intellectual inquiry into the workings of complex ecological economic systems (Hannon and Ruth 1994).

To model and better understand nonlinear dynamic systems requires that we describe the main system components and their interactions. System components can be described by a set of state variables, or stocks, such as the capital stock in an economy, the amount of sediment accumulated on a landscape or the size of a population. These state variables are influenced by controls, or flows, such as annual investment in new capital, seasonal sediment fluxes, or births and deaths that occur in a population during the course of a year. The extent of the controls, the size of the flows, in turn may depend on the stocks themselves and other parameters of the system.

There are various graphical programming languages available that are specifically designed to facilitate modelling of nonlinear, dynamic systems. Among the most versatile of these languages is the graphical programming language STELLA II (Costanza 1987, Richmond and Peterson 1994 and Hannon and Ruth 1994). STELLA II runs in the Macintosh and Windows environments.

A STELLA II dynamic systems model consists of three communicating layers that contain progressively more detailed information on the structure and functioning of the model (Figure 14.1). The high level mapping and input-output layer captures high level maps and facilitates user interaction through input and output devices. This layer is most appropriate for defining the structure of the model and to enable non-modellers to easily grasp the model structure, to interactively run the model and to view and interpret its results. The ease of use of the model at this aggregate level of detail thus enables individuals to become intellectually and emotionally involved with the model (Peterson 1994).

Models are constructed in the next lower layer. Here, the symbols for stocks, flows and parameters are chosen and connected with each other. STELLA II represents stocks, flows and parameters, respectively, with three particular symbols.

Icons can be selected and placed on the computer screen to define the main building blocks of the computer model. The structure of the model is established by connecting these symbols through information arrows.

Once the structure of the model is laid out on the screen, initial conditions, parameter values and functional relationships can be specified by simply clicking on the respective icons. Dialogue boxes appear that ask for the input of data or the specification of graphically or mathematically defined functions.

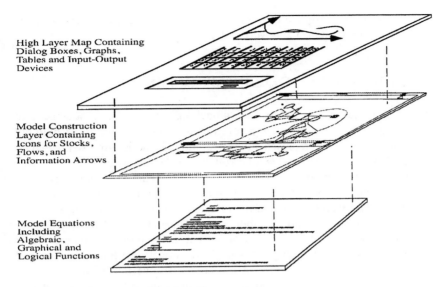

High Layer Map Containing
Dialog Boxes, Graphs,
Tables and Input-Output
Devices

Model Construction
Layer Containing
Icons for Stocks,
Flows, and
Information Arrows

Model Equations
Including
Algebraic,
Graphical and
Logical Functions

Figure 14.1   *Stella II, Modelling environment*

Equally easy is the generation of model output in tabular or graphical form through the choice of icons. With the use of sliders, a user can also immediately respond to the model output by choosing alternative parameter values as the model runs. Subsequent runs under alternative parameter settings and with different responses to model output can be plotted in the same graph or table. Thus, the modelling approach is not only dynamic with respect to the behaviour of the system itself but also with respect to the learning process that is initiated among decision makers as they observe the system's dynamics unfold. Subsequent runs under alternative assumptions help point towards aspects of the system that may be insufficiently understood, may prompt further model development and help stakeholders to systematically evaluate their perceptions of the workings of a system. The process of learning by doing experiments on the computer rather than the real world system gives model users the opportunity to investigate the implications of their assumptions for the system's dynamics and to assess their ability to make the *right* decision under alternative assumptions.

The lowest layer of the STELLA II modelling environment contains a listing of the graphically or algebraically defined relationships among the system components together with initial conditions and parameter values. These equations are solved in STELLA II with numerical techniques. The equations, initial conditions and parameter values can also be exported and compiled to conduct sophisticated statistical analyses and parameter tests

(Oster 1996) and to run the model on various computing platforms (Costanza *et al.* 1990 and Costanza and Maxwell 1991).

A THREE-STEP MODELLING PROCESS

We advocate the use of a three-step modelling process. The first stage is to develop a high generality, low resolution *scoping and consensus building* model involving broad representation of all the stakeholder groups affected by the problem. STELLA II and similar software make this process feasible. This first stage scoping model can be used to answer preliminary questions about the dynamics of the system, especially its main areas of sensitivity and uncertainty and thereby to guide the research agenda in the second stage.

The second stage *research* models are then more detailed and realistic attempts to replicate the dynamics of the particular system of interest. This stage involves collecting large amounts of historical data for calibration and testing and a detailed analysis of the areas of uncertainty in the model. Resolution is medium to high, depending on the results of the scoping model.

The third stage is aimed at models that can be used to answer particular *management* questions. These models must be based on the previous two stages and can simply be the exercising of the research models to produce future scenarios, or they can be a further elaboration of the research models that allow them to be applied to management questions. In general, these will be medium to high resolution models.

Each of these stages in the overall modelling process has useful products, but the process is most useful and effective if followed in the order described. Too often we jump to the research or management stage of the process without first building adequate consensus about the nature of the problem and without involving the appropriate stakeholder groups. Below we discuss these three stages in more detail, before describing some case studies of how they have been used.

Scoping and Consensus-Building Models

The potential to use modelling as a way to build consensus has been greatly expanded in recent years by the advent of new, much easier to use computers and modelling software as described above. It is now possible, with graphic, icon-based modelling software packages such as STELLA II, to involve a group of relative modelling novices in the construction of relatively complex models, with a few people competent in modelling acting as facilitators. Using STELLA II and projecting the computer screen onto the wall or sharing a model via the internet, the process of model construction can be transparent to a group of diverse stakeholders. Participants can then both follow the model construction process and contribute their knowledge to the process. After the basic model structure is developed, the program requires more detailed decisions about the functional connections between variables. This process is also transparent to the group, using well-designed dialogue boxes and the potential for both graphic and algebraic input. The models that result from this process are designed to capture as much realism as possible. Once preliminary versions of the model have been constructed, it can be run to develop understanding of its dynamics and sensitivity, to compare its behaviour to data for the system and to help decide where best to put additional effort in improving the model. This can be thought of as an initial scoping step that facilitates broad-based input and consensus.

Research Models

Based on this initial consensus-building model development stage, which focuses on generalism as described above, it may be appropriate and desirable to move to a more realistic and/or precise modelling stage. This stage could involve more traditional experts and is more concerned with analyzing the details of the historical development of a particular system with an eye toward developing specific scenarios or policy options in the next stage. It is still critical to maintain stakeholder involvement and interaction in this stage with regular workshops and meetings to discuss model progress and results.

While integrated models aimed at realism and precision are large, complex and loaded with uncertainties of various kinds (Costanza *et al.* 1990, Groffman and Likens 1994, Bockstael *et al.* 1995), our abilities to understand, communicate and deal with these uncertainties are rapidly improving. It is also important to remember that while increasing the resolution and complexity of models increases the amount we can say about a system, it also limits how accurately we can say it. Model predictability tends to fall with increasing resolution due to compounding uncertainties as described above (Costanza and Maxwell 1993). What we are after are models that optimize their effectiveness (Costanza and Sklar 1985) by choosing an intermediate resolution where the product of predictability and resolution (effectiveness) is maximized.

Management Models

It is also necessary to place the modelling process within the larger framework of adaptive management (Holling 1978) if it is to be effective. We need to view the implementation of policy prescriptions in a different, more adaptive way that acknowledges the uncertainty embedded in our models and allows participation by all the various stakeholder groups. *Adaptive management* views regional development policy and management as *experiments*, where interventions at several scales are made to achieve understanding and to identify and test policy options (Holling 1978, Walters 1986, Lee 1993, Gunderson *et al.* 1995). This means that models and policies based on them are not taken as the ultimate answers, but rather as guiding an adaptive experimentation process with the regional system. More emphasis is placed on monitoring and feedback to check and improve the model, rather than using the model to obfuscate and defend a policy which is not corresponding to reality. Continuing stakeholder involvement is essential in adaptive management.

This third stage of 'management' models is focused on producing scenarios and management options in this context of adaptive feedback and monitoring and based on the earlier scoping and research models.

CASE STUDIES

In this section we briefly describe a set of case studies that embodies some or all of the characteristics of the three-stage modelling process outlined above. The purpose of this section is to illustrate the wide range of environmental issues to which scoping and consensus-building modelling has been applied and to indicate the various degrees to which stakeholder involvement has been achieved in model development. We begin with case studies that solicited from stakeholders specific information to be included in the models and that shared the models throughout the modelling process with the contributors through a series of conversations, mailings and presentations. We also present examples of cases in which less formal workshop meetings for scoping and consensus building have been conducted in which a group of stakeholders convened to collectively develop models for scoping and consensus-building purposes. Some of the models presented here have been followed up with more detailed research and management models.

US IRON AND STEEL PRODUCTION

Using STELLA II software, a model has been developed of iron ore mining, processing and raw steel production for the aggregate US iron and steel industry with the goal to identify the industry's future likely profiles of material and energy use.[2] The iron and steel industry is the single largest energy consumer in the industrial sector of the economy and characterized by large-scale operations that require significant capital investment to change their structure and functioning. The high degree of interconnectedness among the various production stages often makes necessary technological adjustments at one stage in response to change elsewhere in the industry. For example, many vertically integrated steel plants have been retiring their coke ovens, replacing them with imported coke and decreasing the production of pig iron, in which coke is used to reduce iron ores. The decline in pig iron production from blast furnaces requires a shift in raw steel production technologies away from those that use pig iron as their main input if overall raw steel output is to be maintained (Sparrow 1983, Ross 1987 and Ruth 1997). This typically meant movement towards electric arc furnaces, whose main energy input is electricity. The overall effect of the changes in technologies at the various production stages is a significant change in the industry's energy use profile, accompanied by an increase in the fractions of energy purchased elsewhere rather than produced by the industry itself. The latter affects the industry's influence on its supply and cost of energy.

The large investments that are required for the implementation of new technologies and the many interdependencies among the various production stages make it necessary for decision makers to anticipate long-term trends in demand of the industry's products and supply of raw materials and energy. By the same token, to move towards sustainable industry practices requires that managers and policy decision makers are able to explore the implications for the industry's material and energy use profiles under a wide range of scenarios about changes in demand and the speed at which technologies can be adapted (Ruth 1993).

The goal of the scoping and consensus-building modelling of US iron and steel industries was to capture the feedbacks among various production stages in the industry in terms of material and energy use. Particular attention was given to changes in material and energy flows in response to changes in input materials, technical change at the various production stages and changes in demand for raw steel. A series of informal, iterative interviews with industry experts, members of industry associations and consultants was carried out to arrive at a model structure that is sufficiently detailed to capture the various feedbacks and sufficiently simple to be easily communicated to non-expert modellers. Significant agreement was already present at the outset of the

---

[2] The model was developed by Matthias Ruth under the auspices of Roy F. Weston Inc., a management consulting company in West Chester, Pennsylvania, USA, and in close cooperation with members in industry, industry organizations and industry experts in research institutions, involving informal interviews and presentations at various stages of the model development.

model development process on the system boundaries that define the respective production stages and on the key material and energy types to be included in the model. Based on this consensus, the model captures mining, pig iron production and raw steel production and modules for own electricity generation and coke production. The structure of the model is outlined in Figure 14.2 (Ruth 1995 and Weston and Ruth 1995).

To generate consensus on the specification of material and energy use at the various production stages and the feedback processes that occur among them, engineering information from various sources was used and supplemented with time series data derived from published sources. These quantifications provided a benchmark for model runs. To explore industry's profiles of material and energy use under alternative assumptions, the model was set up to be run in an interactive modelling mode that enables decision makers to choose different parameter settings based on their understanding of the industry. Additionally, the model was designed to investigate the implications that various rates of change in the demand for the industry's products and in technologies may have on material and energy use at individual production stages and by the industry as a whole.

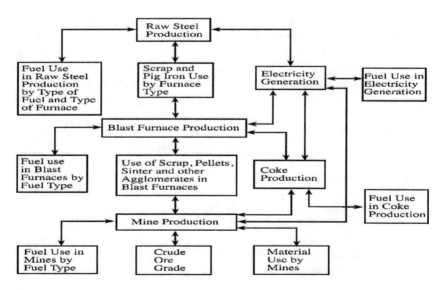

Figure 14.2   Structure of the US iron and steel model

The discussions with industry experts prior to setting up the model and running it indicated a prevailing assumption that even though crude ore reserves are finite, absolute amounts are large and ore grades sufficiently high to not pose a constraint on industry in the long run. Various model runs refuted this view of the industry. The model indicates over a wide range of reasonable assumptions that although there is no shortage of ore in the US, declines in ore grade lead to increases in total energy consumption per ton of raw steel output that is unlikely to be compensated for by improvements in technology, even in the presence of further increased recycling rates and only moderate increases in demand. Valuable insight was also generated with regard to changes in the industry's energy mix, technology mix and the time frames over which these changes are likely to occur.

Subsequently, the model has been significantly extended from the model designed for scoping and consensus building to include indirect energy requirements by the iron and steel industry and direct and indirect carbon emissions (Ruth 1997). Further efforts are on their way to work with managers in industry to guide investment decisions at the level of the firm and provide management support.

US PULP AND PAPER PRODUCTION

Similar to the model on iron and steel production, a dynamic modelling project is currently being carried out to trace material and energy flows in the US paper and pulp industry over time (Ruth 1996). The pulp and paper industry is among the leaders in US manufacturing in expressing a commitment to sustainable business practices. Its *Agenda 2020* outlines the industry's path towards sustainability by the year 2020 (AFPA 1994). While the document is strong in vision, it lacks sufficient empirical detail to identify the likelihood for sustainability to be achieved.

Currently, the United States has the highest apparent per capita consumption of paper in the world (approx. 330 kg); demand has been forecast to grow by 2.5 per cent per year over the next decade (Gundersby and Rennel 1992). The industry (SIC 26) ranks eighth among US manufacturing industries in value of shipments (Department of Energy 1994). It accounts for about 3 per cent of total national energy use, or 12 per cent of total manufacturing energy use, out of which 95 per cent is consumed by pulp, paper and paperboard mills (Department of Energy 1994). Based on the energy intensity of its shipments, the paper and allied products industry ranks as the second most energy intensive industry group in the manufacturing sector. 56 per cent of total fuel and electricity use is self-generated, primarily from spent pulping liquors, wood residues and bark. Wood for pulping represents the largest cost of material inputs, accounting for a total of 21 per cent of total material and energy costs. By weight, the industry's output contributes 37 per cent to the municipal solid waste stream (Ince 1994) and contributes with its production processes to local environmental problems through solid waste disposal, emissions to water and air.

The high capital intensity and the resulting economic consequences of equipment replacement reduce the industry's ability to rapidly adopt new production methods (Gilbreath 1995). Yet, rapidly changing social, regulatory and consumer expectations call for flexibility in the industry's choice of technology, material and energy inputs and outputs. Given the industry's lack of short and medium-term flexibility, it is essential that future trends in technology, markets of inputs and outputs and environmental regulation are properly anticipated prior to policy and investment decisions.

How can likely future trends be anticipated and proper management strategies and policies be identified? Expectations of consumers, policy decision makers and resource managers are likely to be based on different assumptions about the industry's ability to make the necessary adjustments, the data and information necessary to evaluate industry performance and likely future markets of inputs and outputs. Thus, to generate consensus on the means necessary for industry to achieve its sustainability goals requires that consensus is generated on the various inputs into the decision making process.

The scoping and consensus-building process of this study is ongoing. In its present form, it involves representatives from paper companies, industry associations, government agencies and research institutions to identify the system boundaries that define the key model components. Special emphasis is placed in the model development process to easily enable replacement of parts of the model and additions to the model as additional stakeholder groups are brought into the discussion.

In the model development process, a set of likely scenarios of industry performance is emerging that is currently being used to assess the realm of the industry's future material and energy use profiles. Several problems and issues have been identified through scoping and consensus-building modelling. First, stabilizing or reducing total energy consumption concomitant with moderate production growth requires that future annual increases in energy efficiency are twice as high as the efficiency improvements achieved for the period 1972-92; a period that was characterized by significant efficiency improvements that where spurred by two oil price shocks and tightened environmental regulations. Second, to maintain or increase the industry's reliance on self-generated energy depends on one or a combination of several approaches: (1) Rapid dissemination of energy saving technology; (2) reduction in the rate of growth of the wastepaper utilization rate; or (3) cessation of the substitution of wastepaper pulp for kraft pulp. However, approaches (2) and (3) lead to increases in total energy consumption and virgin fibre consumption and conflict with other sustainability goals set forth in *Agenda 2020*. Third, increased wastepaper utilization rates lead to a significant replacement of pulpwood by recycled fibre. Nevertheless, total pulpwood consumption may increase as rates of pulpwood replacement are likely to be dwarfed by increased rates of paper and paperboard production, even under the assumption that wastepaper utilization rates reach their technical maxima by the year 2020.

SOUTH AFRICAN FYNBOS ECOSYSTEMS

Perched at the south western tip of Africa is the world's smallest and, for its size, the richest floral kingdom – the Cape Floristic Region. This tiny area, occupying a mere 90,000 km^2, supports 8,500 plant species (of which 68 per cent are endemic), 193 endemic genera and six endemic families (Bond and Goldblatt 1984). Because of the many threats to this region's spectacular flora, it has earned the distinction of being the world's *hottest* hot spot of biodiversity (Myers 1990).

The predominant vegetation in the Cape Floristic Region is fynbos, a hardleafed and fire prone shrub which grows on the highly infertile soils associated with the ancient, quartsitic mountains - mountain fynbos - and the wind blown sands of the coastal margin - lowland fynbos - (Cowling 1992). Owing to the prevalent climate of cool, wet winters and warm, dry summers, fynbos is superficially similar to California chaparral and other Mediterranean climate shrubs of the world (Hobbs, Richardson and Davis 1995). Fynbos landscapes are extremely rich in plant species (the Cape Peninsula has 2,554 species in 470 km^2) and narrow endemism ranks amongst the highest in the world (Cowling, Holmes and Rebelo 1992).

In order to adequately manage these ecosystems several questions had to be answered, including, what services do these species rich-fynbos ecosystems provide and what is their value to society? A two week workshop on valuation of fynbos ecosystems was held July 17-28, 1995 at the University of Cape Town (UCT). The workshop organizers (Robert Costanza and Richard Cowling) brought together a group of faculty and students from different disciplines along with parks managers, business people and environmentalists, in order to take a problem-oriented approach to modelling and valuing the fynbos. The workshop was attended by more than 40 delegates from a wide array of backgrounds, including four universities, two research institutions, two government departments, two conservation agencies, one regional authority, one NGO and one consulting business. Funding was provided by the Pew Charitable Trusts, Foundation for Research Development, National Botanical

Institute and the UCT Visiting Scholar's Fund.

The primary goal of the workshop was to produce a series of consensus-based research papers which critically assessed the practical and theoretical issues surrounding ecosystem valuation as well as assessing the value of services derived by local and regional communities from fynbos systems.

To achieve these ambitious goals, an *atelier* approach was used, which threw the faculty and students together to form multidisciplinary, multicultural teams, breaking down the traditional hierarchical approach to teaching. The workshop format included some lectures but focused on encouraging creative synthesis of ideas by taking a problem-solving approach to the issues under scrutiny. Open space (Rao 1994) techniques were used to identify critical questions and allow participants to form working groups to tackle those questions. Open space meetings are loosely organized affairs which give all participants an opportunity to raise issues and participate in finding solutions.

The working groups of this workshop met several times during the first week of the course and almost continuously during the second week. The groups convened together periodically to hear updates of group projects and to offer feedback to other groups. Some group members floated to other groups at times to offer specific knowledge or technical advice.

Despite some initial misgivings on the part of the group, the loose structure of the course was remarkably successful and by the end of the two weeks, seven working groups had worked feverishly to draft papers. Marjan van den Belt filmed the entire workshop and produced a short video describing the course/workshop.

One of the groups focused on producing an initial scoping model of the fynbos. This modelling group produced perhaps the most developed and implementable product from the workshop: A general dynamic model integrating ecological and economic processes in fynbos ecosystems (Higgins *et al.* 1996). The model was developed in STELLA and designed to assess potential values of ecosystem services given ecosystem controls, management options and feedbacks within and between the ecosystem and human sectors. The model helps to address questions about how the ecosystem services provided by the fynbos ecosystem at both a local and international scale are influenced by alien invasion and management strategies. A monthly time step was selected in order to simulate the seasonal and fire-related dynamics of the fynbos watershed ecosystem over a 50-year period. The model comprises five interactive sub-models, namely hydrological, fire, plant, management and economic valuation. Parameter estimates for each sub-model were either derived from the literature or established by workshop participants and consultants (they are described in detail in Higgins *et al.* 1996). The plant sub-model included both native and alien plants. Simulation provided a realistic description of alien plant invasions and their impacts on river flow and runoff.

This model drew in part on the findings of the other working groups and incorporates a broad range of research by workshop participants. Benefits and costs of management scenarios are addressed by estimating values for harvested products, tourism, water yield and biodiversity. Costs include direct management costs and indirect costs. The model shows that the ecosystem services derived from the Western Cape mountains are far more valuable when vegetated by fynbos than by alien trees. The difference in water production alone was sufficient to favour spending significant amounts of money to maintain fynbos in mountain catchments.

The model is designed to be user friendly and interactive, allowing the user to set such features as area of alien clearing, fire management strategy, levels of wildflower harvesting and park visitation rates. The model should prove to be a valuable tool in demonstrating to decision makers the benefits of investing now in tackling the alien plant problem, since delays have serious cost implications. A research and management modelling exercise may ultimately follow from this initial phase.

LOUISIANA COASTAL WETLANDS

The marshes of coastal Louisiana represent one of the most rapidly changing landscapes in the world. The changing historical sequence of Mississippi River main distributaries have deposited sediments to form the current Mississippi deltaic plain marshes. This delta switching cycle (on average lasting 1500 years) sets the historical context of this landscape. At present, the river is in the process of changing from the current channel to the much shorter Atchafalaya River. The Corps of Engineers maintains a control structure at Old River to control the percentage of Mississippi River flow going down the Atchafalaya. Since about 1950 this percentage has been set at approximately 30 per cent. Atchafalaya River-borne sediment first filled in open water areas in the upper Atchafalaya basin and more recently have begun to build a delta in Atchafalaya Bay (Roberts *et al.* 1980, Van Heerden and Roberts 1980a, 1980b). During the next few decades, new delta is projected to form at the mouth of the river and plant community succession will occur on the recently formed delta and in the existing marshes. At the same time, the overall Louisiana coastal zone has been projected to lose a net of approximately 100 km²/year due to sediment starvation and salt water intrusion (Gagliano *et al.* 1981).

The levee building on the Mississippi and Atchafalaya Rivers, along with the damming of distributaries, has virtually eliminated riverine sediment input to most Louisiana coastal marshes. This change has broken the deltaic cycle and greatly accelerated land loss. Only in the area of the Atchafalaya delta is sediment laden water flowing into wetland areas and land gain occurring (Roberts *et al.* 1980 and Van Heerden and Roberts 1980a, 1980b).

Primary human activities that potentially contribute to wetland loss are flood control, canals, spoil banks, land reclamation, fluids withdrawal and highway construction. There is evidence that canals and levees are an important factor in wetland loss in coastal Louisiana, but there is much disagreement about the magnitude of the indirect loss caused by them (Cleveland *et al.* 1981, Craig *et al.* 1979, Deegan *et al.* 1984, Leibowitz 1989 and Scaife *et al.* 1983). Natural channels are generally not deep enough for the needs of oil recovery, navigation, pipelines and drainage, so a vast network of canals has been built. In the Deltaic Plain of Louisiana, canals and their associated spoil banks of dredged material currently comprise 8 per cent of the total marsh area compared to 2 per cent in 1955. The construction of canals leads to direct loss of marsh by dredging and spoil deposition and indirect loss by changing hydrology, sedimentation and productivity. Canals are thought to lead to more rapid salinity intrusion, causing the death of freshwater vegetation. Canal spoil banks also limit water exchange with wetlands, thereby decreasing deposition of suspended sediments.

Proposed human activities can have a dramatic impact on the distribution of water and sediments from the Atchafalaya River and consequently on the development of the Atchafalaya landscape. For example, the Corps of Engineers was considering extending a levee along the east bank of the Atchafalaya that would restrict water and sediment flow into the Terrebonne marshes.

This situation represented both a unique opportunity to study landscape dynamics and a unique opportunity to build consensus about how the system works and how to manage it. The Atchafalaya landscape is changing rapidly enough to provide time series observations that can be used to test basic hypotheses about how coastal landscapes develop. In addition to short-term observations, there is a uniquely long and detailed history of field and remotely sensed data available on the study area (Bahr *et al.* 1983 and Costanza *et al.* 1983). Solutions to the land loss problem in Louisiana all have far reaching implications. They depend on which combination of solutions are undertaken and when and where they are undertaken. Outside forces (such as rates of sea level rise) also influence the effectiveness of any proposed solution. In the past, suggested solutions have been evaluated independently of each other and in an *ad hoc* manner and without adequate dialogue and consensus among affected parties.

In order to address this problem in a more comprehensive way, we began a project in 1986 aimed at applying the three-stage modelling approach described above. The first stage of scoping and consensus building involved mainly representatives of the Corps of Engineers, the US Fish and Wildlife service, local landowners and environmentalists and several disciplines within the academic community. This stage involved a series of workshops aimed at developing a 'unit model' of the basic processes occurring at any point in the landscape (using STELLA) and at coming to agreement about how to model the entire landscape in the later stages. This stage took about 1 year.

In the second (research) stage an integrated spatial simulation modelling approach was developed (Costanza *et al.* 1988, Sklar *et al.* 1985, Sklar *et al.* 1989 and Costanza *et al.* 1990) that replicated the unit model developed in stage 1 over the coastal landscape and added horizontal flows of water, nutrients and sediments, along with successional algorithms to model changes in the distribution pattern of habitats on the landscape. Using this approach, we first demonstrated the ability to simulate the past behaviour of the system in a fairly realistic way (Costanza *et al.* 1990). This part of the process took about 3 years.

We then entered the third (management) stage of the process and developed a range of projected future conditions as a function of various management alternatives and natural changes, both individually and in various combinations. The research and management model simulates both the dynamic and spatial behaviour of the system and it keeps track of several of the important landscape level variables in the system, such as ecosystem type, water level and flow, sediment levels and sedimentation, subsidence, salinity, primary production, nutrient levels and elevation.

The research and management model was called the Coastal Ecological Landscape Spatial Simulation (CELSS) model. It consists of 2,479 1 km^2 spatial cells to simulate a rapidly changing section of the Louisiana coast and predict long-term (50 to 100 year) spatially articulated changes in this landscape as a function of various management alternatives and natural and human influenced climate variations.

The model was run on a CRAY supercomputer from initial conditions in 1956 through 1978 and 1983 (years for which additional data were available for calibration and validation) and on to the year 2033 with a maximum of weekly time steps. It accounted for 89.6 per cent of the spatial variation in the 1978 calibration data and 79 per cent of the variation in the 1983 verification data. Various future and past scenarios were analyzed with the model, including the future impacts of various Atchafalaya River levee extension proposals, freshwater diversion plans, marsh damage mitigation plans, future global sea level rise and the historical impacts of past human activities and past climate patterns.

The model results were used by the Corps of Engineers and the Fish and Wildlife Service in making decisions about these management options. Because they were involved directly as participants in the process through all three stages, the model results were much easier to both communicate and implement. The participants also had a much more sophisticated understanding of the underlying assumptions, uncertainties and limitations of the model, along with its strengths and could use it effectively as a management tool.

FLORIDA EVERGLADES

The Everglades of Florida, US, is a mosaic of urban, agricultural, marsh and forest habitats in a vast neotropical wetland, with a pattern that has been altered by water management via canals, levees and water control structures. This modelling study was built on the initial experience in Louisiana with the CELSS model. The three-step modelling process was used by first running a series of workshops to come to consensus about: (1) The basic variables to be included (2) the general structure of the 'unit model' (which was developed using STELLA); and (3) the spatial and temporal resolution and other aspects of the overall study (Fitz *et al.* 1993 and Fitz *et al.* 1997).

A spatially explicit research and management model of ecosystem processes and landscape succession was then developed to evaluate landscape response to different water quantity/quality management scenarios.[3] A GIS partitions the model area into 10,000 1 km² grid cells, storing data such as initial habitat types, elevation and water levels. The ecosystem unit model is replicated in each homogeneous cell and parameterized according to the habitat type. The unit model simulates hydrology, growth of periphyton and macrophytes, nutrient cycling and fire, with numerous feedbacks among these components. Water and nutrients flux among the model's raster cells and canal vectors, with controls at management structures that alter water delivery in the system according to management rules. Unit model dynamics respond to the varying water quantity and quality in the landscape mosaic, while the pattern of cell habitat type may change in response to alterations in hydroperiod, nutrient levels and fire effects.

The model sensitivity was evaluated at varying scales, with several biotic (maximum Leaf Area Index, maximum rate of net primary production) and abiotic (evapotranspiration rate, initial concentration of PO_4 sorbed to sediments) parameters having significant influence on model dynamics in terms of water levels, nutrient concentrations, and/or plant biomass. Similarly, variations in forcing functions such as water inflows into the model area and its distribution via control structures altered the landscape. Most components of the model have been calibrated with available data and we are evaluating different algorithms and hypotheses concerning habitat transitions.

---

[3] Visit the web site: http://kabir.umd.edu/Glades/ELM.html for a complete description of the Everglades Landscape Model, the data base and some example scenarios.

The Everglades Landscape Model (ELM) is now one of the tools in a research and management program to aid in focusing research and evaluating changes in water management in the south Florida region. Due to the tight coupling of the urban and agricultural demands with the natural system, an integration of economic forces that influence management decisions is important for holistic analysis of the Everglades. In a similar initiative to that discussed below in the Patuxent River watershed of Maryland, US, we are currently explicitly incorporating the valuation of important system components into the landscape modelling effort.

PATUXENT RIVER WATERSHED, MARYLAND

The Maryland Patuxent River Watershed, which includes portions of Anne Arundel, Calvert, Charles, Howard, Montgomery, Prince George's and St. Mary's counties, has been experiencing rapid urban development and changes in agricultural practices, resulting in adverse impacts on both terrestrial and aquatic ecosystems. Concern peaked when the Patuxent estuary began to experience rapid degradation of water quality and disappearance of sea grass beds in the late 1970s. Since then the Patuxent has been a focus of scientific study and political action in efforts to conserve environmental resources. It is also a model of the larger Chesapeake Bay watershed and serves as an example and test bed for many ideas about managing the entire Bay watershed (Costanza and Greer 1995).

As part of this effort a three-stage modelling project was begun in 1992. This ongoing project is another outgrowth of the initial work with the CELSS model in Louisiana. It uses: (1) Workshops involving the full range of scientific, government and citizen stakeholder groups to develop initial scoping models, to communicate results and to refine and adapt the research agenda; and (2) integrating ongoing and new scientific studies over a range of scales from small microcosms to the Patuxent watershed as a whole. The project is aimed at developing integrated knowledge and new tools to enhance predictive understanding of watershed ecosystems (including processes and mechanisms that govern the interconnected dynamics of water, nutrients, toxins and biotic components) and their linkage to human factors affecting water and watersheds. The goal is effective sustainable ecosystem management at the watershed scale.

Major research questions include: (1) What are the quantitative, spatially explicit and dynamic linkages between land use and terrestrial and aquatic ecosystem structure and function; (2) what are the quantitative effects of various combinations of natural and anthropogenic stressors on watershed ecosystems and how do these effects change with scale; and (3) what are useful ways to measure changes in the total value of the landscape including both marketed and non-marketed (natural system) components and how effective are alternative mitigation approaches, management strategies and policy options toward increasing this value.

The overall model consists of interrelated ecological and economic sub-models that employ a landscape perspective, for this perspective captures the spatial and temporal distributions of the services and functions of the natural system and human-related phenomena such as surrounding land use patterns and population distributions (Bockstael *et al.* 1995). Configuration and reconfiguration of the landscape occurs as a result of ecological and economic factors and these factors are closely intertwined.

The ecological part of the model is based on the Patuxent Landscape Model (PLM), one of a series of landscape level spatial simulation models as discussed above (Costanza *et al.* 1995). The PLM is capable of simulating the succession of complex ecological systems using a landscape perspective. Economic sub-models are being developed to reflect human behaviour and economic influences. The effects of human intervention result directly from the conversion of land from one use to another (wetlands conversion, residential development, power plant siting) or from changes in the practices that take place within specific land uses (adoption of agricultural best management practices, intensification of congestion and automobile emissions, change in urban water and sewer use and storm run-off).

Economic sub-models will characterize land use and agricultural decisions and capture the effects on these decisions of institutional influences such as environmental, zoning, transportation and agricultural policies. The integration of the two models provides a framework for regulatory analysis in the context of risk assessment, non-point source pollution control, wetlands mitigation/restoration and so on. Figure 14.3 shows the relationship of the various model components.

The integrated model will allow stakeholders to evaluate the indirect effects over long time horizons of current policy options. These effects are almost always ignored in partial analyses, although they may be very significant and may reverse many long-held assumptions and policy predictions. It will also allow us to directly address the functional value of ecosystem services by looking at the long-term, spatial and dynamic linkages between ecosystems and economic systems.

BANFF NATIONAL PARK, CANADA

An integrated modelling project was begun for Banff national park in 1994 to address a range of management issues in this ecosystem. A task force with representatives from all the major stakeholder groups in the area (tourism, residents, natural systems, government and so on) was established and several workshops and ongoing projects were initiated. A round table was established to thoroughly discuss the issues among the stakeholder groups and come to consensus on a vision for the park. A futures (scoping) modelling exercise was undertaken as part of this larger project by EERA (Ecological Economics Research and Applications). This exercise utilized STELLA and a series of workshops with the stakeholders and a technical working group they established. The computer model included sectors for the natural ecosystems in the park, three main indicator species (bear, wolf and elk) and the socioeconomic components of the system (for example, tourists, resident population, infrastructure, income and employment). This model is being used to help understand the linkages between human use and ecosystem health and to project scenarios for different management options into the future. These scenarios can then be compared to the vision for the park and ultimately the process will lead to consensus recommendations for park management. A research and management modelling exercise may ultimately follow from this initial phase.

PATAGONIA COASTAL ZONE MANAGEMENT

A similar scoping model exercise using STELLA was undertaken in Patagonia (van den Belt *et al.* 1996) as part of a larger UNEP/GEF and Wildlife Conservation Society funded project, coordinated by the Fundacion Patagonia Natural of Argentina, on managing the Patagonian coastal zone. In this case, workshops were difficult to arrange and stakeholder input was solicited from each stakeholder individually. The model represented the synthesis of these different inputs and it was presented to the complete group of stakeholders at a final workshop.

The model included sectors for penguins (a main tourist draw), hake and anchovies (major food items for penguins and also commercially harvested), coastal and offshore fisheries, the local and international fish markets, tourism and oil pollution. The model can look at the linkages and tradeoffs between these sectors and calculate the total net present value of the coastal zone under different future management scenarios. For example, overfishing harms not only the fisheries sectors, but also tourism through its impact on penguin populations. The model shows that preventing oil pollution is very cost effective since damage to tourism via penguin deaths far outweighs the cost of cleanup and prevention. The model will be distributed to the stakeholders for their own use and further elaboration and more detailed management and research models may follow.

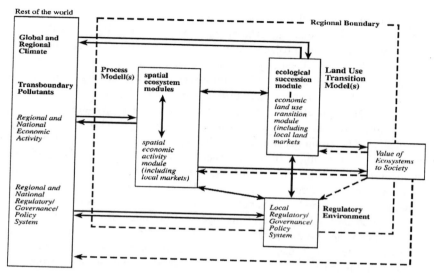

Figure 14.3   *Integrated ecological modelling and valuation framework*

CONCLUSIONS

In each of the case studies described above, the three-stage modelling process enabled us to provide a set of detailed conclusions regarding the management of the respective system. These conclusions were built on models that embodied the input and expert judgment of a broad range of stakeholders. They also offered unique insight into our ability to anticipate a system's dynamics in the light of non-linearities and spatial and temporal lags. Our ability to anticipate those dynamics on the basis of available data and knowledge and to develop consensus about those dynamics is an essential prerequisite for the successful management of complex ecological economic systems. We anticipate that future modelling efforts will increasingly make use of the software tools and the three-step modelling process with stakeholder involvement described in this chapter.

REFERENCES

AFPA 1994. *Agenda 2020: A Technology Vision and Research Agenda for America's Forest, Wood and Paper Industry*. Washington DC: The American Forest and Paper Association.

Bahr, L.M., Costanza, R., Day, J.W. Jr., Bayley, S.E., Neill, C., Leibowitz, S.G. and Fruci, J. 1983. Ecological characterization of the Mississippi Deltaic Plain Region: A narrative with management recommendations. US Fish and Wildlife Service, Division of Biological Services, Washington DC, FWS/OBS-82/69, 189 pp.

Bockstael, N., Costanza, R., Strand, I., Boynton, W., Bell, K. and Wainger, L. 1995. 'Ecological economic modelling and valuation of ecosystems', *Ecological Economics*, 14, 143-59.

Bond, P. and Goldblatt, P. 1984. 'Plants of the Cape Flora', *Journal of South African Botany*, Supplement, 13, 1-455.

Cleveland, C.J., Neill, C. and Day, J.W. Jr. 1981. 'The impact of artificial canals on land loss in the Barataria Basin, Louisiana', in Mitsch, W.J., Bosserman, R.W. and Klopatek, J.M.(eds), *Energy and Ecological Modelling*. Amsterdam: Elsevier pp. 425-34.

Checkland, P. 1989. 'Soft systems methodology', in Rosenhead, J. (ed.), *Rational Analysis for a Problematic World*. Chichester, England: John Wiley and Sons.

Costanza, R. 1987. 'Simulation modelling on the Macintosh using STELLA', *BioScience*, 37, 129-32.

Costanza, R., Fitz, H.C., Maxwell, T., Voinov, A., Voinov, H. and Wainger, L.A. 1995. 'Patuxent landscape model: Sensitivity analysis and nutrient management scenarios'. Interim Report for US EPA Cooperative Agreement #CR 821925010. Institute for Ecological Economics, Center for Environmental and Estuarine Studies, University of Maryland.

Costanza, R. and Greer, J. 1995. 'The Chesapeake Bay and its watershed: A model for sustainable ecosystem management?' in Gunderson, L. H., Holling C. S. and Light, S. (eds), *Barriers and Bridges to the Renewal of Ecosystems and Institutions*. New York: Columbia University Press, pp. 169-213.

Costanza, R. and Maxwell, T. 1991. 'Spacial ecosystem modelling using parallel processors', *Ecological Modelling*, 58, 159-83.

Costanza, R. and Maxwell, T. 1993. 'Resolution and predictability: An approach to the scaling problem', *Landscape Ecology*, 9, 47-57.

Costanza, R. and Sklar, F.H. 1985. 'Articulation, accuracy and effectiveness of mathematical models: A review of freshwater wetland applications', *Ecological Modelling*, 27, 45-68.

Costanza, R., Fitz, H.C., Maxwell, T., Voinov, A., Voinov, H. and Wainger, L.A. 1995. 'Patuxent landscape model: Sensitivity analysis and nutrient management scenarios'. Interim Report for US EPA Cooperative Agreement #CR 821925010. Institute for Ecological Economics, Center for Environmental and Estuarine Studies, University of Maryland.

Costanza, R., Neill, C., Leibowitz, S.G., Fruci, J.R., Bahr, L.M. Jr. and Day, J.W. Jr. 1983. 'Ecological models of the Mississippi deltaic plain region: Data collection and presentation'. US Fish and Wildlife Service, Division of Biological Services, Washington DC, FWS/OBS-82/68, 340 pp.

Costanza, R., Sklar, F.H., White, M.L. and Day, J.W. Jr. 1988. 'A dynamic spatial simulation model of land loss and marsh succession in coastal Louisiana', in Mitsch, W.J., Straskraba, M. and Jorgensen, S.E. (eds), *Wetland Modelling*. Amsterdam: Elsevier, pp. 99-114.

Costanza, R., Sklar, F.H. and White, M.L. 1990. 'Modelling coastal landscape dynamics', *BioScience*, 40, 91-107.

Cowling, R.M. (ed.) 1992. *The Ecology of Fynbos. Nutrients, Fire and Diversity.* Cape Town: Oxford University Press.

Cowling, R.M., Holmes, P.M. and Rebelo, A.G. 1992. 'Plant diversity and endemism', in R.M. Cowling (ed.), *The Ecology of Fynbos. Nutrients, Fire and Diversity.* Cape Town: Oxford University Press, pp. 62-112.

Craig, N.J., Turner, R.E. and Day, J.W. Jr. 1979. 'Land loss in coastal Louisiana (USA)', *Environmental Management*, 3, 133-44.

Deegan, L.A., Kennedy, H.M. and Neill, C. 1984. 'Natural factors and human modifications contributing to marsh loss in Louisiana's Mississippi River deltaic plain', *Environmental Management*, 8, 519-28.

Department of Energy 1994. *Manufacturing Consumption of Energy 1991.* Manufacturing Energy Consumption Survey. Washington DC: Government Printing Office.

Fitz, H.C., Costanza, R. and Reyes, E. 1993. 'The Everglades landscape model (ELM): Summary report of Task 2, model development'. Report to the South Florida Water Management District, Everglades Research Division.

Fitz, H.C., DeBellevue, E.B., Costanza, R., Boumans, R., Maxwell, T. and Wainger, L. 1997. 'Development of a general ecosystem model (GEM) for a range of scales and ecosystems', *Ecological Modelling* (in press).

Gagliano, S.M., Meyer-Arendt, K.J. and Wicker, K.M. 1981. 'Land loss in the Mississippi River deltaic plain', *Transactions of the Gulf Coast Association of Geological Societies*, 31, 285-300.

Gilbreath, K.R. 1995 (draft). 'Life cycle assessment, energy and the environment from a pulp and paper mill's perspective'. Prepared for the ACEEE 1995 Summer Study on Energy Efficiency in Industry, Grand Island, New York, August 1-4.

Granger, C.W.J. 1969. 'Investigating causal relations by econometric models and cross-spectral methods', *Econometrica*, 37, 424-38.

Granger, C.W.J. 1993. 'What are we learning about the long run?' *Economic Journal*, 103, 307-17.

Groffman, P.M. and Likens, G.E. (eds) 1994. *Integrated Regional Models: Interactions Between Humans and their Environment.* New York: Chapman and Hall, 157 pp.

Gundersby, P. and Rennel, J. 1992. 'The global demand/supply outlook for market pulp', *Know-How Wire, Jakko Pöry Client Magazine*, No. 1.

Gunderson, L.C.S., Holling, C.S. and Light, S. (eds) 1995. *Barriers and Bridges to the Renewal of Ecosystems and Institutions.* New York: Columbia University Press, 593 pp.

Hannon, B. and Ruth, M. 1994. *Dynamic Modelling.* New York: Springer-Verlag.

Higgins, S.I., Turpie, J.K., Costanza, R., Cowling, R.M., Le Maitre, D.C., Marais, C. and Midgley, G.F. 1996. 'An ecological economic simulation model of mountain fynbos ecosystems: Dynamics, valuation and management', *Ecological Economics*.

Hobbs, R.J., Richardson, D.M. and Davis, G.W. 1995. 'Mediterranean-type ecosystems: Opportunities and constraints for studying the function of biodiversity', in Davis, G.W. and Richardson, D.M. (eds), *Mediterranean-type Ecosystems. The Function of Biodiversity.* Berlin: Springer, pp. 1-42.

Hogarth, R. 1987. *Judgment and Choice*. Chichester, England: John Wiley and Sons.

Holling, C.S. 1964. 'The analysis of complex population processes', *The Canadian Entomologist*, 96, 335-47.

Holling, C.S. 1966. 'The functional response of invertebrate predators to prey density', *Memoirs of the Entomological Society of Canada*, No. 48.

Holling, C.S. (ed.) 1978. *Adaptive Environmental Assessment and Management*. London: Wiley.

Ince, P. 1994. 'Recycling and long-range timber outlook'. US Department of Agriculture, Forest Service, Rocky Mountain Forest and Range Experiment Station, General Technical Report RM-242, Fort Collins, Colorado.

Kahneman, D. and Tversky, A. 1974. 'Judgment under uncertainty', *Science*, 185, 1124-31.

Kahnemann, D., Slovic, P. and Tversky, A. 1982. *Judgment Under Uncertainty: Heuristics and Biases*. Cambridge: Cambridge University Press.

Kraemer, K.L. and King, J.L. 1988. 'Computer-based systems for cooperative work and group decision making', *ACM Computing Surveys*, 20, 115-46.

Lee, K. 1993. *Compass and the Gyroscope*. Washington DC: Island Press.

Levins, R. 1966. 'The strategy of model building in population biology', *American Scientist*, 54, 421-31.

Leibowitz, S. 1989. 'The pattern and process of land loss in coastal Louisiana: A landscape ecological analysis'. PhD Dissertation, Louisiana State University, Baton Rouge, LA.

Lyneis, J.M. 1980. *Corporate Planning and Policy Design: A System Dynamics Approach*. Cambridge, Massachusetts: Pugh-Roberts Associates.

Morecroft, J.D.W. 1994. 'Executive knowledge, models and learning', in Morecroft, J.D.W. and Sterman, J.D. (eds), *Modelling for Learning Organizations*. Portland, Oregon: Productivity Press, pp. 3-28.

Morecroft, J.D.W. and van der Heijden, K.A.J.M. 1994. 'Modelling the oil producers: Capturing oil industry knowledge in a behavioral simulation model', in Morecroft, J.D.W. and Sterman, J.D. (eds), *Modelling for Learning Organizations*. Portland, Oregon: Productivity Press, pp. 147-74.

Morecroft, J.D.W., Lane, D.C. and Viita, P.S. 1991. 'Modelling growth strategy in a biotechnology startup firm', *System Dynamics Review*, 7, 93-116.

Myers, N. 1990. 'The biodiversity challenge: Expanded hot-spots analysis', *The Environmentalist*, 10, 243-55.

Oster, G. 1996. *Madonna*, http://nature.berkeley.edu/~goster/madonna.html.

Peterson, S. 1994. 'Software for model building and simulation: An illustration of design philosophy', in Morecroft, J.D.W. and Sterman, J.D. (eds) *Modelling for Learning Organizations*. Portland, Oregon: Productivity Press, pp. 291-300.

Phillips, L.D. 1990. 'Decision analysis for group decision support', in Eden, C. and Radford, J. (eds), *Tackling Strategic Problems: The Role of Group Decision Support*. London: Sage Publishers.

Rao, S.S. 1994. 'Welcome to open space', *Training*, April, 52-5.

Rawls, J. 1971. *A Theory of Justice*. Oxford England: Oxford University Press.

Rawls, J. 1987. 'The idea of an overlapping consensus', *Oxford Journal of Legal Studies*, 7, 1-25.

Richmond, B. and Peterson, S. 1994. *STELLA II documentation*. Hanover, New Hampshire: High Performance Systems, Inc.

Roberts, E.B. 1978. *Managerial Applications of System Dynamics*. Portland, Oregon: Productivity Press.

Roberts, H.H., Adams, R.D. and Cunningham, R.H. 1980. 'Evolution of the sand-dominated subaerial phase, Atchafalaya delta, Louisiana', *American Association Petroleum Geology Bulletin*, 64, 264-79.

Robinson, J.B. 1991. 'Modelling the interactions between human and natural systems', *International Social Science Journal*, 130, 629-47.

Robinson, J.B. 1997. 'Of maps and territories: The use and abuse of socio-economic modelling in support of decision-making', *Technological Forecast and Social Change* (forthcoming).

Rosenhead, J. (ed.) 1989. *Rational Analysis of a Problematic World*. Chichester, England: John Wiley and Sons.

Ross, M. 1987. 'Industrial energy conservation and the steel industry of the United States', *Energy*, 12, 1135-52.

Ruth, M. 1993. *Integrating Economics, Ecology and Thermodynamics*. Dortrecht: Kluwer Academic Publishers.

Ruth, M. 1995. 'Energy saving potentials in US iron ore mining and iron and steel production: A dynamic assessment'. Technical Report prepared for Roy F. Weston, Inc., West Chester, Pennsylvania.

Ruth, M. 1996. 'Material and energy flows in the US pulp and paper industry: Are industry practices becoming more sustainable?'. Technical Document, Center for Energy and Environmental Studies, Boston University, Boston, MA.

Ruth, M. 1997. 'Technology change in US iron and steel production: Implications for material and energy use and CO_2 emissions', *Resources Policy* (forthcoming).

Ruth, M. and Cleveland, C.J. 1997. 'Modelling the dynamics of resource depletion, substitution, recycling and technical change in extractive industries', in Costanza, R., Segura, O. and Martinez-Alier, J. (eds), *Getting Down to Earth: Practical Applications of Ecological Economics*. Washington DC: Island Press (in press).

Ruth, M. and Hannon, B. in press. *Dynamic Modelling of Natural Resource Use*. San Diego: Academic Press.

Scaife, W.W., Turner, R.E. and Costanza, R. 1983. 'Coastal Louisiana recent land loss and canal impacts', *Environmental Management*, 7, 433-42.

Senge, P.M. 1990. *The Fifth Discipline*. New York: Doubleday.

Senge, P.M. and Sterman, J.D. 1994. 'Systems thinking and organizational learning: Acting locally and thinking globally in the organization of the future', in Morecroft, J.D.W. and Sterman, J.D. (eds), *Modelling for Learning Organizations*. Portland, Oregon: Productivity Press, pp. 195-216.

Simon, H.A. 1956. *Administrative Behaviour*. New York: Wiley and Sons.

Simon, H.A. 1979. 'Rational decision-making in business organizations', *American Economic Review*, 69, 493-513.

Sklar, F.H., Costanza, R. and Day, J.W. Jr. 1985. 'Dynamic spatial simulation modelling of coastal wetland habitat succession', *Ecological Modelling*, 29, 261-81.

Sklar, F.H., White, M.L. and Costanza, R. 1989. 'The coastal ecological landscape spatial simulation (CELSS) model: Structure and results for the Atchafalaya/Terrebonne study area. US Fish and Wildlife Service, Division of Biological Services, Washington DC.

Sparrow, F.T. 1983. *Energy and Material Flows in the Iron and Steel Industry*. Argonne, Illinois: Argonne National Laboratory, ANL/CNSV-41.

van den Belt, M., Deutsch, L. and Jansson, Å. 1996. 'An integrated ecological economic assessment of the coastal zone of Patagonia: Using modelling as a consensus building tool'. Paper presented at the inaugural conference of the European Chapter of the International Society for Ecological Economics: Ecology, Society, Economy. Université de Versailles, Paris, France, May 23-25, 1996.

Van Heerden, I.L. and Roberts, H.H. 1980a. 'The Atchafalaya delta - Louisiana's new prograding coast', *Transactions of the Gulf Coast Association Geological Society*, 30, 497-506.

Van Heerden, I.L. and Roberts, H.H. 1980b. 'The Atchafalaya delta - rapid progradation along a traditionally retreating coast (South Central Louisiana)', *Z. Geomorph. N.F.*, 34, 188-201.

Vennix, J.A.M. and Gubbels, J.W. 1994. 'Knowledge elicitation in conceptual model building: A case study in modelling a regional Dutch health care system', in Morecroft, J.D.W. and Sterman, J.D. (eds), *Modelling for Learning Organizations*. Portland, Oregon: Productivity Press, pp. 121-46.

Walters, C. J. 1986. *Adaptive Management of Renewable Resources*. New York: McGraw Hill.

Westenholme, E.F. 1990. *System Inquiry: A System Dynamics Approach*. Chichester, England: John Wiley and Sons.

Westenholme, E.F. 1994. 'A systematic approach to model creation', in Morecroft, J.D.W. and Sterman, J.D. (eds), *Modelling for Learning Organizations*. Portland, Oregon: Productivity Press, pp. 175-94.

Weston, R.F. and Ruth, M. 1995. 'A dynamic hierarchical approach to understanding and managing natural economic systems', Working Paper, Center for Energy and Environmental Studies, Boston University, Boston, Massachusetts.

15. Conclusions: Future Horizons for Global Environmental Policy

Andrew Dragun and Kristin Jakobsson

CONCLUSIONS

It is not our intention in this conclusion to write a new treatise integrating the salient and profound insights of the contributions in this volume. Substantively the insights stand on their own in each case as the astute reader will attest. Our objective as editors of this volume has been to facilitate and enable the presentations which have been included here, containing editorialising to a minimum. In this way we have not sought to obtain unanimity of argument or thinking amongst the contributors and it should be clear that there might be many disagreements on theory and issues amongst the contributors.

But there are also a range of recurring concerns and themes that emerge from the contributions and it is our objective in this final chapter to briefly mention some of those themes as somewhat of a platform for further contemplation in this area. For after all, if this volume is concerned with *sustainability in environmental policy* it is the case that we should highlight some of the main issues which our contributors have identified as important for the development of environmental policy in the *future*. Subsequent to identifying such themes, we will then conclude by highlighting, very briefly, the main contributions of the respective chapters.

Some General Issues for Further Consideration

While the range of concerns and insights raised by the respective authors in this volume are indeed very wide, we have restricted our observations here to six recurring themes which appear to provide a categorical statement for future innovations in environmental policy. We should be clear here that this is our small contribution to editorialising in this volume and we do not necessarily expect that the respective contributors would always agree with the list of themes or the overall picture which we think that they provide.

1. Humans destroying the human environment

Fundamentally, there would appear to be almost unanimous concern amongst the contributors, that current human activities are not merely causing environmental discomfort, but they in fact might be destroying the environmental support systems for humanity itself. Consequently, it is generally held that the current structure of human activity is not sustainable and there is a fundamental necessity that humanity - as a whole - changes the way we view the environment and crucially, how we make decisions which impact on the environment.

2. Sustainability IS important

There is a general belief that sustainability is important and that the pertinent issues are very complex. Sustainability is much broader than ecological criteria, involving social and cultural considerations as well. In this setting it is important to apply rigorous methodology which is concise and operational.

3. The accepted wisdom is not working well

Many of the contributors felt that the accepted theoretical wisdom of dealing with issues of sustainability was not working very well or might not even be applicable. In this setting the accepted wisdom might in fact re-enforce the very processes which are causing the destruction of the human environment. Consequently, there is a need to contemplate revision of the accepted wisdom as well as alternative perspectives which might yield insight.

4. The distribution of sustainability is important

Not only are the what and how of sustainability crucial, but the *who is sustained?* is profoundly important. Equity and the distribution of environmental resources is crucial if sustainability is to be achieved. At a practical level this means that the global implications of local resource will need to be considered and that special attention should be given to the poor countries to the extent that they be granted a greater share of the global environmental commons.

5. Innovative institutional approaches are needed

In the light that the current environmental malaise is a function of accepted ways of doing things and possibly redundant or inapplicable institutions, new innovative institutional approaches are needed.

6. Fair decision processes

Most contributors were of the view that ultimately sustainability and an improvement in the human condition were only going to be achieved if there was explicit social attention to the decision making processes generally and with respect to the environment in particular. A consistent recurring theme was the need to *involve* all stakeholders in the environmental decision making process, with an emphasis on a range of criteria including democracy, transparency, fairness, reciprocity and community.

Some Concluding Comments on the Individual Contributions

With a general overview of the main recurring themes in mind it is now appropriate to conclude this volume with attention to some of the specific issues raised by the respective authors.

Professor Daly argues that it is increasingly evident that economic growth is not the answer to problems of poverty and environmental degradation. Natural capital has become limiting and cannot be substituted for to any great degree by man-made capital. Nor is it at all clear that growth will necessarily increase welfare. Overall, consumption must decrease and conservation of and investment in natural capital must increase.

Dr Goodland concludes that the 'profligate, extravagant and inequitable nature of current patterns of development, when projected into the not too distant future, leads to biophysical impossibilities'. To achieve environmental sustainability and greater equality of access to resources will require reducing overall consumption, sharing and population stability.

Mr Ekins develops a methodology to make the concept of environmental sustainability operational as the basis of practical environmental policies. This is a valuable contribution, because, as Dr Goodland observes, it is easy to avoid doing anything to promote sustainability if the concept is not well defined and made operational.

Some responses to improve environmental policy making and implementation mentioned by Professor Tisdell include greater participation in decision making by those directly affected by the policies, greater consideration of the complexities of the systems involved and the use of concepts such as total economic valuation in decision making, although there are no simple solutions which guarantee favourable outcomes. In general policy making approaches need to be more organic and flexible than they have been in the past.

Dr Uhlin looks at a particular sustainability issue - energy use in agriculture, using data from Sweden. He recommends a deeper and more creative consideration of how agricultural resources could be used to capture solar energy. Professor Faucheux also focuses on a particular sector, industry, suggesting the prevention of environmental problems by proactive and positive institutional incentives which lead to beneficial institutional changes.

Distributional issues and valuation are the central concern of the chapters by Professor O'Connor and Professors Dragun and Jakobsson. Professor O'Connor identifies valuation for sustainability as inseparable from the notion of a habitat as a place to live with social and community significance and meaning. Questions of ecological, economic and social sustainability are identified to involve explicit choices of the redistribution of economic opportunity and access through time. Professor Dragun and Jakobsson conclude that welfare economics is often inconsistent in that it cannot always deal with the environmental problems of equity and distribution.

Professor Knetsch discusses the implications for environmental valuation of how people express preferences and make choices. Professor Knetsch suggests that what people actually do is often seriously inconsistent with the assumptions made in most current environmental policy analyses, which may result in systematic understatements of values for environmental goods and too great an allocation of resources to activities with negative environmental impacts.

Professor Shogren uses experimental economics to explore motivations for individuals' behaviour and uses the results to suggest practical environmental policies.

Two of the final three chapters suggest new and innovative institutions to address particular environmental issues. Dr Hodge considers several possible institutional arrangements that can enable interested parties an opportunity to have an influence on resource allocation decisions with respect to species decline of biodiversity. Professor Chichilnisky proposes an International Bank for Environmental Settlements as a means of obtaining market value from environmental resources without destroying them and as a way of ensuring developing countries gain equitable access to resources.

The final chapter by Professors Costanza and Ruth demonstrates how modelling of complex environmental systems can also be used as a tool for building and securing a broad consensus on environmental problems and solutions not only between science and policy practitioners, but also including the stakeholders in the public sphere. The consensus achieved in such processes is seen as a prerequisite for the successful management of complex ecological economic systems.

Subject and Author Index